BCL-3rd ed

The Economic Development of Bangladesh within a Socialist Framework

OTHER INTERNATIONAL ECONOMIC ASSOCIATION PUBLICATIONS

SCIENCE AND TECHNOLOGY IN ECONOMIC GROWTH
LATIN AMERICA IN THE INTERNATIONAL ECONOMY
ALLOCATION UNDER UNCERTAINTY
TRANSPORT AND THE URBAN ENVIRONMENT
MODELS OF ECONOMIC GROWTH
THE MANAGEMENT OF WATER QUALITY AND THE ENVIRONMENT
AGRICULTURAL POLICY IN DEVELOPING COUNTRIES
THE ECONOMICS OF HEALTH AND MEDICAL CARE

The Economic Development of Bangladesh within a Socialist Framework

Proceedings of a Conference held by the
International Economic Association
at Dacca

EDITED BY
E. A. G. ROBINSON
AND KEITH GRIFFIN

A HALSTED PRESS BOOK

JOHN WILEY & SONS
New York – Toronto

First published in the United Kingdom 1974 by
THE MACMILLAN PRESS LTD

*Published in the U.S.A. and Canada
by Halsted Press, a Division of
John Wiley & Sons, Inc., New York*

Library of Congress Cataloging in Publication Data

Main entry under title:

The Economic development of Bangladesh within
    a socialist framework.

"A Halsted Press Book."
    1.   Bangladesh—Economic   conditions—Con-
gresses.
I.   Robinson, Edward Austin George, ed.   II.
Griffin, Keith B., ed.   III.   International Economic
Association.
HC440.8.E26   338'.09549'2   74–8438
ISBN 0–470–72803–5

Printed in Great Britain

Contents

Acknowledgements

The holding of the conference recorded in this volume was made possible by a special grant of the Ford Foundation. To the Foundation itself, and especially to George Zeidenstein, its representative in Bangladesh, the International Economic Association is indebted far beyond their financial assistance, invaluable as it was. Their interest, encouragement, and practical help in overcoming all the many difficulties of holding a conference in Dacca was a constant support.

Within Bangladesh, the Association is deeply grateful to the Government for its permission to hold the conference and to allow its Planning Commission to take a very active part in it. It is deeply grateful also to Mazharul Huq, President of the newly created Bangladesh Economic Association, which collaborated with the International Economic Association in sponsoring the conference; he personally helped us to overcome many of the minor difficulties and obstacles which inevitably confronted us. He obtained for us the great privilege of meeting in the board-room of the Bangladesh Bank, to which our most sincere thanks are due.

The Association seldom expresses its thanks to its own officers. On this exceptional occasion special thanks are due to two of them. Professor Nurul Islam, our Treasurer, found time amid his load of responsibilities as Deputy Chairman of the Planning Commission of the Government of Bangladesh to work out the detail of our programme. Miss Mary Crook, the Administrative Secretary of the Association, had to solve hour-by-hour almost insoluble problems created by shortages of everything from transport facilities to hotel bedrooms and by crises over moneyless arriving participants or missing exit-visas.

On this occasion also the Association is anxious to express its gratitude to all those who accepted at unusually short notice its invitations to participants. If the conference was to contribute, as was hoped, to the thinking going into the first five-year plan, it needed to be held no later than January 1973. Many of those who came had, we know, to postpone other urgent claims on them to take part.

To all participants the most vivid memory of their days in Dacca will unquestionably be the hour of discussion of the problems and difficulties of developing Bangladesh with the Prime Minister, Sheik Mujibur Rahman, and the powerful impression that he made on us all of his grasp of the issues confronting his country. To him and to his people we offer our good wishes and our hope that our deliberations may have made a small contribution to their welfare.

POSTSCRIPT

While this book was going through the final stages of printing off, news has come of the death of Daniel Thorner. A vigorous controversionalist and a devoted friend of Bangladesh, he took a major part in the conference here recorded. There are many Bangladeshi economists who will always have good cause to remember with gratitude his staunch support and help when he was with them in Dacca in their days of danger.

E. A. G. R.

Programme Committee

E. A. G. Robinson

Nurul Islam

B. Csikos-Nagy

Local Secretary in Dacca

Swadesh Bose

List of Participants

FOREIGN

Bulgaria: Konstantin Gabrovski, Research Centre for Planning, Gosplan, Sofia.
Konstantin Kolev, Research Institute, Bulgarian Academy of Science, Sofia.
France: Daniel Thorner, École Pratique des Hautes Études, VI Section (Sorbonne), Paris.
Réné Dumont, Institut National Agronomique Paris–Grignon.
Hungary: Andreas Brody, Institute of Economics, Hungarian Academy of Science, Budapest.
India: Ambika Ghosh, Jadavpur University, Calcutta.
Ashok Mitra, Calcutta.
Arjun Sengupta, Delhi School of Economics.
Japan: Saburo Okita, The Japan Economic Research Center, and the International Development Center of Japan, Tokyo.
Akira Takahashi, University of Tokyo, and the International Development Center of Japan.
Norway: Just Faaland, World Bank, Dacca.
Poland: Jozef Pajestka, Planning Commission, Warsaw.
Jan Lipinski, Central School of Planning and Statistics, Warsaw.
U.S.S.R.: Vladimir A. Kondratiev, Institute of World Economy and International Relations, U.S.S.R. Academy of Sciences, Moscow.
Ilya Redko, Institute of Oriental Studies of the Academy of Sciences of the U.S.S.R., Moscow.
United Kingdom: Esra Bennathan, University of Bristol.
Paul Streeten, Queen Elizabeth House, Oxford.
Michael Lipton, Institute of Development Studies at Sussex University, Brighton.
U.S.A.: Gustav Ranis, Economic Growth Center, Yale University, New Haven.
Hollis B. Chenery, International Bank for Reconstruction and Development, Washington, D.C.
Jaroslav Vanek, Cornell University, Ithaca.
Yugoslavia: Branko Horvat, Institute of Economic Sciences, Belgrade.
Alexander Bajt, University of Ljublijana.

BANGLADESH

Nurul Islam
A. F. A. Husain
R. H. Khondker
Mosharraf Hossain
Rehman Sobhan
Muzaffar Ahmad   } Planning Commission, Government of
Shamsul Islam   Bangladesh, Dacca.
A. R. Khan
Mahfuzul Huq
S. A. Rahim
K. H. Imam

S. R. Bose
Mohiuddin Alamgir   } Bangladesh Institute of Development
A. N. M. A. Rahman   Economics, Dacca

M. N. Huda   ⎫   Department of Economics, University of
Anisur Rahman   ⎬   Dacca
Iftikhar Ahmed   ⎭

Abdullah Farouq, Department of Commerce, University of Dacca.
M. K. Chowdhury, Department of Economics, Jahangirnagar University.
M. B. Duza, Department of Sociology, Chittagong University.
S. A. Kabir, Bangladesh Bank, Dacca.
A. K. Siddique, Bangladesh Bank, Dacca.
Mazharul Huq, President, Bangladesh Economic Association, Dacca.

OFFICIALS

E. A. G. Robinson, Cambridge University.
Keith Griffin, Magdalen College, Oxford.
Mary Crook, I.E.A. Secretariat, Paris.

Introduction

E. A. G. Robinson

I

The conference recorded in this volume was in a number of respects unique. It represented the first occasion on which the International Economic Association had studied the development of a single country rather than a much wider region. It was the first occasion on which an International Economic Association Conference had been organised in close collaboration with those actually responsible for a country's development. It represented a conference originally planned in one context and finally held in a wholly different one.

The conference was first conceived at a time when Bangladesh did not yet exist as an independent nation. A number of economists of Bengali extraction had been forced to take refuge in India or further abroad during the war of liberation. Some of these were members of the research staff of the Institute of Development Economics which had been transferred from Karachi to Dacca during the previous months. Some were members of the teaching staffs of what are now the universities of Bangladesh. As a contribution towards the task of sustaining and encouraging these refugees the International Economic Association agreed to plan a conference on the subject of 'The Economics of Extreme Poverty – a case study of East Pakistan'. Many of those who contributed papers to the conference we ultimately held had been invited to take part in this original project.

The turn of the wheel made this earlier concept of the conference irrelevant. Within a few months all or most of the economists concerned had returned to Dacca, and a number of them found themselves carrying new responsibilities for planning in a much more practical way the future economic development of Bangladesh. In particular, Professor Nurul Islam, the Director of the Institute, had become Deputy Chairman under the Prime Minister of the Planning Commission of the Government of Bangladesh. Others were either members of the Planning Commission or of its staff. The Institute of Development Economics was finding its feet again and beginning to frame a new research programme.

This turn of the wheel, however, made thinking about the economic future of Bangladesh more urgent rather than less urgent. A small group of economists, well aware of their lack of practical administrative experience, had found themselves faced with a large measure of responsibility not only for thinking out the long-term policies that can best contribute to the development of Bangladesh, but also at the same time for dealing with the innumerable day-by-day problems and crises that were confronting a new country, just escaped from war, faced by serious shortage of foodgrains, with a badly damaged transport system, with inadequate financial reserves and a break-down of its foreign trade arrangements.

It was in these circumstances that Nurul Islam suggested to me in September 1972, at another conference of the International Economic Association, that we should revive the idea of the conference to study the development of Bangladesh. But our concept of it was now a very different one. What we now had in mind was a conference at which the members and staff of the Bangladesh Planning Commission and the Institute of Development Economics would present as objectively as possible the problems and issues of development which appeared to them to need solution, and a group of foreign economists with experience in actual problems of economic development would discuss possible solutions, the methods of handling these problems in different parts of the world, the institutions that had been created to handle them, and so on. The concept, that is to say, was that the conference should be a vehicle for putting at the disposal of those planning Bangladesh development as wide a range of knowledge and experience as might be possible.

We accepted, however, from the first one very important constraint. The new government of Bangladesh had already decided that the framework of development was to be that of a socialist state. At the urgent request of the Bangladesh Economic Association, the executive committee of the International Economic Association agreed to this constraint. It was imposed not to introduce an element of politics but to exclude it. We were anxious to avoid a continuous stream of argument and recrimination as to whether it would be better for Bangladesh to adopt socialist or capitalist policies. That issue had become *chose jugée* – irrelevant to our discussions. All who were invited came to the conference prepared to treat it as such and we used the words 'within the framework of a socialist economy' as an essential part of the title of the conference.

It was, nevertheless, very far from clear what exactly might be meant by 'a socialist framework'. It had been clear from the first that Bangladesh was not adopting uncritically any one of the familiar frameworks of the U.S.S.R., of Communist China, of Poland, of Roumania or any other prototypes. Among ourselves we sometimes spoke of Yugoslavia as something nearer to a model. But that meant no more than that Bangladesh must be expected to work out her own compromise between a controlled economy and a price-guided economy. When on the last day of the conference we were given the opportunity of discussing the problems of developing Bangladesh with the Prime Minister, Sheik Mujibur Rahman, he was asked what was meant by Bangladesh socialism. His answer was 'socialism as we shall practise it in Bangladesh'. This was not, as I understand it, a quick and clever repartee to a troublesome question. It was a perfectly accurate reflection of the practical and pragmatic attitude of the Bangladesh government to its problems.

The constraint of 'a socialist framework' did, however, affect the form and composition of the conference. The experience that was relevant to the planning of Bangladesh development was as likely to be found in the socialist countries of the world as among economists drawn from capitalist or mixed economies. We agreed from the first to invite about half the foreign participants from socialist countries federated to the International Economic Association and about half from capitalist or mixed economies. The ratio was never exact. Economists are not to be regarded as spokesmen for the particular type of economy under which they happen to live. It is not easy to lump countries – India for example – into categories. What is more important is that the conference did very successfully represent a wide spectrum of thinking and experience.

We were singularly fortunate in some very first-rate participants from socialist as well as other countries. Among the former, Jozef Pajestka and Jan Lipinski from Poland, Branko Horvat and Alexander Bajt from Yugoslavia, Andreas Brody from Hungary, to name only a few, admirably combined practical experience with theoretical expertise. This was the more valuable because in many relevant fields the capitalist experience and methods of operation are very much better documented than the socialist experience and the relevant details of actual socialist methods of operation. Outside of the conference itself much of this was made available to the Planning Commission. On the side of capitalist and mixed economies the presence of Hollis Chenery, Gus Ranis, Paul Streeten, again to name only a few, was invaluable. It was equally valuable again to have available through Saburo Okita, Ashok Mitra, Ambika Ghosh and others the relevant experience of Japan and India.

The actual planning and conduct of the conference reflected this concept of it as a vehicle for transmitting relevant thinking and experience. All the papers were written by Bangladesh experts, some of them by members of the staff of the Bangladesh Institute of Development Economics under Swadesh Bose's guidance, some of them by members of the staffs of the universities, some of them by members of the Planning Commission and its staff. To them, it need hardly be said, we were immensely indebted. If the conference was to contribute to the formulation of the first five-year plan while the latter was still at a more or less flexible stage it was necessary to hold it not later than January 1973. This gave only some three months of preparation to writers who were already overloaded with work.

If the conference was to fulfil its objective, however, the comments of the foreign participants had a vital role to play. We so planned the conference that in all except a few cases there should be two commentators on the paper under consideration – one drawn from a socialist country, one from the other countries. This volume prints not only the original paper but also the comments of those specially invited, as well as a record of the discussion. Where the commentator had prepared a full text, that is printed. Where he spoke, as many did, from notes, they have been expanded into a text, which represents, however, a somewhat summarised version of what was said. The record of the subsequent discussion is, as always, a very much abbreviated account of very much longer and more detailed argument.

Perhaps I may comment at once that arguments never, in my recollection, divided between capitalists and others. There were nearly always Bangladeshis, socialists, others on both sides of what was often a practical and pragmatic argument about the success or lack of success of particular policies or experiments.

There is one final point regarding the working of the conference that needs to be stressed, if only because it was incomprehensible to the local Press of Dacca. We were not a body of advisers. We were not trying to reach agreement as to the advice that we should collectively give to the government of Bangladesh. Bangladesh is an independent sovereign country and it would be an impertinence for a group of foreign economists to press on it advice for which they had not been asked. Our purpose – our sole purpose – was to ensure that the economists working in the Planning Commission or the research institutes of Bangladesh should be as well-informed as possible in tendering their own advice, based on all their own special knowledge, to the government. It was as individuals and not in any collective capacity that we were trying to do what we could to help. We never attempted to reach a collective conclusion or recommendation, and I can attach no meaning to the result of a majority vote among a group that made no pretensions to proportionate representation of the universe of opinions. It would, moreover, have been a flagrant transgression of the first article of the I.E.A.'s Statutes – that it is 'established with purely scientific aims' – if we had attempted to reach political conclusions and to give political advice, and we never dreamed of doing so.

II

May I come now to the conference itself, as recorded in this book? My comments must, I think, be very personal, provocative and argumentative and must be read as such. I cannot escape having views of my own on the problems of developing Bangladesh or judging the contributions of others by the criterion of whether they seem to me sensible and practicable in the light of the urgent needs of Bangladesh. I hope that others will forgive me if they think I am wrong-headed. As I see it there is only one criterion by which to judge any policy. Is it the best policy for Bangladesh, in all its existing circumstances?

The central problem is the poverty of Bangladesh. In a world of changing exchange rates it is never easy to know exactly where Bangladesh might come in a league-table of statistics of national incomes per head translated into dollars at official rates of exchange – one of the most questionable methods of measurement that has ever been used. At the present, post-devaluation, rate of exchange income per head in Bangladesh is unquestionably among the very lowest of the very low – low in the lowest decile of world incomes per head.

I emphasise this because I think the conference too often lost sight of the fact. Some of us had done a lot of previous work in Asia. Many, and almost all of our socialist participants, were visiting Asia for the first time. Bangladesh in January was, as always, lovely, green, apparently fertile. It is all too easy to forget that it is support-ing some 1400 persons per square mile – twenty-five times as many as the average of the United States, nearly twice as many as Belgium or the Netherlands, two and a half times as many as the United Kingdom, more than three times the average of India. It is too easy to forget that it is an almost wholly agricultural country which, through population growth, has slipped into the position of import-ing year by year one-eighth of its food needs.

The central problem, let me repeat, is that of extreme poverty. The problem of planning is how to escape from poverty, how to maximise the growth rate of the economy consistently with doing what is possible to mitigate the effects of inequitable distribution of income, inadequate social services, maldistribution of land, and institutions which tend to perpetuate these things. In retrospect I regret that the conference did not have before it a paper that rubbed its nose in these problems and constraints and looked forward to the possible income growth of the future. Those best qualified in the Planning Commission were overloaded with official work. Dr Alamgir had already taken on his willing shoulders a far heavier load than it was proper to impose. In this volume as published he has generously agreed to do something to fill the gap for a reader who is not otherwise familiar with the background and I would like to express our gratitude to him.

Given the circumstances and constraints of Bangladesh – given that 94 per cent of the population is rural, that about 85 per cent of all manpower is engaged in agriculture and 55 per cent of national product is generated in agriculture – what is the maximum economic growth that it is at all reasonable to assume? It must be borne in mind that the base from which modern manufacturing industry starts is a tiny fraction of the national income – now about 6 per cent of the whole. The service industries are largely engaged in providing services to or based on agriculture and reflect its growth. In the short term the practicable rate of national income growth cannot greatly exceed the rate of growth that is possible in agriculture.

I stress this because I myself feel sceptical whether some of the rates of growth bandied about in the conference are really capable of achievement. I hope I am wrong. It would certainly be folly to do anything that might make impossible anything that is within the range of possibilities; it would be folly to set targets lower than those which might be achieved with greater energy. My own private attempts to estimate, which will be published elsewhere, suggest an annual growth rate of about $5\frac{1}{2}$ per cent as a practicable target. Hollis Chenery in the discussion of Chapter 4 will be found to suggest 5 to $5\frac{1}{2}$ per cent as the probable range. I believe that work in the Planning Commission has led to a not widely different figure. I found it disturbing that so experienced a commentator as Branko Horvat was convinced that Bangladesh could grow by 8 per cent a year. I wish I could think he was right. He, like others, basing himself on the experience of European socialist countries, was convinced that there is a great deal of under-utilised capacity, needing no investment other than in working capital to bring into effective use. Undoubtedly there is plentiful under-utilised labour. But there is little or no under-utilised land except so far as more land can be made usable by investment in pumps and irrigation and in ordinary times (the shortage of cotton yarn for handlooms was a temporary phenomenon) no great amount of under-utilised capacity outside the small sector of modern industry. I would myself want to take Jozef Pajestka's wise advice to exploit all opportunities and show people in their villages that change and progress are occurring. But I remain a little sceptical as to whether increased effective demand will evoke a large volume of increased production without corresponding investment. My doubts are, I think, the stronger because there was a time when I firmly believed that this would happen in India and events proved me wrong.

The central problem, then, is agricultural development and development of all the various inputs that are necessary for its success – fertilisers, tubewells, transport facilities, credit facilities. We accepted this, and the priority that such development will need to be given. The very interesting papers by Swadesh Bose and by Rahim and Islam introduced us to these issues.

The debate in regard to agricultural policy turned largely on land reform. Here there was sharp division of views. There seemed to be three alternatives open to the government: to begin immediately with a policy of collectivisation, designed quickly to improve agricultural efficiency and production and to embody from the first the principles of socialism; to accept a policy of creating a socialist state based on a peasant agriculture and to proceed immediately to redistribute land more equally; to accept the fact of peasant agriculture and to postpone till later any more vigorous attack on land reform than is already embodied in the rule that land holdings shall not exceed 100 dighas (33 acres).

The first alternative commended itself, as can be seen in Chapters 2 and 3, to Anisur Rahman and Mohiuddin Alamgir, but was not much discussed in the conference. We were mostly concerned with the immediacy or otherwise of land reform within a system of peasant agriculture. The argument was principally concerned with two issues: what would be the effect on short-term agricultural output of measures to redistribute land holding? Is administrative talent the shortest of all Bangladesh shortages, and if so was land reform the most valuable use to which it could be devoted?

There were fears about the short-term effects. On the one hand the improvements of the green revolution were believed to have been largely concentrated on bigger farms, since lumpy investment in tube-wells and other farms is necessary and bigger farmers have had better access to credit. Others accepted the need to overcome this difficulty through co-operatives and in other ways, but regarded this difficulty as not insuperable. Ashok Mitra was able to tell us that in India yields had increased rather than diminished. Many participants were convinced that immediate land reform was urgent. The doubts of others derived principally from a feeling that an energetic drive to improve the agricultural infrastructure was a precondition of the very necessary achievement of self-sufficiency in foodgrains without loss of output of cash-crops and that the over-stretched district administrations ought to be concentrating on that rather than on the immensely complicated issues of re-drawing village-by-village all the farm boundaries.

The issues involved are in reality political and concerned with priorities. Our own concern (though we may, perhaps, have strayed sometimes outside it) was with the possible economic effects of alternative decisions.

Just how worried one may be about agricultural development depends on just how worried one is about population growth, and its effects on acreage per head and on food supplies not only in the remote future but well within the working lives of those born today. I found myself in profound agreement with Dr Duza and I continue to think that he is right in being as deeply worried as he is. A country as poor as Bangladesh, with population growth somewhere between 2·8 and 3·0 per cent a year, comes nearer to one's nightmares of Malthusia than almost any other country in the world – an agricultural country that cannot feed itself. I found myself – I know he will forgive me – in violent disagreement with Daniel Thorner and what seemed to me too facile preparedness to disregard what I believe to be the most serious problem of Bangladesh today. As I see it, it is not merely a problem of starvation and malnutrition, desperately serious as those are. It is the fact that, of the scanty development resources of Bangladesh, something like three-quarters must go into providing equipment for the growing population. I myself cannot see an escape from extreme poverty consistent with the present rate of population growth. I was worried to see any playing down of the need for an immensely active population policy.

What in these circumstances should the industrial policy be? The papers by Rehman Sobhan and Muzaffar Ahmad give between them a very good picture in the first case of the present thinking about the future industrial framework and in the second case of what already exists in the way of industrial capacity. But it is well to remember how small is the present capacity, with large-scale modern industry generating no more than 6 per cent of G.N.P., as contrasted with some 12 per cent in Pakistan. Muzaffar Ahmad's paper very rightly draws attention to the gaps in supplies and the opportunities for industrialisation. He draws attention also to the rather depressing prospects for jute. I fully agree that at no great distance ahead very active industrialisation will be the right way to use resources and to provide a means of drawing people out of agriculture. But I remain sceptical whether this should have a high priority in the first five-year plan. In the present critical situation I believe that the first short-term priority is to make agriculture more productive and that industrialisation should be judged by its contribution to that. What the discussion in this field seemed to me to lack was a clear view of the constraint imposed by potential savings and by the claims likely to be imposed on industrial investment in what I would regard as the prior claims of agricultural infrastructure.

III

This brings me back to the attempts made to estimate Bangladesh's resources and particularly the saving potential. In the volume as it is now printed I have, as has been said above, persuaded Mohiuddin Alamgir to expand his study of Bangladesh's resources and to look into the future as well as the past, so that a reader may better appreciate the difficulties that confront the country. The paper we had before us in the Conference (like that now printed) was in one short-term respect extremely gloomy. His analysis of the past showed that in 1968–9 the total investment of East Pakistan (both fixed and in stocks) had represented about 13·9 per cent G.D.P.; of this about 10·5 per cent had been financed from domestic saving and about 3·4 per cent (just under a quarter of the whole) from capital inflow. Of the domestic saving he estimated that about six-tenths came from the non-corporate private sector, about three-tenths from government saving and about one-tenth from the corporate sector. When Dr Alamgir tried to look ahead for each of these sources, very properly assuming in the first stage the absence of policy changes other than those implicit in the political changes already determined, he came out with estimates of total savings which, when related to probable G.D.P.s, represented even in the later years of the first plan only some 8–9 per cent. If one takes something not much less than a 13 per cent total investment ratio as an objective, one comes out with an assumed capital inflow considerably higher than that of 1968–9 in a world very different from that of the development decade.

For my own part I would assume changes of policy which can push the total domestic savings ratio back to a figure higher than that of 1968–9. But equally I find myself sharing the view widely voiced in Bangladesh that it may be better to accept a slightly lower and less capital-intensive plan rather than one which must involve so large a capital inflow that marginal lenders must be attracted and their inevitably more stringent strings accepted.

These issues affect inevitably one's attitude also to trade policies and to the constraints on development that are likely to be imposed by foreign earnings. If one assumes a large inflow of capital, financing a large part of the necessary import of capital goods, one need not greatly worry about the adequacy of domestic exports in a world in which the great traditional exports of Bangladesh – jute and jute manufactures – are expanding only very slowly. If one is doubtful about the dimensions of the capital inflow that can be negotiated on acceptable terms, the need to increase exports, to save imports and to adjust the economic structure to these ends becomes very much more urgent and very much more likely to limit the scale of the practical plan.

It is at the present moment extremely difficult to forecast the future balance of payments because in the past Pakistan took some 35 per cent of Bangladesh exports and provided some 45 per cent of imports in the form of trade within a single country and on the basis of the protection that existed within it. Some of the previous exports to West Pakistan will be difficult to sell on similar terms in world markets. On the other hand many imports can be bought more favourably and the overall terms of trade may be no worse. The guessing of exports is the Achilles' heel of all planning. It is because of the over-optimistic guesses of many other plans (not least those of my own country) in respect of exports that I feel nervous whenever any planner seems (as I felt Mohiuddin Alamgir and Hasam Iman to be doing) to be trying to see what exports might be desirable rather than calculating with decent caution what they are really likely to be. It may be possible to alter the picture for jute by negotiation with India. It may be possible to develop, on the basis of natural gas, fertiliser and other exports. But these are hopes. In the meantime I fear that pressures from the balance of payments will reinforce policies of import-saving.

Once again I am myself somewhat pessimistic, I hope unnecessarily. I cannot see probable Bangladeshi economic policies being very attractive to a United States that is increasingly critical of all aid-giving, and I cannot see the capital inflow that would be necessary for a brave plan becoming available without American aid, without the preparedness of American-based international agencies to raise capital for it in American markets, and without a considerable participation of American-based international corporations. Thus I would, I think, be less optimistic than Dr Alamgir on this score also, more inclined to accept a slightly more modest plan and more than a little ashamed of a world which produces these results. Once again I would like to hope that I shall be proved wrong.

IV

I come finally to social services. Their present inadequacy is horrifying to anyone who starts with a background of the social services that exist in Europe or America. Less than half the population over the age of five is literate. Disease is endemic with inevitable effects on productivity. There are about 7500 persons per doctor and hardly any medical assistants. It seems obvious that more investment in human capital is badly needed. But once again one finds oneself driven to ask where in the priorities of extreme poverty even this desperately necessary investment should rate. Is it even more necessary than investment to increase food?

It is the terrible difficulties of establishing priorities in a situation in which the opportunity cost of the most urgent action is frighteningly high in terms of other action forgone that I felt the conference was evading.

The question that needs, I feel convinced, to be asked is the one I tried to raise in the last session. In a country with massive unemployment, need the opportunity costs be high? If the unemployed students and the underemployed rural manpower are there, can they be mobilised and set to work with little or no more entitlement to consumption than they already enjoy? Can the rural infrastructure be created by some process which extracts a surplus and returns it in exchange for work? Can an education service and a rural medical service be provided by students and doctors who accept for a few years the duty of national social service and perform it without having to be cajoled into it by middle-class consumption levels? Can schools be built on a do-it-yourself basis by local communities anxious to obtain education for their children? These are the problems I would like to see explored. A solution along these lines might allow social services as well as rural infrastructure at an almost negligible opportunity cost.

V

A major problem for Bangladesh, to which in retrospect I think we paid too little attention, is how in a world of very rapid population growth one can simultaneously solve the problems of economic development and modernisation and the problems of creating employment for the very large numbers entering the labour force each year as well as for the very large numbers of already existing unemployed and underemployed, living in most cases in the rural areas and creating almost insoluble problems of housing, sanitation, public services if they move in large numbers to the cities.

It is with the practical problems of turning the economist's over-facile incantation of low-capital-intensity industrial development into workable and reasonably productive engineering hardware that the world has had, hitherto, so singularly little success. The longer-term development of Bangladesh, like that of India, Sri Lanka,

Indonesia and many other Asian, African and West Indian countries, depends on greater success than we have yet achieved in this field.

But our very lack of success emphasises the immediate need to focus development, so far as is practicable, on things that can efficiently be done in the rural areas themselves to improve agricultural productivity and to increase incomes through better supply of agricultural inputs and services, better irrigation, better rural transport facilities, combined with expansion of agro-based small-scale industries.

VI

I have deliberately been provocative. I hope that my worries are exaggerated, that Branko Horvat turns out to be more nearly right than I, that the resources available for development turn out to be sufficient to make it possible to combine the solution of the food problem with more industrialisation and more social service than I believe to be possible. I hope that good sense and good leadership will help to make the population problems of Bangladesh less frightening than I find them.

If our conference has done something to stimulate thinking and clarify these problems of Bangladesh, those of us who took part in it will be delighted. For in one thing we were beyond all question unanimous – our desire to see the growth of a vigorous, healthy and viable Bangladesh.

1 The State and Prospects of the Bangladesh Economy [1]

Nurul Islam

DEPUTY CHAIRMAN BANGLADESH PLANNING COMMISSION

I

Bangladesh is an old land but a new nation. On the one hand, it is beset with problems inherited from years of underdevelopment and neglect in the past; on the other hand, the tragic circumstances under which Bangladesh was born as an independent nation have created a new set of problems. The ravages of the war of liberation in 1971 followed closely on the heels of an unprecedented cyclone in 1970, which devastated the coastal areas of Bangladesh. The state of the economy of Bangladesh as it emerges after one year bears the marks of both years of neglect as well as of the damages and destruction caused by the recent war.

A vast majority of people in Bangladesh live in poverty and a substantial number of them live in crushing poverty. Per capita annual income in 1969–70 in current prices was no higher than $50 to $60 and 20 per cent of the population earned no more than $15 to $18 per capita per annum. About half the population suffer from serious inadequacy in calorie-intake, while over 80 per cent suffer from some kind of deficiency in vitamins. Rice and wheat, but mostly rice, provide two-thirds of the average calorie-intake; average diet lacks diversification and is short of protective elements. Life expectation at birth is no more than 49 years for men and 47 years for women. Infant mortality is over 140 per thousand as compared to 20 in developed countries. Literacy is no more than 20 per cent. Housing, specially in the rural areas, for the great bulk of the population is rudimentary and barely provides protection against nature. In urban areas, an average family of 5·6 members shares a 1·5 roomed house, more than 70 per cent of which are temporary constructions without any sanitary facilities, 80 per cent without water connection and 97 per cent without electricity.

Over the past two decades, income per capita has hardly registered

[1] This is a somewhat enlarged and up-dated version of the account of the current situation in Bangladesh and of the problems facing the country that Professor Nurul Islam gave to the Dacca Conference at its first session in order to provide a background to its subsequent discussions (Ed.).

any increase. Seventy-four million people live squeezed in a land area of 55,000 square miles, representing a density of about 1400 per square mile. Population increases by about 2·8–3·0 per cent per annum and at this rate of increase would exceed 150 million by the end of the century. Agriculture contributes 56 per cent of the gross national product and provides over 80 per cent of employment. 90 per cent of the population live in the rural areas. While available statistics on employment are inadequate, it is estimated that about 30 per cent of the population are underemployed or unemployed. There is not only open, urban unemployment and a large number of landless rural labour, but also underemployment, widespread low-productivity and under-utilisation of labour throughout the economy of Bangladesh. Although over 80 per cent of the population work in agriculture and 90 per cent of the acreage is devoted to the production of rice, a high rate of population growth coupled with a stagnant agriculture has led to a steadily rising food shortage which was about 1·5 million tons in 1959–60, estimated at 15 per cent of the total availability of food in that year. The known and exportable natural resources are extremely limited. Agriculture suffers from a lack of diversification, rice, jute and tea, being the main crops.

The main component of income – agriculture – is subject to uncertain performance and erratic fluctuations. The rate of investment in the late 1960s comprised between 10 per cent and 11 per cent of G.N.P.; the rate of domestic savings was no more than 6 to 7 per cent of the G.N.P. The ratio of tax-revenue to G.N.P. was about 4 per cent and hardly 1 per cent was derived from direct taxes.

Physical infrastructure, in particular the transport and communication system, has suffered from serious neglect in the past. Even though the first railway line in Bangladesh was laid in 1862, she had before liberation no more than 1800 miles of railway lines (representing only about 3·3 miles of railway per hundred square miles of area), with about 500 locomotives, 1172 passenger coaches and 1700 freight cars. There were only 2400 miles of metalled roads (high-type motorable), about 2300 passenger cars, about 6000 buses and 10,000 trucks. The total number of road vehicles was about 70,000, a tiny figure in relation to a population of 74,000,000. In a country criss-crossed with rivers, streams and channels, there are no more than 5000 miles of river routes. The port of Chittagong and the anchorage at Chalna have a handling capacity of not more than 370,000 tons of cargo per month. While the numerous water courses traditionally provided the main avenues of commerce, they also constituted formidable obstacles to the development of other means of surface transportation. They require many costly road and rail bridges, or involve alternatively time-consuming ferry trips. The short stretch between Dacca, the capital, and Comilla, the main town in the Eastern region – a distance of 60 miles and the most travelled road in the country – takes four hours to traverse and has three ferry crossings *en route*.

The poverty of the economy of Bangladesh is not only reflected in the poor state of the transport and communication system but also in its narrow base of natural resources, and a lack of diversification of the economy. Large-scale manufacturing contributes only 6 per cent and construction and housing account for no more than 15 per cent of the G.D.P. In the large-scale industrial sector, 75 per cent of the industrial output originates from jute processing. Bangladesh has no major known natural resources excepting natural gas; the possibility of exploitation of a limited quantity of coal and limestone on economic terms is under investigation.

II

The war and its aftermath in 1971 have dealt a severe blow to the economic structure of Bangladesh. The blow was severest at points where the structure was weakest: in the physical infrastructure. According to one estimate, the total loss of physical assets due to the war amounted to takas 1257 crores, of which takas 329 crores was in the public sector and takas 928 crores in the private sector. In the public sector 43 per cent of the loss was in the transport sector and 20 per cent was in the agricultural sector. To mention a few outstanding cases of loss in the transport sector, about 300 road bridges and 300 railway bridges were destroyed; half of the trucks and buses were destroyed; the ports of Chittagong and Chalna suffered heavy damage and were blocked with sunken vessels; the inland waterways were also obstructed by a large number of sunken river craft; two major railway bridges, one linking the western region with the northern region, and the other linking the main port of Chittagong with the capital city and the rest of the western region, were damaged. In the private sector 90 per cent of the loss was in housing.

The war had a deep impact on the villages in Bangladesh, which bore the major brunt of the exodus of 10 million refugees to India, of the dislocation of about 20 million people within the country and of the eventual resettlement of 30 million. The rural economy was affected in at least four principal ways. First, there was an immediate and substantial decline in the output of rice, jute and tea; second, stocks of food, seed and inputs were run down; third, productive capacity, including draft animals, implements, fishing boats and nets, irrigation pumps and appliances, was destroyed or damaged; fourth, the transport facilities and the workshops and buildings of the agricultural administrative services were lost. Finally, all important land and water development projects were interrupted.

The task of relief and rehabilitation was gigantic. The new government faced this task with courage, and with considerable outside assistance. It was handicapped by the limited ability of its administrative structure, which had to be geared up from the level of a limited provincial administration to that of a national administration. The process of adjustment to the challenge of creating a national administration was hampered by the lack of experienced administrators, many of whom were, and still are, stranded in Pakistan.

The large majority of the damaged road and railway bridges have been temporarily repaired on a makeshift basis, but in many of them more permanent repair work requires to be carried out over a period of time. The two major ports have been cleared for the movement of the minimum necessary number of ships; additional salvage operations are now being conducted, to widen the channels for future expansion of the movement of ships and to prevent silting and change of course of main water flows in the rivers. The public expenditure on relief, rehabilitation and reconstruction between January 1972 and June 1973 is expected to amount to takas 290 crores or $400 million. The immediate problem in the aftermath of war has been an acute shortage of food caused by a fall in agricultural production and by depletion of stocks, both public and private.

The most important single problem of relief during 1972 has been the severe food shortage, amounting to about 3 million tons, if provision was to be made for an end-year stock of 600,000 tons. Thanks to international efforts, about 2·4 million tons have been procured during this period, more than 90 per cent of which has been obtained under grant. The international voluntary aid agencies also helped in providing supply of other protective food items, including baby food, medicines, shelter materials and clothing for the refugees and displaced persons. In view of the disrupted state of transportation in Bangladesh, a major part of the task of distributing food has had to be undertaken by the UNROD with transport equipment supplied directly by them.

While the task of relief and rehabilitation has been under way, development activities could not be brought to a standstill. There were a large number of ongoing development projects which had to be reactivated during the year. Takas 366 crores were earmarked for the reactivation of these ongoing development projects. Thus, for the period January 1972 to June 1973 as a whole, public sector expenditure which was earmarked for relief, rehabilitation and development was about takas 660 crores.

A large part of this expenditure was met from external assistance. Between December 1971 and November 1972 the commitment of external assistance was as follows:

		(Million $)
Bilateral credits		227·41
Bilateral grants		520·47
(*a*) Food	200·81	
(*b*) Non-food	319·66	
Multilateral grants		164·45
(*a*) Food	60·00	
(*b*) Non-food	104·45	
Voluntary agencies		84·63
		996·960

Even though the commitment was large, actual disbursement of aid has been rather slow excepting in the case of food aid. The flow of disbursement of project aid is notoriously slow. The time lag between the signing of a loan agreement and that of the project agreement, involving detailed discussions between technical and financial experts from the donor countries and the executing agencies in the recipient country, is often quite considerable. Even in the case of reactivation of the on-going projects the time lag has been sometimes quite considerable. The actual flow of equipment and commodities, after their specification is finalised and banking arrangements are made, involves an additional lag. During July–December 1972 only about takas 16 crores of imports (about U.S. $21 million) have been received under the system of licensing. The figures of actual disbursement of project aid and unlicensed commodity aid in the public sector are yet to be made available.

III

In terms of recovery of output and production, the slowest rate of recovery has been registered in the agricultural sector. This is partly due to the slow rate of rehabilitation of the institutional framework and administrative services, including the extension of credit and arrangements for delivery of inputs. It has been partly due to the failure of rainfall. This was 40 per cent below normal in this crop year, seriously affecting the Aman crop of 1972. It was partly due also to late arrival of imports of fertilisers and delays and inadequacies in the system of distribution. Added to this was the loss of draft animals caused by war and its aftermath, which led to inadequate and/or inefficient tilling of land. There has, as a consequence of all these factors, been a major shortfall in the principal crop – the Aman crop – during 1972, which constitutes 60 per cent of the total rice production. The new high yielding rice varieties, which were expected to cover 2·2 million acres, in fact barely covered 1·7 million acres and that too, without the adequate supplies of water and fertiliser required to make them fully effective. Moreover, a large number of pumps and tubewells suffered from lack of repair and maintenance and from inadequate supply of diesel oil. During 1972 there was thus more than a 20 per cent shortfall in production compared with 1969–70. Rice and wheat output, which was roughly 11·8 million tons during 1969–70, declined to 9·7 million tons during 1971–2, and is not expected to be more than 10·2 million tons during the whole calendar year 1973. The food shortage, which during 1972 had been about 3 million tons, is estimated at about 2·5 millions for the year 1973.

An increase in production is being sought primarily through an extension of irrigated areas and the use of new varieties of seeds. In Bangladesh out of 33 million acres of deltain plain, only about 22 million acres are cultivated, of which one-third is heavily flooded every year. The flooded areas are unsuitable for new varieties of seed. Eighty per cent of the remaining area is without water for cultivation during the non-monsoon. The flood protection schemes are not only expensive but also suffer from a long gestation lag; not all aspects of the technological and economic problems of flood control have been so systematically mastered as to produce feasible and efficient flood control schemes. During 1971–2 only 1·1 million acres of land were under irrigation, under the tubewell and low lift programmes. The Plan for 1972–3 aimed to increase the irrigated area to a total of 1·53 million acres. The area under new varieties during 1969–70 was about 1·5 million acres (0·6 million acres of the Aman crop, 0·8 million acres of the Boro crop and 0·1 million acres of the Aus crop) and the Annual Plan 1972–3 postulated an increase to 3·5 million acres (2·2 m. Aman, 1·1 m. Boro and 0·2 m. Aus). In view of the fact that the cropped area under rice production was about 25 million acres, the expected area under new varieties is no more than 6 per cent of the cropped area, and the area under irrigation does not exceed 4·5 per cent of the cropped area. It is the limited supply of irrigation water which at present restricts the Boro crop (the winter crop) cultivation to no more than 2·18 million acres. The cropping intensity is thus only about 1·49 per cent.

The large-scale industrial sector has achieved partial recovery, mainly in the field of jute and cotton textile manufacturing. Because of the acute shortage of imported raw materials and spares in the rest of the industrial sector, the pace of recovery has been rather slow. The comparison of actual output in 1972 with that in the last normal year, i.e. 1969–70, is handicapped by the fact that (*a*) there has been addition to capacity since 1969, and that (*b*) the monthly figures of production for the years 1969–70 to match the corresponding figures in the current year are not easily available. Two things stand out from the analysis done so far: (*a*) monthly average production during July–October 1972 has recorded significant increase over the January–June 1972 level in all the major industries; this has been associated with an increased utilisation of capacity; (*b*) while jute and cotton textile output has recovered to the extent of 80 per cent, as indicated by a comparison of average monthly output of July–October 1972 with average output of 1969–70, in other industries, heavily dependent on imported raw materials, recovery has varied from about 25 per cent in beverages and pharmaceuticals to 40–50 per cent in basic metals, oil products and tobacco; recovery has also been slow in some industries based on local raw materials, such as paper and board (45 per cent), wood products (20 per cent) and sugar (50 per cent) because of inadequate supply of local materials, due to disorganisation in the domestic production of raw materials. This survey is limited to the nationalised sector, which covers about 86 per cent of the industrial assets as valued in 1969–70. The performance of the private sector is not known at the moment. In none of the fifteen industries covered in the survey except one does capacity utilisation on a single-shift basis exceed 65 per cent. In nine cases, the rate of utilisation is below 30 per cent. In the remaining industries the rate of utilisation has varied between 40–65 per cent.

IV

There is one area in which Bangladesh has had to undergo a significant readjustment, in terms both of direction and of institutional arrangements. Bangladesh is short of domestic supplies of many critical raw materials as well as of many essential consumption goods. Large volumes of miscellaneous intermediate and consumer goods used to be imported from Pakistan: raw cotton, cotton textiles of all varieties, and oilseeds are examples of essential items for which Bangladesh depended on Pakistan. Similarly, important export items, such as jute goods, tea, newsprint and paper, matches and leather used to be exported to Pakistan. On independence,

Bangladesh has had to find new sources of supply for her imports and new markets for her exports. Secondly, many of the private importers in Bangladesh were Pakistanis, who operated exclusively in Bangladesh or operated in both wings with head offices in Karachi; on independence they disappeared from the scene. Prior to liberation, even when a large proportion of import licences were issued to Bengalis, they were in fact utilised by these Pakistani traders; the former sold them at a profit to the latter who had the expertise in import trade, had trading connections abroad, and above all had command over financial resources. This class of importers with trading skill and resources ceased to function after independence. There was a lack of knowledge among the Bengali traders of the world markets for a number of key commodities which had previously been imported from Pakistan. Thirdly, the banking connections with international financial centres had to be built up; all the major banks were owned by the Pakistanis, and on independence they were taken over by the government. They had to build up an independent relationship with foreign banks and financial centres. Fourthly, there were two significant changes in the institutional framework of foreign trade in Bangladesh: first, about 80 per cent of the export trade (which in any case consists of raw jute and jute goods) and about 70 per cent of import trade is now in the hands of the public agencies; second, in so far as private importers are allowed in the import trade, the vacuum partly caused by the departure of Pakistani importers has been met by inducting a large number of new traders who have been issued a small amount of licences each, ranging from takas 1000 to takas 20,000 (which has recently been revised upwards to takas 5000 to takas 35,000). Even though the number of private importers is very large (about 29,000, including 5000 importers inducted during the past year) the total volume of imports handled by them is relatively small. The Bangladesh Trading Corporation, the state agency, has expanded its operations starting from a volume of takas 10 crores to about takas 65 crores. The existence of a large number of importers, each importing a small amount, has resulted in delay and inefficiency in the import trade. Most of the small importers have no skill in importing and no contact with trading centres abroad. The time lag involved in the transfer of import licences from new traders, who on political considerations have been spread uniformly throughout the length and breadth of the country (10 importers per thana) to the professional importers, by means of sales and resales through a chain of intermediaries, has caused inordinate delay in the flow of imports.

The inadequate recovery in industrial production, the shortfall in agricultural production and the disorganisation and disruption in the transport sector has affected the revival of exports, on the one hand, and interrupted the flow of essential imports, on the other. As far as import requirements are concerned, due to disturbance and the war of liberation during 1970–2, there was a backlog of demand for spare parts and for equipment and machinery to replace the existing capital stock. This factor has seriously handicapped utilisation of capacity in all the sectors of the economy, ranging from idle pumps and tubewells in the agricultural sector to broken-down buses, trucks and railway wagons and industrial plant and machinery.

The recovery in exports has been restricted by a large number of factors, outstanding amongst which are the disruption of internal transport, inadequate shipping facilities and banking facilities. The major problem relates to the export of tea, the world price of which is about 30 per cent less than the cost of production and about half the domestic price, prevailing in the pre-liberation period, in the protected market of Pakistan. Recovery in the exports of matches, newsprint and paper industries and of sea-fish, specially prawns, has been very slow partly because of high cost and partly because of inadequate production. While the exports of hides and skins have recovered, those of tanned leather have not yet shown the same trend.

V

As the foregoing analysis brings out clearly, before liberation Bangladesh was one of the poorest, least developed countries of the world. The ravages of the war of liberation and its aftermath aggravated the problems of underdevelopment. With a large and rapidly increasing population, low per capita income, narrow resource base and lack of a diversified economy, Bangladesh faces a formidable challenge in the task of generating a momentum of economic growth.

In order to ensure a standard of life consistent with minimum human dignity for the masses of the people, Bangladesh needs to generate a rate of growth of G.N.P. at least between 5 and 6 per cent per year. Given the rate of growth of population, it would provide no higher than 2 per cent rate of increase in per capita income. At this rate of growth of per capita income Bangladesh will require about four decades to double her per capita income, unless in the successive Five Year Plans she is able to raise the rate of growth of income far above 5 per cent or unless she is able to curtail drastically the rate of growth of population.

A realistic appraisal of the future prospects of the economy of

Bangladesh would lead one to accept the fact that Bangladesh will in all probability remain one of the poorest countries of the world for some years to come. In the immediate future she must address herself energetically to the task of mobilising domestic resources for development; she must increase the domestic savings rate over the next five years from the present 5 to 6 per cent to about 13 to 14 per cent. This minimum level of domestic effort is essential if she is to keep the requirements of foreign assistance within realistic limits of availability, on the one hand, and domestic constraints, both social and political, on the use of foreign aid on the other. Undoubtedly, she would need to increase progressively total development outlay to about 20 per cent of G.N.P. by the end of the next five years, if she aims to attain a growth of G.N.P. of 5 to 6 per cent per year. This would necessitate an increase to the ratios both of both foreign assistance and of domestic savings to G.N.P. during the next five years or so. These are not in absolute terms very ambitious targets. But compared to the low level of savings and investment in the past two or three abnormal years of dislocation and disruption of the normal economic activity, they may appear to be very ambitious.

The pattern and magnitude of economic growth in Bangladesh has to be conceived in two stages: In the first phase, Bangladesh has to stage a recovery of her economy to the level of the last normal year – 1969–70. This would largely be a matter of improvement of organisation and management and of an increase in the utilisation of existing capital stock. In the next phase, she has to attain a tolerable rate of growth over the benchmark period, which will result mainly from the development outlays undertaken during the next five years. It is along these lines that the strategy of the First Five Year Plan of Bangladesh is being designed.

VI

Bangladesh faces a severe domestic savings constraint on her development efforts. This is due to paucity of domestic savings caused by a low level of income, absence of a large modern sector of the economy with an investible surplus, and a weak institutional structure for mobilising private household savings. In view of the fact that the largest segment of the modern economy is in the public sector and that investment in infrastructure, specially in the agriculture, will be undertaken mainly by the government, Bangladesh would need to mobilise a large amount of private savings for investment in the public sector. Investment requirements in the public sector would far exceed the savings which will be directly generated in the public sector. The task of mobilisation of private savings is not an easy one; she would have to develop and organise new and modern financial institutions as well as devise and implement efficient and wide-ranging fiscal instruments.

Bangladesh also faces a foreign exchange constraint which may indeed appear as a predominant constraint, even if the country succeeds in mobilising the expected amount of domestic savings. This is due to the fact that, on the one hand, her exports are few and face a stagnant world demand and, on the other, her require-ments of imported raw materials and capital equipment increase more than in proportion to the rate of increase in investment. This is due to the limited domestic resources and absence of a diversified economic structure. While, in the long run, diversification of exports would remain the principal goal of her policy, in the immediate future, Bangladesh would have to rely on a substantial increase in her traditional exports, mainly raw jute, jute goods, tea, hides and skins and leather. At the same time she has to pursue a policy of import substitution in such fields as cotton textiles, cement, fertiliser, sugar, pharmaceuticals and chemicals. These are important and significant areas of import substitution which are found economically justified, if an appropriate rate of exchange is used to calculate the costs and benefits of import substitution.

VII

The major thrust of the development efforts in Bangladesh has to be directed towards the agricultural sector and related activities, with emphasis on projects and techniques which are labour-intensive. The high priority which is attached to rural development is war-ranted by the fact that the largest portion of national income, as well as of employment, originates in agriculture; it is also in this sector that significant manifestations of poverty exist. Thus, any attempt to reduce poverty, to increase income and to expand employ-ment opportunities must start with the agricultural sector. In the foreseeable future, any attainable rate of industrialisation is unlikely to make a dent in either poverty or unemployment in Bangladesh.

Bangladesh needs to accord very high priority to population control and planning. Admittedly, the results of family planning measures will take time before their effects on the rate of growth of population are felt. What is necessary is political and adminis-trative commitment at the earliest moment to the policy of popula-tion control. It will be necessary to demonstrate the seriousness of commitment by a substantial investment of financial resources and of manpower in the family planning programme. An appropriate institutional framework for a successful family planning programme which is suitable to the socio-economic conditions in Bangladesh has to be developed. There is no escape from experimenting with new institutional arrangements, so that changes in techniques and methods can be introduced as experience in this field accumulates. At present, health and family planning services are integrated and it is expected that other institutions and agencies in the field of social welfare, education, agricultural extension – institutions, that is, which impinge on the life, living and the attitudes of the population – will be harnessed for the purposes of motivating the masses for the control of the family size.

In the field of agriculture, the greatest importance attaches to the reduction of dependence on imports of foodgrains as soon as possible. New technologies, involving improved varieties of seeds, combined with regulated supply of irrigation and fertiliser, is expected to expand the domestic production of foodgrains by some 40 per cent within the next five years, provided institutional and administrative problems can be satisfactorily solved. The institutional requirements range from an efficient delivery system for the supply of inputs to the multitude of farmers, spread throughout the length and breadth of the country, to the provision of credit, marketing and extension facilities. The enormity of this task is highlighted by the fact that, in order to accelerate growth consistently with social justice and equity, it is necessary to direct efforts to the small farmers and landless labourers. The institutional problems in organising them for efficient production are more difficult than if the increase in production was to be mainly realised from a few big farms. The main reliance will need to be on co-operatives and farmers' groups at the village level, working in collaboration with local government institutions as a catalytic and dynamic agent in the task of co-ordination and leadership.

Moreover, at the policy level, there is need to resolve the difficult problems of choice between the objective of self-sufficiency in foodgrains and the production of other agricultural crops which either provide exports or constitute the basis of a diversified nutritional diet.

In the field of industry, factor endowments and need for import substitution are likely to lead Bangladesh to emphasise labour-intensive, small-scale industries which can be integrated, on the one hand, with agriculture, and on the other hand, with the large-scale manufacturing sector. The limited size of the domestic market for a wide variety of industrial products which preclude the possibilities of large-scale mass production, the high cost of transportation and communication, the limited financial ability of private entrepreneurs to mobilise resources, and the need to avoid concentration in a few urban centres and the consequent large capital-intensive investment in physical infrastructure, all underline the important role that the small-scale industrial sector should play in Bangladesh. The objective is to identify in each industry those processes and activities which could be split up for relegation to the small-scale sector.

The pattern of industrialisation should be so designed as to produce domestically, so far as is consistent with considerations of cost and efficiency, the components of the minimum consumption basket conceived in terms of food, clothing, shelter, education and health. It should provide import substitutes for fertilisers, pesticides, irrigation equipment and agricultural implements. The areas which require an immediate improvement in efficiency and in the utilisation of capacity are the agro-based industries such as jute, sugarcane, tobacco, tea, hides and skins. Large-scale industry will be developed primarily in those areas where the choice of technology is limited, where efficiency considerations arising out of economies of scale are overwhelming, and where capital-intensive technology, specially in the export sector, is imperative. Import-intensive industries can only be warranted in areas where value added in domestic processing of the imported materials is substantial. The pattern of future industrialisation must take into account the new possibilities of specialisation and division of labour through economic collaboration with India.

VIII

The constitution of Bangladesh lays down that the economy shall be built up on socialist lines. It provides for three types of ownership – private, co-operative and state. The limits to and scope of each type of ownership will be determined by law. The bill of fundamental rights does not include the right of private property, which is subject to regulation by law, in any manner it likes. As of today, 86 per cent of the industrial assets in the large-scale manufacturing sector, 70–80 per cent of foreign trade, a large segment of the inland water transport and the entire banking and insurance companies, excepting foreign-owned banks, are in the public sector. In so far as ownership of land is concerned, a ceiling of 33 acres per family has been installed. In the private sector, a ceiling on salaries up to takas 2000 has been imposed. As far as incomes in the private sector are concerned, the intention is to deal with them through fiscal policy. A Pay Commission is currently examining the desirable and efficient pattern of income distribution.

In its attempt to build a socialist framework for its economy, with a large number of publicly owned and managed productive and trading enterprises, Bangladesh faces two sets of issues:

(1) How to manage the new institutions in the considerably expanded public sector so as to ensure efficiency, equity and incentives?

(2) How to meet the difficult development situation in Bangladesh in terms of generating an acceptable rate of growth of per capita income and of employment opportunities?

The problems with which we are faced in the management of nationalised enterprises are:

(i) What is the optimum degree of decentralisation?

(ii) What will be the role of material and financial incentives which can ensure initiative and enterprise in the public sector and produce optimum operational results?

(iii) What is the role of markets and prices in an economy where a large part of the economic system is publicly operated and owned?

These are inter-related issues, a satisfactory solution of which seems to us to provide a key to the success of experiments on which Bangladesh has embarked.

The optimum degree of decentralisation affects not only the relationship between units of public enterprises and the regulating and administrative ministries of the government but also the relationship between the national government and the local government for the purposes of optimum geographical decentralisation of planning and implementation of development activities. In the field of industry, for example, enterprises have been grouped together by type of industry in a number of sector corporations (there are 10 of them). We are now working on evolving a satisfactory degree of distribution of functions and responsibilities between the individual industrial enterprises and the sector corporations, on the one hand, and between the sector corporations and the ministry, on the other hand.

The constitution provides for the role of local government in development activity in planning, financing as well as implementing development works. For many projects, specially in the health and education sector, one aspect of the mobilisation of resources at the local level is through local institutions and enterprises. The inter-relationships between the national government and local governments, as and when they are established, in terms of feedback on implementation and resources mobilisation, have yet to be worked out.

On the question of markets and prices, the basic issue with which we are confronted is whether a change from private to public ownership necessarily implies a corresponding increase in the role of direct quantitative controls on production and trade. Should there be more than one unit in the same activity? And if so, should there be competition between units? For example, should there be many independent banks or insurance companies now that they have been nationalised? Should there be one agency conducting foreign trade, or multiple agencies competing with each other? If there is to be competition between units in the public sector, what will be the nature and criteria of competition? Is there anything called wasteful competition in the context of competing public enterprises? Do they maximise profits and, if so, how does one take care of the divergence between social and private costs or benefits? Should one rely on the traditional prescription of taxes and subsidies as one does in a private enterprise economy?

We have also been concerned with the evolution of the most efficient system of incentives in the public sector enterprises. Now that maximisation of private or personal profits is not the driving and motivating force in the nationalised sector, how does one ensure that the managers of enterprises are motivated to exercise initiative and enterprise? An appropriate system of incentives must affect not only the managers of public enterprises but also the workers at all levels.

2 Priorities and Methods for Socialist Development of Bangladesh[1]

Md. Anisur Rahman

UNIVERSITY OF DACCA

I. INTRODUCTION: THE DIALECTIC

According to standard theory in the Marxist–Leninist tradition, the political philosophy of Bangladesh, as reflected in its constitution, suffers from internal contradiction by aiming to attain socialism through traditional parliamentary democracy. The constitution provides, on the one hand, for a 'nationalised public sector embracing the key factors of the economy', which should logically include the bulk of agriculture and hence by far the greater part of the economy; for payment for one's work according to the socialist principle 'from each according to his abilities, to each according to his work'; and for emancipating the peasants and workers from 'all forms of exploitation' that does not presumably exclude exploitation of labour by capital in the classical Marxian sense. It provides also, on the other hand, that the state shall only 'endeavour', 'to create conditions in which, as a general principle, persons shall not be able to enjoy unearned incomes', and also permits of private ownership of the 'means of production and distribution within such limits as may be prescribed by law'. It provides, finally, for parliamentary democracy of the traditional western variety where socialists and non-socialists, the exploiter and the exploited, have equal rights but unequal opportunities to seek election and grab power.

It should be fascinating to observe how this contradiction unfolds its dialectic. Until resolution of this dialectic, unfortunately, the planners of Bangladesh will be in the unenviable position of having to plan without a clear political consensus, and without any firm commitment from relevant quarters to provide the necessary political support to their plan. Hence planning for socialist development of Bangladesh at this stage can only serve to indicate a direction and mobilise progressive forces in its favour, and thereby make the planners' own contribution to the dialectic; the course of actual development may thus only be influenced, but not determined, by such planning.

[1] The paper is presented in the author's personal capacity and does not necessarily represent the views of any agency he is associated with.

II. THE URGENCY OF SOCIALISM

Quite apart from its ideological merits, the specific socio-economic environment in Bangladesh makes socialism the only system capable of harnessing its abundant labour force fully for sustained productive work. In a private-enterprise economy employment and the wage-structure are determined by cash market returns from employment and the relative supply of labour of various categories. The general level of poverty in Bangladesh makes the market return from employment generally low, so that a large pool of labour will remain unemployed for a long time to come if employment is left to private enterprise. This will keep the wages of unskilled and semi-skilled labour depressed while the more scarce skilled technical and managerial labour receives a high premium. The resulting income-differential will be too high and the size of the unemployed pool of labour itself too large, to constitute a state of social equilibrium, and the energy of unskilled and semi-skilled labour will be engaged more in unproductive struggles and lawlessness to reduce this differential rather than in productive work. The generally high level of political consciousness of Bengali labour, and the compact geography of the land where unrest spreads quickly, strengthen further the disequilibrium forces.

The disequilibrium tendency has already reached near explosive character in Bangladesh. The massive increase in the labour force in the next decade or so, which cannot be limited by the best efforts at population control because of the lag between a fall in the growth rate of population and its effect on the supply of labour of the relevant working age, will further intensify the problem. There is no solution to this problem but to organise this huge labour force for constructive work, and this can be done only by socialist methods and institutions available to a socialist and not to a private-enterprise economy. The sooner this is realised and efforts directed in this direction, the less costly will be the country's inevitable transition to socialism.

III. SOCIALIST CADRES AND ADMINISTRATIVE REFORM

The very first task in socialist reconstruction of Bangladesh is to build political and administrative cadres committed to socialism and familiar with its philosophy, principles and methods. Socialism hardly has had a place traditionally in the education system of Bangladesh which has produced its present leadership class – political, administrative and intellectual. Individual exceptions apart, this leadership elite of the country can hardly be expected to exhibit the knowledge and other qualities required of a socialist leadership. The pace and quality of the post-war reconstruction effort have also betrayed the inadequacy of the traditional administration in mobilising men and materials on an emergency footing.

The foremost priority for socialist development of Bangladesh must therefore be to draw up a programme for the building of socialist cadres in the ruling party as well as in the government administration. These cadres will combine in them knowledge in socialist principles, the methods and experience of socialist reconstruction of traditionally non-socialist societies, an innovative quality necessary to adapt these methods and experiences to the particular heritage, culture and socio-economic environment in Bangladesh, and the ability to organise people for collective work by conventional and unconventional methods through dynamic leadership and living fellowship with the common man. The building of such cadres will involve a process of training followed by a period of watching before final enlistment. Until a decisive step is taken in this direction the task of socialist development in Bangladesh cannot be said to have started. Urgent reform is also needed in the work procedures and attitudes of the bureaucracy that would change the concept of administration from that of file-disposals to one of action and problem-solving.

IV. SHARED AUSTERITY

No less urgent is early and decisive action to restore faith in the destiny of the nation which is at the moment struggling to get back its bearing after a devastating liberation war, the economic shortages that inevitably follow such a war, and the degeneration of economic and social morals that naturally threaten a nation after such a major convulsion.[1] Shortages of varying degrees have occurred in Bangladesh before, and are frequent phenomena generally in the Third World. What distinguishes Bangladesh today from other such economies, including Bangladesh of the past, is that the liberation war has destroyed the set of traditional values that sustain the traditional pattern of distribution of scarce goods however inequitable they are. This has released two forces. One is the evil, which has stepped into the vacuum as if with a vengeance. Thus, for

1

[1] 'All the elements of disintegration of the old society . . . are bound to "reveal themselves" during such a profound revolution. And these elements of disintegration *cannot* "reveal themselves" otherwise than in an increase of crime, hooliganism, corruption, profiteering and outrage of every kind. To put these down requires time and *requires an iron hand*.' – V. I. Lenin in Apr 1918 ('The Immediate Tasks of the Soviet Government', *Collected Works*, vol. 27, p. 264).

example, adulteration has reached a criminal height that was hard even to conceive previously. The other is the consciousness that a system cannot and should not be accepted unless it appears to be just. While essentially a good and progressive force, its reaction to the evil and the unjust has been without proper guidance, disorderly and often destructive.

No development plan can be implemented until this state of moral crisis and chaos can be ended, and a minimum order and respect for an agreed set of social and economic codes brought back into society. This requires that stern action must be taken against the corrupt and the criminals irrespective of the social and power strata they may come from. This also requires that economic hardships be shared, so that there may develop a sense of solidarity among the various sections of the people. Thus a programme of shared austerity must be launched that will be in consonance with the difficult economic situation the country is passing through.

A programme of shared austerity is needed not only to tide over the immediate post-war difficulties but also to face the hard choice between consumption and accumulation for long-run development with the limited resources at the disposal of the nation, and in the new environment of social consciousness where poverty and affluence can no longer exist side-by-side without an explosive confrontation. This does not mean that individual incomes or consumption should all be equal against the very socialist principle of distribution according to work. This does, however, mean that life styles grossly out of line with the social average be curbed, and in particular the demonstration of superfluous consumption amidst mass hardship must be eliminated. Thus sumptuous hotel dinners, the exhibition of costly jewellery and dress, and the display of surplus motor space speeding past long queues for heavily overloaded public transport, to mention only a few, must be limited severely.

All socialist contries have observed a period of shared austerity in the initial phases of their economic development, in order both to maximise the rate of accumulation and to distribute the 'consumption fund' as equitably as possible. Even a non-socialist country like the United Kingdom exhibited exemplary austerity at all social levels in the period of reconstruction after the Second World War. Bangladesh has yet to emulate these examples as it must, not only because of moral reasons, but also because social and economic development in the framework of a stable social order cannot be expected otherwise. Poverty becomes tolerable and constitutes a force of progress only if it is shared; otherwise it becomes only a force of anarchy and destruction.

In a programme of shared austerity the distribution system becomes of paramount importance and must, at least in respect of the more essential commodities, be taken over by the state as early as possible. A vital element of planning at this stage must be to design an institutional set-up for regimented state procurement and distribution of the essential commodities. Once more, the availability of motivated political and administrative cadres to manage the system will be of crucial importance. It may not be an exaggeration to say that this is the most important and challenging immediate task, the success or failure in which will measure the capability of any leadership in steering the country through the difficult task of socialist reconstruction.

V. REFORM OF OWNERSHIP

A regimented distribution system is necessary in the early phases of socialist reconstruction in order to bring down the existing wild differences in consumption standards traditionally prevalent in the society. Such consumption disparities, however, are the result of an unjust system of property ownership which should be reformed early in order to remove the sources of unearned incomes. Once this is done, the distribution of consumption may be left to be determined by the socialist principle of income distribution according to work after resources are set aside for accumulation.

In phasing the reform of the pattern of ownership, a distinction may be made between ownership of rentier property both rural and urban and that of productive enterprises. The former is unrelated with production efficiency, and can and should be socialised at the very earliest.[1] The socialisation of ownership of productive enterprises should be done in stages keeping in view the state's managerial capacity to run these efficiently. Over-riding political considerations may, however, dictate early socialisation of such property even at some initial cost in terms of efficiency; such consideration may arise, for example, from a desire to act before vested interests can consolidate their position and make the very process of socialisation difficult. The necessary judgement rests essentially with the political leadership and is an exercise that has to combine considerations of efficiency with those of political dialectics.

The specific task of land reform is urgent for reasons of productive efficiency, equity and more fundamentally for reconstructing rural life from its present near-feudal individualistic and passive traditions to a creative and forward-looking collective living force. Land reform also needs to be phased, however, in order to handle gently

---

[1] Exceptions may be made only on humanitarian grounds for cases where property rent provides the only or major source of income of persons unable to work or those for whom the state cannot immepdiately rovide suitable work.

the small and middle peasants' traditional attachment to land-ownership. The first phase of land reform should be restricted to reducing the land-ownership ceiling to a more equitable and efficient size than at present, the organisation of surplus land into demonstration collective farms, and putting all the weight at the command of the government to make these a success. For this, the training of motivated cadres in the management of collective farms, preferably drawn from subsistence or small peasant families, is of the highest priority.[1]

VI. FOUNDATION OF LONG-RUN SELF-ASSURED GROWTH

The most important technical task of planning for socialist development in its very early phases is to design structural changes in order to build the foundation for long-run self-assured growth of the economy. Self-assurance for a developing nation is defined for the present purpose as a position where a nation is prepared to dispense with external assistance rather than submit to donors' dictates.[2] Without such self-assurance, genuine economic and social development in line with the culture and aspirations of a nation's own people is not possible.

This requires a plan for full utilisation of the nation's own resources, including labour which has to be productively employed for even more fundamental reasons already discussed. The major structural change needed for this is the adaptation of technology. Traditionally, the technology in Bangladesh has developed in response to a price structure that has not reflected the relative resource scarcities even in terms of conventional accounting, to the extent that the price of imported technology in the form of debt servicing has in general not been considered. This price structure is in any case irrelevant now for choice of technology, in view of the social necessity of mobilising resources by non-market methods mentioned earlier. The choice of technology in the high-skill sectors has also traditionally been influenced by the training and outlook of the managerial and engineering class who have been educated at home and abroad in institutions not oriented to the development of indigenous technology, and in an environment where greater prestige is

---

[1] Detailed discussion in this regard is available in a study in the Planning Commission on Land Reform.

[2] See the author's 'Perspective Planning for Self-Assured Growth: An Approach to Foreign Capital from a Recipient's Point of View', *Pakistan Development Review*, vol. 8, no. 1 (Spring 1968) (A Russian summary and discussion appeared in B. S. Fomin, *Ekonometrichiskie Theorii i Modeli Mezhdunarodnykh Ekonomicheskikh Otnoshenii*, Iedatelstvo Myshl (Moscow, 1970).

associated with sophisticated capital-intensive imported machines. The switch to indigenous and semi-indigenous technology wherever feasible and socially efficient will not be easy unless these traditional attitudes can be changed. This will need an entire change in cultural values, and hence wide social campaigns to glorify the innovation and use of indigenous technology and the dignity of labour at all levels, and the creation of technological adaptation cells in each relevant sector with the task of scientific exploration of socially more efficient technology.

Major educational reform will be necessary to support the programme for change in technology. The dignity of labour cannot be taught in the class-room: it has to be taught in the field. Change in curricula at the school, college and university levels is imperative to take the students to the fields to engage directly in productive work, in the construction sector and in workshops, and to get them to play a part in making and innovating tools with indigenous resources.

The impact of such reorientation in education will be salutary in many directions: to the extent that students can be mobilised for works programmes at less cost than hired labour, it will directly reduce the average capital cost of construction, and thereby reduce the colossal waste of resources inherent in the present education system, which is geared to produce more unemployable graduates than productive workers. The programme will also change cultural values to lift the status of labour where it must be lifted to reach the ideals of socialism and to attain the specific objective of technological adaptation as a step to building the foundation of long-run self-assured growth; and it will have an inspiring effect on the entire social environment as the student community will once more emerge as the major instrument of purposeful social change.

Building the foundation of long-run self-assured growth also involves the early development of social infrastructure, such as power and transport, technical and managerial manpower, and the development of heavy industry in areas of long-run comparative advantage. These are well-known principles of socialist development and need not be elaborated.

With its finite and already overburdened land space, the long-run viability of the nation depends crucially on successful population control. For this, methods have to be adopted more decisive than any hitherto adopted in the sub-continent. The challenge has to be picked up *socially*. The educational system, the information media, rural co-operatives, the village panchayet and other such institutions all have to be mobilised to this end, and social techniques of population control devised and used through these institutions to supplement, and where appropriate substitute for, the traditional individual-oriented extension approach.[1]

VII. QUICK-YIELDING PROGRAMMES

With the plan to build the foundation of long-run self-assured growth should be integrated a plan for attaining early self-sufficiency in essential mass consumption goods. This should particularly include rapid increase in agricultural output, fish and poultry, and a programme for several-fold increase in the production of cloth in small and cottage industries spread all over the country. Other light industries using local inputs and supported by rural electrification should be designed wherever such possibilities exist.

A countrywide spread of such industries in small units will bring industry closer to agriculture, provide employment where living is cheaper, cater to local needs more speedily and surely than urban-based large factories can, and contribute to even overall development of all the localities in the country.

A programme for functional mass literacy and barefoot medical care should constitute integral parts of plans in the education and health sectors, in order to strike a balance between conventional sophisticated training and service which is time-consuming and costly, and cruder but disciplined pragmatic methods which are faster to acquire and cheaper to serve.[2]

VIII. THE MOBILISATION OF RESOURCES

Traditional discussions on resource mobilisation by western development economists have virtually degenerated into an estimation of aid requirement after a cursory and unimaginative estimation of so-called domestic savings. Ruling elites themselves in many developing countries have been preoccupied with the easier course of mobilisation of external rather than domestic resources. The arithmetic value of external resources in supplementing domestic resources for development is indisputable. Foreign assistance should be sought, particularly from countries sympathetic with the ideology of the nation, and assistance specifically for programmes of structural change should be particularly welcome. But a nation that seeks

[1] Cf. an assessment, prepared for the Planning Commission by the United Nations Relief Operation in Dacca, on 'Population Planning in Bangladesh'.

[2] A highly innovative experiment in low-cost, self-help-oriented medical care has been launched in Savar in a project called the 'People's Health Centre' where school and college students are being given para-medical training to assist the centre on a purely voluntary basis.

external assistance *as a substitute for harnessing its own resources* is a nation without self-respect and an easy prey to unholy designs of donor nations whose motives for wanting to bail out such a nation must be questioned.

Properly organised and inspired, the abundant labour force of Bangladesh can do wonders, as has been demonstrated during the liberation war. While population control remains imperative for long-run viability of the nation, it would be stupid not to regard the existing population and the inevitable increase in the labour force in the next decade as an asset. Harnessing this labour force fully for productive work must be the focal point of the country's entire development effort. As suggested earlier, this is also the only positive way to steer the liberated people of Bangladesh who have attained a new manhood through the war and will destroy if they are unable to construct.

The first step in this direction is to stop relief to all able-bodied adults except in sudden emergencies and call them to work and earn their bread. This is where imaginative socialist leadership can be at its best by organising unemployed labour in doing productive community work against a daily ration of essentials. There is no end to such work that can be devised for every locality and can be done with little or no implements, and keep fully engaged all labour which the traditional market-mechanism is unable to absorb.

Ways and means must also be found to utilise under-employed labour more fully with least addition to the social cost of such utilisation. Unlike the student force, which in the present education system is also under-employed and can be 'coerced', as already suggested, to do directly productive work as a part of the curriculum, the conventionally defined under-employed labour cannot be coerced into doing extra work without extra remuneration. Such extra remuneration will constitute an extra burden on the society, and will be beyond the taxation power of the government if conceived on any significant scale. It will at the same time be a pity if labour power available to the society is allowed to be wasted. The way out lies in *organising voluntary labour or mobilising purchasing power over under-employed labour by appropriate social (community) incentives.* It should be possible, for example, to tie the approval of local development projects for the purpose of government assistance to local contributions either in cash or in labour. Thus, for instance, a community offering voluntary labour to build a road, school, hospital or factory may be given other material support for the project on a priority basis; a community which contributes to an entire project in cash or kind may be given a fluid development grant for another project of its own choice; the location of state-financed factories in the villages may be made contingent on the villagers building the auxiliary road connecting the factory to the nearest market on a voluntary basis, and so on. Such methods should generate a spirit of competition among various local communities in contributing voluntary labour and other resources and also stimulate the spirit of self-help whose economic and social importance needs no elaboration.

In assessing the productive potentials of the people of Bangladesh, the better half of the country's population should not be forgotten. No plan for resource mobilisation and socialist development of Bangladesh can be complete without a programme for liberating the creative energies of the country's women from the chain of traditional taboos and for engaging them in nation-building side-by-side with its men. This is also, in the ultimate analysis, the surest way of controlling population growth.

IX. CONCLUSION

The foregoing discussion brings out some of the more strategic structural, institutional and cultural changes necessary for sustained socialist development of Bangladesh. A good part of the country's first medium-term development plan must consist of programmes for qualitative change and unorthodox methods of sectoral development and resource mobilization. Targets and instruments for such planning and their inter-relationships are not as readily quantifiable as are the more conventional econometric concepts. Nor can conventional macro-growth indices like growth in G.N.P. be meaningfully projected from planned action in these directions. The very concept of G.N.P. as traditionally defined and measured excludes capital formation and flows that are 'intangible' by the conventional tools of measurement; hence a pre-occupation with growth of G.N.P. will be out of place in a situation where change in the quality and content of the nation's intangible capital is considered to be of fundamental importance in redirecting the economic and social course of the nation.[1] Similarly, a pre-occupation with material balances should be avoided in the early stages of development planning for the country. The calculation of material balances would rest on a very tenuous foundation anyway when institutions are in transition; appropriate institutions, moreover, can absorb

[1] For a theoretical discussion of the inadequacy of national income as a measure of social welfare see James Mirrlees, 'The Evaluation of National Income in an Imperfect Economy', *The Pakistan Development Review*, vol. 9, no. 1 (Spring 1969), and the present author's 'National Income and Social Values', *The Bangladesh Economic Review* (Jan 1973).

material imbalances while material balancing is no substitute for the former, which alone will sustain genuine development in the long run.

Institutional and cultural change, and a plan for changing the entire social landscape that socialist development planning for Bangladesh must involve, cannot be imposed from the top. One important task of socialist political and administrative cadres will be to guide local communities into discussions of the issues involved in socio-economic development and in particular the need for maximum self-help, and *to steer them through progressive resolutions of their own* in the implementation of which they will then naturally be more committed. Talents for such cadres exist, but they will need to be picked out, and trained before they are sent out to the villages. The local government's responsibility in providing the organisational leadership and support for such self-help-oriented community development will be heavy. The vision and the direction must, however, come from the top leadership whose command and examples alone can unite and inspire the cadres and the organs of administration at all levels in working collectively for the challenging task of socialist development.

3 Priorities for Development and Allocation of Resources

Mohiuddin Alamgir
BANGLADESH INSTITUTE OF DEVELOPMENT ECONOMICS[1]

I. INTRODUCTION

(i) Background

Since the impact of growth brings about changes in the relationships among economic and institutional variables, planning is necessary to bring order into the chaos that is created by the unco-ordinated growth of these variables. The most important function of planning is to bring about the harmonisation of a large number of socio-economic variables moving in different directions pursuing their own targets, which are sometimes in conflict with one another. The task of the planner has to be geared towards attaining this objective. However, planning defined as the process of preparing a set of decisions for future action pertaining to social and economic development along a prescribed course, has some uncertainty associated with it.

The future (short term and long term) course of social and economic development should be determined within the framework of a welfare function, reflecting the aspiration of all sections of the country's population. The welfare function – the variables to be included – is determined through a political process which may be democratic or otherwise. The Central Planning Authority itself, in consultation with the political authority, can take decision regarding the welfare function. In fact only in a socialist economy is the Central Planning Authority in a position to work out a sensible welfare function for the society and at the same time to ensure that all of the individual sections of the economy will follow the directions from the top. By a socialist economy is meant here one that socialises the the entire production or a significant part thereof, and also socialises

[1] The author is grateful to his colleagues Dr S. R. Bose, Mr Kholiquzzaman Ahmad, Mr Atiqur Rahman, Mr S. R. Osmani and Mr Chowdhury Anwaruzzaman for helpful discussion on various aspects of the paper. Mr Osmani has given particular assistance in the collection and presentation of data. Any credit for the paper should be shared by all, although errors and omissions remain the responsibility of the author.

an objectively determined essential element of the total consumption-set. This definition is slightly different from the classical definition of socialism as well as that of communism.

For a developing economy like Bangladesh, which cannot afford any waste of resources, and which aims at establishing an egalitarian society based on the principle of equality of opportunity and an equitable distribution of national income, a framework of the free enterprise system along the lines of the western capitalist countries can be summarily rejected. The alternative model of a mixed economy, defined as partial planning of production under central control and a relatively dominant role played by the private sector, should be ruled out on the basis of Bangladesh's past experience under the planning framework of the erstwhile Government of Pakistan. Thus the declared objective of the political authority in Bangladesh to establish a socialist order, and to formulate a development plan within that framework, is a step in the right direction. The more important task, however, of incorporating functional content into this otherwise laudable objective, remains to be accomplished.

It is important to note that planning under socialism involves both economic and social planning. The blueprint of the plan should include policy prescriptions affecting not only economic institutions but also social institutions. Planning in Bangladesh will henceforth necessitate fundamental changes in all institutions and, above all, measures to bring about changes in the attitude of the people. Thus 'social planning' will have to be directed towards developing right-minded agents of socialism. The term 'social planning' is used to imply physical and ideological mobilisation of human resources within the country. This is certainly very important for a country with as vast a population base as that of Bangladesh. Physical mobilisation is a process by which the active part of the population is trained and gainfully employed.

Gainful employment, in the context of a transitional society like that in Bangladesh, implies not only that the marginal productivity of labour should be greater than zero, but also that each individual should be able to adjust to the new demands placed on him by the society. In particular, he should be a willing participant in the task of bringing about the desired institutional changes in the country with a minimum of conflict among various social groups. This is where political and ideological mobilisation is absolutely essential. It is the task of the political and the planning authority to provide for the basic ideological training of the people. This is necessary, in addition to technical training, because, as pointed out above, for a healthy social and economic development every individual must be able to act successfully as a social agent apart from being an economic agent of production.

(ii) *Statement of the Problem*

It is with the above background that one has to discuss the problem of determining priorities for development and allocation of resources in Bangladesh. What will be attempted in the following pages is to suggest an analytic framework within which sectoral priorities and resource allocation should be determined. It should be emphasised here that the objective of any type of planning is to put the available resources to their best use in terms of the ultimate objective. A resource-poor region like Bangladesh would naturally seek to minimise the cost of attaining a given objective in each sector. On the other hand, from a global point of view, the problem is one of attaining the optimum of the social welfare function, subject to a number of socio-economic resource- and structure-constraints. What will be the relative weights attached to the development of the different sectors of the economy will depend, on the one hand, on the explicit objective of the planner, and on the other on the scarcity of basic resources, such as capital, foreign exchange and labour. Thus the macro-economic calculus of priority determination will not only incorporate a social objective but must also reflect the scarcity of basic resources.

In reality, the task of resource allocation is very complicated. The planner, while allocating resources, has at the same time to formulate a number of sub-plans. These sub-plans are like sub-routines in a large programme for a computer. The implicit tasks associated with resource allocation are formulation of: the production plan; the investment plan; the consumption plan; the distribution plan; and finally the plan for accumulation of funds out of current income. The problem of resource allocation and determination of sectoral priorities is integrated into these sub-plans. It then clearly follows that the analytic framework of the planner must be such as to incorporate as its components the sub-plans mentioned above; it will be through the working of these plans that desirable resource allocation will be effected.

(iii) *Assumptions*

A number of assumptions are made so that the following discussion can have some relevance to the actual planning process in Bangladesh. First, it is assumed that Bangladesh will continue to be a socialist state no matter which political groups may be in power. Second, the commitment of the political authority towards socialism will be such that it will place its entire weight behind any policy required to realise socialist objectives. Third, a rigorous plan will be formulated immediately for ideological orientation of the proletariat (workers and peasants) so as to ensure maximum co-operation from them in the process of socialisation. Fourth, the top hierarchy of the Central Planning Authority will be composed of dedicated socialists who have a very close political contact with the executive authority. This requirement is extremely important for two reasons: (1) the responsible planners should continue to provide intellectual guidance to the political leadership in matters of economic and social development; (2) an atmosphere of mutual confidence must prevail at all times to ensure a smooth functioning of the decision-making process at the top. This is needed to ensure that the plan has the complete backing of the political leadership. Fifth, in terms of formulating the economic and social plan and the policies related to its execution, the Central Planning Authority must be the supreme authority among all administrative departments of the government. Other agencies (departments) of the government will be responsible for seeing through the execution of the plan as well as for providing continuously inputs to the planning process.

(iv) *Perspective for Resource Allocation*

It should be pointed out that planning is a continuous process so that the optimal time horizon for formulating a plan is the infinite time horizon. Infinity is, however, always a difficult entity to handle, whereas planning must go on and decisions will have to be taken every day on various issues. The planner is confronted with the diffi-cult choice of allocating his time to immediate problems and keeping in abeyance all decisions regarding the distant and not-so-distant future, or formulating a set of decisions for future action over a predetermined time perspective during which policies will remain invariant unless changes are warranted by changes in the assumed state of exogenous variables. In this paper it is postulated that the Central Planning Authority will work with two different time perspectives in view, one being short relative to the other. Ac-cordingly, two frameworks will be required, one to formulate the short-term plans and the other the long-term plan. Purposely nothing is being laid down as to the duration of each. The short-term plan will, however, be concerned with the actual decision-making process pertaining to social and economic development. The period will be short enough to ensure the stability of the underlying values of different parameters and the structural relationships among the variables within the economy. On the other hand, the long-term plan will be designed to provide an indication of a desirable growth path of the economy. The time perspective will inevitably be so long that basic parameters will change and significant structural changes will take place within the economy. There is no *a priori* reason why the period of the long-term perspective (indicative) plan should not be longer than what is considered to be of direct interest to the present working generation, although socialists may hotly debate this point among themselves.

It is important that the short-term plans are formulated within the long-term perspective because the policies pursued over a short period may have serious implications for long-term development and this cannot be evaluated without an analytic framework exclusively related to the latter. The potential for social welfare maximisation may not always be realised and serious imbalances may occur within the economy in the future, if the short-term policies are framed without considering long-run implications. On the other hand, as mentioned above, it is only through the short-term plan that the actual acts of production, consumption, accummulation and invest- ment are realised. Furthermore, short-term plans provide the basis for revising the assumptions and consequently the level of decision variables underlying the perspective plan. At the end of each short- term plan, new information will be generated which could then be incorporated into the perspective plan. In fact, one could conceivably revise the perspective plan every year or every month (the computa- tional and related expenses may, however, be prohibitive) as the work on the successive short-term plans progresses. It is not un- likely that over time some modifications of the underlying social objective will take place. Thus the framework for the long-term perspective plan should be flexible enough for all contingencies to be easily incorporated. For convenience, it is assumed here that the short-term plan of Bangladesh will cover a period of five years, i.e. 1973–4 to 1977–8 which incidentally is also the perspective of the Bangladesh Planning Commission for the First Five Year Plan. The long-term planning horizon is taken to be thirty years, although no changes would be needed in what is said below if the length of this period were different.

II. PREPARING THE SHORT-TERM PLAN

In a socialist economy, planning is not passive but active, in the sense that the plan incorporates all aspects of national life and that policies are framed to execute all decisions of the plan under the direct supervision of the political leadership. Thus in the formulation of the plan a greater degree of harmonisation among all variables and institutions is necessary. The flows to and from each branch must be co-ordinated in such a manner that all the basic objectives of the plan are realised. In this sense, a complete synchronisation of the

physical and financial flows within the economy must be achieved.
The primary targets of the planner are better formulated in physical
terms, and the corresponding production plan should also be formulated in physical terms in so far as practicable. The financial implications of the plan will have to be worked out simultaneously, since
price and income policies are closely related to it. Furthermore, the
resources to be allocated are not always available in physical form
although they are all ultimately transformed into the flow of goods
and services. Thus it is necessary to retain all types of financial
institutions in a socialist economy. Money, credit, banking and
insurance have very important roles to play in a socialist economy.
This is more so for a country like Bangladesh, where the volume of
trade is a significant proportion of the gross national product. An
elaborate financial basis of all economic activities must be present so
that international transactions can be smoothly carried out.

(i) *Objectives of the Planner*

It will perhaps be agreed by all concerned, that the state in a socialist
economy must directly control all basic industries. These industries
are those which are engaged in the production of essential consumption goods, intermediate and capital goods, in an open economy all
export goods, and finally all essential services. The operation of the
non-basic industries, producing goods and services and their inputs,
for what can be called residual consumption, though included in the
plan, need not be centrally controlled. As a matter of fact, this
provides an area where some element of private enterprise and
initiative can be retained within the bounds set by the Central
Planning Authority.

The nature of central control indicated above will be required in
Bangladesh, if the realisation of what is considered by the author a
reasonable social objective is to be achieved. The social objective of
the planner in Bangladesh should be to raise the living standard. The
living standard can be raised only after the basic minimum consumption needs of the people have been met. Therefore, the implicit
welfare function should have as its argument variables representing
the different items of residual consumption. The plan should be
so formulated that this function is maximised subject to certain
constraints. One of the important constraints is, of course, the
satisfaction of basic minimum consumption needs. In the short-term
plan other important constraints will include: realisation of a given
export target based on a realistic forecast; maintaining a reasonable
level of government expenditure (including those on education,
health and housing); attaining a given level of employment; achieving
an equitable distribution of income; and finally, ensuring an

adequate rate of accumulation of investible surplus out of current national income.

(ii) *Components of the Plan*

The schematic flow diagram presented below identifies the principal components of the economy and explains the process of determination of the short-term development plan. As pointed out before, the components include:

(1) minimum consumption bundle – physical goods and services;
(2) required government consumption;
(3) exportables;
(4) intermediate demand;
(5) investment bunch;
(6) foreign sector;
(7) production plan;
(8) manpower and education;
(9) distribution plan;
(10) accumulation plan.

The minimum consumption bundle includes goods and services that are objectively considered a minimum requirement for sustenance and efficient economic activity of the population. In the first instance, these requirements will be determined by some given criteria in terms of calorie requirements and other requirements determined on the basis of past experience and the experience of other countries.

For maintaining state activities in administration and other fields, some minimum expenditure will have to be incurred every year during the short-term plan. Every government department should be able to provide information on this minimum requirement. It may be pointed out here that this will include requirement of essential services consumed by the population, such as education, health and housing.

For the short-term plan, it should be possible for the planners to determine export targets of various commodities on the basis of realistic projection. The list of items should be fairly comprehensive so as to include all major and minor items of exports.

Intermediate demand will include only those commodities which will be embodied as raw materials into the production of various commodities and services.

The investment bunch covers the requirement for investment in various sectors originating from demand for consumption, exports, skill production, educational production and intermediate production as well as creation of new capacity for the future.

The foreign sector will include an estimate of all import demands, originating from final and intermediate use of various types of commodities and services.

The production plan will be derived from all the components mentioned above. It will consist of a statement of the required levels of domestic production of all commodities and services during the period covering the short-term plan.

The manpower and educational plan will spell out the requirement for various types of schemes and the corresponding requirements for educational inputs. The educational demand, however, will also originate from the social demand for education itself. It is, therefore, very important to integrate the manpower and educational plan into the economic plan. Furthermore 'social planning' as referred to above, can be implemented only through the educational plan.

The distribution plan is the most important component of planning under socialism. This will determine on the one hand the distribution of national income among various sectors of the economy and on the other between present consumption and investment. The first type of distribution – distribution among sectors – will have to be carried out in such a way that a greater degree of equality is achieved among all individuals. This will be very closely related to the minimum consumption requirement, in the sense that income of every individual must be enough to pay for the minimum consumption bundle; and in addition, since the objective of the planner is to maximise residual consumption, some amount should be distributed to enable individuals to exercise their consumer sovereignty in purchasing items of residual consumption.

The accumulation plan will consist of measures to allocate a part of the national income to acquiring assets which will help to increase residual consumption in the future. The most important thing to be decided in this plan is what proportion of the total accumulation of services shall be carried out individually and what proportion corporately.

(iii) *Planning Institutions*

The planning institution that is responsible for formulating the development plan has been referred to here as the Central Planning Authority. It is suggested that the top hierarchy of this institution should be composed of experts in social and economic planning with adequate political orientation. It is perhaps desirable that they also be the members of the central politburo so that it shall become easy for them to take account of the reaction of the political leadership towards various social and economic measures incorporated into the short-term and the long-term plan.

The lower echelons of the planning institution should be composed of both political and technical personnel. The political personnel will be entrusted with the responsibility of incorporating political content into all projects where it is necessary. At the same time socio-political inputs into the planning process will also be provided by them. On the other hand, technical personnel will fill in the technical details of the plan. They will on the one hand ensure the overall consistency of the plan and, on the other hand, work out the technical feasibility of the different projects to be included in the plan.

The entire planning institution will be divided into a number of divisions, each responsible for planning the development of the different sectors of the economy. There should, however, be very close co-ordination among these divisions. While working out the plan there will, of necessity, be continuous horizontal flow of information. The entire success of the plan will depend on ensuring the smoothness of this flow. The structure of the Bangladesh Planning Commission is similar to what is described above as desirable. What is perhaps left to be ensured is close co-ordination between the political leadership and the top hierarchy of the planning institution on the one hand, and on the other hand, close co-ordination and smooth flow of information among all divisions.

(iv) *Working of the Schematic Flow*

The schematic flow diagram is presented here to facilitate the understanding of the process of formulation of the short-term plan. This framework is distinct from other analytic frameworks in the sense that it cannot be easily solved entirely by a computer; rather the solution has to be worked out by a trial and error method through the effort of the different divisions of the planning institution. However, it may be possible to obtain a solution for any particular component with the help of an analytical framework that allows for computer solution. A brief description of the working of the schematic flow will elaborate this point. The top cell contains the first round estimate of the exogenous variables of the system. These include minimum consumption bundle ($\bar{C}^p$), required state consumption ($\bar{C}^G$), residual consumption ($\bar{C}^r$) and exportables ($\bar{X}$). These estimates are made by, say, the General Economics Division of and relevant agencies outside the planning institution. All other sectoral divisions will take these estimates as given data and will proceed to work out the corresponding intermediate (I), import (F) and investment (K) requirement. They will do this by analysing the schedule of projects already available with them. If necessary, they will also work out the possibility of incorporating new projects, which may be undertaken during the planning period. These

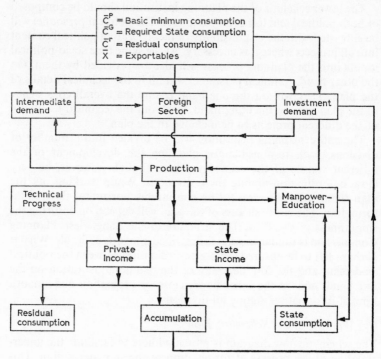

FIG. 1 Schematic flow diagram of short-term plan

individual project analyses will enable them to determine the investment inputs and intermediate demand of all types. However, at this stage, as pointed out above, a continuous feedback of information into each division will be necessary from all other divisions and outside agencies.

From the above will emerge the production plan (Y) for domestic sectors which is to be carried out during the planning period. The plan will also spell out the annual phasing of the different projects. From the production plan one can then work out the requirement of various types of skills and the corresponding educational inputs. This will, however, depend on the relationship between different types of skill and output of commodities and services on the one hand, and on the other hand, the relationship between the educational input and output of the various skill production processes. So it will be necessary for the manpower and educational division of the Planning Commission to determine the analytic form of the skill production function and the educational production function. It can be seen from the lower portion of the schematic flow that the educational plan must also include minimum social demand for education.

It should be pointed out that the production plan must be flexible enough to take advantage of exogenously given technological progress. In other words, after the formation of the plan there should be provision for new ideas being incorporated as the plan progresses. What can happen in reality is that a project which was included initially may have to give way to another, technologically and economically superior, which is designed later in the plan period.

Production will give rise to income. Here the top hierarchy of the planning institution, in consultation with the political leadership, will have to decide upon the following:

(a) distribution of national income between the private sector (V_1) and the state sector (V_2);

(b) distribution of total private sector income among all individuals;

(c) distribution of national income between current consumption and capital accumulation.

Total private sector income will by definition, equal the cost of the minimum consumption bundle, plus the value of services provided by the state on account of education, health and housing ($e\bar{C}^G$), plus the residual income (X) to be allocated by the private individual between consumption of residual (C^r) items and saving (S_1) to finance permissible private investment in financial and non-financial assets. Income of the state will then equal total income (V) minus private income. So the political leadership will have to decide upon the magnitude of X, the residual income of the private sector.

Out of the state income a portion will go to pay for the required state consumption and the residual will go into the accumulation fund. Thus the accumulation fund will consist of saving of the state and saving of individuals. In deciding upon X, the political leadership will have to decide on the extent of control it wants to maintain over the accumulation fund. If the state decides to socialise the entire production, then it must have complete control over the disposal of the accumulation fund. Alternately, if some activities are left in the hands of private individuals, then a portion of the accumulation fund will have to be allowed to be used according to the preference of the latter.

It is obvious that the accumulation fund is the domestic resource for financing the investment plan. At this stage, a comparison of investment and domestic saving will reveal the need for external capital inflow, if any, and this will also be reflected in a difference between import requirement and export earning, although *ex ante* these two gaps need not be equal. If the requirement of the foreign capital inflow exceeds the limit set by economic and political criteria then there will be a need for revision in the initial estimates of the exogenous variables. The economic criterion referred to above need not be anything more than a comparison between the stream of benefits over time flowing from foreign capital inflow and the cost (including interest payment and amortisation) thereof. The political criteria will, of course, have to be spelled out by the political authority.

The axe of revision of the initial values of exogenous variables will usually have to fall on the residual consumption and state consumption, although revision of the export target cannot be completely ruled out. Thus through this process of revision, the maximum feasible level of residual consumption within the given socio-economic and political constraints will be determined.

III. SOME QUESTIONS RELATED TO THE SHORT-TERM PLAN

(i) *Determination of the Objectives – Some Quantitative Estimates*

An attempt will be made here to present some initial estimates of basic consumption requirements and feasible export targets for the First Five Year Plan of Bangladesh. Estimates of consumption items and major exports will be presented in financial terms. No estimate will be presented on residual consumption or state consumption because time did not permit me to go into these. Admittedly, the minimum consumption requirement presented here has not been worked out as carefully as it might otherwise have been.

In fact, the present exercise in projecting the consumption requirement of some essential commodities for the short-term plan of Bangladesh is not consumption planning in the usual sense. A consumption plan is supposed to indicate how supply should be manipulated through production and import in order to satisfy the consumption requirement estimated independently of supply. One basis of projecting the consumption requirement is to estimate the income-elasticity of demand for individual items and to project the expected income of the consumers of those items. This is known as projection-type consumption planning. Further sophistication can be introduced in such an exercise by estimating what additional supply will have to be ensured so as to keep prices at a socially desirable minimum level. This is relevant for an economy that allows for complete consumer sovereignty. Clearly, a country like Bangladesh cannot afford this. An alternative basis of calculating the consumption requirement is to find out what level of food consumption is sufficient to provide the essential nutrient values in terms of calories, proteins, vitamins, etc. This is known as a nutrition-oriented plan.

The common feature between the projection-type plan and the nutrition-type plan is that in both the cases consumption requirement is projected independently of supply, and then suggestions are made to adjust supply to satisfy the consumers. What is done here, however, is quite different. In many cases an independent projection of supply for 1972–3 was made and then the implicit consumption was taken as the minimum that should be maintained over the first plan. For some of the items, at least, independent assumptions about the consumption requirement were made and the working out of the implicit production was left to detailed planning.

In general, the per capita requirement in 1969–70, as given in the Fourth Five Year Plan of pre-March, 1971, Pakistan, was accepted as the norm, since it appeared quite reasonable. This general rule was not followed, however, for a few items, such as sugar, where independent estimates of the consumption requirement were made on purely *a priori* reasoning. The reason why independent estimates were made about the consumption requirement of some of the items is that these estimates are not widely divergent from the consumption implication of our supply projections, so that the flexibility required to adjust supply to consumption is not too much to expect. For the rest of the items, either an independent consumption norm could not be found or where it could be found, the flexibility required to adjust supply to the norm was considered to be too much to expect during the short and difficult span of the coming years. That is why the per capita consumption implications of our supply projections have replaced the independent norms as the assumed per capita consumption requirement for those items. The same consideration of the flexibility of supply in relation to the time-span also lay behind the discarding of nutrition-oriented consumption planning in some cases. The time-span was also a very important factor in determining the educational and health requirement. The minimum consumption bundle is presented in Table 1.1.

The following assumptions regarding population were made to establish the relationship between per capita and total consumption requirements. The population in 1971–2 was taken as 75 million, and assuming 3 million deaths during the liberation struggle and a population growth rate of 3 per cent, the population for different years during the first plan was projected.

No attempt has been made here to present a minimum requirement of housing because a reliable estimate of present housing needs was not available. It will be necessary to undertake immediately a

TABLE 1.1

THE MINIMUM CONSUMPTION BUNDLE

Description of goods and services	Assumed per capita consumption per annum (lb.)	Minimum requirement for 1973–4 (000 tons)	Minimum requirement for 1974–5 (000 tons)	Minimum requirement for 1975–6 (000 tons)	Minimum requirement for 1976–7 (000 tons)	Minimum requirement for 1977–8 (000 tons)
Rice	341·40	11,934	12,292	12,661	13,040	13,432
Wheat	39·30	1,374	1,415	1,457	1,501	1,546
Pulses (excluding gram)	6·70	234	241	248	256	264
Vegetables (including potatoes,)	67·20	2,349	2,419	2,492	2,567	2,644
Milk	21·04	375	758	780	804	828
Fats and oils	3·34	117	120	124	128	131
Sugar and molasses	3·50	122	126	130	134	138
Meat	6·00	210	216	223	229	236
Fish	24·60[a]	860	836	912	940	968
Salt	8·40	294	302	312	321	330
Kerosene	1·03 (gallons)	297	305	315	324	334
Cotton cloth	10 (yds.)	783 (m. yds.)	807 (m. yds.)	831 (m. yds.)	856 (m. yds.)	881 (m. yds.)
Education	—	5·00[b]	4·10[b]	4·40[b]	6·14[b]	7·33[b]
Population assumption (millions)	—	78·30	80·65	83·07	85·56	88·13

[a] Exclusive of subsistence consumption.
[b] New enrolment at primary level (in millions).

housing census so that the requirement over the First Five Year Plan can be realistically estimated.

(ii) *Evaluation of Projects – Pricing of Output and Input*

It is clear from the above that in giving a final shape to the short-term development plan, it will be necessary to evaluate a large number of projects in different sectors. The evaluation of projects should be carried out in such a manner that the benefit is expressed in terms of total consumption (basic and residual) gains and costs in terms of true scarcity of all factors of production. Under a free market economy, willingness of the consumer to pay for a commodity or service may be taken as an indication of the consumption benefit of final products while for intermediate products the consumption gains of the ultimate consumers will be reflected in producers' willingness to pay. It may be pointed out here that, since the plan requires that items of basic consumption must be provided, projects taken up for evaluation in the first round, will be only those related directly or indirectly to basic consumption supplies.

Market prices are sometimes accepted as consumers' and producers' willingness to pay. However, in Bangladesh this will be misleading for three reasons. First, market prices of all commodities reflect a demand pattern which is the result of the existing income distribution that is to be regarded as highly skewed. Second, a large requirement of the economy is non-monetised where output is consumed either in or after the process of production; the market price would possibly be different if the entire output was marketed. Third, at present because of the operation of certain unusual social and economic factors following the liberation struggle the relative price structure has changed sharply as compared with that prevailing in the pre-liberation period, and there is a likelihood that in equilibrium there will be shifts in these prices. For all these reasons, for the purpose of project evaluation the use of existing market prices will not be desirable.

It is, therefore, suggested that all final output and intermediate products be evaluated in terms of international prices. The international price of any commodity will reflect the opportunity cost of producing at home instead of importing. It is assumed that international prices are insensitive to quantities bought and sold. There are two problems associated with this procedure: (1) At what rate should the international price be converted into a domestic price? This points to the problems of determining the shadow price of foreign exchange which will be discussed later. (2) The international price may differ from one source to another. In such a case a weighted average of the different prices should be taken. The weights should be the proportion of supply in the international market that originates from any particular source.

Some remarks should be made now on the pricing of primary inputs, such as capital, labour and foreign exchange, in the evaluation of projects. A large volume of literature is available on this topic. What will be said below will draw heavily from these writings. It has been emphasised over and again that primary inputs' prices should be such as to reflect their true scarcity. The best way to derive these prices for a country like Bangladesh would be to use a trial and error method in the sense that a price should be initially decided upon by the Central Planning Authority on the basis of past experience; if this price leads to surplus or deficit of the amount of resource consumed then the price should be revised accordingly. Some suggested initial prices are as follows. (1) For capital, a weighted average of the various existing interest rates can be taken as a first approximation; the weights should be the proportion of total volume of credit should be different for different types of skill. For example, for an unemployed unskilled labourer the price will be equal to the cost of the minimum consumption bundle plus a transfer cost if he is coming from any source in the last years. (2) For labour, this price moved from one region to another. It should be noted that the shadow price of an unemployed unskilled labourer has not been taken to be zero as is sometimes assumed. The reason is simply that given the present level of development in Bangladesh, and given capital and other resources, the amount of employment of the above type of labour in any particular project could never be pushed to an extent so as to make marginal productivity of labour zero; for different types of skilled labour a differential in the residual income (transfer payment) will have to be maintained in order to reflect differences in productivity; existing wage differentials may not be good indicators since they reflect different bargaining powers of the different groups of labour as well as the impact of the institutions which will undergo changes in the process of socialisation. A correction will be necessary to take account of these factors. (3) Finally for foreign exchange the first approximation to the shadow price would be the official exchange rate inflated by a weighted average of the rates of tariff and subsidy on various types of imports and exports respectively; the weights are the value of imports and exports of different commodities as a proportion of the total; this implies that with any change in the rate of tariff or export subsidy the initial shadow price of foreign exchange used for project evaluation changes.

(iii) *Strategy of Investment*

Investment provides the only link between the present and the future.

In the context of development planning and allocations of resources, it is necessary to arrive at a carefully determined set of decisions that reflect the underlying strategy of investment of the plan. There is a fundamental problem here additional to that of deciding about the distribution of national income between consumption and investment or accumulation. The basic question is that of allocating the accumulation fund between investments which will aid, directly or indirectly, in the raising of consumption standards during the short-term plan period and those whose benefit spills over partially or entirely into other planning periods. Alternatively it is a decision between creating capacity for the present and that for the future. To give concrete examples, what should be the strategy regarding investment in education, heavy machinery complex or a large-scale irrigation project? All of these have long gestation periods and they are characterised by 'dual' time lags. The first lag is the usual investment capacity utilisation lag. For education this lag exists between the time when investment takes place in a certain level of education and the time when the first enrolment is possible. The second lag involves the time between the enrolment and the actual addition to the labour force. For a heavy machinery complex this lag will refer to the time between the production of a unit of machinery and the generation of an ultimate flow of consumption benefit from it. The gestation period mentioned above, thus, can cover more than one planning period. Therefore, it is clear that the desirability of such investment projects cannot be determined within the context of the short-term plan. This points towards the need for a long-term perspective plan from which one can derive criteria for selecting investments which have serious implications for long-term development. Bangladesh must be very careful in this respect. It just cannot afford to make mistakes in formulating the strategy of investment. In its anxiety to meet the very short-run reconstruction and rehabilitation requirements, the Central Planning Authority must not ignore the long-term needs of development.

Within the Bangladesh context the problem mentioned above can be tackled in two ways. First, an investment growth constraint should be incorporated into the short-term plan.

The investment growth constraint will reflect the planner's concern for the well-being of the future generation and will be expressed in terms of lower limits on investment in fields which have implications for long-term development. Second, all investment proposals other than those affecting the basic consumption bundle within the short-term plan period should be evaluated and priorities determined in terms of discounted net present value of benefits (measured by contribution to the consumption stream). In that case there is no need for the General Economics Division to provide a set of $\bar{C}^r$s as mentioned above, this will come out as a consequence of the final short-term plan formulation.

(iv) *Realisation of the Production Plan – Institutional Framework*

In Bangladesh today, the following means of production have been socialised: all major industries with fixed assets of takas 1·5 million and more; all concerns of absentee owners; organised transport; banks and insurance companies other than those managed and owned by foreigners. Sterling tea gardens have also not been socialised. Thus it is clear that only a small fraction of the total production activity falls under the direct control of the state. In particular, the production of all major items of the basic consumption bundle that originate from agriculture is almost entirely in private hands. So, the relevant question here is how one shall go about realising the production plan that is spelled out by the Central Planning Authority in its short-term plan. In other words, what is the guarantee that what the individuals produce will add up to the production targets for all the different commodities as given in the plan? Given the present context of Bangladesh, this appears to be a rather weak link in the framework for the short-term plan discussed above.

In the non-agricultural sector the problem can be solved easily by the immediate socialising of all other basic industries still left in private hands. The question, however, remains one of efficient management of these industries. In point of fact, Bangladesh is already facing difficulty on this front. During the initial phase when a separate cadre of managers are not available, there does not seem to be any other alternative than to retain the services of the capitalist managers (owner-managers or salaried managers) of the past. In the meanwhile arrangement must be made for the training of management personnel to take up assignments in the socialised institutions. The training, as pointed out before, must consist of both technical training as well as political and ideological. It must be recognised that the human element in the process of socialisation is extremely important. Socialism can never be established without socialist men. Therefore, all individuals who will be holding responsible positions in various socialised institutions must be developed into mature agents of socialism.

However, in order to ensure efficiency and increasing productivity in all establishments, it is necessary to introduce reward (in the form of bonus) for good work or penalty (in the form of demotion, cut in salary or termination of job) for less than normal performance. Bangladesh must start pursuing these policies, if the political leadership intends to capitalise on the fading initiative of the people.

As for agriculture, when it is producing basic food items there does not seem to be any simple solution. It is composed of a large number of privately owned farms and a large part of the agriculture sector is outside the market economy. Ownership of land is far from being equal and policies related to agricultural development are not carefully formulated, affect different groups of farmers differently, and often give rise to serious social imbalances from which many undesirable consequences follow. For example, the 'agricultural revolution', in terms of introduction of new techniques, in the absence of appropriate institutional changes, is likely to benefit only the farmers with large holdings and to increase the number of surplus farmers. Under these circumstances there may be difficulty in realising the target set by the Central Planning Authority.

Furthermore, there is often delay in the spread of new ideas because of the presence of large numbers of decision-makers who are often excessively cautious. The task of increasing the rate of diffusion of new technology among farmers has been a major concern of planners for a long time. Bangladesh needs to introduce new techniques and ensure their rapid diffusion if something like an agricultural revolution is to be brought about within a reasonable period of time. The delay caused by individual decision-making may prove too costly. Thus it is essential that some mechanism be devised so that the state can obtain a greater degree of control over individual decision making. Without such a measure there will be no way of ensuring that the target production of the basic consumption bundle from agriculture will be achieved. The author feels that collectivisation of agriculture in Bangladesh is the answer to this problem. To spell this out more clearly, the entire agriculture of Bangladesh will be organised into a number of collectives. There will be one or more representatives of the state in the management of the collectives. These representatives will be trained extension workers and they will be responsible for seeing through the implementation of the production plan of the Central Planning Authority. Clearly the reorganisation of agriculture in Bangladesh along the lines suggested above will not be achieved very easily. It will require elaborate planning and extensive popularisation of the concept of collective farming among the rural masses. Hopefully, the Bangladesh Central Planning Authority will find enough talents within the country to undertake this job.

(v) *Generation of Income and its Distribution – the Accumulation (Savings) Fund*

Production activities of all types generate income. On the one hand the income will have to be distributed between consumption and investment and on the other will have to be distributed among all the individuals of the country. These two types of distribution problem were referred to above in section II. The first type of distribution is, as pointed out above, to a great extent dependent on purely political considerations. The political considerations are reflected in the basic consumption bundle of goods and services, residual consumption as well as state consumption.

What is really most important for Bangladesh is the distribution of the second kind. This is, however, sometimes linked with the first, although in a somewhat distorted way. It is often quite fallaciously argued by growth-minded economists that, in order to ensure a high rate of growth of income over a long period of time, consideration of attaining a more equitable distribution of income must be postponed in the initial phase. In point of fact, it is said that some degree of inequality is necessary in order to ensure a higher rate of saving and consequently a higher rate of growth of income. Now, it is not very clear that aggregate saving is reduced by a more equitable distribution of income. Pre-March 1971 Pakistan followed a policy of generating a higher level of income in the capitalist sector in order to generate higher saving. A study by the author on savings in Bangladesh during the Pakistani regime reveals that the capitalist sector contributed only a small proportion of total saving and also that the rate of saving out of gross profit was not as high as is often claimed by proponents of high-capitalist-saving theories. What is more important, the proponents of the above policy ignore the potential danger inherent in pursuing this policy for too long. The socio-political turmoil that is likely to result from the accumulated discontent of the masses will produce complete dislocation of economic activities, so that even after a decade of development a country may find itself back in the position it started from in terms of production, consumption, saving and investment. The history of the development of the economy of erstwhile Pakistan and the consequences that followed should be a case in point.

In a capitalist or a mixed economy, it is not clear whether a more equitable distribution will raise the level of savings. On the other hand, for a socialist economy it can be asserted with some degree of confidence that a more equal distribution of income can be made consistent with a higher level of savings, simply because of the dominant role that is played by the state in the mobilisation of domestic saving. In the context of a socialist Bangladesh, the state can use the following instruments to affect a higher savings out of national income: (i) holding back the surplus of the state enterprises; (ii) mobilising surplus from collective farms; (iii) direct taxes, levies and tolls. The most important question – how to achieve a more equitable distribution of income – still remains unanswered.

In a socialist economy, where plans are formulated on the basis of a minimum consumption bundle, the problem of distribution of income is somewhat simplified. In all the socialised sectors the profit, rent and interest income belong to the state and only the wage fund remains to be distributed among workers. The wage fund consists entirely of the minimum consumption bundle (value) and the residual income which, as pointed out before, will be distributed in a manner such that payments to different types of skill reflect differences in their productivity. However, it should be noted that the difference between the lowest and the highest wage should not be very wide.

One cannot talk about the distribution of income in the agriculture sector without referring to the distribution of land holdings. An equitable distribution of agricultural income can only come from an equitable distribution of land holding. The collectives, as suggested above, can be formed only after a redistribution of land holding has taken place. Within each collective, the source of earnings (in physical or in financial terms) of the members would be the rent on the land owned and the wage for the labour contributed. It follows from the above that the total of this income must include the minimum consumption bundle and a residual income.

So far as income distribution in other non-socialised non-agricultural sectors is concerned, there does not seem to be any other alternative but to fall back upon instruments such as direct taxes and lump sum transfers in order to bring about a more equitable distribution of income.

A word should be added here on the mechanism of procuring and distributing the minimum consumption bundle. For services (education, health and housing) the problem is easily solved since the state can distribute most of these services under its direct supervision. Housing can be provided sometimes in the form of the state first building a housing complex and then renting it out to people, or by the alternative of providing a housing subsidy to those who wish to have their own. In order to avoid inequity in housing services, strict quality and size control will have to be enforced. As for other items, the source of procurement will be state production, surplus of collectives and import. Distribution to consumers will have to be affected through direct rationing all over the country since this appears to be the only way of ensuring that the minimum consumption bundle will be made available to all individuals. In the context of Bangladesh both internal procurement of surplus and total distribution of commodities through a system of country-wide rationing will be a very difficult task to be performed during the early phase of socialism. Past experience with internal procurement and rationing has been of much smaller magnitude. An elaborate machinery of institutions and personnel will have to be created in order to initiate the programme of the distribution of the minimum consumption bundle. This will represent another challenge to be met by the Bangladesh Central Planning Authority.

IV. THE LONG-TERM PERSPECTIVE PLAN

What has been said thus far has left aside the question of determining the long-term perspective within which the short-term policies are to be formulated. It was implicitly assumed that the overall strategy of the short-term plan had been formulated within the framework of a long-term perspective plan, so that the only task that remained to be accomplished was to work out the details of the different components of the short-term plan. In this section the analytic framework of the long-term perspective plan will be presented. Although no attempt has yet been made to implement the model empirically, the author from past experience of the working of models of a similar nature can state confidently that this is a suitable framework for a country such as Bangladesh and that existing data, with some alteration and additions, will permit empirical implementation of the model. The model has the following broad characteristics:

- (*a*) The model is formulated, along traditional lines, as a constrained optimisation problem. It is assumed that both the maximand, which represents an index of social welfare, and the set of constraints are linear functions in terms of the structural variables.
- (*b*) The set of constraints include those: (i) concerning the economic system; (ii) concerning the educational system; (iii) concerning skill-creating activities; (iv) concerning the interrelationship between the economy and education.
- (*c*) The model is dynamic; it extends over a finite horizon and the time is considered discretely.
- (*d*) Explicit production functions have been formulated to describe production activities related to education, manpower and economy.
- (*e*) This is a single model: no attempt is made to divide Bangladesh into different regions; this extension, however, should not be too difficult once more data are available.
- (*f*) The model recognises some boundary constraints indicated by the historical process of development as experienced in different countries of the world over time.
- (*g*) The model recognises the difference between tied aid and untied aid; the total volume of aid and its composition are decision variables within some given bound in the model.

(*h*) The model incorporates the distribution of national income between private income and state income as decision variables.

(*i*) The model includes the following choice elements: (i) commodities can be produced at home or imported from abroad; (ii) non-repeating students may either join the labour force or they may continue education; (iii) for the production of skill, choice exists among various types of graduates and dropouts; (iv) in skill production, choice also exists between drawing persons directly from subsidiary job training activities; (v) at certain levels, the supply of graduates can be increased either by increasing the enrolment or by reducing the dropout rate.

ALGEBRAIC FORMULATION OF THE MODEL

In the description of the model, time subscripts are omitted except where they are essential for clarity.

(*a*) Welfare Function

It is defined as the discounted sum of residual consumption.

$$\sum_t \sum_j C^r_j\, W + \sum_i \sum_j t_{ji}\, I_i\,(T)W_T + i$$

C^r_j = Private residual consumption item j.
W = Discount parameter.
I_i = Gross fixed investment in i th sector.
t_{ji} = Investment – consumption transformation coefficient.

(*b*) Constraints

(i) *Structure of Residual Consumption*

Residual consumption is treated as a composite commodity and it is distributed among individual items by a fixed proportion.

$C^r_j j = c'_j C^r$. For some $_j$, $C^r_j = 0$.
C^r = Total residual consumption.
$c'_j j$ = Proportion of residual consumption going into j th commodity.

(ii) *Basic Consumption Bundle*

$\bar{C}j$ = $\bar{C}^p j + \bar{C}^G j$. For some j, $\bar{C}j = 0$.
$\bar{C}j$ = Exogenously determined basic requirement of the state and the private sector.
$\bar{C}^p j$ = Private basic consumption requirement.
$\bar{C}^G j$ = Basic consumption requirement of the state.

(iii) *Total consumption*

$$C = \sum_j (C^r_j + Cj)$$

(iv) *Monotonicity Requirement*

It is required that total residual consumption should be non-decreasing.

$$C^r(t) \geqslant C^r(t-1), \quad t \neq 1.$$

(v) *Commodity Balance*

Supply of each commodity should be greater than or equal to demand.

$$Y_j + d_j M_j \geqslant \sum_i a_{ij} Y_i + \sum_i b_{ij} I_i + C^r_j + \bar{C}_j + X_j + \hat{I}_j + m_{ij} M_j$$

Y_j = Domestic production of commodity.
M_j = Import of commodity.
X_j = Export of commodity.
$\hat{I}_j$ = Investment in working capital of type j.
a_{ij} = Input – output coefficient.
b_{ij} = Capital – output ratio.
m_{ij} = Trade/Transport requirement for import.
d_j = Ratio of price of import (at official exchange rate) to domestic production cost.

It is possible to make the changes in a_{ij} endogenous by expressing it as a function of investment output ratio which is taken to be a surrogate for technical progress.

$$a_{ij} = f(I_{i/Y_i})$$

Export levels are determined by specifying upper bounds.

$$X_j \leqslant \bar{X}_j \text{ for some } j.$$

Working capital requirement is determined as a function of output, consumption, export and investment.

$$\hat{I}_j = f(Y_1, ..., Y_j; \quad C_1, ..., C_j; \quad X_1, ..., X_j; \quad I_1, ..., I_j)$$

(vi) *Capacity Constraint*

Domestic production in any sector can not exceed the capacity available.

$$Y_j(t) \leqslant K_j(O) + \sum_{\tau=lj}^{t-lj-1} \delta_j{}^{(t)} I_j(t-r) - \sum_{=1}^{t-1} D_j(\tau)$$

K_j = Capacity available in sector j.
D_j = Depreciation of capacity in sector j.
$\hat{I}_j$ = Investment capacity utilisation lag in sector j.
δ_j = Fraction of time period for which capacity is available for use.

(vii) *Structural Constraint*

It has been observed by many writers that, over time, developing economies reveal certain pattern of changes in the proportional importance of various components of the economy. These changes were found to be closely correlated with per capita income. Although each developing country had specific reasons for following a given time path, yet from an analysis of a cross section of comparable countries, it is possible to discover an upper and a lower bound for the movement of the various components, e.g. proportion of gross domestic product originating in any sector, the proportion of labour force being employed by any sector. The rationale behind incorporating these bounds is that there are no known peculiarities of Bangladesh such that it might fall outside these bounds. The bounds can be expressed as follows.

In terms of sectoral gross domestic product,

$$\frac{\sum V_j}{V} \leqslant f^u(y) \text{ or } \bar{P}_j$$

and

$$\frac{\sum V_j}{V} \geqslant f^L(y) \text{ or } \underline{P}_j$$

In terms of sectoral labour force,

$$\frac{\sum L_j}{L} \leqslant g^u(y) \text{ or } \bar{g}_j$$

and

$$\frac{\sum L_j}{L} \geqslant g^L(y) \text{ or } \underline{g}_j.$$

V_j = Value added in sector j.
V = Total value added.
L_j = Labour force in sector j.
L = Total labour force.
y = Per capita income.
$\bar{P}_j, \underline{P}_j$ = Exogenously given upper and lower bound to the proportion of value added in sector j.
$\bar{g}_j, \underline{g}_j$ = Exogenously given upper and lower bound to the proportion of labour force in sector j.

(viii) *Foreign exchange*

Total import bill and debt repayment liability should equal export earnings and foreign capital inflow.

$$\sum_j M_j(t) + R(t) = \sum_j x_j(t) + F_1(t) + d' F_2(t) \quad 0 < d' < 1.$$

$$F(t) = F_1(t) + F_2(t).$$
$$F(t) = F_1(t) + F_2(t).$$
F = Total foreign capital inflow.
F_1 = Untied capital inflow.
F_2 = Tied capital inflow.
R = Debt repayment liability.

(ix) *Requirement for Self-Reliance*

New capital inflow in the terminal year will be zero.

$$F_T = 0$$

(x) *Upper Bound on Periodic Debt Liability*

$$R(t) \leqslant 0 \cdot 10 \sum_j X_i$$

(xi) *Capital*

Investment should equal saving plus foreign capital inflow.

$$S + F = \sum_j k_j I_j + \sum_j \hat{I}_j$$
$$S = S_p + S_G$$

S = Total saving.
S_p = Saving by private sector.
S_G = Saving by the state.
k_j = Capital – output ratio for sector j.

Private saving function

$$S_p = f_p(x)$$

x = Residual private sector income.

In this function parameter estimates from data reflecting capitalist income distribution, should be corrected.

Determination of private sector residual income.

$$x = V_1 - (C^p{}_j + eC^G{}_j).$$

V_1 = Total private sector income.
e = Proportion of state consumption on account of education, health and housing.
V_1 = $V - V_2$.
V_2 = State income.

V = Total income

$\quad = \sum\limits_{j} v_j\, Y_j.$

V_j = Value added coefficient.

$\quad = 1 - \sum\limits_{i} a_{ij}.$

(xii) *Skill constraint*

The constraints concerning the skill production and demand are related to both the educational system and the economic system. As pointed out before, the skill production activity requires input from the educational system (primarily graduates and dropouts). However, in the case of farmers and manual workers inputs can be drawn directly from the uneducated population. On the other hand, the demand for various types of skill is generated from the activities in the economic system. In each time period the supply of a particular skill is composed of the initial stock, new graduates and dropouts joining the labour force during the planning period, uneducated workers and dropouts from the teacher stock. Two types of leakages are to be taken account of. The first arises due to death and the second due to retirement. It is suggested that the choice among various sources for the formulation of a particular skill is determined by the relative productivities of workers with different educational background. The relative productivity coefficients are used to convert the units of graduates and dropouts into efficiency units. The demand for labour is a function of the level of output of the different sectors and the labour output coefficients, which is also expressed in efficiency units. So, this supply and demand relationship provides the most important link between the economic system and the educational system. The skill constraint can be written as,[1]

$$\sum_{j=1}^{8} l_{sj}\, V_j(t) \leqslant L_s(t)$$

$$L_s(t) = (l-\alpha)^t\, L_s(0) + \sum_{\tau=1}^{t} (l-\alpha)^{t-\tau}$$

$$\sum_{p=1}^{7} e_{ps}\, w_{ps}\, W_{ps}(\tau)\pi_{ps}$$

$$+ \sum_{p=1}^{7} g_{ps}\, Z_{ps}\, Z_{ps}\, \phi_{ps} + \beta^0{}_s\, W^0{}_s(\tau).$$

Where,

$L_s(t)$ = Total supply of labour skill s in period t;

$L_s(0)$ = Base period supply of labour skill s;

[1] The above approach to deriving skill constraint is due to Irma Adelman [1]. The basic logic is further elaborated and extended in M. Alamgir [2].

α = Rate of mortality including retirement;

l_{sj} = Labour output coefficients;

$W^0{}_s$ = Number of uneducated labourers in skill s;

$W_{ps} Z_{ps}$ = Fraction of time for which graduates and dropouts are available for work force. Normally less than 1 in the initial period and 1 in all future periods;

π_{ps} = Relative productivity of a graduate of school type p as a worker in the skill group s. It expresses the productivity of a worker with educational background p as a fraction of the sum of productivity of all admissible types of worker;

ϕ_{ps} = Relative productivity of a dropout from school type p as a worker in the skill group s;

$\beta^0{}_s$ = Relative productivity of the uneducated labour in skill s.

It is assumed that uneducated workers join the labour force at the beginning of each time period. Further, the uneducated workers into skill s in period t are drawn from the potential stock of the period $t - 1$. This is because this potential stock is residual among the school age population and fall into the age-group 5–9. But here it is assumed that the minimum age of entry into the work force is 10. Accordingly, the following distributional relationship for uneducated workers is included.

$$\sum_{s=1}^{2} W^0{}_s(t) \leqslant (1 - r_0) W^0(t - 1)$$

Where

r_0 = Leakage due to mortality, household work (mostly women), etc.

(xiii) *Educational Flow Constraints*

Graduates from each level of education can either be intermediate input (continuing students) or final output (teachers and workers). Dropouts, on the other hand, cannot by definition be intermediate inputs but they can be used as primary input. So, the distributional relationship for graduates can be written as

$$(1 - g_p) P_p N_p(t - 1) - \sum_{q=1}^{6} c_{pq} N_{pq}(t) - \sum_{s=1}^{5} e_{ps} W_{ps}(t) - \sum_{r=1}^{6} f_{pr} T_{pr} = 0.$$

and for dropouts as

$$g_p P_p N_p(t - 1) - \sum_{s=1}^{5} g_{ps} Z_{ps}(t) - \sum_{r=1}^{6} K_{pr} V_{pr}(t) = 0$$

$$g_p = f_g(E^p{}_d)$$

where

N_p = Enrolment in schools of type p;

N_{pq} = Graduates from schools of type p entering schools of type q;

W_{ps} = Workers of skill class s originating from schools of type p;

T_{pr} = Graduates from schools of type p becoming teachers in schools of type r;

Z_{ps} = Dropouts from schools of type p who enter labour skill s;

V_{pr} = Dropouts from schools of type p who become teachers in schools of type r;

g_p = Dropout rate from schools of type p;

P_q = Labour force participation rate (including continuation probability of students) for persons from school type p – it takes account of leakages due to mortality, housewifery, etc.;

$c_{pq}{}'$ e_{ps}, f_{pr}, g_{ps}, k_{pr} = 1 or 0, indicating whether or not entrance into the category (of students, teachers and workers) is permitted to persons with the given educational background.

$E^p{}_d$ = Additional expenditure on education to reduce dropout rates in level p.

Further, there is a population flow constraint expressed as following,

$$N_1(t) + W^0(t) = \bar{p}(t)$$

where:

$N_1(t)$ = Enrolment in the primary level in period t;

$W^0(t)$ = Potential new addition to the stock of uneducated workers;

$P(t)$ = School age population in period t.

Basic education and health

$$N_p \geqslant \bar{N}^p$$

(xiv) *Educational Stock Constraints*

There are three different types of stock constraints corresponding to teachers, building and equipment. They put upper bound to the total enrolment at different levels.

The teacher constraint is expressed as

$$u_r t_r N_r(t) \leqslant (1 - \lambda_r)^t T^0{}_r + \sum_{\tau=1}^{t} \sum_{p=1}^{6} (1 - \lambda_r)^t - f_{pr} T_{pr}(\tau) + \sum_{r=1}^{t} \sum_{p=1}^{6}$$
$$(1 - \lambda_r)^{t-\tau} K_{pr} V_{pr}(\tau)$$

where

$T^0{}_r$ = Stock of teachers of type r at the start of the plan;

t_r = Teacher–student ratio;

u_r = The conversion factor expressing the time required by educational process r as a fraction of the planning period. Such adjustment is necessary to express the fact that if the length of the particular course is more or less than a planning period, less or more than a single student may be educated during the period. This factor also takes account of the repeater rates at each level;

λ_r = Rate of attrition (due to death and retirement) of teachers.

The building and equipment stock constraints are similar to the teacher constraints.

The equipment and building constraints are

$$\sum_p u_p \, n'_p \, (t) \, N_p \, (t) \leqslant (1 - \delta'_j) \, t - 1 \, K^0{}_{j,3} + \sum_{\tau=0}^{t-1} (l - \delta'_j) \, I_{j,3} \, (\tau)$$

and

$$\sum_p u_p \, n_p \, (t) \, N_p \, (t) \leqslant (1 - \delta_j) \, t - 1 \, K^0{}_{j,4} + \sum_{\tau=0}^{t-1} (1 - \delta_j) \, I_{j,4} \, (\tau)$$

where,

n'_p = Equipment–student ratio expressed as takas worth of equipment needed for enrolling one student;

n_p = Building–student ratio expressed as takas worth of building capacity needed for enrolling one student;

j = 9, 10, 11. Index for type of capacity;

j = 9 represents capacity for primary and secondary schools;

j = 10 represents capacity for higher secondary schools and primary training institutes;

j = 11 represents capacity for university and secondary teacher training colleges.

The summation on the left-hand side extends over different educational levels within each group.

$K^0{}_{j,3}$ = Equipment stock of type j available at the start of the plan;

$k^0{}_{j,4}$ = Building capacity of type j available at the start of the plan;

δ'_j = Rate of depreciation of the equipment of type j;

δ_j = Rate of depreciation of the building of type j.

(xv) *Terminal Constraints*

Investment in school equipment

$$I_{j,3}(T) \geqslant (1 + \bar{g}_1) I_{j,3} (T-1)$$

Investment in school building

$$I_{j,4}(T) \geqslant (1 + \bar{g}_1) I_{j,4} (T-1)$$

Investment in basic consumption items

$$I_j(T) \geqslant (l + \bar{g}_2) I_j (T-1) \text{ for some } j.$$

$\bar{g}_1$, $\bar{g}_2$ and $\bar{g}_3$ = Exogenously gives growth rate of investment.

V. CONCLUSION

An attempt has been made to present a framework for formulating a short-term and long-term development plan for Bangladesh within the context of a socialist economy. The framework will it is hoped, be a convenient tool towards determining priorities for development and allocation of resources in Bangladesh. No attempt has, however, been made to implement the model empirically. This task is left for the Central Planning Authority in Bangladesh.

From what has been discussed above it seems clear that the establishment of a true socialist order in Bangladesh will not be an easy task. The task becomes more difficult since a large number of fundamental institutional changes will be required. In the process of a socialist development, both human and material factors will be equally important. Given technology and resources, it is the human element that will be the sole carrier of the principles of socialism. Without an active and dedicated co-operation from all sections of the population the worth-while goals of socialism will remain unrealised. Therefore, it is imperative on Bangladesh, if it is to emerge as a socialist state, to embark upon the task of creating socialist men.

REFERENCES

[1] Adelman, I., 'A Linear Programming Model of Educational Planning: A Case Study for Argentina', in Irma Adelman and Erik Thorbecke (ed.), *The Theory and Design of Economic Development*. (Baltimore: Johns Hopkins Press, 1966).
[2] Alamgir, M., 'A Planning Model for East Pakistan, with Special Reference to Manpower and Education', an unpublished Ph.D. dissertation at Harvard University, 1971.

[3] Alamgir, M., 'Some Theoretical Issues in Economic, Manpower and Educational Planning' (mimeo), Bangladesh Institute of Development Economics, 1972.

[4] ——. 'Alternative Approaches to Educational Planning – Their Relevance to a Developing Economy' (mimeo), Bangladesh Institute of Development Economics, 1972.

[5] ——. 'Resources for Development,' a Paper presented at the International Economic Association Conference on the Economic Development of Bangladesh within the Framework of a Socialist Economy in Dacca Bangladesh, 6–13 Jan, 1973. (Chapter 4 below).

[6] Bose, S. R., 'A Few Comments on Professor Huda's Conference Address: "Planning Experiments in Pakistan"', *The Pakistan Development Review*, vol. VIII, no. 3 (Autumn 1968).

[7] Dickinson, H. D., 'Price Formation in a Socialist Community', *Economic Journal*, vol. XLIII (June 1933).

[8] Dobb, M. H., 'Economic Theory and the Problem of a Socialist Economy', *Economic Journal*, vol. XLIII (Dec 1933).

[9] Durbin, E. F. M., 'Economic Calculus in a Planned Economy', *Economic Journal*, vol. XLVI (Dec 1936).

[10] Hayek, F. A. Von (ed.), *Collectivist Economic Planning* (London: Routledge, 1935).

[11] Khan, A. R., 'Some "Notes on Planning Experience in Pakistan"', *The Pakistan Development Review*, vol. VIII, no. 3 (Autumn 1968).

[12] Knight, F. H., 'The Place of Marginal Economics in a Collectivist System', *American Economic Review*, Supplement to vol. XXVI (Mar 1936).

[13] Kantorovitch, L. V., *The Best Use of Economic Resources*, translated from the Russian by P. F. Knightsfield (Cambridge; Harvard University Press, 1965).

[14] Lange, O. and Taylor, Fred M., *On the Economic Theory of Socialism* (New York: McGraw-Hill Book Company, 1964).

[15] Lenner, A. P., 'Statics and Dynamics in Socialist Economics', *Economic Journal*, vol. XLVII (June 1937).

[16] Mahmood, A. N. M., *Essays on Political Economy* (Dacca, 1970).

[17] United Nations, *Long Term Planning*, Papers presented to the Seventh Meeting of Senior Economic Advisors to E.C.E. Governments (New York, 1971).

[18] United Nations, Industrial Development Organisation, *Evaluation of Industrial Projects*, Project Formulation and Evaluation Series, Volume I, Selected Studies Presented at the Interregional Symposium on Industrial Project Evaluation Held in Prague, Czechoslavakia, 11-29 Oct. 1965. (New York, 1968).

Discussion of Papers by
M. Anisur Rahman and Mohiuddin Alamgir

COMMENTS ON THE PAPERS BY JAROSLAV VANEK

I have read with a good deal of interest both papers but because this is my first contact with this country and in fact my first visit to Asia, I do not have the perspective which would allow me to present a truly competent discussion of the two papers. In view of this I will restrict myself to a few basic comments. Then, in order to be constructive, I will move in the direction of my comparative advantage and outline some key points which the Bangladesh policy makers ought to be aware of in introducing labour participation and self-management in general.

Alamgir's paper, presenting a short-run consistency planning procedure and long-range optimising planning procedure, impresses me as a technically competent piece of work. Given the obvious data problems and problems of implementation, the latter procedure especially may not remain much more than an academic exercise. The former procedure, however, if combined with experienced judgement, is likely to become a useful tool in providing broad year-to-year consistency checks between the resources and needs of the Bangladesh economy. It is this part, in my opinion, that should be given by far the greater significance and to which a greater analytical effort should be devoted. The complexity of the economic problems at hand and the problems of implementation may make it necessary, at least in the initial years, to restrict the number of objectives to an absolute minimum, perhaps including only considerations of maximum (if not full) employment and fulfilment of some minimum nutritional targets. The question raised in my mind by Alamgir's paper is whether the procedures developed do not imply a greater degree of centralisation and command within the economy than the Bangladesh authorities are either capable of implementing or willing to accept.

To be quite frank, Anisur Rahman's paper made me feel more at ease than that of Alamgir, perhaps because the first author has been away from the abstractly-oriented classrooms of American universities for about ten years. Indeed, Rahman's discussion demonstrates a considerable – and in my view entirely correct – understanding of the real situation of Bangladesh and contains the necessary elements – perhaps the only possible elements – for resolving the critical conditions of the economy. Rahman's central points are of such importance that they deserve brief restatement. As I read them, Rahman's specific recommendations imply much more than planning, however perfect it may be; they call for a fundamental change of attitude – perhaps change of heart is a better term – on the part of the authorities and of all Bengalis.

Specifically, what is necessary is (1) the introduction of a fundamentally socialist economy; (2) the development of socialist cadres who would be able to carry out an administrative reform; (3) what he calls the sharing of poverty, that is, significant income and wealth redistribution; (4) reform of ownership, particularly in the larger agricultural holdings; (5) self-sufficiency in the long run; (6) what he terms fast-yielding emergency programmes to increase output in agriculture; and (7) last but by far not least, full utilisation of labour resources. These are the cornerstones of the proposed economic reform, and if any one is grossly overlooked, given the seriousness of the situation, the fulfilment of the aspirations of the young Bengali nation will be jeopardised.

Let us now become more specific and speak about the first pre-condition, that of a socialist economy, and go from there to the problems of participation and self-management, since, as I understand it, not only from the two papers presented here but also from the other papers before the conference, these are of priority in Bangladesh.

The first thing we must realise is that the postulate of socialism for development in Bangladesh, which has been posited as fixed before the conference, and with which most of us here present wholeheartedly agree, should never be taken as the final aim and purpose in itself. Rather it should be understood as an optimal expression of something that is truly fundamental and as such can be posited as the key axiom of an ideal society anywhere in the world. That basic postulate or axiom is the liberation of man, both political and economic, or what we may refer to as total or *integral humanism*. It is this fundamental principle towards which the young Bangladesh nation and state must strive.

In the economic sphere, this fundamental principle of humanism implies two things, their importance being such that both should be taken as fundamental rights of man. The first is the right to work, intimately involving the right to decent minimum living conditions. This is of absolute urgency in this country and should be carried out at any cost with the shortest possible delay. The other implication of the fundamental principle, the second basic right suggested, is what we may call full economic self-determination of all working men or, in a more concrete and practical expression, self-management. Now economic self-determination and self-management have assumed historically a variety of forms, and several other possibilities can also be imagined in theory. Some of these forms can be very efficient, indeed the most effective forms of economic organisation of any kind, but others, as is amply demonstrated by history, can be ineffective sometimes to the degree of dooming to failure all efforts to introduce producer co-operation and self-management.

If I can share any of my knowledge usefully with my Bangladesh hosts, it is precisely in this area of identifying the forms of economic participation and self-management which are highly effective and which could play a central role in getting under way true and human economic development in Bangladesh. I will summarise here in ten separate points what I would call the necessary conditions of an optimal and viable self-managed economy, and by implication of an optimum and viable socialist organization. Of course I cannot go into full justification and reasoning behind each of the points, but this I have done very carefully and in considerable detail in my published writings.

These necessary conditions are:

(1) All control, management and income (after payment of all costs and taxes) should always remain in the hands of those who work in a given enterprise, the underlying operational rule being a fully democratic rule on the basis of equality of vote. The philosophical and moral basis of this must always remain the work in common of a group of men and nothing else, in particular not, as was often the case with traditional producer co-operatives, some kind of ownership of shares or basic contributions. This is nothing but an expression of the fundamental humanist principle.

(2) Whenever, on grounds of static or dynamic economies of scale, division of labour and co-operation in an enterprise are necessary,[1] social or socialist ownership and funding of capital assets is necessary. But of course that ownership does not imply control, which by condition No. 1 remains in the hands of the working collective.

(3) While capital, or more precisely the source of financial capital, does not command any right of control, it is entitled to adequate remuneration at a rate reflecting the relative scarcity of capital in the economy. Such a rate in my judgement might be quite high in Bangladesh, perhaps well in excess of 10 per cent.

(4) Conditions 1, 2 and 3 are equally applicable to productive land which for all practical purposes can be treated as capital. The only exception here is that the payment of rent or income of land should be conditioned by the attainment of necessary minimum subsistence of those who work on the land. For example, a payment of 10 per cent on the value of land might reduce the income per farm labourer to unacceptably low levels.

(5) The returns to capital and land should in their entirety, or at least predominantly, be earmarked for accumulation, that is creation of new capital assets and not for individual consumption of any kind. In this way the fundamental problem of accumulation facing all developing economies is resolved, while at the same time the objection to personal capital income (that is, non-labour income) on distributional grounds is eliminated. It can be shown that the rates of accumulation attainable through this method are quite considerable.

(6) In principle the returns charged on capital should be the same for all users. This guarantees an optimal allocation of capital resources.

(7) It is imperative to establish an organisation or institution on the national level (which can be decentralised to any degree according to need), whose function would be to guarantee the fulfilment of the two above-noted basic rights of economic self-determination and full employment. More specifically, this agency would be charged with supervision but not control of the capital market, promotion and expansion of new firms or sectors according to national plans, the co-ordination and spreading of information regarding alternative investment projects, technical

[1] It seems to me that Anisur Rahman's advocacy of collective exploitation of land is based on such dynamic economies of scale, modernisation and technical change being impossible on the present very small, sometimes fragmented, individual holdings.

and other assistance to the new groups desiring to form self-managing firms, and supervision designed to secure in the long run the equalisation of income per worker (of course of equal skill) among industrial branches. This organisation would be the active arm of the national planning agency or ministry. Its fundamental objective must be the promotion of the social good of the participatory sector and of the whole economy, and never profit maximisation or other conventional objectives of private capitalist firms.

(8) To minimise the need for the services of this institution, it is advisable that existing firms be given priority in using the funds which they are paying as interest on capital for the purpose of their own expansion or creation of new firms.

(9) In general, but especially in young countries interested in rapid accumulation and the efficient flow of resources, the depreciation allowances of the self-managed firms should also be collected and added to the national investment fund and allocated according to optimality criteria. Of course, to protect the interest of the firms contributing their depreciation allowances, the authorities and the national organisation must guarantee automatic availability of these funds when actual replacement of plant and/or equipment (on which the depreciation allowances were paid) is required.

(10) The optimal form of the self-managed economy or sector is one based on the market mechanism, in the sense that all firms act to the best advantage of their working collectives, while using prices in all product and factor markets as objective signals when making decisions. But of course the authorities can and indeed ought to exercise influence over the individual firms of the participatory sector by means of non-discriminatory tools such as tax policies of all kinds, or price ceilings and other price controls. Price regulation in particular should be used whenever a significant degree of monopoly power exists in a given industry.

COMMENTS ON THE PAPERS BY BRANKO HORVAT

My ignorance of Bangladesh is considerable and I ought to keep quiet and listen. My remarks will be brief and tentative; they are merely first reactions to the papers.

A vast range of topics is covered in the two papers: income distribution, planning models, the definition of socialism, the institutional system, constraints and the organisation of planning, etc. I would like to make a few specific comments on the papers and then explore more generally some of the major issues.

First, I do not agree with Anisur Rahman that socialism and parliamentary democracy are contradictory. All serious Marxists agree on this point. If exploitation is abolished there is nothing wrong with equal political rights. Next, I do not agree with Dr Alamgir's dangerous but common assumption that the state must have complete control over the accumulation fund. This is not necessary. I do agree very strongly with Alamgir, however, that policy should be concerned with social institutions as well as with resource allocation, and neglect of institutions accounts for the failure of many plans. Alamgir's paper, however, does not explain how policies and institutions are to be wedded in Bangladesh.

Both authors favour collectivisation of agriculture, seemingly on grounds that this is necessary for state control. This view is mistaken. Collective farming is not necessary for control. Desired behaviour in agriculture can be induced not by giving orders but by other means. In fact, giving orders is not quite a socialist attitude.

As regards the planning model in Alamgir's paper, I do not think an infinite time horizon makes sense in the real world. The lower limit to the time horizon should be that component of the plan which has the longest gestation period, e.g. advanced training. The upper limit is fixed by uncertainty. No one claims to be able to see clearly beyond, say, twenty-five years. Bangladesh should not make a long-term plan in order to fulfil it. The purpose of a plan is to enable the government to make decisions *now* in the best way. Hence it is only the annual plan that one attempts to fulfil. Alamgir's model starts from consumption needs and builds up the plan from these. We have found this not to be an efficient approach in practice in Yugoslavia. Our experience suggests that it is better to start from the side of production and to attempt to use given resources as completely as possible.

Let me now turn from the papers to a consideration of the strategy of socialist institution building. In general I agree with Professor Vanek, but it is very hard to define humanism. Instead I will put forward another approach.

Socialism means basically an equitable society: equal rights and equal opportunities. This can be achieved if every individual is equal in his three social roles of producer, consumer and citizen. Producers are equal if ownership is social and management is self-organised by the workers. Consumers are equal if what one receives is equal to what one contributes. Citizens are equal if the distribution of political power is equal. These are pre-conditions for socialism.

There are also developmental pre-conditions for socialism which are as important as the institutional ones. I shall list the three most important. First comes universal education, i.e. equal access to education up to the amount each person can absorb. This eliminates all class differences. Next is high productivity. This is necessary to make it possible to have enough leisure for everyone to participate in ruling his own society – both at the firm and in the political sphere. Last, it is necessary to have experience in political democracy.

Can we build socialism in Bangladesh? According to orthodox dogmatists the answer is 'no'. Good-hearted idealists, on the other hand, would say it is possible regardless of conditions. But we can do better than this. All roads lead to socialism; the problem is to choose the road which leads to socialism in the fastest way. The problem is to discover the road for Bangladesh.

There are a few hints on how to find this road, but one must not underestimate the immensity of the task. My basic assumption is that the war of liberation was a key to the socialist revolution because it has made institutions more flexible and opened up more options. One must move quickly, however, before institutions crystallise again. It is the task of the leadership to choose the proper course while institutions still are in a state of flux.

The proper approach is to concentrate on the broad sector of the population, namely, the peasants. This must be a socialist society for the peasants. It is alleged that peasants are conservative, anti-growth and anti-innovation and that therefore collectivisation is necessary. It is said that peasants are reactionary and petty bourgeois. It is claimed that small holdings prevent a rise in productivity and that therefore large farms are essential. It is said that peasants are fanatics about possessing land. All of these statements are contrary to the facts and are merely products of the imagination. The Yugoslav and Chinese revolutions were peasant revolutions; Japan has small and efficient farms, etc. Peasants are an integral part of the forces leading to socialism; they do not form part of the forces opposed to socialism.

DISCUSSION

There was a lively debate about the economic and political purposes of planning, about the need for idealism and inspiration versus pragmatism and realism, and about the general orientation of the economy.

Jozef Pajestka emphasised that planning must not be an intellectual exercise. Planners and politicians must have a common language in which to engage in a useful dialogue. Models were unlikely to be useful. The time period of a plan and its general character cannot be determined by planning techniques and gestation periods. Plans are in part political documents which have a political impact. He was sympathetic to the idea that social, institutional and structural change are the key to development in Bangladesh. Macro-economic aggregates did not provide a sufficient focus for planning. Social purpose must be integrated into all activity. Building the nation and building self-confidence in the nation are vital. At present there is a lack of optimism in Bangladesh and there is a need to tap the creative abilities of the people. If the nation is to be mobilised the planners must present inspiring objectives, among which income distribution is terribly important.

Ashok Mitra remarked that the neighbouring country, India, was suffering from an epidemic of oral socialism. He cited four examples in which rhetoric and reality were in conflict. First, the government does not have confidence in itself that it is capable of managing the foreign trading sectors. As a result, in effect, the state protects existing businesses and grants them privileges. This raises costs and deceives the public. Second, the foodgrain distribution programme is confined almost exclusively to urban areas and the middle classes; agricultural labourers and small deficit farmers are left out of the system. Third, the state has nationalised moribund industries in the private sector which no longer are capable of earning a profit. Industrialists themselves have launched campaigns for nationalisation. Moreover, the prices of products produced in public sector enterprises are low and thereby private industrial customers are subsidised. Lastly, the leaders have preached abstinence but in their private lives they have not practised it. The leaders must exercise more restraint. Even so, it is difficult to mobilise the masses unless there is a political consensus and this is difficult to achieve in a multi-party parliamentary system.

We have much to learn from the experience of China, North Korea and North Vietnam, said *Réné Dumont*. Academic work should be combined with manual work, even at the primary school level, otherwise it will not be possible to mobilise the people. Civil servants and politicians should be required to labour in a village. It is unrealistic to imagine that Western civilisation is possible in Bangladesh. This should be faced squarely and, for instance, the private automobile should be banned; only bicycles should be permitted.

Austin Robinson was concerned that there is a danger of being too brave, too inspiring and too ambitious. It is necessary to remember that Bangladesh is a very poor country. *Gustav Ranis* said Bangladesh needs a 'pragmatic' socialism. Can one really do away with automobiles in Bangladesh? We must not overestimate the changes that have occurred since the war of liberation and we must be realistic about what can be achieved. The effort put into development will respond to the discipline of ideology, but attention must also be paid to the quality or efficiency of effort. *A. Ghosh* asked about the grassroot organisation of socialist leaders and how cadres were recruited and trained.

The social parameters within which decisions have to be made was explained by *Rehman Sobhan*. Socialist development, he said, reflects an interaction of objective and subjective forces. Traditional forces hostile to social change are weak in Bangladesh. The country never had a significant indigenous capitalist class. In the rural sector there is no traditional feudal class. The dialectics are between the middle peasant and the landless workers plus small cultivators. The country also does not suffer from a traditional military machine. Lastly, there are no tribal or caste problems. Socially and culturally Bangladesh is a highly homogenous nation. The only people who might be termed 'exploiters' are those engaged in trading and it is in this sector that the next thrust toward socialist transformation will come. The government does not have many options; these are constrained by the objective conditions.

Turning to agriculture, *Michael Lipton* suggested that the path to socialism might mislead Bangladesh (as Preobrazhensky and Stalin were misled in the U.S.S.R.) into squeezing savings and cheap food out of the rural areas into industrial investment on the grounds that the latter but not the former is nominally 'socialist'. Bangladesh has over 80 per cent of its workforce in agriculture, producing about 55 per cent of G.N.P., yet agriculture is allocated only 20–30 per cent of planned development expenditures. The danger of further squeezing agriculture, where people are poorest and returns to investment highest, is severe. The best remedy is to find efficient ways of removing exploitation from agriculture, so that it becomes a sector that socialists would judge worthy of high resource inputs. Since, over the range of one to forty acres, both employment and output per acre rise as holding size falls, efficiency as well as equity indicate the desirability of redistributing land. There is however no case for collectivisation or co-operative joint farming, since such methods have usually reduced output.

Lipton agreed with Alamgir that the new agrarian structure should meet minimum nutritional requirements. Foodgrain self-sufficiency, however, will not of itself help because it replaces imported wheat, largely fed to poor people in ration shops, by lower protein rice largely consumed on the farm. It will be necessary to identify groups in need and seasons of most serious exposure to hunger and to plan to bring food and jobs to such families. Research and production incentives will be necessary for low-cost sources of calories (e.g. sweet potatoes) and proteins (e.g. pulses) as against high-cost sources such as dairy products and even perhaps rice.

In reply to the debate *Alamgir* agreed that short-term policy making is the most important aspect of planning. He has no objection to building up a plan frame from the production side, provided that one is certain the minimum consumption bundle is available for the people. The danger of beginning with a production plan is that this will lead us back to an excessive emphasis on G.N.P. and rates of growth.

Anisur Rahman observed that the conference consisted of two groups of people, one ignorant of Bangladesh and the other of socialism. Socialism is in the air but has yet to land on the ground. What he was doing in his paper was to dream and try out ideas. The average elected representative of the people is unlikely to have a clear understanding of socialism. One of the tasks of planners is to try to understand what socialism means and then project their vision in the confidence that the people will respond. He agreed that the country needs a social purpose, but we should have to experiment for some time. He was not advocating collective farms in a narrow sense but social ownership of land. A small farmer would not give up his land unless he wished to do so voluntarily. Only the surplus land from the larger landowners would be taken over.

He thought the concept of a minimum subsistence level of consumption was too vague to be helpful to planners. Moreover, there was a danger that with such an approach the country would end up with an absurd requirement that could be met only by massive external assistance, which in turn might result in undesirable political and social consequences. The nation is short of resources; we must produce as much as we can and share it fairly without becoming over-dependent on foreign assistance. It is important, however, not to become preoccupied with material balances and G.N.P. Institutional changes will convert calculations into mis-calculations. Society must learn to absorb shortages, to anticipate that there will be shortages without always knowing which specific goods will become in short supply. If one reads history one finds little discussion of material imbalances being an important impediment to development. The question asked of the planners in twenty years will be 'did you get your institutions right?'

4 Resources for Development

Mohiuddin Alamgir[1]

BANGLADESH INSTITUTE OF DEVELOPMENT ECONOMICS

I. INTRODUCTION

The size of the First Five Year Plan of Bangladesh and the potentiality for future growth will be determined by the availability of resources for development. Before formulating the plan it is necessary to carry out a careful assessment of the resources that can be mobilised from within and outside the country. This is important in view of the fact that, like other developing countries, Bangladesh suffers from a vicious circle of poverty with low levels of income and saving.

From the point of view of the entire economy, resources for development are made up of physical and financial components. Physical resources are represented by the unutilised productive capacity, human skill, natural resources, such as minerals, gas, hydro-electricity potential, and non-monetised real assets in agriculture. Financial resources are represented by the net financial asset acquisition of various sectors of the economy including the foreign sector. However, for economic development financial resources are relevant only to the extent that they can be transformed into real investment either through mobilisation of idle productive potential of the economy so as to increase output or through imports of productive capital equipment. In this paper all aspects of resource mobilisation will be examined except human resources and the existing excess industrial capacity. It is assumed that in the process of new asset acquisition (both financial and physical) an attempt will be made by all concerned in Bangladesh to assure a more satisfactory level of utilisation both of excess industrial capacity and of human resources. Nothing definite, however, can be said about the latter, in the absence of a comprehensive manpower planning. But one can state with some confidence that a part of the

[1] The author is grateful to his colleagues Mr Atiqur Rahman, Mr Naimuddin Chowdhury, Mr S. R. Osmani, Mr Chowdhury Anwaruzzaman, Mr A. B. M. Shamsul Islam and Mr Karimullah Bhuiyan without whose help this paper could never have been completed.

Editorial Note. This paper has been considerably revised and extended since the conference, particularly in those sections (pp. 95-end) which deal with future trends.

new resource mobilisation, particularly in the foreign sector, will be devoted to ensuring a higher level of utilisation of the existing idle capacity in industry.

For the purpose of the present analysis, resources are divided under two heads, domestic and foreign. Domestic resources are represented by the total saving potential of the economy. They include all types of real and financial (net) asset acquisition. Real asset acquisition, however, is shown here only for the non-corporate private sector. For other sectors, the financial equivalent of real investment from domestic sources is shown. The actual real asset acquisition by any sector may exceed its saving in financial terms if it is a net borrower from other sectors, which is usually true of both the corporate sector and the government sector.

Foreign resources are composed of the country's own foreign exchange earnings through exports and the inflow of foreign capital. An assessment of the potential foreign resources is important for two reasons. First, in addition to the savings constraint, the foreign exchange constraint constitutes an important bottleneck for economic development of a country like Bangladesh. In many cases, domestic saving cannot be transformed into productive investment without supplementary capital goods imports to be financed either from export earnings or through foreign aid. Second, a realistic policy formulation in terms of choice of technique or determination of sectoral priorities is not possible without a careful projection of the availability of foreign resources during the plan period. Furthermore, if a society places a high premium on self-sufficiency, it must develop a set of consistent criteria for the acceptance of foreign aid. Consistency refers, of course, to the realisation of the social objectives of planning. Thus a thorough analysis of the role of foreign aid is not possible without exploring the potential for expanding exports of the country concerned as well as assessing the probable attitude of prospective donors towards meeting the need of the recipient country for foreign capital on the terms desired by the latter. In this paper, the primary emphasis will be on the foreign exchange earning potential of Bangladesh, although a few comments will be added later about the terms and conditions under which foreign capital inflow or foreign aid can be accepted. This will, however, be supplemented by some preliminary estimates of the foreign aid requirement during the First Five Year Plan of Bangladesh.

Section II will attempt an indirect estimate of domestic savings in Bangladesh over the period 1959/60–1969/70. A direct estimate of domestic saving in Bangladesh over the same period by sector of origin will be presented in Section III. Foreign exchange earnings of Bangladesh during 1959/60–1969/70 will be analysed in Section IV.

Section V presents an outlook for domestic resources mobilisation during the First Five Year Plan. Sections VI-VII discuss the prospects of foreign export earnings and capital inflow during the First Five Year Plan. Some conclusions follow at the end.

II. AN INDIRECT ESTIMATE OF DOMESTIC SAVING IN BANGLADESH, 1959/60–1969/70

This estimate is taken primarily from a study by Alamgir and Berlage. The indirect approach, otherwise known as the investment method of saving estimation, is derived from the *ex-post* national income identity which states that saving equals investment, including net foreign investment of the economy. Expressed in another form the saving–investment gap equals the export–import gap or the net deficit or surplus in the current account of the balance of payments. Thus if independent estimates of investment and the trade gap are available, one can easily estimate the total domestic saving of the economy.

In Table 4.1 an indirect estimate of gross national saving in Bangladesh is presented. Figures are presented in both current and constant prices. The series of gross national products as presented by Alamgir and Berlage differs from the official series of the Central Statistical Office (C.S.O.). The authors start with the official data provided by the Central Statistical Office and carry out a number of adjustments to them. The first represents a correction for the fact that the official data over-estimate the rice (*Aman* variety) production and under-estimate jute production. Secondly, the C.S.O. methodology for estimating value-added in large-scale and small-scale manufacturing has been rejected in favour of new methods which represent a significant improvement. In the case of large-scale manufacturing, the C.S.O. applied the quantum index of manufacturing (1959–60 = 100) to the benchmark value-added for 1959–60 based on the Census of Manufacturing Industries (C.M.I.) 1959–60 and adjusted for under-coverage and miscellaneous charges such as water, stationery, telephone, bank charges, insurance premiums to obtain estimates of value-added in later years. Alamgir and Berlage used the direct information as given in subsequent censuses for individual years to estimate value-added in large-scale manufacturing after making adjustments for under-coverage, indirect taxes and other charges. For small-scale manufacturing, the C.S.O. used data on value-added per worker and the total number of workers to estimate value-added for 1959–60 and applied somewhat arbitrarily determined rates of 'real growth' in order to derive estimates of value-added for later years. The C.S.O.'s estimate of value-added per worker as well as

TABLE 4.1

AN INDIRECT ESTIMATE OF GROSS NATIONAL SAVING IN BANGLADESH: 1959–60 to 1969–70

(Takas millions)

	At current market prices						At constant market prices of 1959–60					
	G.N.P.	Total fixed investment	Stock forma-tion	Total investment	Net capital inflow	Regional savings	G.N.P.	Total fixed investment	Stock forma-tion	Total investment	Net capital inflow	Regional savings
1959–60	14,490	810	170	980	42	938	14,490	810	170	980	42	938
1960–1	16,357	951	68	1,019	477	542	15,283	856	66	922	424	498
1961–2	17,491	1,234	89	1,323	347	976	16,445	1,038	83	1,121	199	922
1962–3	18,527	1,622	96	1,718	488	1,230	16,709	1,285	90	1,375	281	1,094
1963–4	18,706	2,056	68	2,124	797	1,327	18,268	1,567	66	1,633	331	1,302
1964–5	20,672	2,120	142	2,262	950	1,312	18,651	1,557	128	1,685	498	1,187
1965–6	22,870	1,961	147	2,108	728	1,380	19,496	1,388	120	1,508	311	1,197
1966–7	26,456	2,355	372	2,727	814	1,913	19,548	1,646	263	1,909	478	1,431
1967–8	28,197	3,181	179	3,360	862	2,498	21,323	2,197	138	2,335	455	1,880
1968–9	29,880	3,345	329	3,674	1,016	2,658	21,950	2,113	233	2,346	372	1,974
1969–70	32,630	4,011	386	4,397	1,100	3,297	22,394	2,568	265	2,833	568	2,265

Source: M. Alamgir and L. Berlage, *An Analysis of National Accounts of Bangladesh*, Research Monograph No. 1 (Forthcoming), Bangladesh Institute of Development Economics, Dacca.

total number of workers was very unsatisfactory since it was based on a survey of Karachi and a limited survey of rural areas in Bangladesh. Alamgir and Berlage made use of the results of more comprehensive surveys conducted later by the Bangladesh Small Industries Corporation (B.S.I.C.), the Bangladesh Bureau of Statistics and the C.S.O. to obtain estimates of value-added per worker and of the total number of workers in 1961–2 and 1969–70. These figures were interpolated and extrapolated backward to obtain a revised series of value-added in small-scale manufacturing in Bangladesh. Thirdly, the value-added in trade was corrected to reflect the adjustments made in value-added in agriculture and manufacturing. Finally, the official figures did not include certain unallocated items, such as banking and insurance, central government and the Pakistan International Airlines. The value-added from these sectors was divided between Bangladesh and Pakistan on the basis of 25 per cent and 75 per cent respectively.

The fixed investment series is basically that estimated by the C.S.O. This is a new fixed investment series which differs from the one estimated earlier by the Pakistan Planning Commission. The C.S.O. series follows an improved methodology and has wider coverage. The only problem has been that the series extended back only to 1963–4. Using a number of assumptions Alamgir and Berlage extended the series back to 1959–60. The stock formation series is obtained by dividing the Pakistan Planning Commission's estimate for the whole country in the proportions of total fixed investment. Figures for net capital inflow were estimated on the basis of data provided by a report of a panel of economists on the Fourth Five Year Plan of Pakistan.

Savings at current prices have been estimated as the difference between the total investment (fixed + changes in the stock) and the net capital inflow. Since the pre-March 1971 Pakistan figure for stock formation is somewhat arbitrarily divided between Bangladesh and Pakistan, the resultant saving estimate may be different from the actual; the difference, however, is unlikely to be significant. In the constant price account, total savings of the economy were obtained as the difference between gross national product at market prices and total consumption. Thus there is an asymmetry in the method of estimating savings at current and constant prices.

Some general remarks can be made on the basis of the current price data in Table 4.1. It would appear that investment grew as a proportion of gross national product over the period 1959–60 to 1963–4 except for 1960–1; this was followed by a somewhat erratic trend to 1965–6, after which there was a consistent upward trend. The average rate of saving reveals a very erratic trend over the entire

Second Five Year Plan period of Pakistan; but in the period following it rose consistently from 6·3 per cent in 1964–5 to 10·1 in 1969–70,
except in 1965–6 when it was slightly lower than the year before.
This was achieved in Bangladesh despite the increasing defence
expenditure of the central government following the 1965 Indo-
Pakistan conflict. The marginal rate of saving during the Third Five
Year Plan period (19·7 per cent) was higher than that achieved
during the Second Five Year Plan Period (17·8 per cent).

An interesting feature is to be observed if one studies the relative
importance of domestic saving and foreign capital inflow in total
domestic investment over the entire period. Bangladesh contributed
over 60 per cent towards investment out of her own resources except
in 1960–1 and 1963–4. If one compares these figures with the average
for the whole of pre-March 1971 Pakistan, as given in the *Final
Evaluation of the Second Five Year Plan*, Bangladesh comes out more
favourably in terms of lesser dependence on the external assistance.
Alternatively, one may say that, had Bangladesh received a more
equitable share of the foreign capital (e.g. on the basis of relative
populations), then with the given level of domestic savings a higher
rate of growth of investment and income could have been realised.

Two savings functions have been estimated from the data given
in Table 4.1. Savings in current and constant prices have been
expressed as functions of gross national product in current and
constant prices. The estimated parameters of the saving functions
are given below:

(1) Constant prices (figures are in takas hundred million)
$$S_{\overline{IND}} = -20·39^a + 0·181^a Y_1$$
$$(3·76) \quad (7·45)$$
R^2 = 0·86, Standard error of estimate = 4·16.

(2) Current prices (figures are in takas hundred million)
$$S_{\overline{IND}} = -13·74^a + 0·135^a Y_2$$
$$(4·59) \quad (10·60)$$
R^2 = 0·93, Standard error of estimate = 2·46

where S and Y represent national savings and Gross National
Product respectively.

The above relations imply a marginal propensity to save of 13·5
per cent when estimated from the current price data and 18·7 per cent
when estimated from the constant price data. These figures appear to
fall within the range observed for developing countries. For India, a

[a] Significant at 1 per cent level.
[b] Significant at 5 per cent level.
Figures within parentheses represent *t*-statistic.

simple linear relation of indirect estimates of saving to national income produced a marginal propensity to save of 14·5 per cent at current prices and 17 per cent at constant prices.[1]

III. DIRECT ESTIMATES OF DOMESTIC SAVING IN BANGLADESH 1959–60 TO 1969–70

The direct estimate of saving in Bangladesh was reached by aggregating the savings of different groups in the economy. Three different saver groups have been identified in this study. These are (*a*) the non-corporate private sector (including private limited companies), (*b*) the corporate sector and (*c*) the government sector. This grouping was made on the basis of two considerations: firstly to obtain an idea about inter-sectoral flow of resources and to identify and determine the effectiveness of the various instruments of saving in mobilising resources and in effecting resource transfer from one sector to another; secondly in the light of availability of data.

The saving of any economic unit can be defined as its excess of current income over current consumption expenditure. It can be estimated as the earned surplus or as the change in earned net-worth during a given period. The earned surplus can be measured from the current account of the economic unit while change in net-worth is estimated from the balance sheet. In estimating the change in net-worth all capital gains or losses are excluded.

Thus the concept of saving adopted here is close to what is known as the social accounting concept as contrasted with the business accounting concept and the cash flow concept. This also appears to be consistent with the definition of the various components of the national income accounts in Bangladesh.

The savings estimate presented here represents the gross saving of the various sectors of the economy in Bangladesh. No attempt has been made to derive the corresponding net saving figures because of the difficulties involved in estimating depreciation in Bangladesh. A summary of gross saving for the various sectors mentioned above, for the period 1959–60 to 1969–70 is presented in Table 4.2. Over the entire period under consideration, the non-corporate private sector's contribution to total savings in Bangladesh was the highest; it was always more than 55 per cent of the total. While the absolute magnitudes of savings varied from year to year in the cases of the corporate sector and of the government sector, the non-corporate private sector savings showed a consistent upward trend over time. Within the

---

[1] *Saving in India 1950–51 to 1961–62*, National Council of Applied Economic. Research (New Delhi, 1965), p. 19.

TABLE 4.2

GROSS SAVINGS IN BANGLADESH: 1959/60–1969/70

(Takas millions at current prices)

	1959–60	1960–1	1961–2	1962–3	1963–4	1964–5	1965–6	1966–7	1967–8	1968–9	1969–70
A. Non-corporate Private Sector	623·2 (69·4)	674·0 (64·7)	678·7 (56·1)	788·2 (72·5)	1,053·1 (67·0)	1,126·8 (63·6)	1,393·7 (65·3)	1,399·9 (64·0)	1,439·5 (60·7)	1,651·5 (65·7)	2,044·6 (69·5)
B. Corporate Sector	77·1 (8·6)	75·8 (7·3)	125·1 (10·3)	133·1 (12·2)	182·7 (11·6)	201·0 (11·3)	249·2 (11·7)	215·6 (9·9)	257·7 (10·9)	279·1 (11·1)	284·6 (9·7)
(i) Non-financial companies	53·3 (5·9)	49·1 (4·7)	94·6 (7·8)	97·3 (8·9)	142·1 (9·0)	152·1 (8·5)	190·8 (8·9)	146·0 (6·7)	184·6 (7·8)	193·6 (7·7)	183·1 (6·2)
(ii) Financial companies	23·8 (2·7)	26·7 (2·6)	30·5 (2·5)	35·8 (3·3)	40·5 (2·6)	48·9 (2·7)	58·4 (2·7)	69·6 (3·2)	73·1 (3·1)	85·5 (3·4)	101·5 (3·5)
C. Government Sector	197·6 (22·0)	291·8 (28·0)	406·0 (33·6)	166·4 (15·3)	335·6 (21·4)	446·5 (25·1)	492·2 (23·1)	570·6 (26·1)	672·5 (28·4)	584·4 (23·2)	611·1 (20·8)
D. Gross National Savings	897·9 (100)	1,041·6 (100)	1,209·8 (100)	1,087·7 (100)	1,571·4 (100)	1,774·3 (100)	2,135·1 (100)	2,186·1 (100)	2,369·7 (100)	2,515·0 (100)	2,940·3 (100)

Sources: Tables 8 to 12 in the Appendix.

Note: Figures in parentheses represented the percentage distribution of total saving by sector of origin.

corporate sector the contribution of non-financial companies appears to be more important than that of financial companies. Savings of the individual sectors are discussed briefly in the following pages.

A. *The Non-corporate Private Sector*

The non-corporate private sector includes all households (both farm and non-farm), unincorporated enterprises engaged in all types of economic activities, non-private organisations and private limited companies as defined in the Companies Act, 1913. The reasons for including private limited companies in the non-corporate private sector is that their balance sheets have not been available so that their savings could not be estimated separately and included in the corporate sector. Savings of the non-corporate private sector were estimated as their increased net-worth, i.e. increases in financial assets less liabilities plus increases in their real assets. Table 4.3 presents separate estimates of financial and non-financial asset accumulation of the non-corporate private sector. These estimates are, however, only approximate since numerous assumptions have had to be made in order to generate data on savings. No data were available on the following: provident funds and benefit funds of industrial workers; individual holdings of gold and jewellery; changes in stocks of physical assets; real investment in non-mechanised transport equipment; real investment in buildings by non-corporate private business. Under-coverage of the savings estimate due to the above omissions were assumed to be 10 per cent of the total non-corporate private sector savings, and thus the estimate based on the available data was increased accordingly. Details of financial and non-financial asset accumulation by types of asset in the non-corporate private sector are presented in Appendix Tables 1–10.

As pointed out above, the total saving of the non-corporate private sector increased consistently over the period 1959–60 to 1969–70. A major part of this saving was accumulated in the form of non-financial assets. However, despite some year-to-year fluctuations, the proportion of savings in financial assets increased during the Third Plan period as compared with the Second Plan period of the former Government of Pakistan. This implies on the one hand a shift in individual asset preference and, on the other, an increase in the flow of funds from the non-corporate private sector to other sectors of the economy.

A separate saving function was estimated for the non-corporate private sector. The results indicate that the marginal propensity to save in the non-corporate private sector is only 8·6 per cent. This rate is undoubtedly very low judged by any criteria. It is lower than

TABLE 4.3

NON-CORPORATE PRIVATE SECTOR SAVING IN BANGLADESH 1959/60–1969/70

(takas 000s at current prices)

	1959–60	1960–1	1961–2	1962–3	1963–4	1964–5	1965–6	1966–7	1967–8	1968–9	1969–70
A. Financial Assets											
1. Currency holding	42,200	43,600	1,800	–53,600	219,800	205,300	40,800	21,500	127,800	185,500	121,800
2. Bank deposits	36,800	39,000	57,000	156,000	177,000	174,000	307,000	397,900	13,400	157,500	121,800
3. Postal saving scheme	18,212	32,727	25,462	24,359	23,776	43,380	16,893	15,390	16,441	33,384	40,341
4. Provident fund	23,792	31,201	39,328	32,713	48,343	52,002	63,807	79,544	34,339	71,910	63,262
5. Live insurance	11,813	13,741	16,952	20,868	25,756	32,577	38,852	44,679	53,825	62,447	67,034
6. Corporate share holding	8,258	8,512	17,530	12,437	24,028	21,714	8,499	23,746	19,210	28,974	30,080
7. Co-operative societies	278	23,830	7,520	6,226	–2,112	–3,485	27,992	–3,960	36,333	22,871	209,369
8. National investment trust fund	–	–	–	766	1,792	2,163	1,262	1,427	1,086	1,604	1,701
9. Prize bonds	–	4,580	4,580	4,580	4,580	4,580	1,040	1,040	1,040	1,040	1,040
10. Gross financial asset acquisition (Row 1+2+3+4+5+6+7+8+9)	141,353	197,191	170,172	204,349	522,963	532,201	506,091	581,266	303,474	565,230	827,727
11. Total financial liability or dissaving	50,094	97,506	126,321	120,447	225,503	381,585	133,780	279,348	157,072	259,985	195,500
12. Total saving in	91,259	99,685	43,851	83,902	297.460	150,646	372.311	301.918	146.402	312.726	620.006

equipment											
15. Non-monetised investment	121,000	137,000	142,000	149,000	141,000	149,500	109,100	138,000	193,500	198,700	204,100
16. Housing construction (rural and urban)	115,556	130,000	137,778	143,333	145,556	155,889	199,778	189,889	214,333	186,000	165,000
17. Total saving in non-financial assets	475,267	513,129	573,165	632,657	659,917	878,856	894,667	970,757	1,162,230	1,189,640	1,238,691
18. TOTAL SAVING (Row 12 + 17)	566,526	612,814	617,016	716,559	957,377	1,029,502	1,266,978	1,272,675	1,308,632	1,502,366	1,858,697
19. Total saving adjusted for under-coverage	623,179	674,095	678,718	788,215	1,053,111	1,132,452	1,393,676	1,399,943	1,439,495	1,652,603	2,044,567
20. Savings in financial assets as a percentage of total saving (Row 12 as a percentage of Row 19)	15	15	6	11	28	13	27	22	10	19	30

Source: Tables 8 to 10 in the Appendix.

that obtained for India (9·0 per cent).[1] The Indian estimate, it may be pointed out, does not include private companies as does that of Bangladesh.

Non-corporate private sector saving in the form of financial asset acquisition is derived by subtracting changes in financial liability from changes in financial assets. This procedure slightly over-estimates the non-corporate private sector saving because no account has been taken of the sale of real assets, corporate shares or both by this sector to other sectors.

Percentage-wise breakdown of the gross financial asset acquisition by the non-corporate private sector in Bangladesh as given in the Appendix, Table 9, reveals that currency holdings and bank deposits are the most important forms of asset acquisition by the private sector. These two together represented more than 50 per cent of the total financial asset acquisition by the non-corporate private sector in all years except 1960–1 and 1961–2. Contractual saving in the form of provident funds and life insurance are next in importance. The proportion of savings in the small saving scheme, which represents a form of capital receipt (unfunded debt) of the government, seems to have declined over the period. Corporate share holdings maintained a stable proportion of the total gross financial asset acquisition of the non-corporate private sector.

An attempt has been made to find out the determinants of the financial asset acquisition of the non-corporate private sector. For this purpose a number of relationships were estimated through least square regression. The results are presented in the following table.

Determinants of Financial Assets

F_N = Net financial asset in ten million taka;
F_G = Gross financial asset in ten million taka;
Δ_M = Changes in money supply in ten million taka;
E = Visible exports in hundred million taka;
E' = Total export receipts in hundred million taka;
I = Import in hundred million taka; and
i = Inter bank call rate.
    S.E.E. represents standard error of estimate.
    All figures are in current prices.

[1] *Op. cit.*, p. 53. The non-corporate private sector saving function for Bangladesh is given by:
$$S_{NC} = -5·435^b + 0·086^a Y_{NC}$$
$$(-3·244)\ (10·526)$$
$$R^2 = 0·92,\ \text{standard error of estimate} = 1·33.$$

Where, S_{NC} and Y_{NC} are non-corporate private sector savings and disposable income respectively, expressed in taka hundred million at current prices.

(1) $F_N = 10 \cdot 830 + 6 \cdot 245^c \Delta M$ $R^2 = 0 \cdot 22$ S.E.E. $= 16 \cdot 007$
     $(1 \cdot 197) (1 \cdot 579)$

(2) $F_N = -49 \cdot 904^a + 3 \cdot 524^a E$ $R^2 = 0 \cdot 61$ S.E.E. $= 11 \cdot 297$
     $(2 \cdot 637) (3 \cdot 749)$

(3) $F_n = -25 \cdot 897^b + 2 \cdot 036^a I$ $R^2 = 0 \cdot 65$ S.E.E. $= 10 \cdot 652$
     $(2 \cdot 108) (4 \cdot 113)$

(4) $F_n = -100 \cdot 955^b - 38 \cdot 935i + 0 \cdot 242^a I$ $R^2 = 0 \cdot 69$
     $(1 \cdot 840)$ $(1 \cdot 163)$ $(3 \cdot 063)$
     S.E.E. $= 74 \cdot 865$

(1) $F_G = 16 \cdot 670^b + 12 \cdot 775^a \Delta M$ $R^2 = 0 \cdot 54$ S.E.E. $= 15 \cdot 884$
     $(1 \cdot 860)$ $(3 \cdot 260)$

(2) $F_G = -48 \cdot 889^b + 4 \cdot 557^a E$ $R^2 = 0 \cdot 61$ S.E.E. $= 14 \cdot 631$
     $(1 \cdot 995)$ $(3 \cdot 744)$

(3) $F_G = -29 \cdot 487^b + 2 \cdot 957^a I$ $R^2 = 0 \cdot 82$ S.E.E. $= 9 \cdot 856$
     $(2 \cdot 594)$ $(6 \cdot 456)$

(4) $F_G = -699 \cdot 723^a - 75 \cdot 211^a i + 0 \cdot 451^a I$ $R^2 = 0 \cdot 97$
     $(14 \cdot 673)$ $(4 \cdot 887)$ $(12 \cdot 528)$
     S.E.E. $= 34 \cdot 407$

(5) $F_G = 39 \cdot 239^b + 3 \cdot 615^a E'$ $R^2 = 0 \cdot 64$ S.E.E. $= 14 \cdot 014$
     $(1 \cdot 908)$ $(4 \cdot 012)$

[a] = Significant at 1 per cent level
[b] = Significant at 5 per cent level
[c] = Significant at 10 per cent level
(Figures within parentheses represent *t*-statistic).

Variables chosen to explain the variation in the financial asset acquisition of the non-corporate private sector were money supply, exports, imports and interest rates. Since different rates of interest were prevailing in the country, the inter-bank call money rate was taken as a proxy for the variation in the overall interest rate during the period under consideration. As expected, functions related to the gross financial assets acquisition perform better than those related to the net financial asset acquisition. When regressed alone, the coefficient of money supply, exports and imports turned out to be significant at a 5 per cent level and the percentages of the total variation in gross financial asset acquisition explained by these variables separately were 54, 61 and 82 respectively. In a multiple regression incorporating interest rates and imports, the percentage of the variation explained was higher (97 per cent). However, the co-efficient of the interest rate was now significant only at a 10 per cent level. Attempts were made to introduce money supply and exports into the relationship but a good result could not be obtained because of high multi-collinearity between the explanatory variables.

A significant correlation between money supply and gross financial asset acquisition is not surprising since currency holding and bank deposits constitute the largest proportion of total savings in financial assets. Export and import being determined by the level of economic activity in the economy, are likely to influence gross financial asset acquisition in the same direction. This happens for two reasons. Firstly the volume of both exports and imports in Bangladesh had an expansionary effect on the money supply and thus on the gross financial asset acquisition. Under normal circumstances imports are a leakage out of domestic income and should influence money supply in the opposite direction. But in Pakistan imports contained a large quantity of foodgrain under PL-480 which created counterpart funds in domestic currency. Thus it makes sense that the coefficient of import was found to be positive. Secondly the level of economic activity reflected in the volumes of the imports and exports, affects the flow of funds from the non-corporate private sector to other sectors of the economy. As the corporate and government investment increased, a greater amount of resources was transferred out of the non-corporate private sector and the holding of gross financial assets of this sector increased.

B. *The Corporate Sector*

The corporate sector includes all public limited companies as defined under the Companies Act 1913. The following types of companies, have been distinguished:

(1) Non-financial companies, primarily engaged in manufacturing, trade and transport activities.

(2) Financial companies, which include the State Bank of Pakistan, all scheduled banks incorporated in Pakistan, insurance companies and various other investment and credit institutions, e.g. the Pakistan Industrial Credit and Investment Corporation (P.I.C.I.C.), the House Building Finance Corporation (H.B.F.C.), the Agricultural Development Bank of Pakistan (A.D.B.P.), the Industrial Development Bank of Pakistan (I.D.B.P.) and the Co-operative Societies. Data were, however, not available for all non-financial companies, and in the case of financial companies and some non-financial companies data were available only for the whole of pre-March 1971 Pakistan. It was, therefore, necessary to make some assumptions for adjusting the available total figures to account for under-coverage, and for dividing total Pakistan figures to arrive at a separate saving estimate for Bangladesh.

Corporate saving has been estimated by examining the balance-sheet and/or profit and loss account of the various companies.[1]

When estimated from the balance-sheets, corporate saving equals the net increase in assets less net increase in all types of liabilities with adjustment for capital gains and losses. Alternatively, when saving is calculated from the profit and loss account it is equal to the excess of current income over current expenditure including dividend distribution. To be more specific, gross saving of the corporate sector equals gross profit less tax provision and dividend payment. In the case of insurance companies, however, a direct method had to be applied to estimate saving. Saving of the insurance companies in the form of changes in life fund during a year was treated as an item of non-corporate private sector saving. The proportion of saving for insurance companies included under corporate sector saving consists of the change during a year in the profit and loss account, in the general reserve and other reserve funds and in the investment fluctuation account.

A summary of gross saving by the corporate sector in Bangladesh over the period 1959–60 to 1969–70 is included in Table 4.4. Gross saving of non-financial companies with separate account for Bangladesh was adjusted upwards on the basis of the ratio of paid-up capital of the companies for which data were available to the total paid-up capital. Gross saving of non-financial companies without separate account for Bangladesh was divided between Bangladesh and Pakistan in the following manner:

(1) 30 per cent of the gross saving of P.I.A. was allocated to Bangladesh;
(2) 50 per cent of the National Shipping Corporation was allocated to Bangladesh;
(3) saving of various oil companies was divided on the basis of the proportion of imported petroleum and petroleum products in the two regions.

Of the financial companies only the Co-operatives had a separate account for Bangladesh. As for others, the basis of allocation was the following: (1) 30 per cent of the gross saving of the State Bank of Pakistan; (2) 40 per cent of the saving of the insurance companies; (3) on the basis of the proportion of loans advanced in the case of scheduled banks and investment and credit institutions.

[1] Primary sources of data were the Registrar, Joint Stock Companies, Bangladesh; *Banking Statistics of Pakistan, Currency and Finance, Monthly Bulletin of the State Bank of Pakistan; Balance Sheet Analysis of the Joint Stock Companies listed on Karachi Stock Exchange;* Annual Reports of BIDC and other financial investment and credit institutions; *Statistical Year Book of Pakistan.*

TABLE 4.4

A SECTORAL BREAK DOWN OF GROSS SAVING BY THE CORPORATE SECTOR IN BANGLADESH: 1959/60–1969/70
(takas 000s at current prices)

	1959–60	1960–1	1961–2	1962–3	1963–4	1964–5	1965–6	1966–7	1967–8	1968–9	1969–70
A. Non-financial											
1. Jute	110	11,759	42,000	41,400	56,343	52,559	67,930	20,848	45,140	63,543	49,207
2. Textile and allied industry	1,400	3,046	1,800	4,200	5,200	5,561	6,344	5,000	8,100	21,242	828
3. Sugar industry	—	—	—	—	6,400	4,000	8,400	2,600	7,286	–18,544	–4,273
4. Paper and paper board industry	—	9,100	11,600	11,400	14,300	14,900	14,000	6,300	15,778	21,721	8,861
5. Chemical, pharmaceutical, fertiliser industries	—	—	43	172	918	2,693	10,202	18,683	22,300	8,326	9,213
6. Iron, steel, dockyard, engineering and oil industries	—	500	500	900	1,900	1,100	2,200	3,200	–9,600	–19,035	–29,933
7. Miscellaneous industry	1,266	5,749	5,579	5,495	4,921	4,652	5,401	12,866	4,917	10,194	145
8. Gross saving of non-financial companies with separate account for Bangladesh	2,776	30,154	61,522	63,567	89,982	85,465	114,477	69,497	93,921	87,447	34,048
9. Gross saving of non-financial companies with separate account for Bangladesh adjusted for under-coverage	46,822	40,205	82,567	85,073	120,348	113,953	152,712	94,641	126,802	121,729	92,668
10. Gross saving of some companies without separate account for Bangladesh	6,461	8,850	12,060	12,180	21,800	38,110	38,100	51,400	57,790	71,860	90,457
11. Total gross saving of non-financial companies	53,283	49,055	94,627	97,253	142,148	152,063	190,812	146,041	184,592	193,859	183,125

Item											
2. Scheduled banks incorporated in Pakistan	3,592	5,253	5,349	6,810	10,356	13,714	17,312	17,136	21,346	26,683	33,354
3. Insurance companies	596	−623	−88	2,506	1,016	5,580	801	3,569	3,032	5,325	5,325
4. Pakistan Industrial Credit and Investment Corporation	273	379	423	620	1,206	−70	2,730	2,948	3,541	6,382	6,263
5. House Building Finance Corporation	111	182	299	354	798	1,306	1,125	1,623	435	32	2,756
6. Agricultural Development Bank of Pakistan	—	—	292	816	652	616	291	345	637	1,116	1,726
7. Industrial Development Bank of Pakistan	—	—	639	943	1,353	1,188	1,283	3,369	4,059	3,831	4,689
8. Co-operative societies	−151	517	1,630	3,115	1,960	2,135	3,057	2,661	2,925	3,418	4,061
9. Total gross savings of financial companies	23,762	26,645	30,388	35,497	40,586	48,903	58,439	69,576	73,115	85,521	101,515
C. Total gross saving by the Corporate sector in Bangladesh (A. 11 + B. 9)	77,045	75,700	125,015	132,750	182,734	200,966	249,251	215,617	257,707	279,380	284,640

Sources :

1. Registrar, Joint Stock Companies, Dacca.
2. *Balance Sheet Analysis of Joint Stock Companies Listed on Karachi Stock Exchange*; State Bank of Pakistan, various issues.
3. Annual Reports, Pakistan Industrial Development Corporation.
4. *BIDC in Figures*, Bangladesh Industrial Development Corporation, Dacca.
5. *Annual Report*, State Bank of Pakistan, different years.
6. *Banking Statistics of Pakistan*, State Bank of Pakistan, various issues.
7. *Pakistan Insurance Yearbook*, Controller of Insurance, various issues.
8. *Annual Report*, Pakistan Industrial Credit and Investment Corporation, different years.
9. *PICIC at work*, Pakistan Industrial Credit and Investment Corporation, 1965.
10. *Annual Report*, House Building Finance Corporation, different years.
11. *Annual Report*, Agricultural Development Bank of Pakistan, different years.
12. *Nine Years of IDBP*, Industrial Development Bank of Pakistan.
13. *Pakistan Statistical Yearbook*, 1968, Central Statistical Office, Government of Pakistan.
14. *Annual Departmental Report for the Year*, 1967–8, 1968–9 and 1969–70, The Registrar of Co-operative Societies, East Pakistan, Dacca.

As can be seen from Table 4.4 the contribution of the non-financial companies in the total saving of the corporate sector was much higher than that of the financial companies. In all years, non-financial companies contributed more than 60 per cent of the total corporate sector's saving. However, with the growth of the economy the contribution of the financial companies has increased over time.

A separate saving function[1] relating corporate saving to corporate income (excluding insurance companies and co-operative societies) defined as the gross profit, indicates a marginal propensity to save of 69·8 per cent. This is clearly much higher than that realised by other sectors and also closer to what was claimed by the Planning Commission of the erstwhile Government of Pakistan. However, it should be pointed out that the total saving of the corporate sector has in fact been depressed because of the inclusion of many companies under the B.I.D.C. management which incurred heavy losses in many years. Table 4.4 reveals that the sugar industry and the iron, steel and engineering industries dissaved in a number of years. Such a high rate of saving was realised due to tax concessions accorded to many industries by the government as well as the policy of the enterprises to give out a small proportion of their earning to shareholders as dividend payment especially in early years of operation.

C. *The Government Sector*

The government sector in this study includes only the accounts of the erstwhile Pakistan Central Government and the Provincial Government of East Pakistan. Saving of the local bodies could not be estimated because of non-availability of data. Government saving can be measured from the annual budget documents which contain detailed information on receipts and expenditure. Tables 4.5 and 4.6 present estimates of revenue receipts and expenditure of the Government of Bangladesh and the Pakistan Central Government. Gross public saving was estimated as the excess of total revenue receipts over total revenue expenditure.

Revenue receipts include collection under the provincial head as well as under the central head. Data on tax and non-tax revenue of the Bangladesh Government was easily available but separate data on the collection of revenue within Bangladesh under the central head were not usually published. The first attempt was made in a document,

---

[1] The saving function is given by, $S_c = -0·107 + 0·698^a Y_c$ $R^2 = 0·98$
$$(1·125) \quad (21·22)$$
Standard error of estimate $= 0·103$. S_c and Y_c are corporate saving and income respectively in takas hundred million/current prices.

An Analysis of Financial Resources and Development Potential in East Pakistan (Planning Department, Government of East Pakistan) to record the Central Government revenue receipts raised in East Pakistan for the period 1947–8 to 1959–60. The second source for such data is *The Budget in Brief, 1970–71*, which gives figures of important central taxes by point of collection. The above sources are, however, likely to under-estimate the contribution of Bangladesh since some of the burden of taxes could be shifted away through transfer of income to West Pakistan by both individuals and businesses. Since there were no data available on the magnitude of income transfer between Bangladesh and West Pakistan no attempt has been made to allow for this factor. Furthermore, in the case of indirect taxes the burden could be shifted from the point of collection so that the actual contribution might come from the region other than where the tax had been recorded. Such a shift could be measured from the nature of the commodities exchanged through interwing trade, but this was not attempted here. Thus all that has been done has been to add up the recorded figures for the tax collection under different heads from Bangladesh. *The Budget in Brief, 1970–71* contained data for 1960–1 to 1968–9. For 1959–60, data were taken from the Planning Department document mentioned above and for 1969–70 the pre-March 1971 Pakistan figure which was obtained from *The Budget in Brief, 1971–72* was divided between Bangladesh and Pakistan in the same proportion as that of 1968–9. This may have introduced some bias but the difference is likely to be minor.

Interest receipts of the Pakistan Central Government have been allocated on the basis of the proportion of the estimated capital expenditure in Bangladesh. Interest receipts exclude inter-governmental interest payments; this has been done in order to avoid double counting.

Revenue expenditure of the Bangladesh Government was taken from budget documents. Revenue expenditure of the Pakistan Central Government after deducting 50 per cent of the development expenditure in the revenue account was allocated between Bangladesh and Pakistan on the following basis:

(a) Direct Demand on Revenue:

25 per cent of the amount shown under 'Pak General' in *Combined Finance and Revenue Accounts of the Central and Provincial Governments* (C.F.R.A.) plus the amount shown under East Pakistan was taken as total expenditure in Bangladesh on account of collection of central taxes. For years for which C.F.R.A. was not available, the relevant figures in B.I.B. were divided on the basis of the average trend revealed in other years.

TABLE 4.5

ESTIMATES OF REVENUE RECEIPTS OF BANGLADESH: 1959–60 TO 1969–70
(takas millions at current prices)

	1959–60	1960–1	1961–2	1962–3	1963–4	1964–5	1965–6	1966–7	1967–8	1968–9	1969–70
A. Tax Revenue	535·5	654·2	747·1	703·0	960·1	1,119·7	1,449·2	1,407·5	1,487·5	1,648·8	1,810·3
1. Customs	182·6	194·3	226·1	237·9	304·5	408·2	371·1	463·4	501·1	542·6	547·4
2. Central excise	88·4	118·3	122·0	125·9	159·2	180·0	198·3	305·2	403·2	507·3	612·5
3. Sales	67·6	111·3	121·0	124·1	184·6	193·3	505·4	233·7	170·3	214·1	211·6
4. Income and corporation	53·0	65·3	71·6	78·1	115·2	135·3	143·7	155·0	162·4	128·2	176·1
5. Estate duty	0·1	0·3	0·2	0·2	0·2		0·2	0·2	0·3	0·3	0·3
6. Wealth and gift					1·1	1·2	1·0	1·4	1·3	2·5	1·9
7. Central rehabilitation[a]	4·5	5·6	6·5	3·6	0·7	12·4	13·0	12·7	9·4	11·8	11·8
8. Provincial excise	9·7	10·7	12·6	13·7	13·5	16·4	17·1	18·0	18·4	18·8	20·6
9. Agricultural income	12·5	15·0	10·4	10·8	16·4	14·6	15·8	18·7	17·7	19·6	25·5
10. Land revenue	93·5	108·3	145·5	76·6	130·3	121·5	134·3	146·9	149·1	137·1	134·9
11. Provincial rehabilitation	1·9	3·2	2·5	2·7	5·3	6·0	6·6	4·0	4·3	4·6	6·1
12. Urban immovable property tax	0·9	1·1	1·4	1·5	1·5	1·2	1·5	2·2	3·2	5·4	7·2
13. Salt	—	—	—	—	—	—	—	—	—	—	—
14. Other taxes[b]	20·8	20·8	27·3	27·9	27·9	29·4	41·0	46·1	46·7	56·5	54·6
B. Non-Tax Revenue	298·6	358·8	443·1	312·7	508·4	624·0	611·0	601·7	840·6	790·5	953·4
1. Stamps and registration	55·5	57·8	57·7	55·5	54·7	57·3	72·4	85·7	92·2	104·2	123·8
2. Other heads[c]	218·0	227·7	262·0	187·9	295·5	299·8	327·2	296·7	355·6	304·8	369·6
3. Interest receipts	25·1	38·6	58·9	22·3	121·5	192·4	177·3	199·0	309·5	371·0	445·2
4. Foreign aid and grants from central government	—	34·7	64·5	47·0	36·7	74·5	34·1	20·3	83·3	10·5	14·8

rehabilitation tax represents the sum of taxes collected under the two heads mentioned above.

[b] Major items under this head are entertainment tax, jute tax, motor vehicles, etc.

[c] It includes collections under forest, irrigation and navigation, civil administration, civil works, electricity schemes, railways, posts and telegraphs, currency and mint and other miscellaneous receipts.

Sources:

1. *Combined Finance and Revenue Accounts of the Central and Provincial Governments in Pakistan* (Karachi, Manager of Publications, published annually), for different years.

2. *Annual Budget of the Central Government of Pakistan*: for different years.

3. *Civil Budget Estimates*, Finance Department, Government of East Pakistan: for different years.

4. *Detailed Estimates of Revenue and Receipts*, Finance Department, Government of East Pakistan: for different years.

5. *Budget in Brief, 1970–71 and 1971–72*, Ministry of Finance, Government of Pakistan.

6. *Economic Survey of East Pakistan, 1963–64 and 1969–70*, Finance Department, Government of East Pakistan.

7. Unpublished work of N. N. Chowdhury at the University of California, Berkeley.

TABLE 4.6

ESTIMATES OF REVENUE EXPENDITURE IN BANGLADESH: 1959-60 TO 1969-70
(takas millions at current prices)

	1959-60	1960-1	1961-2	1962-3	1963-4	1964-5	1965-6	1966-7	1967-8	1968-9	1969-70
A. Bangladesh Government											
1. Direct demand on revenue (expenses of revenue collecting departments)	57·3	60·1	60·7	74·1	103·4	110·8	106·1	112·7	97·0	82·7	87·9
2. Direct account of irrigation, navigation, embankment and drainage works	0·3	–	–	–	–	–	–	–	4·3	4·2	20·0
3. Railway	–	–	–	32·0	54·7	45·3	–	34·7	60·1	–	–
4. Civil administration	182·3	243·1	281·0	299·7	326·9	383·4	474·4	353·7	438·8	544·2	608·3
5. Pensions, stationery, printing and miscellaneous expenditure	45·2	50·1	37·0	53·1	73·1	62·6	58·3	45·0	53·2	84·8	69·6
6. Civil defence[a]	0·5	0·6	0·6	0·7	0·3	0·3	0·7	0·7	0·6	0·7	0·8
7. Development expenditure (including central government)	37·6	39·5	68·6	81·9	141·0	181·4	187·3	207·0	261·5	303·8	400·3
8. Total (1+2+3+4+5+6+7)	323·2	393·4	447·9	541·5	699·4	783·8	826·8	753·8	915·5	1,020·4	1,186·9
B. Pakistan Central											

Government also)											
11. Civil administration	91·2	94·7	99·4	83·1	104·9	103·7	106·8	105·6	116·0	125·2	159·2
12. Civil works	20·3	21·3	20·9	12·5	15·3	18·1	27·2	31·5	34·1	40·2	48·3
13. Miscellaneous – pensions, stationery and printing, contribution to central and special fund for rehabilitation	24·7	23·8	23·8	13·8	18·5	39·8	53·8	36·4	36·1	54·8	51·8
14. Defence	104·3	111·2	110·9	95·4	115·7	126·2	285·5	229·4	218·7	242·7	274·9
15. Other heads	7·5	1·5	0·2	0·2	55·7	61·4	40·9	12·3	18·6	3·3	2·0
16. Total (9+10+11+12+13+ 14+15)	313·3	327·8	336·3	307·8	433·5	513·4	741·2	684·8	740·1	834·5	965·7
17. Total revenue expenditure (8+16)	636·5	721·2	784·2	849·3	1,132·9	1,297·2	1,568·0	1,438·6	1,655·6	1,854·9	2,152·6
18. Total revenue receipts	834·1	1,013·0	1,190·2	1,015·7	1,468·5	1,743·7	2,060·2	2,009·2	2,328·1	2,439·3	2,763·7
19. Gross public savings	197·6	291·8	406·0	166·4	335·6	446·5	492·2	570·6	672·5	584·4	611·1

Source:
1. *The Budget in Brief, 1971–72*, Ministry of Finance, Government of Pakistan.
2. Unpublished work of N. N. Chowdhury at the University of California, Berkeley.

a Only fifty per cent of the total amount shown in budget is taken as revenue expenditure.

(b) Debt Services:

These figures (and also those for interest receipts) were taken from a study by N. N. Chowdhury at the University of California, Berkeley. He assigns 20 per cent of the central interest payments on debt raised abroad to Bangladesh and divides interest payments raised domestically on the basis of the proportion of capital expenditure by the central government allocated to Bangladesh.

(c) Civil Administration:

This was allocated, in general, on a 30/70 basis, except for expenditure on the north-west frontier region of which none was allocated to Bangladesh and expenditure on foreign affairs of which 20 per cent was allocated to Bangladesh.

(d) Currency and Mint:

Since the entire activities related to this item were located in Pakistan, none was allocated to Bangladesh.

(e) Civil Works:

50 per cent of the total Pakistan figure was allocated to Bangladesh.

(f) Miscellaneous:

30 per cent of the total Pakistan figure was allocated to Bangladesh.

(g) Defence:

Only 10 per cent was allocated to Bangladesh.

(h) Other Heads:

50 per cent was allocated to Bangladesh.

(i) Development Expenditure:

Of the total development expenditure in the revenue account, 50 per cent was assumed to be actual revenue expenditure, while the other 50 per cent was taken to be capital expenditure. This is quite consistent with what is shown in the C.F.R.A. Of the revenue expenditure 50 per cent was allocated to Bangladesh.

In the absence of any recorded data, the estimate of the gross public saving derived from the above is undoubtedly conjectural. However, as a first approximation they seem to be quite acceptable. The government saving function[1] relating saving to government income (total revenue receipts) implies a marginal propensity to save

---

[1] Government saving function is given by, $S_G = -0.21 + 0.241^a Y_G$, $R^2 = 0.86$
$$(0.35) \quad (7.29)$$
and standard error of estimate = 0.684. S_G and Y_G are government saving and income respectively in takas hundred millions at current prices.

of 24·1 per cent which is indeed very impressive. This is not very surprising in view of the fact that the Pakistan Central Government made a very subtle use of the fiscal mechanism to transfer resources from Bangladesh to Pakistan.

By aggregating over the estimates of saving of the different sectors estimates of total domestic saving in Bangladesh were obtained. The comparison of direct and indirect estimates of domestic saving in Bangladesh over the period 1959–60 to 1969–70 is presented in Table 4.7. A separate aggregate saving function was also estimated on the basis of direct estimate and the result is presented below. This function relates the direct estimate of saving to gross national product at current market prices. Variables are measured in hundred million takas.

$$S_D = -6·692^a + 0·110^a Y_D, \quad R^2 = 0·98 \text{ and standard error of}$$
$$\quad (3·20) \quad (12·40)$$
estimate $= 0·87$.

S_D and Y_D are direct estimates of national savings and gross national product respectively.

TABLE 4.7

A COMPARISON OF DIRECT AND INDIRECT ESTIMATE
OF DOMESTIC SAVING IN BANGLADESH:
1959/60–1969/70
(takas millions at current prices)

Year	Direct Estimate	Indirect Estimate
1959–60	898	938
1960–1	1042	542
1961–2	1210	976
1962–3	1088	1230
1963–4	1571	1327
1964–5	1774	1312
1965–6	2135	1380
1966–7	2186	1913
1967–8	2370	2498
1968–9	2515	2658
1969–70	2940	3297

Source: Tables 4.1 and 4.2.

The estimated marginal propensity to save has turned out to be 11·0 per cent which is somewhat lower than what was obtained in the saving function estimated from the indirect method. It is to be hoped that the recording and collection of basic data will improve over time so that a closer correspondence can be obtained between savings estimates by the alternative methods.

IV. FOREIGN EXCHANGE RESOURCES OF BANGLADESH
1959–60 TO 1969–70

A brief review of the foreign exchange earnings of Bangladesh will be presented in this section. It should be noted that in the past, trade with Pakistan did not involve any foreign exchange transaction. But since in the future all trade will involve payment and receipt in hard currency, it is necessary to analyse the past pattern of trade on a combined basis, treating trade with both Pakistan and other countries as foreign trade. In order to identify the differences in the composition of exports to Pakistan and to other countries, the data have, however, been presented separately in Table 4.8.

A careful analysis of the export performance is necessary because, for some commodities for which Pakistan was the most important market, Bangladesh will have to find alternative outlets until such time, at least, when trade channels with Pakistan may be reopened. It assumes even greater importance due to the fact that many decisions regarding investment for capacity creation in export industries are closely related to finding a suitable market for the product. In the event that no alternative market can be found, it may be necessary to disinvest in those industries and transfer mobile resources to alternative uses. Major export commodities for which Bangladesh is now looking for suitable alternative markets are, tea, paper and paste board and matches.

There appears to have been an upward trend in the export earnings of Bangladesh over the period 1959–60 to 1969–70. Foreign exchange earnings from visible exports in current prices increased at an annual compound rate of 6 per cent. However, this compared rather un-favourably with the rate of growth of gross domestic product at current factor cost, which was 8·3 per cent. The corresponding figures at constant prices are 2·7 per cent[1] and 4·3 per cent respectively. Clearly in real terms the growth of exports has substantially lagged behind the growth of the gross domestic product. Comparing foreign (other than Pakistan) with regional exports (with Pakistan) it is found that the latter grew faster than the former. An analysis of the commodity composition reveals that raw jute and jute manufactures contributed more than 65 per cent towards the total export earnings of Bangladesh during the period under consideration. However, over time the share of jute manufactures increased considerably while earnings from raw jute exports remained stagnant around takas 750 million. It is interesting to note that the export market of tea shifted during this period as Pakistan replaced other

[1] Foreign (other than Pakistan) and regional (with Pakistan) export series were deflated separately by unit value of exports and the G.D.P. deflator respectively.

countries as the major buyer. One of the redeeming features (perhaps the only one) was the growth in invisible earnings. This presumably was due to an increase in the remittances of Bengalis from abroad. Entitlement to a more realistic exchange rate under the bonus scheme may have helped to increase the amount of remittances from abroad. During the period under consideration two policy measures were designed to play a key role in expanding foreign (other than Pakistan) export earnings of Bangladesh: (1) allowing a more realistic exchange rate for some exportables and (2) favourable treatment of export industries in terms of tax credit and import licensing. However, in the light of growth performance of exports, as discussed above, one can have serious reservations regarding the effectiveness of these policies in expanding exports. One may add here, though, that under-invoicing of exports may have played some part in an under-estimation of the growth in export earnings as reflected in the official statistics.

V. DOMESTIC RESOURCES FOR DEVELOPMENT DURING THE FIRST FIVE YEAR PLAN AND THEIR MOBILISATION[1]

A. *The Economy of Bangladesh 1972–3 to 1977–8*

In order to make an attempt at projecting the resources available to Bangladesh, it is necessary to review the progress of the economy since liberation as well as to predict the future pattern of growth. Growth and domestic resource mobilisation are interdependent, although one can study the growth prospect independently of the latter since the estimated gap between the investment requirement and possible domestic resource mobilisation can, in theory at least, be filled by foreign capital inflow. Thus up to a given limit (usually set by physical and socio-political constraints) any growth rate of the economy can be sustained if adequate foreign capital is forthcoming. It is necessary, however, to take a careful look at the structure of the economy and investment allocation should be so geared that it creates a foundation for a long-term sustained growth with an increasing dependence on domestic resources for financing development expenditure.

[1] This section of this chapter and the subsequent sections have been considerably expanded from the paper presented to the Conference in order to provide a reader of the present volume with a fuller picture of the potential resources of Bangladesh. It must be made clear that the forecasts here printed are Dr Alamgir's own responsibility and may differ significantly from those of the Government of Bangladesh – Editor.

TABLE 4.8

FOREIGN EXCHANGE EARNINGS OF BANGLADESH: 1959/60 – 1969/70
(takas millions at current prices)

	1959–60	1960–1	1961–2	1962–3	1963–4	1964–5	1965–6	1966–7	1967–8	1968–9	1969–70
A. Foreign (other than Pakistan)	1,080·0	1,259·0	1,300·0	1,249·0	1,224·0	1,268·0	1,514·0	1,667·0	1,484·2	1,542·7	1,670·0
Exports of Bangladesh:											
Total	729·1	841·0	849·5	792·9	752·5	845·3	863·1	897·8	758·9	730·7	762·4
(i) Raw jute and jute cuttings											
(ii) Tea	34·5	1·1	21·3	6·4	–	10·0	11·0	0·8	–	–	–
(iii) Hides and skins	40·3	28·6	26·6	26·3	25·9	20·1	27·8	3·8	2·1	0·2	0·2
(iv) Jute manufacturers	213·8	310·8	311·9	306·0	314·0	292·3	565·3	626·3	605·5	655·9	768·3
(v) Leather	2·4	3·7	11·9	5·6	6·8	12·4	24·8	51·8	43·1	75·2	60·0
(vi) Cotton twist yarn and fabrics	9·4	6·3	–	0·3	5·2[a]	4·2	4·1	3·1	11·3	25·6	26·5
(vii) Other commodities	50·5	67·5	78·8	111·5	119·6	83·7	17·9	83·4	63·3	55·1	52·7
B. Foreign (with Pakistan)	362·4	363·5	402·0	474·0	511·2	537·1	651·8	738·0	784·9	871·3	923·4
Exports of Bangladesh:											
Total	72·6	80·3	89·0	90·3	100·0	104·9	137·5	135·8	154·7	158·3	159·2
(i) Jute manufactures											

(iv) Leather	25·2	15·3	11·4	17·6	22·1	22·6	23·2	24·7	27·6	29·7	28·1
(v) Matches	25·1	26·3	30·9	24·9	28·5	26·2	39·6	29·5	31·7	42·6	44·7
(vi) Tea	118·9	109·6	116·3	152·8	164·1	185·4	243·5	291·2	228·9	257·1	243·3
(vii) Other commodities	69·2	80·4	73·4	109·9	112·4	96·5	121·7	171·4	239·0	265·5	339·0
C. Invisible Receipts	83·3[b]	116·7[b]	164·0	163·8	223·3	257·4	292·1	291·0	335·1	408·1	441·4
D. Total Foreign Exchange Resources of Bangladesh: (A+B+C)	1,525·7	1,739·2	1,866·0	1,886·8	1,958·5	2,062·5	2,458·0	2,696·0	2,604·2	2,822·1	3,034·9

[a] Export during the period July 1963 to May 1964.

[b] The Panel Report listed in the sources below did not contain data of invisible receipts for the years 1959–60 and 1960–1. Data from other sources were not reconcilable with the Panel Report figures. Therefore a linear time trend was fitted by least-square regression to the receipts data to obtain figures for 1959–60 and 1960–1.

Sources:
1. *Monthly Statistical Bulletin of Bangladesh*, March 1972. Bangladesh Bureau of Statistics, Government of Bangladesh, Dacca.
2. *Economic Survey of East Pakistan*, various issues, Ministry of Finance, Government of East Pakistan.
3. *Statistical Digest of Bangladesh*, 1970–1. Bangladesh Bureau of Statistics, Government of Bangladesh, Dacca.
4. *Pakistan Statistical Yearbook*, 1968, Central Statistical Office, Government of Pakistan.
5. *Reports of the Advisory Panel for the Fourth Five Year Plan*, 1970–75, vol. I, Planning Commission, Government of Pakistan.

Since the war of liberation the economy of Bangladesh has been operating at a level much lower than the level attained during the last normal year before liberation, 1969–70. In fact, the actual level of output in some sectors during 1972–3 has been anywhere between 10 and 30 per cent below the level of 1969–70. In this, two factors seemed to have played the most dominant role. First, an exceptional drought affected the production of the major rice crops (*aus* and *aman*) and early rain affected the output of the *boro* crop. The performance of other crops was no better, so that on the whole it is estimated that agricultural output in 1972–3 was 17 per cent below that of 1969–70. Second, in other sectors production was lower due to labour-management problems, shortage of raw materials and spare parts, destruction of capacity during the liberation struggle and similar causes. While domestic production was lagging, imports also failed to augment the supply of essential commodities, thus resulting in a phenomenal rise in all prices. Both shortage of resources and institutional bottlenecks (delay in issue of licences, absence of experienced importers, lack of international contact and lack of planning in setting priorities for essential importables) were responsible for inadequate performance in imports. Reduction in the total availability of consumables and raw materials and increase in money

TABLE 4.9

GROSS DOMESTIC PRODUCT OF BANGLADESH:
1969–70 and 1972–3
(takas millions at current factor cost)

	1969–70	1972–3	1972–3 at 1969–70 Factor Cost
1. Agriculture	17922	27933	14875
2. Mining	5	10	5
3. Industry	2061	3338	1307
(a) Large Scale	965	1602	627
(b) Small Scale	1096	1736	680
4. Construction	1743	1530	1133
5. Utilities	274	328	298
6. Transport	1959	2841	1959
7. Trade	2932	4193	3812
8. Banking and Insurance	250	350	325
9. Ownership of Dwellings	1662	2243	1725
10. Public Administration	1179	1356	1233
11. Services	1346	1817	1397
12. Gross Domestic Product	31333	45939	28069
1969–70 = 100	(100·0)		(89·6)

Sources: 1. 1969–70 value-added – M. Alamgir and L. Berlage, *An Analysis of National Accounts of Bangladesh*, op. cit.

2. 1972–3 value-added – see Appendix 2.

supply (since liberation money supply has increased by 83 per cent) is reflected in the wholesale price index which stood at 205 in 1972–3 with 1969–70 as the base. The index of agricultural products was 187·78, while that of industrial products was 255·46.

With the above background an attempt is made in Table 4.9 to estimate the gross domestic product of Bangladesh for the year 1972–3 at current factor cost. The detailed methodology is described in Appendix 2. A separate column is also added showing the gross domestic product at 1969–70 factor cost. The First Five Year Plan has the twin task of first ensuring a recovery of the economy to the benchmark level (1969–70) and then of realising a growth target. All economic variables are likely to behave differently during the period of recovery and the period of growth. One must apply different co-efficients and cost calculations while determining the input (domestic and foreign) requirements for these two periods. The entire phasing of investment allocation will depend on adequate allowance being made for the different character of these two periods.

For the purpose of projecting the growth of the economy of Bangladesh over the First Five Year Plan period, the year 1973–4 is defined as the recovery phase while the period 1974–5 to 1977–8 is defined as the development phase. This is not to say that there will be absolutely no growth in any sector during 1973–4 over the level of 1969–70 (the benchmark). In point of fact, sectors which are already well ahead in finishing the reconstruction phase during 1972–3 will experience some growth while others will presumably reach the level of 1969–70 in real terms. 1973–4 will thus constitute the base year from which the economy will hopefully take off into the development phase.

Accordingly, in Table 4.10, the projected level of gross domestic product by sector for the year 1973–4 is presented as the starting point. The underlying sectoral assumptions for the projection are as follows. Value-added in agriculture, manufacturing and construction sectors is projected to be the same as in 1969–70 except for price changes. On the basis of recent performance, utilities and transport sectors are assumed to attain a real growth of 10 and 8 per cent respectively over 1969–70. In trade, it was assumed that the present scarcity mark up will continue; value-added in 1973–4 was estimated by applying the 1972–3 ratio of value-added in trade to that in agriculture and manufacturing to the values-added in these two sectors in 1973–4. A similar procedure was adopted to estimate the value-added in the service sector, the ratio in this case being value-added in service to value-added in other sectors. As indicated earlier, the realisation of the target G.D.P. of 1973–4 implies the following assumptions. (*a*) All necessary replacement investment has

TABLE 4.10

PROJECTED GROSS DOMESTIC PRODUCT BY SECTORS
(takas millions at 1972-3 factor cost)

	1973-4	1977-8	Annual Percentage Rate of Growth
1. Agriculture	33654 (59·5)	40907 (56·2)	5·0
2. Manufacturing	5278 (9·3)	7261 (10·0)	8·3
3. Construction	2356 (4·2)	3979 (5·5)	14·0
4. Utilities	361 (0·6)	748 (1·0)	20·0
5. Transport	3068 (5·4)	3873 (5·3)	6·0
6. Trade	5192 (9·2)	7064 (9·7)	8·0
7. Services	6617 (11·7)	9002 (12·4)	8·0
8. Gross Domestic Product	56526 (100·0)	72834 (100·0)	6·5

Note: Figures within parentheses are percentage distribution of gross domestic product by sector. They may not add up to 100 due to rounding errors.

been undertaken by the beginning of 1972-3. (*b*) Additional capacity creation, whenever necessary, has also been completed. These two assumptions are quite realistic in view of what is known about the recent performance of the economy. It may be pointed out here, that in this analysis a one-year lag between investment and output increase is assumed. (*c*) The drought experience of 1972-3 will not be repeated. (*d*) In the manufacturing sector better utilisation of capacity will be ensured through removal of institutional and physical bottlenecks. To be more precise, much can be achieved only by ensuring better labour–management relations, adequate incentive for all engaged in production activities, and smooth flow of spares and raw materials.

Table 4.10 also presents a projection of gross domestic product by sector for the year 1977-8 the terminal year of the First Five Year Plan. The basis of sectoral growth rates is twofold. First, an evaluation of the past trend indicated a feasible path that can be followed if no structural change is attempted. Secondly, an analysis of the desirable structural change over the next five years was undertaken on the basis of the experience of other developing countries which are similarly endowed with natural resources as Bangladesh but which have already experienced a certain amount of development. The spirit of this approach was derived from work done by Dorfman,

Alamgir and Tabors[1] at the Harvard University Center for Population Studies. A combination of the two considerations stated above produced a set of sectoral growth rates which seem to be within the feasible region for Bangladesh (assuming, of course, that the implicit foreign capital will be forthcoming) and which are consistent with the experience of other comparable developing countries in terms of maintaining intersectoral balance during the process of growth.

TABLE 4.11

SECTORAL CAPITAL INCOME COEFFICIENTS
(at 1972–3 prices)

	Capital/Income Ratio
1. Agriculture	1·00
2. Manufacturing	3·50
3. Construction	0·30
4. Utilities	7·50
5. Transport	3·90
6. Trade	1·50
7. Services	3·00

The next step in assessing the need and potential for domestic resources involved estimation of total gross investment requirement during the First Five Year Plan period. For this purpose a set of incremental gross capital/income ratios by sector were derived from the studies done by MacEwan,[2] Khan[3] and Tabors.[4] These were supplemented by recent information on capital requirement for capacity expansion in different sectors as revealed from the work done at various government agencies including the Planning Commission. The sectoral capital/income coefficients are presented in Table 4.11; these were used to derive estimates of gross investment requirement by sector in different years of the First Five Year Plan.[5] These estimates are presented in Table 4.12. Two assumptions were used to arrive at these figures: (1) the investment output lag was

[1] R. Dorfman, M. Alamgir and R. Tabors, *A Framework for Long-term Economic Planning in Bangladesh*, Harvard University Center for Population Studies (Mimeo), 1972.

[2] Arthur MacEwan, *Development Alternatives in Pakistan* (Harvard University Press, 1971).

[3] A. R. Khan, 'The Possibilities of the East Pakistan Economy during the Fourth Five Year Plan', *The Pakistan Development Review*, vol. IX, no. 2 (Summer 1969).

[4] R. D. A. Tabors, Cross-national Approach to the Derivations of Capital Income Coefficients, Harvard University Center for Population Studies (mimeo), 1972.

[5] The sectoral capital/income coefficients include working capital investment as well as gross fixed capital investment.

assumed to be one year; (2) in the post terminal year all sectors were assumed to maintain the growth rate achieved during the plan period.

TABLE 4.12

GROSS INVESTMENT BY SECTOR
(takas millions at 1972–3 prices)

		1973–4	1974–5	1975–6	1976–7	1977–8	Total
1.	Agriculture	1683	1767	1855	1948	2045	9298
2.	Manufacturing	1533	1661	1798	1948	2109	9049
3.	Construction	199	113	129	147	167	655
4.	Utilities	542	650	780	936	1123	4031
5.	Transport	718	761	807	855	906	4047
6.	Trade	623	673	727	785	848	3656
7.	Services	1588	1715	1852	2001	2161	9317
8.	Total	6786	7340	7948	8620	9359	40053
9.	Total Investment as proportion of G.D.P.	11·8	12·2	12·4	12·6	12·9	

From Table 4.12 one can observe that during the First Five Year Plan agriculture claims the biggest share of investment with services sector disaggregated into government and other services. Total investment as a percentage of G.D.P. remains almost stagnant at around 12 per cent. This is less than what was achieved during the end of the Third Five Year Plan of the erstwhile Government of Pakistan. This is primarily because a very realistic approach has been followed in determining the possibilities of the Bangladesh economy during the First Plan and in keeping the necessary capital inflow within reasonable bounds. As will be seen shortly, given the available indication, one cannot possibly be very optimistic about the potential domestic resource mobilisation in Bangladesh over the course of the next five years.

B. *Resources for Development 1973–8*

Domestic savings is divided into two types: (1) private saving and (2) public saving. This is done in view of the fact that the government of Bangladesh has nationalised a major portion of the corporate sector. Therefore, public saving is defined as savings by the government sector and by the nationalised sectors. Savings from the rest of the economy is defined as private saving. Assuming that the government will allow the small shareholders of the nationalised sectors to retain their right to earn a dividend, it is possible to re-classify the total savings of Bangladesh as presented in Table 4.2, under only two heads. This exercise was done for 1963–4 and 1968–9 and the results are presented below.[1]

[1] Public savings = Govt. savings + savings by sugar industry + 80 per cent of savings by Jute, Textile and Allied; Chemical, Fertilisers, etc.; Iron, Steel etc.; Paper and Board, etc., industries + savings by non-financial companies without

(Takas millions at current prices)[a]

	1963–4	*1968–9*
Private saving	1,015·6 (5·6)	1,638·2 (5·7)
Public saving	555·8 (3·0)	876·9 (3·1)

[a] Figures in brackets show the ratios of savings to G.D.P. at current factor cost.

1963–4 was chosen because the coverage in data for that year was much wider than any other previous year while 1968–9 was the last year for which a satisfactory coverage in data for all sectors was obtained. Reclassification of savings estimates along the lines suggested above is essential in order to make the projection of the domestic resource availability relevant for the working of the Bangladesh economy in the future. From this one can determine the required intersectoral flow of funds and also identify the appropriate instruments to mobilise domestic resources for public sector investment.

It emerges clearly from the above table that both public and private saving measured in current prices increased substantially over the period under consideration. However, in real terms the growth is not as impressive as it seems otherwise. If one uses the wholesale price index to deflate both private and public saving then one gets the former growing at 3·4 per cent per annum, the latter at 2·8 per cent per annum and the total saving at 3·1 per cent per annum. The corresponding rates in current prices were 10·0 per cent, 9·5 per cent and 9·9 per cent respectively. A more interesting comparison would be between the ratios of private and public saving to G.D.P. and their movement over time. Although in both periods, private saving is relatively more important than public saving in total saving, as a percentage of Gross Domestic Product at current factor cost, there does not seem to have taken place any structural shift in saving in Bangladesh in terms of its sectoral origin. This has interesting implications for projection of domestic savings by sector in the future. As will be explained below, government's policy perspective will play a very important role.

In a country like Bangladesh which is aspiring to establish a socialist order, the relative importance of the private and public saving in the accumulation of investment fund will be determined by the policy perspective of the political authority. It was argued by the

---

separate account for Bangladesh + savings by financial companies + 50 per cent of savings by private companies. Savings by private companies is assumed to be equal to the total gross savings by non-financial public companies with separate account for Bangladesh.

Private savings = Total gross national savings − total gross public savings.

TABLE 4.13

DOMESTIC RESOURCES DURING THE FIRST FIVE YEAR PLAN OF BANGLADESH

(takas millions at 1972–3 prices)

	1972–3 (Revised Budget Estimate)	1973–4 (Budget Estimate)	1974–5	1975–6	1976–7	1977–8	Total (1973–4 to 1977–8)
1. Revenue Receipts							
Customs	1,000·0	1,420·0	1,533·6	1,656·3	1,788·8	1,931·9	8,330·6
Excise	620·5	986·2	1,134·3	1,304·2	1,499·9	1,724·9	6,649·5
Sales	300·0	460·0	517·5	582·2	655·0	736·8	2,951·5
Income and corporation taxes (including agricultural income tax)	83·6	156·3	169·4	183·7	199·1	218·8	924·3
Land revenue	35·0	45·0	45·0	45·0	45·0	45·0	225·0
Stamps and registration	103·0	107·0	116·1	126·0	136·7	148·3	634·1
Interest receipts	7·4	232·5	267·4	307·5	353·6	406·6	1,567·6
Other revenues	173·4	186·2	198·3	211·2	224·9	239·5	1,060·1
Additional taxes and fees	–	239·9	600·0	1,100·0	1,750·0	2,550·0	6,239·9
Total	2,322·9	3,833·1	4,581·6	5,516·1	6,653·0	7,998·8	28,582·6
2. Revenue Expenditure							
Revenue collecting department	134·3	148·0	155·4	163·2	171·3	179·9	817·8
Civil administration	879·1	1,041·9	1,146·1	1,260·7	1,386·8	1,525·4	6,360·9
Defence	250·0	470·0	517·0	568·7	625·6	688·1	2,869·4
Civil works	94·5	94·6	104·1	114·5	125·9	138·5	577·6
Education	450·1	584·4	701·2	841·5	1,009·8	1,211·8	4,348·7
Health	120·7	141·7	184·2	239·5	311·3	404·7	1,281·4
Interest payment	81·1	97·2	106·9	117·6	129·4	142·3	593·4
Others	242·3	375·2	412·7	454·0	499·4	549·3	2,290·6
Total	2,252·1	2,953·0	3,327·6	3,759·7	4,259·5	4,840·0	19,139·8
3. Revenue Surplus	70·8	880·1	1,254·0	1,756·4	2,393·5	3,158·8	9,442·8
4. Nationalised Sector	102·1	280·0	797·0	876·7	964·4	1,060·8	3,978·9
5. Private Sector	–	2,012·0	2,679·0	2,853·0	3,039·0	3,241·0	13,824·0

author in a separate paper presented at this conference, that the income policy of the government will reflect its thinking about the role to be played by different saver groups within the economy. This decision in turn will depend on the extent to which the government wants to retain control over the accumulation fund. Furthermore, policy directives are necessary to indicate the willingness of the government to restrict the growth in public consumption so as to raise the magnitude of surplus on its own account.

In the absence of a clear policy perspective as mentioned above, projection of the domestic resources by sector of origin can only be very tentative. An attempt is made in Table 4.13 to present a preliminary estimate of domestic saving in Bangladesh during the First Five Year Plan, on the basis of a number of somewhat arbitrary assumptions.

For 1973–4, figures were taken from the budget document.[1] It is assumed that budget estimates represent the best guess on revenue earnings and expenditure of the government. As for prices, although the Planning Commission is hopeful that with a better performance of the economy wholesale prices during First Plan will be somewhat below the level attained in 1972–3, yet it is assumed here that in 1973–4 there will not be any significant change in the price level over the previous year. Thus the budget estimates of revenue earnings and expenditure for 1973–4 can be taken as at constant 1972–3 prices. For other years, the basis of projecting revenue receipts under different heads is given below. All projections are made in constant 1972–3 prices. These projections are made with the existing taxes and tax rates. Possible yields from additional taxes are shown separately.

(i) *Customs revenue* is assumed to grow at 8 per cent per annum with the existing tariff rates It is based on the following considerations. The ratio of imports to G.D.P. during 1969–70 was 11·5 per cent but it went down to about 8 per cent in 1972–3 and also in the latter case the proportion of low tariff imports was high. During the First Plan it is projected that the proportion of low tariff imports will decline and, with increasing amounts of development imports, the ratio of imports to G.D.P. will rise gradually above the level attained in 1972–3 and stabilise at the level of 1969–70 by the end of the First Plan so that the rate of growth of customs revenue at the existing rates is likely to be more than that of G.D.P. (6·7 per cent).

(ii) *Excise duty* is assumed to grow at a rate of 15 per cent per

---

[1] Budget estimates for 1973–4 have been available since the first draft of this paper was prepared and presented at the I.E.A. Conference in Dacca. These are incorporated in the revised version in order to ensure that the projections in this paper do not turn out to be way out of line of the actual operation of the economy of Bangladesh.

annum. This is lower than what was obtained over the period 1965/6–1969/70 but higher than the rate of growth of value added in manufacturing. A general review of the structure of industries shows that it will be desirable to concentrate on the industries that produce major excisable items so that they are likely to grow at a higher rate than overall manufacturing.

(iii) *Sales tax* will grow at a rate of 12·5 per cent per annum. In keeping with the past trend, the rate of growth in sales tax collection is assumed to be higher than the rate of growth of customs revenue.

(iv) *Income and corporation tax* is assumed to grow at a rate of 8·4 per cent per annum after 1973–4. This is derived from the assumption that taxable income will grow at the rate of 7 per cent per annum over the First Five Year Plan and the elasticity of tax receipts with respect to income is 1·2. The rate of growth of taxable income in the past was observed to have risen more than the rate of growth of G.D.P. and the same trend is assumed to continue in the future. The elasticity figure was obtained in the case of income tax payable by individuals during the Third Plan in pre-March 1971 Pakistan.

(v) Receipts from *land revenue* were assumed to remain the same over all years during the First Plan.

(vi) During the sixties *receipts from stamps and registration* increased by about 8·5 per cent per annum and between 1972–3 and 1973–4 are projected to grow at 3·9 per cent according to revised budget and budget estimates of the two years respectively. During the remaining years of First Plan it is projected to grow at 8·5 per cent as experienced in the sixties. In fact, this also closely approximates the rate of growth of non-agricultural value added in both periods.

(vii) For 1973–4, the budget estimate of *interest receipts* is placed above the level given by the revised budget of 1972–3. It is, therefore, indicated that the receipt of interest from outstanding loans from the government as well as from new loans to be given out will pick up the trend realised in the period before liberation. However, the growth is likely to be somewhat lower because of the higher base and because an economy drive by the government may discourage unproductive loans. Thus it is assumed that in the remaining years of the First Plan, interest receipts will grow at a rate of 15 per cent annually. This may be compared with a 20 per cent annual growth over 1965/6 to 1969/70.

(viii) *All other receipts* were assumed to grow at a rate of 6·5 per cent per annum, which is the rate of growth of G.D.P. over 1973–4 to 1977–8.

(ix) In the absence of any other indication from the government in terms of its thinking on *additional tax measures*, the estimate of the Planning Commission is accepted here as possible amounts of additional tax revenue due to tax rate changes and new tax proposals.

Revenue expenditure has mostly been projected on the basis of past trends while keeping in mind the fact that some of the functions of the government have expanded due to the emergence of Bangladesh as a new nation. Furthermore, expenditure on education and health have been projected to grow at a much higher rate (20 and 30 per cent respectively) than what was obtained ever before. This is consistent with the declared objective of the political leadership to extend education and health to every village. For other types of expenditure the following are the assumed rates of growth

Revenue collecting department	5
Civil administration	10
Defence	10
Interest payment	10
Other	13

Government saving is then derived easily as the excess of revenue receipts over revenue expenditure in the current account and this is also shown in Table 4.13. Government saving increases from takas 880·1 million in 1973–4 to takas 3,158·8 million in 1977–8 representing 3·6 fold increase over the First Plan. Table 4.14 below shows

TABLE 4.14

Year	Tax receipts as per cent of gross domestic product	Government saving as per cent of government income
1973–4	6·0	23·0
1974–5	6·8	27·4
1975–6	7·8	31·8
1976–7	8·9	36·0
1977–8	10·1	39·5

Source: Table 4.13.

the tax receipts of the Government as a percentage of G.D.P. over the period 1973–4 to 1977–8. It is assumed that 50 per cent of receipts from other revenue represent receipts from taxes. In a separate column the ratio of government saving to income (total revenue receipts) is also shown. Tax receipts as a percentage of G.D.P. go up from a meagre 6·0 per cent in 1973–4 to 10·1 per cent in 1977–8 which represents an improvement over the trend observed in the 1960s[1] although the overall performance in terms of revenue mobilisation through fiscal means does not compare favourably with

[1] See M. Alamgir and L. Berlage, op. cit.

other developing countries.[2] The average rate of government saving starts at the level realised during the Second and Third Five Year Plan of the erstwhile Government of Pakistan but improves over time to reach the level of 39·5 in 1977–8.

For the nationalised sectors, saving in 1973–4 is projected at takas 280 million in the budget estimate for the year 1973–4. This is far below the level of 1968–9 at 1972–3 prices. However, during the course of the next two years the level of efficiency in the operation of public sector enterprises is likely to pick up, so that the contribution from the nationalised sector towards the national investment fund will reach the level of 1968–9 adjusted for price changes. For the remaining years of the First Plan, the saving of the nationalised sector is assumed to grow at the rate of 10 per cent per annum which is slightly above the rate of growth of industrial and financial companies in the public sector. The underlying assumption is that the state will be recovering a fixed percentage return on capital owned in public sector enterprises but this proportion will increase over the First Plan.

The private sector now includes a part of the non-corporate private sector as defined earlier and that part of the corporate sector which is not nationalised. In terms of G.D.P. of 1969–70 this sector accounts for about 90 per cent of the G.D.P. and its realised average rate of saving was slightly above 6 per cent. It is assumed that this sector will maintain its share of total G.D.P. over the First Five Year Plan. But due to the dislocation in economic and social life following liberation, and particularly the price rise, it is unlikely that the past saving performance of this sector can be repeated. It is, therefore, conservatively estimated that the annual average rate of saving of this sector will be 4 per cent in 1973–4 and will then rise to 5 per cent the next year and stabilise at that level till the end of the Plan period. Thus private sector saving is estimated to go up from takas 2,012 million in 1973–4 to takas 3,241·0 million in 1977–8 representing a 61 per cent increase over the Plan period.

The overall picture of the domestic resource position that emerges from the above discussion does not appear to be very promising. As can be seen from Table 4.13 the total amount of domestic resources available for investment over the First Plan is takas 27,246 million only. In Table 4.15 total domestic saving is expressed as a percentage of G.D.P. in order to indicate the extent of saving effort by different

[2] As far back as in 1959–60, total tax receipts as a percentage of G.D.P. were 10 for Ceylon, 10·8 for Columbia, 10·1 for India, 29·0 for Chile, 15·6 for Costa Rica, 12·9 for Kenya, 10·7 for Korea and 10 for Thailand. These figures are estimated from U.N. *Yearbook of National Accounts 1967*, Department of Economic and Social Affairs, United Nations (New York, 1968).

sectors of the economy during different years of the First Plan. The average rate of saving goes up from 5·6 per cent in 1973–4 to 10·2 in 1977–8, the last year of the First Plan. These can be compared with the rates achieved during the Second and Third Five Year Plan of Bangladesh when the average rate of saving fluctuated between 4 and 10 per cent of gross domestic product.

TABLE 4.15

SAVING AS A PROPORTION OF GROSS DOMESTIC PRODUCT
(takas millions at 1972–3 prices)

Year	Saving	Gross domestic product	Saving as a percent of gross domestic product
1973–4	3172	56526	5·6
1974–5	4730	60200	7·9
1975–6	5486	64113	8·6
1976–7	6397	68281	9·4
1977–8	7461	72834	10·2

Source: Tables 4.10 and 4.13.

Figures for total investment in Table 4.12 can now be combined with estimates of total saving to find out the implicit required capital inflow over the First Plan. This is shown in Table 4.16 below. For

TABLE 4.16

REQUIRED CAPITAL INFLOW FOR THE FIRST PLAN ON THE BASIS OF EXISTING TRENDS
(takas millions at 1972–3 prices)

Year	Investment	Saving	Capital inflow	Capital inflow as per cent investment
1973–4	6786	3172	3614	53·3
1974–5	7340	4730	2610	35·6
1975–6	7948	5486	2462	31·0
1976–7	8620	6397	2223	25·8
1977–8	9359	7461	1898	20·3
Total (1973–8)	40053	27246	12807	32·0

the Plan as a whole, about one-third of the total investment will have to be financed by external resources. This clearly represents a higher proportion than that realised during the Second and Third Plan of the Pakistan Government. But, net capital inflow as a proportion of total investment declines substantially over the First Plan as it moves from a rather high level of 53·3 per cent in the first year of the Plan to 20·3 per cent in the last year.

Nevertheless, what emerges from this discussion is that if Bangladesh wants to formulate an ambitious development plan which does not depend too much on foreign capital inflow, some more fundamental measures will have to be undertaken to mobilise domestic resources. These measures will involve basic institutional changes so as to ensure first, the realisation of a higher amount of surplus on government's own account and on the account of nationalised sector and second, a significant resource transfer from the private sector. These point towards the need for (1) austerity on the part of the government, (2) efficiency in the management of nationalised sector and finally (3) an intelligent use of income and price policy in addition to fiscal policy to effect a greater amount of resource transfer from the private sector to the public sector.

Domestic financing of the public sector investment will come from net capital receipts in addition to revenue surplus and the surplus of the nationalised sector. A major part of the net capital receipts (Appendix, Table 13) represent funds out of private saving which are placed in the hands of the government for development expenditure.

It is clear from Appendix, Table 13 that, net domestic capital receipts from Bangladesh increased substantially over the period 1959/60 to 1969/70. The annual compound rate of growth of net domestic capital receipts at current prices was about 10 per cent. Domestic debt (permanent debt, floating debt and unfunded debt)

TABLE 4.17

DOMESTIC CAPITAL DURING THE FIRST FIVE YEAR PLAN OF BANGLADESH
(takas in millions at 1972–3 prices)

	1972–3 (Budget estimate)	1973–4	1974–5	1975–6	1976–7	1977–8	Total (1973–4 to 1977–8)
1. Domestic debt	635	699	768	845	930	1023	4265
2. Accretion to reserve fund	24	199	203	207	211	215	1035
3. Recovery of loans and advances	26	168	202	242	290	348	1250
4. Others receipts	5	47	47	47	47	47	235
5. Net domestic capital	–	1113	1220	1341	1478	1633	6785

registered a rate of growth of 10·3 per cent per annum while receipts on account of the recovery of loans and advances increased by 23 per cent.

Table 4.17 presents a projection of net capital receipts for the First Five Year Plan period of Bangladesh. These were calculated on the assumption of no basic change in policies underlying capital receipts and liabilities. Needless to say that policy changes will warrant changes in these projections. Rates of growth applied to different components of net domestic capital receipts were primarily derived from past trends and are given below:

Domestic debt	10
Accretion to reserve fund	2
Recovery of loans and advances	20
Others	0

From the above it is then possible to derive an estimate of the total domestic resources available for public investment during the First Five Year Plan. These estimates are given below in Table 4.18.

TABLE 4.18

DOMESTIC RESOURCES FOR PUBLIC SECTOR
DEVELOPMENT EXPENDITURE DURING FIRST PLAN
(takas millions at 1972–3 prices)

	1973–4	1974–5	1975–6	1976–7	1977–8	Total
1. Revenue surplus	880	1254	1756	2394	3158	9442
2. Surplus of the nationalised sectors	280	797	877	964	1061	3979
3. Net domestic capital receipts	1113	1220	1341	1478	1633	6785
4. Total	2273	3271	3974	4836	5852	20206

Source: Tables 4.13 and 4.17.

Total domestic resources available for the public sector programme during the First Plan are thus estimated to be takas 20,206 million. To this one can add the total amount of foreign capital inflow to obtain an estimate of the total resources available for development expenditure in the public sector. In the past a part of the foreign capital, in the form of foreign private investment, was available for the private sector but the present policy of the government is that all foreign private investment in Bangladesh must be undertaken in collaboration with the government. Thus the estimated total resources for the public sector are takas 33,013 million, which represents 82 per cent of the total gross investment during the First Plan. The share of public sector expenditure in the total development expenditure of Bangladesh during the Third Plan of the erstwhile Government of Pakistan was 68 per cent. A more dominant role of the public sector in future is consistent with the declared objective of the government to bring about economic development of the country within the framework of a socialist economy.

VI. FOREIGN EXCHANGE RESOURCES DURING THE FIRST FIVE YEAR PLAN

An analysis of exports of Bangladesh over 1959/60–1969/70 reveals that while there is some prospect for export expansion along certain lines, the task will not be an easy one. Bangladesh has a very narrow export base and its major exports are facing hard competition from substitutes as well as alternative sources of supply. Furthermore, in the cases of certain exportables for which the only market in the past was Pakistan, a vigorous export drive will be necessary to find markets elsewhere.

As will be explained later in greater detail, there is need to increase the efficiency in many export industries if we are to maintain comparative advantage in terms of both quality and price. For example, efficiency in the jute manufacturing industry must be increased if Bangladesh wants to maintain or increase its share of exports in the international market. Bangladesh tea is not of a very high quality and given the natural conditions, there is not much scope to improve the quality. What is more disconcerting is that the price that Bangladesh tea is fetching in the international market is far below the cost of production. If this continues and no effort is made to reduce cost by increasing efficiency at various levels in tea production, a large amount of export subsidy will be necessary for the industry to break even. It is well known that once a subsidy of this kind is given, it continues. This will imply an increasing domestic resource cost per unit of export. In fact, a point may come when it will be desirable to give up tea production altogether. This point will, of course, depend on the extent of over-valuation of the domestic currency. The basis for projection of major exportables is given below.

Raw Jute and Jute Goods

In making projections about export of raw jute and jute goods the following points must be considered carefully.

(*a*) Export of raw jute and jute goods are interrelated. The available export of raw jute will normally depend on the total production and the domestic absorption. Given the excess capacity in the jute manufacturing industry there is scope for a large domestic absorption of raw jute so that there may not be as much exportable surplus as is stipulated in the plan. This is very important, since according to one World Bank study the price elasticity for jute goods is around 2 which indicates that our jute goods can find a market if the pricing (exchange rate) policy is rationalised. Since expansion of the output of manufactured goods can take place without expansion of capacity, there is a strong case for diverting more raw jute into domestic absorption rather than export expansion.

(*b*) One should therefore be careful in determining the desirable exchange rate for raw jute exports, although the need for maintaining a reasonable domestic price cannot be denied if an adequate supply is to be ensured. In the case of jute manufacturing, however, a revision of the present exchange rate policy is perhaps warranted; but this must be preceded by a careful analysis of the cost structure of various lines of production in the industry. Without a clear picture of the extent to which productive efficiency can be improved and cost per unit of output reduced or stabilised, nothing can be said about the degree of subsidy required by the industry in terms of a favourable exchange rate. In the present state of the jute manufacturing industry one way to reduce cost would be to improve capacity utilisation, if possible even above the level attained in the last normal year (1969–1970). This has obvious implications for the consumption of raw jute domestically and for its export, as was mentioned earlier. Furthermore, the plan should emphasise the production of jute manufactures in lines other than the present sacking, hessian and the small quantity of carpet backing. Thus, even without substantial additional investment, production and export of jute manufactures can go up to 800 thousand tons in 1977–8, implying an absorption of about 1 million tons of raw jute. So, if the production target of raw jute is about 1·7 million tons in 1977–8, as indicated by the plan, the exportable surplus of it remains at 700 thousand tons. It may be emphasised here that the production plan required to sustain the export plan for jute as discussed above can be realised only if the net productivity (profitability) of jute cultivation is maintained at a competitive level with alternative uses of land. This calls for an increase in yield as well as a rational price support policy.

(*c*) Jute is the only important resource that Bangladesh has at this moment. Therefore, it must be pushed to its logical frontier in terms of export expansion, preferably in the form of jute manufactures. It never pays to be a raw material supplying region while opportunity exists for its domestic exploitation. It is absolutely necessary to take a very cautious approach in regard to jute *vis-à-vis* India and other raw jute and jute textile producers. The optimum policy for Bangladesh, assuming it can maintain a high level of productive efficiency, would be to expand domestic production and export of jute goods as much as is feasible. If necessary, the entire amount of raw jute may be used up in the process of domestic production of jute goods. The other policy must be to seek export markets through aggressive salesmanship and appropriate pricing policy. So, the future of Bangladesh jute exports lies in healthy competition with all other

TABLE 4.19

PROJECTION OF EXPORTS OF BANGLADESH 1973–4 TO 1977–8
(value figures at 1972–3 prices)

	1969–70 (actual)		July 1972 – May 1973 (actual)		1973–4	
	Quantities	Values (takas millions at current prices)	Quantities	Values (takas millions)	Quantities	Values (takas millions)
1. Raw jute and jute cuttings (000 tons)	626·2	762·4	443·7	884·1	639	1,248
2. Jute manufactures (000 tons)	521·0	927·5	381·3	1,270·3	521	1,735
3. Tea (million lbs.)	60·0	274·4	50·0	75·1	60	90
4. Newsprint (tons)		0·2	13,089	17·4	27,300	37
5. Fish (tons)		88·1	1,434	25·3	31,835	161
6. Leather (tons)		28·8	8,633	124·0	10,000	143
7. Spices (000 tons)	2,980·0	30·0	0·36	3·4	2,980	28
8. Cotton twist yarn		20·5	negligible	N.A.		30
9. Paper (000 tons)	27·0	40·0			27	21
10. Matches (000 gross boxes)	6,500·0				5,000	34
11. Furnace oil, jute batching oil and naphtha (tons)						17
12. Other visible exports		305·4		N.A.		305
13. Invisibles		441·4		13·3		441
14. Total		3,034·9		N.A.		4,290

TABLE 4.19
(Continued)

PROJECTION OF EXPORTS OF BANGLADESH 1973–4 TO 1977–8
(value figures at 1972–3 prices)

	1974–5		1975–6		1976–7		1977–8	
	Quantities	Values (takas millions)	Quantities	Values (takas millions)	Quantities	Values (takas millions)	Quantities	Values (takas millions)
1. Raw jute and jute cuttings (000 tons)	626	1,223	614	1,199	601	1,174	589	1,150
2. Jute manufactures (000 tons)	573	1,909	630	2,099	694	2,312	763	2,542
3. Tea (million lbs.)	62	93	64	96	66	99	68	102
4. Newsprint (tons)	30,030	41	33,033	45	36,336	49	39,970	54
5. Fish (tons)	39,797	201	49,747	252	62,183	315	77,725	393
6. Leather (tons)	10,800	154	11,664	167	12,597	180	13,604	195
7. Spices (000 tons)	3,427	33	3,941	38	4,532	43	5,212	50
8. Cotton twist yarn		32		35		38		41
9. Paper (000 tons)	30	23	33	25	36	27	40	30
10. Matches (000 gross boxes)	5,250	36	5,513	38	5,788	40	6,078	42
11. Furnace oil, jute batching oil and naphtha (tons)		18		20		22		24
12. Other visible exports		351		404		495		534
13. Invisibles		477		515		556		601
14. Total		4,591		4,933		5,350		5,758

producers and not in entering into cartel arrangements with any one of them in order to protect our own inefficiency or the inefficiency of the other party.

With the above observations one may now turn to the problem of the projection of exports of raw jute and jute manufactures. Production of raw jute during 1973–4 is projected at 1250 thousand tons which was the level attained in 1969–70. Present indications are that the jute manufacturing industry will be producing about 85 per cent of the 1969–70 output in 1972–3 and with adequate measures taken, 1973–4 will probably restore the output level of 1969–70. Consumption of raw jute in 1969–70 was 611 thousand tons. Assuming the same batching efficiency, there will be no change in raw jute consumption by industries and the exportable surplus of raw jute in 1973–4 can be placed at 639 thousand tons which is slightly above the level of export in 1969–70. With India emerging as an important buyer there should be no problem in exporting this amount by the end of 1973–4. At the prevailing export price of 1972–3, the value of raw jute exported in 1973–4 will be takas 1248 million. This and other export projections are shown in Table 4.19.

For the remaining years of the First Plan period, it is assumed that the quantity of raw jute export will decline by 11 per cent and this is assumed to be spread equally over every year. The reduction in the volume of exports is consistent with the increased domestic demand as well as reduction of foreign demand due to emerging importance of substitutes.

During July 1972–May 1973, the quantity and value of exports of jute manufactures were 443·7 thousand tons and takas 884·1 million respectively. During the fiscal year 1973–4, the volume of exports of jute manufactures is projected to reach the level of 1969–70. Export of jute goods is projected to grow at a rate of 10 per cent per annum, a major part of which will be contributed by hessian and carpet backing. Thus at 1972–3 prices the export earnings of Bangladesh from jute manufacturing is projected to go up from takas 1735 million in 1973–4 to takas 2542 million in 1977–8.

Tea

Tea exports, as was shown above, depend very much on the pricing policy, which can be formulated only after questions of policy regarding subsidy and exchange rates have been answered. In fact debate has been going on in the country as to whether the tea industry can survive without some adequate relief in the form of subsidy cum favourable exchange rate, since the present production cost per lb. (takas 3·00) is far above the average auction price in Chittagong (expected to be takas 2·00, which in turn is somewhat higher than that prevailing in 1972–3). Here again, a careful analysis of cost structure together with an examination of the possibilities of productivity increase must be undertaken, if one is to formulate a rational policy for the future development of the tea industry.

During July 1972–May 1973, 50 million lbs. of tea were exported at a value of takas 75·1 million. It is assumed that during the First Plan a better price for tea will be obtained by improving the quality. The assumed price is takas 2·25 per lb., which is lower than both Indian and Ceylonese export auction price prevailing in 1970; the difference is to make allowance for inferior quality. It is assumed that during 1973–4, the level of export of tea will reach the 1969–70 level (i.e. 60 million lbs.) and it is assumed to grow at a rate of 3 per cent per annum which is the approximate rate of growth of production during 1966–70. Thus at the 1972–3 prices, the value of tea exports will rise from takas 90 million in 1973–4 to takas 102 million in 1977–8.

Newsprint

Export during July 1972–May 1973 was 13,089 tons at a value of takas 17·4 million. Total exports during the fiscal year 1972–3 are assumed to be takas 20 million, which is 67 per cent of the amount agreed upon under a barter deal with India. Another 10 per cent export is taken to consist of low grammage writing paper, thus implying a shortfall of 23 per cent in the stipulated export to India. The export price is assumed to be takas 1329 per ton which prevailed during July 1972–May 1973.

It is assumed that newsprint production will be restored to the 1969–70 level (39 thousand tons) in 1973–4. And given the export possibility to India it will be allowed to expand at a rate of 10 per cent per annum. Export is placed at 70 per cent of production each year in keeping with the past experience.

Fish

Export of fish to countries other than India during July 1972–May 1973 was 1434 tons at a value of takas 25·3 million. With some special effort the final level of exports during 1972–3 could go up as high as takas 39 million. To this, the amount of exports to India, worth takas 90 million, which was agreed under a barter deal was added to obtain an estimate of total exports of fish during 1972–3. The underlying price assumption for the export of fish to India was takas 3978 per ton.

The value of exports to countries other than India is assumed to grow at an annual average rate of 25 per cent which is slightly less than that experienced during the Third Plan period of the erstwhile

Government of Pakistan. It is assumed that the export price of 1972–1973 will be maintained throughout. The quantity of exports to India is assumed to grow at an annual rate of 25 per cent which is about 50 per cent of the average annual rate of growth during the peak years of fish trade with India (1957–8 to 1962–3). The export price for India is assumed to be the same as that of 1972–3.

Leather

The export of tanned leather during July 1972–May 1973 was 8683 tons at a value of takas 124 million. On this basis, the export during the full year July 1972–June 1973 should be takas 135 million. But such a figure cannot form a valid basis for a future projection, since a significant portion of the exports during 1972 came out of stocks. This can be easily seen from the following statistics. Whereas export of leather in the whole of the normal year was to the tune of takas 88·1 million, the export during the difficult first nine months of 1972 was more than that, nearly takas 94·3 million. Some of the difference in the level of receipts can, however, be explained by the difference in prices of the two periods.

It is therefore projected that the export in 1973–4 will be at the level of the normal year 1969–70, that is 10 thousand tons; if this is valued at the price of 1972–3, the total earnings from exports of leather come to about takas 143 million.

On the basis of an analysis of the growth of exports of tanned leather during the sixties it seems reasonable to assume that over the First Five Year Plan period leather exports will grow at an annual rate of 8 per cent. This appears to be consistent with the probable expansion of the tanning industry, with the likely improvement in the collection of hides and skins as well as the local demand for these materials.

Spices

Exports during 1969–70 were 2980 thousand tons at a value of takas 28·79 million and the corresponding figure for July 1972–May 1973 was 360 tons at a value of takas 3·4 million.

It is assumed that exports will recover during 1973–4; the projected level of export for this period is put at 2980 tons, which was the level of 1969–70. At the price of 1972–3 the value of this export is takas 28·1 million. For the remaining years of the First Plan, export is projected to grow at an annual rate of 15 per cent which is slightly less than the rate achieved (25 per cent) during the Third Five Year Plan of Pakistan.

Cotton Twist Yarn and Fabrics

Exports during 1969–70 were about takas 30 million and the corresponding figure for July–September 1972 was 0·8 million. The export level for the period July 1972 to June 1973 is projected to be takas 10 million. However, it is expected that during the first year of the First Five Year Plan (i.e. in 1973–4) the export level will reach the takas 30 million mark. For the remaining years of the First Five Year Plan it is assumed to grow at an annual compound rate of 8 per cent at 1972–3 prices. This figure is the average of the projected rates of growth of cotton cloth and cotton yarn for pre-March 1971 Pakistan, as given in the Fourth Five Year Plan document.

Paper

Export of paper has been negligible during July 1972–May 1973 and on this basis the exports during 1972–3 are also likely to be very negligible. It is, however, assumed that the 1969–70 level will be regained in 1973–4. The realised export price for the first year of the plan is assumed to remain at the level of 1969–70 and this is assumed to be maintained over the First Plan. The quantity exported is, however, assumed to grow at the rate of 10 per cent per annum.

Matches

In 1969–70, 6·5 million gross boxes were exported to Pakistan at a value of takas 40 million. It is expected that a part of this amount will be marketed elsewhere during the First Five Year Plan. Export is projected to be 5 million gross boxes in 1973–4 at a value of takas 34 million, the underlying price assumption being that the taka price of exports will remain the same as the price of export to Pakistan in 1969–70. Quantity of exports is assumed to grow at a moderate rate of 5 per cent per annum during the First Five Year Plan.

Petroleum Products

Exports of furnace oil, jute batching oil and naphtha in the past were not significant. Under the barter deal with India, Bangladesh is, however, assumed to export these items to the value of takas 15·0 million during July 1972–June 1973. Given the capacity of Eastern Refinery in Chittagong and the domestic demand, it can be safely assumed that export can rise at a rate of 10 per cent per annum, maintaining the price of 1972–3.

Other Visible Exports and Invisibles

Both these items have been projected on the basis of the past trend.

Total exports of Bangladesh are thus projected to go up from takas 4290 million to takas 5758 million, i.e. a 34 per cent increase over the First Five Year Plan. It can be seen from Table 4.20 that as a

TABLE 4.20

TOTAL EXPORT AND IMPORT POSSIBILITIES FOR
BANGLADESH 1973–4 to 1977–8
(takas millions at 1972–3 prices)

Year	Exports	Capital inflow	Imports	Exports as a per cent of G.D.P.
1973–4	4290	3614	7904	7·6
1974–5	4591	2610	7201	7·6
1975–6	4933	2462	7395	7·7
1976–7	5350	2223	7573	7·8
1977–8	5758	1898	7656	7·9
Total	24922	12807	37729	

Source: Tables 4.15, 4.16 and 4.19.

percentage of Gross Domestic Product, however, export earnings
remain stable at around 8 per cent. During 1969–70, the corresponding figure was 10 per cent. One can take the figures for the implicit
capital inflow from Table 4.16 and add them to the export earnings
in order to obtain a estimate of the amount of imports that can be
financed during the First Plan. It is interesting to note that the share
of domestic financing of imports goes up from 54 per cent in 1973–4
to 75 per cent in 1977–8. These figures can be compared with 75
per cent which was the average proportion of the domestic financing
of imports during the Third Plan of the former Government of
Pakistan.

VII. THE INFLOW OF FOREIGN CAPITAL

A few notes may be added here on the magnitude and nature of
foreign capital inflow that is desirable from the point of view of the
long-term development of Bangladesh. The first annual plan of
Bangladesh for the year 1972–3 proposed a total expenditure of
takas 5172 million for reconstruction, rehabilitation and development. Of this total requirement of takas 5172 million, as much as
takas 3750 million was expected to be financed from abroad. In
other words 73 per cent of the capital expenditure was expected to
be met out of foreign loans and grants. This undoubtedly was a very
high proportion by any criteria, although it is quite understandable in
view of the urgent need to meet the immediate relief, rehabilitation
and reconstruction expenditure with a very narrow domestic resources basis. In future, when the present needs of reconstruction
expenditure are no longer there, Bangladesh must be able to
manage with less dependence on foreign capital inflow. It is, however,
very difficult to put an *a priori* limit on the desirable volume of

foreign capital inflow in any particular area. This will have to be determined by political as well as economic criteria. Stated in simple terms, the economic criterion should be that the benefit stream-flow from the given amount of foreign capital must be greater than the cost in terms of interest payment and amortisation. The following general principles may be suggested as possible guide-lines for defining the terms of foreign assistance from the point of view of Bangladesh:

(1) Bangladesh should try to arrange as much assistance as possible on a grant basis. But in view of the recent trend of the nature of foreign capital inflow, one should not depend on it too heavily beyond the period of reconstruction.
(2) Bangladesh should try to persuade the capital exporting country to accept payment in takas so far as practicable.
(3) Bangladesh should insist on expanding trade relationships with large capital-exporting countries so that it may be possible for Bangladesh to make a part of the payment in terms of non-traditional exports.
(4) Bangladesh should seek to enter into agreements for loans which would have a loan grace period of, say, seven years or more.
(5) In negotiating loans, Bangladesh must ensure the protection of its right to choose the sources of supply of materials and services against the credit.
(6) Bangladesh should arrange for loans for periods not less than twenty years.
(7) Bangladesh should not accept interest rates higher than the central bank discount rate prevailing at the time of negotiation.

In regard to foreign private capital inflow the following policy measures are suggested:

All foreign investment should be in collaboration with the government and ownership will vest in the government. This is consistent with the aspirations of Bangladesh as a socialistic economy. Bangladesh must apply a set of economic criteria to determine the desirability of foreign private investment. The criteria should have the following components.

(a) All projects involving foreign private capital must be evaluated in terms of their net contribution towards the social objective as given in the short-term and the long-term plan.
(b) Special emphasis should be placed on the net balance of payment effect of foreign private investment. The net balance of payment effect of a project is positive if the initial capital inflow

plus accumulated rate of interest over the life of the project and the net foreign exchange earning (or saving) exceeds the discounted present value of repatriated profit, capital and appreciated value of capital. The acceptability of a project will be determined by the size of the net balance of payment effect.

(*c*) In terms of macro-economic inter-sectoral allocation of resources, each project involving foreign private capital must compare favourably with domestic projects in terms of its use of domestic resources per unit of export earning or saving of foreign exchange.

The above principles must, however, be elaborated within the political perspective of the country. Political leadership should provide some guide-line reflecting its thinking on foreign capital inflow.

VIII. CONCLUSION

Bangladesh is about to launch its First Five Year Plan, reflecting the hopes and aspirations of a newly emerging nation which is desperately trying to break through the vicious circle of war destruction, social conflict and a dismally low level of standard of living. In any resource-poor region like Bangladesh it is unlikely that large resources will be available to be mobilised for development. Given all its limitations, Bangladesh must not spare any effort to increase the level of domestic resource availability to the highest level that is practicable.

An attempt has been made above to estimate the domestic resources over the First Five Year Plan of Bangladesh. This has been done in the light of the experience of the past, although some account has been taken of possible institutional changes within the economy during the next few years. The conclusion reached is that out of her own resources alone, Bangladesh could sustain a development plan of takas 27,246 million at 1972–3 prices (Table 4.16). At the same time the projection of foreign exchange resources indicates that Bangladesh can be expected to sustain a level of import at takas 24,922 million over the First Five Year Plan on its own account. It is hoped that to these resources something like takas 12,800 will be added in the form of an inflow of foreign capital. There will be many revisions of these estimates as new data become available. It is hoped that this first exercise will prove to be a good starting point for further work.

APPENDIX 1

TABLE 1

NON-CORPORATE PRIVATE SECTOR SAVINGS IN THE FORM OF CURRENCY HOLDINGS AND BANK DEPOSITS IN BANGLADESH 1959–60 TO 1969–70
(takas millions at current prices)

	1958-9	1959-60	1960-1	1961-2	1962-3	1963-4	1964-5	1965-6	1966-7	1967-8	1968-9	1969-70
1. Currency in circulation	1,155·8	1,202·7	1,251·1	1,253·1	1,193·5	1,437·7	1,665·8	1,711·1	1,735·0	1,877·1	2,083·2	2,281·5
2. Change in currency in circulation	–	46·9	48·4	2·0	–59·6	244·2	228·1	45·3	23·9	142·1	206·1	135·3
3. Changes in currency holding of non-corporate private sector	–	42·2	43·6	1·8	–53·6	219·8	205·3	40·8	21·5	127·8	185·5	121·8
4. Demand deposits	392·6	420·0	475·0	540·0	670·0	815·0	975·0	1,064·9	1,366·2	1,323·3	1,340·0	1,457·6
5. Time deposits	151·0	185·0	195·0	225·0	355·0	505·0	635·0	988·3	1,204·4	1,307·6	1,329·1	1,597·6
6. Total deposits (Row 4 + Row 5)	543·6	605·0	670·0	765·0	1,205·0	1,320·0	1,610·0	2,053·2	2,570·6	2,630·9	2,669·1	3,055·2
7. Deposits held by non-corporate private sector	326·2	363·0	402·0	459·0	615·0	792·0	966·0	1,273·0	1,670·9	1,657·5	1,815·0	2,108·1
8. Changes in deposits held by non-corporate private sector	–	36·8	39·0	57·0	156·0	177·0	174·0	307·0	397·9	13·4	157·5	293·1
9. Total saving in bank deposits and currency (Row 3 + Row 8)	–	79·0	82·6	58·8	102·4	396·8	379·3	347·8	419·4	141·2	343·0	414·9

Sources:

1. *Statistical Digest of East Pakistan*, 1968, East Pakistan Bureau of Statistics, Dacca, 1968.
2. *Statistical Digest of Bangladesh*, 1970–1, Bangladesh Bureau of Statistics, Dacca, 1971.
3. *Monthly Statistical Bulletin of Bangladesh*, March 1972, Bangladesh Bureau of Statistics, Dacca, 1972.
4. *State Bank Bulletin*, State Bank of Pakistan, various issues (published monthly).
5. *Banking Statistics of Pakistan*, State Bank of Pakistan, various issues (published annually).

Note: Currency in circulation does not include one taka notes issued by the Ministry of Finance.

TABLE 2

INDIVIDUAL SAVING THROUGH POSTAL SAVING SCHEME IN BANGLADESH 1959–60 TO 1969–70
(takas thousands at current prices)

	1959–60	1960–1	1961–2	1962–3	1963–4	1964–5	1965–6	1966–7	1967–8	1968–9	1969–70
Savings bank											
(1) deposits	110,280	128,602	133,691	136,439	143,523	150,040	137,009	138,238	121,241	128,513	131,885
(2) withdrawals	111,716	121,287	132,523	130,556	139,112	132,571	140,316	142,325	127,695	132,427	135,861
Cash certificates											
(3) discharged	134	111	33	41	13	19	28	25	8	6	1
(4) discharged	7	6	2	2	2	2	1	1	1	–	–
(5) issued	–	–	–	–	–	–	–	25,879	37,097	56,380	61,991
(6) discharged	–	–	–	–	–	–	–	123	5,052	5,407	7,708
National savings certificates											
(7) discharged	997	745	509	247	50	84	15	33	7	8	17
Pakistan defence savings certificates											
(8) discharged	279	78	48	9	4	15	3	12	1	3	4
Pakistan savings certificates											
(9) discharged	4,789	2,944	2,240	2,480	3,641	3,584	4,604	3,780	2,316	706	596
National development savings certificates											
(10) issued	23,292	25,032	23,991	20,750	25,785	27,658	27,536	8,083	15,651	24,010	19,958
(11) discharged	1,229	2,838	4,445	5,219	7,064	7,281	8,534	18,975	8,834	10,058	10,610
(12)	3,691	7,112	7,580	5,624	4,354	9,237	5,796	8,464	16,441	–	–
Savings (1−2−3−4+5−6−7−8 −9+10−11+12)	18,212	32,727	25,462	24,359	23,776	43,380	16,839	15,390	–	33,384	40,341

Sources:

1. *Monthly Statistical Bulletin*, Central Statistical Office, Government of Pakistan, various issues.
2. *Combined Finance and Revenue Accounts of the Central and Provincial Governments of Pakistan*, Karachi, various issues.
3. *Budgets of the Central Government in Pakistan*, different years.
4. *Detailed Estimates of Revenue and Receipts*, Finance Department, Government of East Pakistan, different years.
5. *Details of Demand for Grants and Charged Expenditure (Non-Development)*, Finance Department, Government of East Pakistan, different years.

TABLE 3

NON-CORPORATE PRIVATE SECTOR SAVING IN PROVIDENT FUNDS IN BANGLADESH 1959-60 TO 1960-1
(takas thousands at current prices)

	1959-60	1960-1	1961-2	1962-3	1963-4	1964-5	1965-6	1966-7	1967-8	1968-9	1969-70
I. Pakistan (Central) Government employees											
(1) Total contribution	17,545	17,868	19,668	14,196	22,196	27,753[a]	33,309	52,750	20,986	15,073[b]	7,615[b]
(2) Interest	2,838	2,833	3,338	3,214	3,858	4,389	7,064	8,317	8,413	9,602	10,078
(3) Disbursement	10,728	9,595	9,493	9,797	9,913	13,880	17,848	24,532	27,901	–	–
II. Bangladesh Government employees											
(4) Total contributions	11,370	12,558	13,683	14,425	17,862	21,700	22,610	24,131	25,106	26,064	25,988
(5) Interest	2,214	2,211	2,489	2,706	3,146	4,406	5,192	6,583	6,275	6,623	8,665
(6) Disbursement	7,637	5,748	5,941	6,566	8,227	12,700	11,826	17,058	17,040	16,064	18,327
III. Employees of educational institutions											
(7) Total contributions	3,639	3,815	4,730	5,693	6,705	7,650	9,047	10,958	12,586	14,317	14,916
(8) Net contributions	1,892	2,747	3,548	4,156	4,828	4,743	6,423	6,246	7,174	9,163	9,397
IV. Employees of other institutions											
(a) Tea plantation employees											
(9) Total contributions	–	68	1,616	1,688	1,741	1,774	1,889	1,975	2,085	2,154	2,847
(10) Interest	–	–	17	66	147	218	317	402	544	757	955
(11) Disbursement	–	–	7	34	92	168	213	326	393	497	559
(b) Other institutions											
(12) Net contribution	6,298	8,259	10,410	8,659	12,797	13,765	16,890	21,056	9,090	19,035	16,603
V. Total saving (1+2+4+5+8+9+10+12 −3−6−11)	23,792	31,201	39,328	32,713	48,343	52,002	63,807	79,544	34,339	71,910	63,262

Sources:
1. *Combined Finance and Revenue Accounts of the Central and Provincial Governments of Pakistan*, Karachi, various issues.
2. Budgets of the Central Government of Pakistan, different years.
3. *Details of Demand for Grants and Charged Expenditure (Non-Development)*, Finance Department, Government of East Pakistan, different years.
4. Controller, Bangladesh Plantation Employees Provident Fund, Dacca.

[a] Estimated – average of 1963-4 and 1965-6.   [b] Net provident fund contribution, i.e. total contributions less disbursements.

TABLE 4

NON-CORPORATE PRIVATE SECTOR SAVING IN THE FORM OF LIFE INSURANCE IN BANGLADESH 1959-60 TO 1969-70

(takas thousands at current prices)

	1959	1960	1961	1962	1963	1964	1965	1966	1967	1968	1969	1970
		1959-60	*1960-1*	*1961-2*	*1962-3*	*1963-4*	*1964-5*	*1965-6*	*1966-7*	*1967-8*	*1968-9*	*1969-70*
Life fund at the end of the year (1) Pakistan (Insurance companies)	159,937	187,124	256,249	319,366	371,531	450,943	538,616	644,386	771,816	899,021	1,061,851	1,252,984
Life fund at the beginning of the year (2) Pakistan (Insurance companies)	133,814	158,782	220,482	275,468	315,220	376,117	445,276	533,310	647,585	737,319	887,435	1,064,922
Net change in life fund during the year (3) Pakistan (Insurance companies)	26,123	28,342	35,767	43,898	56,311	74,826	93,340	111,076	124,231	161,702	174,416	188,062
(4) Bangladesh (34% of (3))	8,882	9,636	12,161	14,925	19,146	25,441	31,736	37,766	42,239	54,979	59,301	63,941
Net change in life fund (5) Pakistan (Postal life insurance)		6,386	7,106	8,523	9,581	8,655	9,969	10,253	11,689	13,041	13,268	13,633
Net change in life fund (6) Bangladesh (Insurance companies)		9,259	10,899	13,543	17,036	22,294	28,589	34,751	40,003	48,609	57,140	61,621
Net change in life fund (7) Bangladesh (Postal life insurance)		2,554	2,842	3,409	3,832	3,462	3,988	4,101	4,676	5,216	5,307	5,413
Saving (6+7)		11,813	13,741	16,952	20,868	25,756	32,577	38,852	44,679	53,825	62,447	67,034

Sources:
1. *Pakistan Insurance Yearbook* (1959 to 1970) (Karachi: Manager of Publications).
2. Postal Life Insurance Department, Dacca.
3. Bangladesh Insurance Corporation.

Notes:
A Pakistan refers to pre-March 1971 Pakistan.
B Moving average method has been used to convert the date from calendar year basis to financial year basis.
C Insurance companies include foreign and local life insurance companies.
D Life fund figures at the beginning and end of 1970 were estimated by applying the rate of increase between 1968 and 1969.

TABLE 5

NON-CORPORATE PRIVATE SECTOR INVESTMENT IN SHARES (PAID UP) OF JOINT STOCK COMPANIES IN BANGLADESH 1959–60 TO 1969–70

(takas thousands at current prices)

	1959–60	1960–1	1961–2	1962–3	1963–4	1964–5	1965–6	1966–7	1967–8	1968–9	1969–70
1. Paid-up capital of newly registered companies in Bangladesh	3,758	1,012	6,530	5,337	16,328	9,614	3,629	9,521	2,085	3,604[a]	4,710[b]
2. Capital invited in Karachi stock exchange	45,000	75,000	110,000	71,000	77,000	121,000	48,700	142,250[c]	171,250[c]	253,701[c]	253,701[d]
3. 10 per cent of (2)	4,500	7,500	11,000	7,100	7,700	12,100	4,870	14,225	17,125	25,370	25,370
4. Investment in shares of joint stock companies[e] (1+3)	8,258	8,512	17,530	12,437	24,028	21,714	8,499	23,746	19,210	28,974	30,080

Sources:

1. *Monthly Bulletin of Statistics*, January 1969, East Pakistan Bureau of Statistics.
2. A. Ghafur, 'Financial Asset Accumulation by Non-Corporate Private Sector in Pakistan: 1959–60 to 1965–66', *The Pakistan Development Review* (Spring 1969).
3. *Current Economic Position and Prospect of Pakistan*, Vol. II, International Bank for Reconstruction and Development.
4. *Banking Statistics of Pakistan 1968–69*, State Bank of Pakistan.

[a] Data were available for the first six months only on authorised capital and for first two months on paid-up capital. The ratio of paid-up capital to authorised capital was applied to the six-month data on the latter and the resultant figure was doubled to obtain estimate of paid-up capital for the whole year.

[b] Average of 1965/6 – 1968/9.

[c] Includes non-financial companies and banks with their head office in Karachi.

[d] No figure being available, 1968–9 figure was used.

[e] Data on the increase in paid-up capital of old companies as well as intercompany subscription were not available. It was assumed that they cancelled each other out.

TABLE 6

NON-CORPORATE PRIVATE SECTOR SAVING THROUGH CO-OPERATIVE SOCIETIES IN BANGLADESH
1959–60 TO 1969–70
(takas thousands at current prices)

	1958–9	1959–60	1960–1	1961–2	1962–3	1963–4	1964–5	1965–6	1966–7	1967–8	1968–9	1969–70
1. Share capital	28,583	27,690	31,500	41,020	36,947	42,186	45,512	54,744	56,824	70,176	73,863	88,603
2. Loans and deposits held	74,629	126,350	173,800	182,150	236,227	256,923	257,392	290,431	334,994	475,460	585,335	905,468
3. Total (1+2)	103,212	154,040	205,300	223,170	273,174	299,109	302,904	345,175	391,818	546,196	659,198	994,071
4. Change in (3)	—	50,828	51,260	17,870	50,004	25,935	3,795	42,271	46,643	154,378	113,002	334,873
5. Loans advanced to individuals	23,753	37,140	53,330	45,590	49,106	48,959	39,712	34,451	46,106	89,508	105,737	141,045
6. Loans advanced to societies	29,336	56,350	123,390	74,010	76,829	62,296	41,565	62,415	72,715	159,795	177,956	243,340
7. Loans repaid by individuals	13,137	20,490	43,510	40,010	30,057	29,858	30,317	36,586	12,064	51,703	74,927	87,807
8. Loans repaid by societies	28,893	22,450	105,780	69,240	52,100	53,350	43,680	46,001	56,154	79,555	118,635	171,074
9. Saving (4+7+8−5−6)	—	278	23,830	7,520	6,226	−2,112	−3,485	−27,992	−3,960	36,333	22,871	209,369

Sources:
1. *Pakistan Statistical Yearbook 1968*, Central Statistical Office, Government of Pakistan.
2. *Annual Departmental Reports* (1967/68 to 1969/70), Registrar of Co-operative Societies, Government of East Pakistan.

TABLE 7

DIS-SAVING OF THE NON-CORPORATE PRIVATE SECTOR IN BANGLADESH 1959-60 TO 1969-70

(takas thousands at current prices)

	1959–60	1960–1	1961–2	1962–3	1963–4	1964–5	1965–6	1966–7	1967–8	1968–9	1969–70
1. Loans from the government during the year	19,220	23,785	26,300	32,350	43,770	2,925	5,669	2,840	18,375	47,094	10,234
2. Loans from the government repaid during the year	5,464	5,998	6,375	3,858	9,340	8,740	15,750	11,946	7,415	18,739	30,761
3. Net loans (1 – 2)	13,756	17,787	19,925	28,492	34,430	–5,815	–10,081	–9,106	6,230	28,355	–20,527
4. Interest paid to government	349[a]	440[a]	554[a]	699	883	1,212	1,189	2,528	3,193	6,257	1,760
5. Net loans of A.D.B.B. during the year	78,001[b]	15,400[b]	16,649	14,989	14,057	7,394	6,886	12,504	26,339	28,143	48,632
6. Net loans of H.B.F.C. during the year	2,310[c]	3,129[c]	4,771[c]	8,052[c]	21,517[c]	41,059	28,577	22,880	13,390	8,728	9,180
7. Net loans of B.R.R.F.C. during the year	19	–46	–49	–40	–20	35	279	365	387	422	398
8. Total of (row 5+6+7)	10,129	18,483	21,371	23,001	35,554	48,488	35,742	35,749	40,116	37,293	58,210
9. Non-corporate sector liabilities to banks	26,083	57,452	82,232	63,612	152,064	333,990	96,282	249,048	102,222	180,468	148,446
10. Non-corporate sector liabilities to insurance companies	–223	3,344	2,239	4,643	2,572	3,810	10,648	1,129	5,311	131	19,832
11. Total dis-saving (Rows 3+4+8+9+10)	50,094	97,506	126,321	120,447	225,503	381,585	133,780	279,348	157,072	252,504	207,721

Sources
1. *Detailed Estimates of Revenue and Receipts*, Finance Department, Government of East Pakistan, various issues.
2. *Explanatory Memorandum on the Budget of the Government of East Pakistan*, various issues.
3. *Statistical Digest of East Pakistan 1968*, East Pakistan Bureau of Statistics, Government of East Pakistan.
4. *Statistical Digest of Bangladesh 1970–71*, Bangladesh Bureau of Statistics, Government of Bangladesh.

[a] Extrapolated backwards by using growth rate between 1962–3 and 1963–4.
[b] Estimated by applying recovery to loan ratio of 1961–2 to total loan disbursed in 1961–2.
[c] Estimated by applying recovery to loan ratio of 1964–5 to total loan disbursed in 1964–5.
[d] Calendar year figures were converted to fiscal year by using moving average method.

TABLE 8

NON-CORPORATE PRIVATE SECTOR SAVING IN THE FORM OF FINANCIAL ASSET ACQUISITION IN BANGLADESH 1959–60 TO 1969–70

(takas thousands at current prices)

	1959–60	1960–1	1961–2	1962–3	1963–4	1964–5	1965–6	1966–7	1967–8	1968–9	1969–70
1. Currency holding	42,200	43,600	1,800	−53,600	219,800	205,300	40,800	21,500	127,800	185,500	121,800
2. Bank deposits	36,800	39,000	57,000	156,000	177,000	174,000	307,000	397,900	13,400	157,500	293,100
3. Postal saving scheme	18,212	32,727	25,462	24,359	23,776	43,380	16,839	15,390	16,441	33,384	40,341
4. Provident fund	23,792	31,201	39,328	32,713	48,343	52,002	63,807	79,544	34,339	71,910	63,262
5. Life insurance	11,813	13,741	16,952	20,868	25,756	32,557	38,852	44,679	53,825	62,447	67,034
6. Corporate share holding	8,258	8,512	17,530	12,437	24,028	21,714	8,499	23,746	19,210	28,974	30,080
7. Co-operative societies	278	23,830	7,520	6,226	−2,112	−3,485	27,992	−3,960	36,333	22,871	209,369
8. National investment trust fund	—	—	—	766	1,792	2,163	1,262	1,427	1,086	1,604	1,701
9. Prize bonds	—	4,580	4,580	4,580	4,580	4,580	1,040	1,040	1,040	1,040	1,040
10. Gross financial asset acquisition (Rows 1+2+3+4+5+6+7)	141,353	197,191	170,172	204,349	522,963	532,231	506,091	581,266	303,474	565,230	827,727
11. Total financial liability or dis-saving	50,094	97,506	126,321	120,447	225,503	381,585	133,780	279,348	157,072	252,504	207,721
12. Non-corporate private sector saving (Row 10−Row 11)	91,259	99,685	43,851	83,902	297,460	150,646	372,311	301,918	146,402	312,726	620,006

TABLE 9

PERCENTAGE-WISE BREAKDOWN OF GROSS FINANCIAL ASSET ACQUISITION OF NON-CORPORATE PRIVATE SECTOR IN BANGLADESH 1959–60 TO 1969–70

	1959–60	1960–1	1961–2	1962–3	1963–4	1964–5	1965–6	1966–7	1967–8	1968–9	1969–70
1. Currency holding	29·85	22·11	1·06	−26·23	42·03	38·57	8·06	3·70	42·11	32·82	14·72
2. Bank deposits	26·03	19·78	33·50	76·34	33·85	32·69	60·66	68·45	4·42	27·87	35·41
3. Row 1+Row 2	55·88	41·89	34·56	50·11	75·88	71·26	68·72	72·15	46·53	60·69	50·13
4. Postal saving scheme	12·88	16·60	14·96	11·92	4·55	8·15	3·33	2·65	5·42	5·91	4·87
5. Provident fund	16·83	15·82	23·11	16·01	9·24	9·77	12·61	13·69	11·32	12·72	7·64
6. Life insurance	8·36	6·97	9·96	10·21	4·93	6·12	7·68	7·69	17·74	11·05	8·10
7. Corporate share holding	5·84	4·32	10·30	6·09	4·60	4·08	1·68	4·09	6·33	5·13	3·63
8. Co-operative societies	0·20	12·09	4·42	3·05	−0·40	−0·66	5·53	−0·68	11·97	4·05	25·29
9. National investment trust	–	–	–	0·38	0·34	0·41	0·25	0·24	0·36	0·28	0·21
10. Prize bonds	–	2·32	2·69	2·24	0·88	0·86	0·21	0·18	0·34	0·18	0·13
11. Gross financial asset acquisition[a]	100·00	100·00	100·00	100·00	100·00	100·00	100·00	100·00	100·00	100·00	100·00

[a] Percentage distribution may not add up to 100 because of rounding error.

TABLE 10

NON-CORPORATE PRIVATE SECTOR SAVING IN THE FORM OF NON-FINANCIAL ASSETS IN BANGLADESH
1959–60 TO 1969–70

(takas thousands at current prices)

	1959–60	1960–1	1961–2	1962–3	1963–4	1964–5	1965–6	1966–7	1967–8	1968–9	1969–70
1. Transport equipment	3,450	7,801	32,202	21,169	23,907	25,261	46,382	3,690	18,077	62,084	46,390
2. Machinery and equipment	235,261	238,328	261,185	319,155	349,454	548,206	539,407	639,178	736,320	742,856	823,201
3. Non-monetised farm investment	121,000	137,000	142,000	149,000	141,000	149,500	109,100	138,000	193,500	198,700	204,100
4. Housing construction (rural and urban)	115,556	130,000	137,778	143,333	145,556	150,889	199,778	189,889	214,333	186,000	165,000
5. Total investment	475,267	513,129	573,165	632,657	659,917	878,856	894,667	970,757	1,162,230	1,189,640	1,238,691

Sources:
1. *Statistical Digest of Bangladesh 1970–71*, Bangladesh Bureau of Statistics, Government of Bangladesh.
2. *Monthly Statistical Bulletin of Bangladesh, May, 1972*, Bangladesh Bureau of Statistics, Government of Bangladesh.
3. *Current Economic Position and Prospect of Pakistan*, vol. II, Statistical Appendix, International Bank for Reconstruction and Development.
4. *Final Evaluation of the Third Five Year Plan*, Planning Commission, Government of Pakistan.
5. *Monthly Foreign Trade Statistics*, Central Statistical Office, Government of Pakistan, various issues.

TABLE 11

GROSS PROFIT AND SAVINGS OF NON-FINANCIAL COMPANIES IN BANGLADESH 1959–60 TO 1969–70
(takas thousands at current prices)

	1959–60	1960–1	1961–2	1962–3	1963–4	1964–5	1965–6	1966–7	1967–8	1968–9	1969–70
A. 1. Number of companies with separate account for Bangladesh covered	9	27	29	40	56	68	76	76	94	98	54
2. Paid-up capital[c]	20,951	267,851	305,500	534,500	646,141	767,920	994,570	1,091,220	1,766,550	1,983,089	1,016,000
3. Gross profit	4,781	56,116	100,848	132,140	133,282	140,640	182,450	117,699	155,558	150,895	53,943
4. Disposal of gross profit											
(i) tax provision	626	7,797	25,189	38,644	23,642	24,205	34,477	22,405	19,517	17,620	10,236
(ii) depreciation	1,491	22,583	26,622	36,872	42,954	43,668	59,694	68,884	113,429	120,602	77,157
(iii) dividend	1,379	18,165	14,137	29,929	19,658	30,970	33,496	27,797	42,120	45,828	9,659
(iv) retained earnings (3 – i – ii – iii)	1,285	7,571	34,900	26,695	47,028	41,797	54,783	613	−19,508	−33,155	−43,109
5. Gross savings in companies covered	2,776	30,154	61,522	63,567	89,982	85,465	114,477	69,497	93,921	87,447	34,048
6. Gross saving in companies adjusted for under-coverage	46,822	40,205	82,567	85,073	120,348	113,953	152,712	94,641	126,802	121,729	92,668
B. 1. Gross savings of companies without separate account for Bangladesh[a] in Pakistan	–	29,500	40,200	40,600	71,800	113,800	114,200	157,800	169,700	206,000	–
2. Gross savings in Bangladesh	6,461[b]	8,850	12,060	12,180	21,800	38,110	38,100	51,400	57,700	71,860	90,456
C. Gross savings by non-financial companies (A. 6 + B. 2)	53,283	49,055	94,627	97,253	142,148	152,063	190,812	146,041	184,592	193,859	183,125

Sources:
1. *Balance Sheet Analysis of Joint Stock Companies Listed in Karachi Stock Exchange*, State Bank of Pakistan, various issues.
2. *B.I.D.C. in Figures*, Bangladesh Industrial Development Corporation, Dacca.
3. *Annual Reports*, East Pakistan Industrial Development Corporation, Dacca, different years.
4. *Registrar, Joint Stock Companies*, Dacca.
5. *Monthly Bulletin of Statistics*, January 1969, East Pakistan Bureau of Statistics.

[a] The companies include Pakistan International Airlines Corporation, National Shipping Corporation, Pakistan Tobacco Company, Pakistan National Oils and Burmah Eastern.
[b] Figure for gross saving is not available for this year. The rate of growth of gross saving over the years 1960/1 to 1961/2 was applied on 1960/1 figure to obtain estimate of gross savings for this year.
[c] In paid-up capital B.I.D.C. fund has sometimes been included for some companies under B.I.D.C. management.

TABLE 12

GROSS PROFIT AND GROSS SAVING OF FINANCIAL COMPANIES IN BANGLADESH 1959–60 TO 1969–70
(takas in thousands at current prices)

	1959–60	1960–1	1961–2	1962–3	1963–4	1964–5	1965–6	1966–7	1967–8	1968–9	1969–70
A. Gross profit in Pakistan[a]	108,278	128,797	149,507	164,737	196,162	220,184	270,035	300,182	321,392	196,293[b]	235,877[b]
B. Disposal of gross profit[a]											
(i) tax provision[a]	18,010	23,026	33,824	42,202	49,166	52,088	62,026	60,595	71,142	25,723[b]	39,356[b]
(ii) depreciation[a]	4,900	4,915	7,065	10,913	11 046	14,564	17,697	21,334	28,952	4,600[b]	8,081[b]
(iii) dividend[a]	11,000	14,350	17,966	20,057	22,906	34,511	24,804	32,759	37,939	10,000[b]	12,450[b]
(iv) retained earnings[a] (A−(i)−(ii)−(iii))	74,368	86,506	90,652	91,565	113,044	119,021	165,508	185,494	183,359	15,597[b]	175,990[b]
C. Gross saving[a] (ii)+(iv)	79,268	91,421	97,717	102,478	124,090	133,585	183,205	206,828	212,311	20,197[b]	184,071[b]
D. Gross saving in Bangladesh[a]	23,317	26,751	28,936	30,176	37,610	41,188	54,581	63,346	67,158	76,715 (50,032)[a]	92,129 (58,775)[b]
E. Gross saving in Bangladesh by insurance companies and co-operatives	445	−106	1,452	5,621	2,976	7,715	3,858	6,230	5,957	8,006	9,386
F. Total gross saving by financial companies in Bangladesh (D+E)	23,762	26,645	30,388	35,497	40,586	48,903	58,439	69,576	73,115	85,521	101,515

Sources:
1. *Annual Report*, State Bank of Pakistan, different years.
2. *Banking Statistics of Pakistan*, State Bank of Pakistan, various issues.
3. *Pakistan Insurance Yearbook*, Controller of Insurance, various issues.
4. *Annual Report*, Pakistan Industrial Credit and Investment Corporation, different years.
5. *PICIC at Work*, Pakistan Industrial Credit and Investment Corporation, 1965.
6. *Annual Report*, House Building Finance Corporation, different years.
7. *Annual Report*, Agricultural Development Bank of Pakistan, different years.
8. *Nine Years of IDBP*, Industrial Development Bank of Pakistan.
9. *Pakistan Statistical Yearbook, 1968*, Central Statistical Office, Government of Pakistan.

[a] Financial companies excluding insurance companies and co-operative societies.
[b] Financial companies excluding insurance companies, co-operatives and scheduled banks.

TABLE 13

NET CAPITAL RECEIPTS OF BANGLADESH 1959-60 TO 1969-70
(takas millions at current prices)

	1959-60	1960-1	1961-2	1962-3	1963-4	1964-5	1965-6	1966-7	1967-8	1968-9	1969-70
I. Domestic debt	212.7	183.2	−68.1	316.3	476.2	237.5	429.7	53.1	682.5	346.1	627.8
(1) permanent	99.8	73.7	9.9	41.6	233.4	75.8	120.0	170.6	87.5	204.4	101.3
(2) floating	85.5	84.1	−112.5	238.1	195.3	107.3	273.5	−165.8	577.2	97.6	477.8
(3) unfunded	27.4	25.4	34.5	36.6	47.5	54.4	36.2	48.3	17.8	44.1	48.7
II. Accretion to reserve funds	−11.3	55.2	89.6	73.4	82.7	99.8	184.9	85.3	116.3	157.5	199.1
III. Deposits and remittances	133.1	59.7	95.2	86.1	70.0	324.3	−54.6	95.2	−3.2	−163.0	−35.9
IV. Recovery of loans and advances	16.5	35.3	58.2	38.0	55.4	59.6	80.9	139.1	148.3	182.4	168.0
V. Other capital receipts	–	–	–	–	–	–	56.6	18.0	23.2	15.7	46.7
VI. Net domestic capital	351.0	333.4	174.9	513.8	684.3	721.2	697.5	390.7	967.1	538.7	1,005.7

Source: *Budget in Brief, 1971-72*, Ministry of Finance, Government of Pakistan.

Note: All intergovernmental transactions are netted out from the above.

APPENDIX 2

METHODOLOGY OF ESTIMATING GROSS DOMESTIC PRODUCT OF BANGLADESH FOR THE YEAR 1972–3

No firm estimate of the gross domestic product of Bangladesh is available for the year 1972–3. An attempt is made here to present a first approximation towards an estimate of 1972–3 G.D.P. at current factor cost. The starting point is, of course, the latest available G.D.P. figure, that is of the year 1969–70. This estimate is due to Alamgir and Berlage who, as described elsewhere in the text, carried out certain corrections to the official series. For the estimate of 1972–3 additional information was collected from different sources so as to extrapolate from the G.D.P. figure of 1969–70. A short discussion of sectoral estimates is given below.

(1) *Agriculture:* Output data on major agricultural products indicate that on the average the production of food and non-food items declined by 17 per cent in 1972–3 below the level attained in 1969–70. It was therefore simply assumed that at constant 1969–70 prices value-added originating in agriculture declined by 17 per cent. This figure was then inflated by the wholesale price index (1969–70 = 100) of agricultural products as constructed by the Bangladesh Bureau of Statistics. Output data were obtained from work done by S. R. Bose at the Bangladesh Institute of Development Economics.

(2) *Mining:* It was assumed that there was no real growth or decline in the mining sector. The constant 1969–70 figure was inflated by the wholesale price index to obtain a 1972–3 current price figure.

(3) *Industry:* The methodology and sources of data are the same as in the case of agriculture. The estimated output decline in 1972–3 over 1969–70 was 35 per cent for large-scale manufacturing (in spite of the fact that in some industries, including fertilisers, steel and ship-building the output level in 1972–3 was above that of 1969–70) and 38 per cent for small-scale manufacturing. The latter was primarily based on the output level of the handloom industries. The price index used in this case was, however, that of all industrial products for both large- and small-scale manufacturing.

(4) *Construction:* Total availability of cement in 1972–3 was 40 per cent less than that in 1969–70. Using the input method one might say that in constant 1969–70 prices, value-added in the construction sector in 1972–3 would be 40 per cent below the level of 1969–70. However, this figure must be corrected due to a large increase in non-cement using construction activities in rural and urban housing following the devastation of the liberation war. It was, therefore, assumed that the value-added in 1972–3 was 35 per cent below 1969–70 and this figure was inflated by the price index of construction materials in order to arrive at the current (1972–3) price estimate.

(5) *Utilities:* This sector includes electricity, gas and water. On the basis of available evidence, it was estimated that the wage bill of the institutions

providing public utility services went up by about 20 per cent. This was taken to represent the difference between current price value-added in 1972–3 and 1969–70 and the value-added originating from the utilities sector was estimated accordingly.

(6) *Transport:* In the transport sector, during 1972–3 there was some decline in the capacity for movement of people while that of goods increased with the additional transport equipment (trucks, minibulkers, burges, etc.) provided by the international agencies and countries to facilitate work on relief and rehabilitation. It would therefore be realistic to assume that the total output in transport remained the same between 1969–70 and 1972–3. Assuming that the change in the transport mix during 1972–3 over 1969–70 did not change the value-added coefficient significantly, the total value-added in the transport sector in 1972–3 was obtained by correcting the 1969–70 figure for underlying price changes. The price index used was an independently constructed index for transport services corrected for differential rate of change in the prices of input and output.

(7) *Trade:* It is estimated that trade margins in 1972–3 were up by 50 per cent as compared with 1969–70. There was, however, a decline of the trade of agricultural and industrial products by about 20 per cent, so that the real increase in the value-added in trade was taken to be 30 per cent in 1972–3 over 1969–70. This figure was inflated by the wage index to arrive at the estimated value-added in 1972–3 prices.

(8) *Banking and insurance:* Considering the fact that banking and insurance activities had to expand significantly both at head office (due to the fact that most head offices were previously located in Pakistan) and branch office level (due to the policy of the government to reach banking service out to the rural areas as far as possible) it is estimated that the value-added in this sector went up in real terms by 30 per cent in 1972–3 over 1969–70. This was further inflated by the wage index to arrive at the current price estimate.

(9) *Ownership of dwellings:* A very simple procedure was followed to estimate value-added in this sector in 1972–3. It was assumed that per capita value-added in this sector remained the same between 1969–70 and 1972–3 so that the latter year's estimate was obtained by first inflating the 1969–70 figure by the rate of growth of population and then by an independently constructed index for rentals. The population figures were taken from work done by Masihur Rahman Khan at the Bangladesh Institute of Development Economics.

(10) *Public administration:* The 1969–70 value-added figure was first raised by the rate of growth of current expenditure of the government of Bangladesh between 1969–70 and 1972–3 and then by the wage index to arrive at the current price estimate of value-added in public administration in 1972–3.

(11) *Services:* The methodology is the same as that developed for ownership of dwellings.

Discussion of the Paper by
Mohiuddin Alamgir

COMMENTS ON THE PAPER BY HOLLIS CHENERY

The paper contains useful background information on what has been happening, but unfortunately, it stops at the point at which interesting questions begin. [1] What should be the target rate of growth? What is to be the role of foreign capital? How great should be the participation of the private sector? Let us consider the experiences of other relevant countries, i.e. of countries moving toward socialism under democratic regimes: India, Sri Lanka and Chile.

The key issue is how much mobilisation of resources is needed. The minimum amount is set by the need to employ the growing labour force. Experience indicates that if the labour force is growing 3 per cent a year, the minimum rate of growth of G.N.P. must be 5 per cent. There are not great inequalities of income in Bangladesh and thus there is not much to redistribute. Moreover, given the weights of the agricultural sector in national product, the rate of growth of G.N.P. cannot be much more than 5 per cent per annum. That is, the range of possibilities is likely to be 5 to $5\frac{1}{2}$ per cent growth per year. The rate of savings in the past has been unable to sustain that growth. Moreover, the social changes envisaged will tend to lower savings. In addition, as the government threatens private industry, the incentive for investment will be reduced. At the same time, the government hasn't the capacity to take over the entire private sector.

In India the private sector has done much better than the public sector. The latter has suffered from inefficient management, low prices, low profits and savings. This is even more true in Chile. The evidence indicates that a rapid move toward socialism leads to slower growth, and this represents a policy dilemma. In Sri Lanka there has been an excess of debate on all aspects of public policy. The party out of power inevitably promises a great deal and then is unable to deliver when it is in office. The result is rising consumption and falling savings. Equality of opportunity and equality of education have been combined with increasing dependence on the outside world to maintain consumption standards. The priorities in Sri Lanka clearly are out of balance and this has resulted in 700,000 people, i.e. 18 per cent of the labour force, being unemployed. In the long run, if present policies persist, the institutions designed to achieve equality will be sabotaged by the unemployed.

One should envisage institutional change as occurring over time. In the next five years the private sector in Bangladesh will provide more than half of total resources for development. This being so, the private sector must be told clearly what are the rules of the game, and the incentives provided by government must be adequate to enable it to perform its function.

A difficult decision confronting the government is how dependent to be

---

[1] *Editorial Note.* It must be remembered that the discussants did not have the sections of Dr Alamgir's paper now represented by pp. 95-end.

on the outside world. India aims to end net capital inflows by the end of the next plan, but such a policy may entail a heavy cost. It already is evident that Indian economic performance has been adversely affected by the attempt to operate a closed economy before they are capable of doing so. A major problem has been that material balances have not been estimated correctly; bottlenecks have retarded growth, especially bottlenecks in steel and power. In practice, one cannot separate material balances from accumulation. One can, however, use foreign trade to compensate for miscalculations of material balances. The open economy is a great offset to bad planning. In Bangladesh, however, the heavy dependence on jute exports may increase the vulnerability of the economy. For example, when receipts of foreign exchange decline, imported goods will become scarce and this, in turn, may reduce the degree of capacity operation, profits and savings. The problem can be overcome in part by relying on external capital in the near future.

COMMENTS ON THE PAPER BY ALEXANDER BAJT

In my opinion Alamgir has written an interesting paper on the most important topic of the conference. I shall comment briefly on his approach and on the general problem of mobilising resources for development.

It is argued that Bangladesh could finance a development plan over the next five years of roughly takas 17,300 million. This, however, is not sufficient to achieve a satisfactory rate of growth and some foreign aid will be needed. How much foreign aid is required will be determined by economic and political criteria. In the present year about 75 per cent of capital expenditure is financed by foreign capital.

Alamgir's method of analysis is to extrapolate from the past. We must ask ourselves two questions, however. First, how reliable are the data on savings? Many European countries would be delighted to have accurate information similar to the data which have been presented to us. Second, is it legitimate to extrapolate trends from the past when the institutional structure has been and will continue to be altered and transformed? One would normally expect violent breaks with trends to occur in this situation. In particular, I doubt the usefulness for a socialist country of figures on the marginal propensity to save. In a socialist economy a completely different approach to deriving savings estimates should be adopted. This approach would start from the political, institutional and social characteristics of the new economy in making estimates; it would not attempt to calculate ratios of savings in relation to income.

Alamgir's paper is restricted to a consideration of the financial aspects of mobilising resources for development during the First Five Year Plan. Personally, I prefer to talk in terms of real resources, not financial resources. The analysis should begin by considering the factors of production and the possibilities for increasing the degree of their utilisation. The existing utilisation of resources cannot be taken as given; there are 'sleeping forces' in the economy capable of generating growth, provided appropriate institutions are created.

The most serious problem faced by Bangladesh is how to produce more, and in particular, how to produce more food. We sometimes tend to talk too much about distribution and not enough about production. In the end social relations will depend on how successful you are in increasing production. I would place considerable emphasis on qualitative planning and on unorthodox methods of mobilising resources. It would be a mistake to overemphasise material balances and elegant mathematical models. They can distract attention from the major issues. Similarly, one must not look at resources just in terms of capital, labour and land; institutions also are resources. Indeed, I do not agree that a shortage of resources as conventionally defined is a major characteristic of this country.

DISCUSSION

The discussion covered a variety of topics: the feasible rate of growth, actual and potential savings rates, the role of foreign aid, alternative methods of increasing investment and the most appropriate planning methods.

Branko Horvat said that he believed Bangladesh could grow about 8 per cent a year, in contrast to Chenery's estimate of 5 per cent. It should be possible to improve the performance of the agricultural sector and accelerate its growth to 6 per cent per annum. There is excess capacity in the sector and unutilised labour, capital assets and irirgation facilities; greater utilisation of these resources would permit several years of rapid growth. In addition, manufacturing could grow 16 per cent a year. The rest of the economy would follow these two leading sectors and grow about 10 per cent a year. By the end of the first five-year planning period the aggregate growth rate could be 8 per cent, but only if agriculture can expand as assumed. *Jozef Pajestka* replied that whether the growth rate is 5 per cent or 8 per cent is not very important. The essential point is to exploit every possible opportunity and to demonstrate to the people that in their village change and progress are occurring.

The contrast between the historic marginal savings rate (11–13 per cent) and the predicted savings rate for 1973/4 (5–6 per cent) was noted by *A. R. Khan*. The main problem, he thought, lies in the corporate sector. The savings of the nationalised industries are very low and the government has been unable to extract the savings that previously were generated by these enterprises when they were in the private sector. Unless this problem is resolved there is no hope for a high rate of savings. *Jaroslav Vanek* claimed that Chenery overstated his argument that a decline of the private sector leads inevitably to a decline in savings. He suggested that the capital assets of the modern manufacturing sector be taxed 10 per cent annually. This tax, when combined with a 10 per cent depreciation charge, would yield more savings than was generated by the private sector prior to nationalisation. *Gustav Ranis* replied that at present Vanek's policy was not practicable because the public sector enterprises were running at a loss.

Turning to foreign aid, *Keith Griffin* argued that much of the external assistance provided to Bangladesh had been used to sustain current consumption and there was a danger that if this continued there would be a permanent reduction in the domestic resource mobilisation potential. Already the savings effort had been weakened by the abolition of the land tax, by the elimination of the export tax on jute and by the pricing policies of the nationalised enterprises, which have resulted in losses and negative savings. All of these policies, it was suggested, were made easier by the availability of massive amounts of foreign aid. *Anisur Rahman* said the government's initial decision not to accept aid from nations which had not supported the War of Liberation was very exciting. Perhaps it was a pity this decision was reversed, since a policy of self-reliance would have forced the government to undertake institutional change. *Horvat* said that foreign aid was needed not only to finance investment but also to bridge the foreign exchange gap.

When examining unorthodox methods of mobilising resources *Griffin* said two points should be recalled. First, investment need not occur always at the expense of consumption. In Bangladesh it may be possible to increase investment by reducing leisure, by increasing effort and by reducing unemployment, especially seasonal unemployment. Investment and consumption are not necessarily alternatives. Indeed, investment may be complementary to certain types of consumption, e.g. food or medical services. Second, savings and investment are not always independent decisions. Savings may depend in part on investment opportunities. The government should devote as much attention to creating profitable outlets for investment as to reducing consumption (raising savings), especially in agriculture and in the small business sector.

On planning methods, *Vladimir Kondratiev* and *Pajestka* favoured the use of material balances. *Esra Bennathan* agreed, but said elaborate material balances should be avoided; what is needed are rather crude balances that can be prepared quickly and provide a guide as to what is happening in the short run. In addition, we need a simple table that would enable the government to determine the effects of different measures and policies on specified income earning groups. In this way the effect of various policies on income distribution could be analysed. *Horvat* argued that the great advantage of material balances is that they are not sophisticated, but are very simple. Moreover, they force the planner to think in terms of physical resources. If physical resources can be mobilised, savings will be forthcoming automatically. That is, investment produces savings, not the other way round.

5 The Strategy of Agricultural Development in Bangladesh

Swadesh R. Bose

BANGLADESH INSTITUTE OF DEVELOPMENT ECONOMICS

I. THE PROBLEM

Bangladesh is predominantly rural and agricultural. In early 1973, of an estimated population of 75 million at least 90 per cent is rural and 80 per cent (60 million) agricultural.[1] Almost all the poorest people live in rural areas. The average agricultural holdings are small, crop yields poor, and rural wages very low. About two-thirds of the agricultural population are very poor – being either landless or having less than 2·5 acres of holding per household.

Population pressure on the limited agricultural land is already very high. Overall and seasonal underemployment is massive. The problem is compounded by rapid population growth. A continuing high (around 3 per cent) rate of population growth, as is to be expected during the next decade, will further enlarge the agricultural population and reduce cultivated area per worker over the next decade or longer simply because the non-agricultural sector, with its small base, will not be able to absorb the increments in labour force and population. A 3 per cent population growth will annually add over 2 million to the population and about 0·8 million to the labour force. Even as high as 5 per cent non-agricultural employment expansion per year will absorb only about 0·3 million annually, leaving 0·5 million to be absorbed in agriculture every year over the next decade. While in the long run labour absorption will have to take place largely in non-agricultural sectors, agriculture will have to provide much larger productive work opportunities over at least the next ten or fifteen years. Moreover to raise the incomes of a rapidly increasing agricultural population from a limited area of land, output per acre must be raised substantially and rapidly.

An increasing foodgrain deficit has imposed an unbearable burden on the national economy. To eliminate this deficit and to meet the incremental domestic demand generated by rising per capita income and rapid population increase, agriculture must rapidly increase

[1] The proportions are rough estimates. In the Census year of 1961, 95 per cent of the population was rural, and 85 per cent of the labour force was in agriculture.

production of basic foodgrains and other foodstuffs. It has at the same time to supply some of the increased raw material needs of domestic industry, and contribute substantially to the country's balance of payments, both by exports and by import-substitution.

In the foreseeable future the key to the pace of economic growth in Bangladesh is held by agriculture. The relative shares of manufacturing and agriculture in the national product of the country being roughly 8 and 60 per cent respectively, even a high rate of growth of manufacturing can have only a limited impact on the growth of the national economy if agriculture languishes with a low rate of growth. For at least the next decade this simple arithmetic will dictate the need for a development strategy with heavy emphasis on agriculture. Agricultural growth will dominate the pace of total economic growth attained in Bangladesh.

Whether one sees the problem as one of raising rural incomes and providing increased employment opportunities or of meeting increasing demand or attaining a rapid growth of the national economy, growth of agricultural output at about 5 per cent a year is needed, compared with a growth rate of 2·5 per cent per year in the decade of the 1960s.[1] Given the socialist goals of the country, this accelerated agricultural growth consistent with an overall expansion of the economy will have to be achieved while ensuring from the beginning that the agricultural growth becomes broad-based, benefits of growth accrue equitably to poorer sections of the rural population, and does not enrich the larger farmers only. Agriculture thus faces a multiple challenge. Can this challenge be met, and how?

The major constraints to rapid agricultural development are a low land–man ratio, poverty of most farmers and overall resources-scarcity, complexity of natural resources demanding a relatively sophisticated input use for substantial yield increase, weak institutions, inadequate trained manpower and inadequate physical infrastructure to support a massive modernisation drive. At the same time the technological possibilities of the green revolution are really immense.

In evolving a development strategy which can translate into reality the potential of agricultural growth it is of great importance to take into account the human and institutional environment in which agriculture operates, its past growth performance, natural and other constraints as well as the technological possibilities within resources limitation.

---

[1] 1969–70 was the last normal year, the output level of which has not yet been reached.

II. THE PRESENT LAND USE PATTERN

Agriculture in Bangladesh consists mainly of crop production. Next in importance is fishing. Forestry and livestock raising are relatively of minor importance, both in terms of output and employment.

Practically all cultivable land is used. There is hardly any scope for extending agricultural land through opening up virgin land. Total agricultural land (including current fallow) is about 22·5 million acres. Total cropped area with multiple cropping is about 31·5 million acres (see Table 5.1). The area under crops in the aus season (early rainy season, early April–July) is 11·5 million acres, during the aman season (main rainy season, July–November) is about 15·5 million acres (see Table 5.1). The area under crops in the aus season April) is nearly 5 million acres. A considerable part of the agricultural land is not cropped during the aus and aman seasons mainly because of too much flooding during monsoon. Also in the absence of sophisticated fertilisation practices, some land should be kept fallow for part of the year. The above figures show that there is more scope for increasing acreage under crops during the boro/rabi season than during aus and aman seasons.

Irrigation, flood protection and drainage can intensify land use and increase cropped acreage. Irrigation can not only raise cropping intensity but also promote introduction of yield raising inputs and farming practices.

TABLE 5.1

BANGLADESH: ACREAGE, PRODUCTION AND YIELD OF VARIOUS CROPS 1969–70

Crops	Acreage (million acres)	Production (million tons)	Yield (lbs./acre)
Rice	25·49	11·82	1039
(a) Aman	14·84	6·95	1049
(b) Aus [a]	8·46	2·96	784
(c) Boro [b]	2·18	1·91	1953
Wheat [b]	0·30	0·11	780
Other cereals [b]	0·27	0·09	695
Jute [b]	2·46	1·32	1199
Gram and pulses [b]	0·90	0·29	717
Oilseeds [b]	0·86	0·38	986
Tobacoo [b]	0·11	0·04	805
Sugarcane [c]	0·41	7·40	18 tns.
Tea [c]	0·11	63·00	588
Fruits	0·38	1·58	9184
Others	0·47		
Total	31·76		

[a] Aus season.   [b] Boro/rabi season.   [c] Perennial.

III. NATURAL CONSTRAINTS

The limited cultivable land is subjected annually to drought and flooding, and to periodic cyclone and tidal wave. Although on a yearly basis Bangladesh obtains more water than can ever be used effectively on its 35 million acres, there are extreme seasonal variations typical of monsoon climates. During the monsoon season – roughly May–October – there is too much water; and during the virtually rainless dry season – roughly November–April – there is too little. The seasonal rainfall variation is compounded by the mighty rivers having most of their catchment areas outside of Bangladesh.

During the monsoon period the great rivers rise to high levels, and since much of the country has nearly flat topography, extensive flooding is caused either by direct overflows from rivers or by impeded natural drainage. Estimates about the area and the depth of flooding can still not be considered very accurate. But soil and land capability surveys by U.N.D.P./F.A.O. indicate that 30 per cent of the total cultivated area is flooded annually up to depths of 3 ft and above. Two-thirds of the total area are flooded to a depth of more than 1 foot. Although flooding provides water for monsoon crops in large areas and people have adapted farming practices to normal annual flooding, floods curtail crop production to a considerable extent. About 15 per cent of the area which goes deep (about 6 ft or more) under water cannot sustain crops during the monsoon period. In addition to direct damage[1] to crops by varying flood levels, the uncertainty of flooding in terms of area, depth, duration and time of occurrence inhibits long-term agricultural and rural development.

During the long dry season river levels are low. Average rainfall over large parts of the country during this period is only 9 in. to 5 in. which is insufficient to sustain crops without additional irrigation water. Intensive land use throughout the year is not yet possible because of excessive flooding during the monsoon and lack of irrigation facilities for the dry season.

Regional variations are also considerable. The country divides into four roughly equal regions based primarily on hydrological differences, although there are important differences in soils, and land availability. In the north-west – north of the Ganges and west of the Jamuna – the monsoon is shorter and the dry season rainfall is very low; droughts are more serious than floods; surface water is scarce and irrigation has to be based on ground water. In the northeast – the areas between the Meghna, Brahmaputra and Jamuna

[1] Estimates of average annual flood damages vary: in the late 1960s the Planning Dept. (of the then East Pakistan) estimated it at takas 4·5 billion. while recently other experts estimated it as about takas 650 million.

rivers and including the Sylhet basin – the flood problem is most serious. Both droughts in the dry season and floods during the monsoon are serious in large parts of the south-east and south-west regions; floods in these regions are partly tidal in nature. Rainfall ranges from 50 in. in much of the north-west and south-west to 200 in. in parts of north-east and south-east. The agricultural pattern of each region is affected to a large extent by the differing topography, climate and river regimes.

More than any other environmental factor, hydrological conditions determine the present and future agricultural use of land and the cropping pattern in Bangladesh. Because of impeded drainage or flooding, 75 per cent of all agricultural land is suitable only for rice and jute cultivation during the monsoon. But the high yielding new seed-fertiliser technology has not yet been successfully adapted to these conditions. On about 15 per cent of agricultural land nothing can be grown during the monsoon because of deep flooding. Dry-land crops and summer vegetables can be grown on the remaining 10 per cent of land which is high and well drained. Dry season crop cultivation is limited to lands which retain moisture or are irrigated, and can be greatly increased through irrigation facilities. About 15 million acres are considered suitable for irrigated I.R.R.I. boro or transplanted aus. The remaining 7 million acres are suitable for irrigation of dry-land crops if water can be supplied.

Flood Control and Drainage

The U.N.D.P./F.A.O. survey mentioned earlier reached some important conclusions in regard to drainage and flood control problems in Bangladesh. Their findings may be debatable, but are so far the best available. About two-thirds of the country's cultivated land comprises high land and medium high land flooded on average to a depth of 1–3 ft during the monsoon. This land is considered suitable for agricultural intensification through improved seed-fertiliser technology without investment in flood control and drainage works. Selective drainage would improve the agricultural potential of such land, and can be undertaken eventually with increased intensification and sophistication of farming practices. On medium low land (flooded from 3 to 6 ft), which occupies 15 per cent of the cultivated area, drainage and flood control are very desirable but would require sizable drainage and embankment works. On low land (flooded more than 6 ft), which comprises 15 per cent of cultivated area, drainage and flood protection requires major and highly expensive works and is not considered critical for the overall national agricultural growth during the next decade or so, although it has important implications for the affected areas.

Irrigation Potential

Readily usable surface and ground water is available – in technical and economic terms – for irrigating at least 7 million acres; i.e. about one-third of total cultivated area as against less than 1 million acres (or 5 per cent) irrigated at present.

The dry season river flow determines the potential for irrigation with surface water. Any source capable of meeting the dry season irrigation demand will have abundant supplies for the wet season. The period of critical surface water flow is in March and April. Part of this dry season flow must be reserved for other uses: navigation, domestic use, and prevention of further saline water intrusion from the sea.

Minimum surface water flows in rivers in March and April are roughly 250,000 cusec and 335,000 cusec respectively. According to expert estimates, about 40 per cent of this flow, or some 100,000 cusec, can probably be withdrawn from rivers without excessive saline water intrusion. The net river water withdrawals for low lift pump irrigation vary by district; it would be a maximum of 10 cusec per thousand irrigated acres for March or April. Making allowances for conveyance losses, the available surface water can irrigate up to 10 million acres or nearly half the cultivated land. However, surface water use at low cost is severely limited by accessibility of suitable agricultural land to the existing network of rivers and canals, and by the distance low lift pumps can reach. Expert studies have shown that small-scale schemes using low lift pumps and double pumping can expand surface water irrigation up to 3 million acres, provided extraction is made 24 hours of the day in the critical months. More land can be irrigated by diverting surface water through channels at appropriate places. This latter, however, requires large-scale and more costly schemes.

Tubewells permit irrigation of lands which cannot be served by surface water because of distance from rivers. Adequate groundwater resources for irrigation exist in all areas of Bangladesh, except two. One is the southern area – roughly south of the line running between Comilla and Jessore – where the presence of saline groundwater makes impossible any major tubewell development. The other area comprises the deeply flooded Sylhet basin and the surrounding hills in the east. The remaining area of about 22,500 sq. miles (over 40 per cent of the total area) is suitable for tubewell development at depths of between 150 ft and 300 ft. But 25 per cent of this area is seasonally flooded to depths of over 3 ft, and another 9 per cent is occupied by human settlements or water, thus leaving about 14,750 sq. miles or 9·4 million acres of land potentially irrigable from groundwater resources. Recharge conditions are generally excellent. With fewer than 1500 tubewells installed at present, the tubewell development potential is practically unlimited in large acres of the country for the next decade or so.

TABLE 5.2

BANGLADESH: LAND TENURE

	1960		1968	
Type of tenure	*Number of farms*		*Number of farms*	
	(000)	%	(000)	(%)
Owner farms	3730	61	4560	66
Owner-cum-tenant farms	2310	37	2070	30
Tenant farms	100	2	240	4
Total	6140	100	6870	100
	Farm area		*Farm area*	
	(m. acres)	(%)	(m. acres)	(%)
Owner-operated area	17·78	82	17·96	83
Tenant-operated area	3·95	18	3·60	17
(a) Cash rented	(0·42)	(2)		
(b) Share cropped	(3·53)	(16)		
Average size of farms	(acres)		(acres)	
(a) Owner farms	3·1		2·7	
(b) Owner-cum-tenant farms	4·3		4·0	
(c) Tenant farms	2·4		3·0	
(d) All farms	3·5		3·2	

Sources:
1. *Census of Agriculture*, 1960.   2. *Master of Survey of Agriculture*, 1968.

IV. FARM STRUCTURE

Land in Bangladesh is largely owner-operated, although the average land-owning farmer rents in some land (usually on a share-cropping basis) from large or non-cultivating owners. As of 1960, owner farmers represented 61 per cent of total, and the owner-cum-tenant class comprised 37 per cent of total. 82 per cent of farm area was owner-operated, and the remaining 18 per cent is tenant operated (mainly share cropped). Full tenancy is negligible (see Table 5.2).

The average farm size in 1960 was only 3·5 acres of which 3·1 acres were under cultivation. The median size of holding was below 2·5 acres. Farms below 2·5 acres, which can be considered as small, were 51 per cent of total and occupied only 16 per cent of area. The medium-sized farms (2·5 to under 7·5 acres) were about 38 per cent of the total and occupied about 45 per cent of the area. The top

10 per cent of farms (7·5 acres and above) occupied 39 per cent of the area (Table 5.3). Almost all farms including small holdings are highly fragmented. As a result of substantial population increase and the consequent subdivision of holdings, both mean and median farm sizes have declined furthei since 1960.

TABLE 5.3

BANGLADESH: PERCENTAGE OF FARMS AND FARM AREA IN VARIOUS SIZE GROUPS

Size (in acres)		Farms (%)		Farm Area (%)	
		1960	1968	1960	1968
	under 0·5	13	12	1	1
0·5 to	„ 1·0	11	13	2	3
1·0	„ 2·5	27	32	13	17
2·5	„ 5·0	26	26	26	30
5·0	„ 7·5	12	9	19	18
7·5	„ 12·5	7	5	19	15
12·5	„ 25·0	3	2	14	11
25·0	„ 40·0	a		3	3
40·0 and over		a		2	2

Sources: As of Table 5.2.

[a] Less than 0·5 per cent.

Very low yields, small farm land per head or household and a land-use pattern dominated by low-valued crops result in low average income in agriculture. The incomes of a large part of the agricultural population are considerably lower than the average because of their landlessness or smallness of holding, and in some cases, inferior tenurial status requiring crop sharing with the owner. Over 50 per cent of the agricultural households who have holdings (owned or rented) of less than 2·5 acres have lower incomes than average, although cropping-intensity, labour-intensity and output per acre are relatively higher on small farms. About 20 per cent of the rural households are estimated as landless[1] who seek work at low wages but still cannot get adequate employment. Thus about 70 per cent of the agricultural population are very poor.

Growth of agricultural output concentrated mainly on the 10 per cent large farms cannot generate adequate increases in productive employment and incomes of the landless and small farmers who constitute the large majority of the agricultural population. Nor can this achieve the desired rate of overall agricultural growth. Moreover, except for the difference in behaviour caused by inadequate resources, small and medium farmers are no less receptive to productive innovations than large farmers.

[1] According to 1961 Population Census, 17 per cent of agricultural labour force was landless.

V. PAST AGRICULTURAL GROWTH

During the 1950s agricultural output virtually stagnated. Rice production in the 1950s increased at only 0·7 per cent per annum compared with a population growth rate of nearly 3 per cent. This resulted in a steadily increasing foodgrain deficit. Performance of the agricultural sector improved in the 1960s when both rice production and aggregate agricultural production increased at about 2·5 per cent per year. But even then, in the face of a 3 per cent annual population growth the country became increasingly dependent on foodgrain imports, which grew from 0·5 million tons a year in the early 1960s to 1·5 million tons in 1969–70. Production of jute, which is practically the only export crop, declined in the 1950s but registered some increase in the 1960s. But this was associated with a large increase in acreage and a decline in yield. Despite the increase in production, the share of Bangladesh in the world export of jute and allied fibres declined during the 1960s. Since the size of the agricultural population increased faster than the sector output, average income in agriculture declined during the 1960s. In this process the poorer segment of the agricultural population were relatively more impoverished.

There are two main reasons for the poor performance of agriculture in the past: neglect of water resources development for irrigation, flood control and drainage; inadequate efforts to spread improved technology among the broad masses of peasants through education, extension, and supplies of inputs and credit, and to build institutions like co-operatives to overcome hindrances of small farming. In the 1960s irrigated acreage, fertiliser use and institutional credit increased rapidly in percentage terms, but the absolute magnitudes were too low to make a break-through in agricultural production:

	1960–1	*1969–70*
Irrigated area	32,000 acres	860,000 acres (less than 5 per cent of agricultural land)
Fertiliser use	24,000 nutrient tons	234,000 nutrient tons (15 lbs. per cropped acre)
Institutional agricultural credit (Taccavi, Agricultural Development Bank, and Co-operatives Bank)	95 million takas	223 million takas

Institutional credit represents only a small fraction (an estimated 14 per cent in 1966) of total agricultural credit. The greater part of the rest comes from farmers-traders-money lenders. A small portion of institutional credit goes to small farmers, as is indicated by the

TABLE 5.4

BANGLADESH: AGRICULTURAL GROWTH,
1960–1 to 1969–70
(per cent growth per year[a])

Value-added in agriculture at 1959/60 prices	*Rice output*	*Jute output*
2·47	2·45	1·44

[a] Based on least square estimate of 'b' in the equation: Log $Y = a + b$ time.

fact that during the 5-year period ending 1969–70 only 18 per cent of Agricultural Development Bank credit went to small farms below 3 acres.[1]

The development of appropriate rural institutions which can support technological innovations in a setting of small fragmented farms has been very sluggish. A model of village co-operative organisation was developed at the experimental level in the early 1960s at the Academy for Rural Development at Comilla. But co-operatives of this type, which could help to release the smaller farmers from the grip of larger farmers-cum-money-lenders and enable them to adopt improved farming techniques, were spread during the decade to only 23 Thanas and 6000 villages out of 420 Thanas and 65,000 villages in the country. Most of these co-operatives are still confined to the Comilla district.

VI. BROAD OBJECTIVES OF A NEW DEVELOPMENT STRATEGY

The data and analysis presented in earlier sections show that although there is hardly any new land to be opened up in Bangladesh, a large portion of all land and water resources is under-utilised and is capable of radically more intensive development with available technology. Therefore, in order to achieve a high rate of growth of output in agriculture the overall strategy should be based on (i) intensification of land use and increase in crop yields through rapid development of water resources and introduction of improved farming techniques and practices. To achieve the objectives of expansion of productive employment, abolition of mass poverty, reduction of income inequality and more equitable distribution of the fruits of agricultural growth, the development strategy should lay serious emphasis on (ii) introduction of intensive development on all farms, with special efforts directed to small farmers and (iii) redistribution

[1] State Bank of Pakistan, *Agricultural Economics Bulletin* (July–Sept, 1971) (mimeo).

of land from very large farms to small farms which are generally much more labour-intensive. The extreme overall scarcity of resources and the urgency of early acceleration of growth underline the need for using in the near future those means of development, such as high-yielding seeds, fertilisers, pesticides, and low-lift pumps, tubewells, minor drainage and flood protection, which are quick-yielding, low-cost, and labour-intensive while initiating preparation of schemes, such as major flood control works, which are indispensable for longer term development.

Considering the potential of the new agricultural technology (commonly known as the green revolution) in relation to available land and water resources, it does not appear that employment, output and income distribution objectives as stated earlier are seriously conflicting, provided the institutional structure of agriculture is appropriately changed and adequate support is given to small farmers. Firstly, the new seeds-fertiliser-water package is land-augmenting and labour-using. Labour requirement per acre increases by about 70 per cent, and thus overall employment and output are likely to increase considerably as larger areas are brought under the new technology. Secondly, such important inputs as seeds and fertilisers are infinitely divisible and can be used with equal advantage by large and small farmers, if they are provided with irrigation water and adequate credit.

Intensive land use through improved farming techniques: The vast majority of farmers lack adequate resources needed for intensive land use through improved farming techniques using new-seed-fertiliser-water. With adequate farm training and extension, credit and supply of necessary inputs and assured markets, the new technology can be introduced and intensive development made on small-sized holdings.

Co-operatives: In many cases irrigation will be crucial for intensifying agriculture. However, even small-scale irrigation (by low-lift pumps or tubewells) requires lumpy investment, and cannot be adopted individually except probably by the top 10 per cent of farmers having holdings of 7·5 acres and above. Small- and medium-sized farmers do not have adequate surpluses for such investment, and there exists no community organisation which can organise group action by such farmers for developing irrigation around which use of other inputs could spread widely. In such a situation of individualistic small (and highly fragmented) farming it will be necessary for an outside agency to introduce irrigation technology and organise farmers for the joint use of facilities provided. In conditions of Bangladesh this function cannot probably be performed by private outside entrepreneurs, and moreover this will militate against its socialist goals. Thus efforts by the central or local government are necessary for the purpose. Such efforts can potentially ensure that participation in the development process is broad-based. If the jointly used irrigation facility is demonstrated to be profitable, it can act as a catalyst around which co-operative organisations for providing other services to most of the farming community can be built.

The availability of additional water for irrigation can substantially raise agricultural output and income of the cultivator through increased cropping intensity, shift to higher valued (and more labour-intensive) crops in response to market demand, and even more importantly by making possible introduction of improved seeds and fertilisers.

The Comilla co-operative experience[1] shows that this divisible technology has spread virtually to all co-operative members irrespective of farm size, although levels of input use vary. Among co-operative members farm size has significant effect on the extent of winter-cropping. Moreover, when supplementary irrigation water is available, small farmers (below 2 acres) achieve higher cropping intensities than larger farmers. Co-operative members have a much larger proportion of their farm land under irrigation than do non-members among whom winter-cropping is much less on small farms than on large farms.

While replicating the co-operative approach for broad-based agricultural and rural development, certain deficiencies of the Comilla experience should be overcome in order to achieve the objectives stated earlier. In the Comilla co-operative movement very small farmers and landless labourers have not generally participated. In the Comilla Thana, among co-operative members 57 per cent are landless or small farmers (below 2 acres), while among non-members 78 per cent are landless or small farmers.[2] Landless and nearly landless workers obtain some benefit as a result of increased labour demand created by the new technology. But the benefits of output growth can accrue to all groups of the farming community if the base of technological diffusion is further broadened by including small farmers and landless labourers in the co-operatives.

Rapid expansion of small-scale irrigation through low-lift pumps and tubewells and their joint use by small- and medium-sized farmers, organised in co-operatives supported by institutional credit and other services, will strengthen their community organisations and provide

[1] L. Faldlay and M. Esmay, 'Introduction and Use of Improved Rice Varieties; Who Benefits?', Michigan State University (Nov 1970), mimeo. Quoted in Carl H. Gotch, 'Technical Change and the Distribution of Income in Rural Areas', *American Journal of Agricultural Economics* (May 1972).

[2] Ibid.

them with sufficient resources to break the economic hold of the very large farmer-cum-trader-money-lender group, who do not require the joint service provided by the co-operative and are likely to try to make it ineffective.

Extension, credit and input supply: Because of a high degree of illiteracy and inadequate mass communication, extension workers will remain a major source of information on new farming techniques, and hence extension should play a key role in the development strategy. The quality of extension workers as well as the present ratio of less than 1 extension worker per 1000 agricultural households should be improved. Along with this, a shift from the earlier emphasis on the relatively large 'progressive' farmers to the relatively neglected smaller farmers is desirable. In order to obtain higher and quicker returns on extension work, extension methods should be altered to give much greater emphasis on group and mass extension techniques rather than on the individual farmer. For this purpose necessary research and experimentation should be undertaken on a priority basis.

Inadequacy of credit is a serious constraint to the adoption of new technologies which require considerable purchased inputs. The massive administrative problems encountered in advancing a large number of small loans and in collecting repayments afterwards can be substantially overcome if credit is channelled to small-holders through a network of co-operative societies. Expansion of seasonal agricultural credit in this way will be limited by the extent of development of a sound co-operative structure throughout the country, as suggested earlier. The development of co-operative societies may be accelerated by linking the provision of credit and the formation of the co-operative.

Research and experimentation to develop improved seeds and to adapt imported high-yielding seeds should be given high priority over the coming years. Adequate availability of improved seeds shoud be ensured partly by seed multiplication through selected farmers, but as these are adopted by farmers, increasing reliance can be placed on farmer-to-farmer seed distribution. Supply and distribution of other inputs, particularly fertilisers, should be substantially improved. As farmers become increasingly familiar with the new inputs and their effects on output, adequate credit rather than price-subsidy can ensure a rapid increase in the use of such inputs. For this to be achieved it is necessary that the average yield from such input-use is high and the variance low.

Price policy and marketing: The government should help agricultural development by pursuing a price policy which can provide increased incentives to farmers to invest in agriculture and adopt new farming techniques. Farmers would do so if they could expect an attractive return over cost. Given the high yield response to new inputs, they can be assured of an attractive return if it is possible to stabilise prices at reasonable levels, without raising prices very much. Agricultural prices resulting from the operation of the market forces should not be seriously distorted. Apart from misallocation of resources, this will create problems of disposal for export crops such as jute. Moreover, fixation of foodgrain prices at high levels would benefit mainly the large surplus farmers and hit hard the poorer farmers and the urban poor. But inter-seasonal stabilisation of major agricultural prices, while providing incentives to farmers, would encourage and enable smaller farmers to shift from entirely subsistence foodgrain cultivation to production of some higher-valued and more labour-intensive crops, which have favourable long-term market prospects. Although the basis of the agricultural development strategy is mainly increased food production, such a commercial policy will also increase the employment and income of small farmers.

Rather than fix agricultural prices at artificially high levels it would be better to increase returns to producers by improvements in marketing and reduction in transport costs through development of feeder roads and waterways linking remote areas with the important marketing centres. Octroi duties on agricultural products should be abolished to encourage freer movement of goods.

VII. LAND REDISTRIBUTION TOWARDS SMALL LABOUR-INTENSIVE FARMS

One important component of agricultural strategy should be redistribution of land from large farms towards the smaller and more labour-intensive farm units. The fear that this will lead to a sacrifice of output for the sake of more employment is unfounded. Evidence in many developing countries including Bangladesh shows that output and employment for unit of land are higher on small farms than on large farms. This suggests that land redistribution is likely to lead to higher output and employment. Also, as discussed earlier, major inputs of the new technology, being highly divisible, can be adopted with equal advantage by small and large farms. But small farmers using largely family labour would use land more intensively than large farmers.

Major arguments against redistribution of land from large farms to small farms are mainly three: (*a*) it will create a fragmented farm structure which will be impossible to rectify in later years; (*b*) it will reduce marketed output; (*c*) it will reduce investible surplus.

Creation of numerous small holdings over the next few years will give a large number of people an opportunity to earn their livelihood and thus reduce mass poverty in rural areas. Adjustment of individual farming to rapidly increasing population results in more numerous farms of small average size. In such conditions efforts for land consolidation have to be continuous. Further, development of farmers' co-operative will help solve the problem of subdivision of holdings.

Land redistribution is likely to reduce marketed surplus in the very short run. But there is a strong presumption that total output will increase. Also, given the farmers' basic need for certain non-farm products and their likely aspirations to acquire newer types of manufactured goods such as better clothing, transistors or bicycles, it is likely that they will market increasingly larger quantities of the increased output.

It is not at all certain that multiplication of small farms will lead to a decline in savings of farm households. The level of income as the determinant of the proportion of income that an agricultural household saves has been excessively emphasised in literature. In several Asian countries even small farmers have been found to save a substantial portion of their income. It seems that investment opportunities strongly influence rural household savings in economies in which financial institutions are very underdeveloped. In such conditions, saving and investment decisions are taken by the same household. If attractive investment opportunity exists, rural households save in order to finance it. As agricultural investment becomes more profitable as a result of the new technology, redistribution of land may even increase rather than decrease the rate of rural capital formation. In cases where the required investment is highly profitable but lumpy, and hence beyond the capacity of an individual, the co-operative organisation suggested earlier would be able to undertake it.

While one cannot be dogmatic about it, these possibilities of small farming within an expanding system of co-operatives suggest that there is no strong case for retaining all the existing large farms in their present form. But in view of the urgent need for quickly increasing output per unit of land, it would be unwise to break up those large farms which have a higher per acre output than is likely to be obtained on a small farm at present. However, all large farms do not fall in this category. A policy of subdivision of large farms, of say over 12·5 acres, should be pursued. It may be done through legislation. Or alternatively it can at least be encouraged through fiscal measures. For example, introduction of a highly progressive land tax related to the size and the productive potential of the holding would encourage farmers either to use their land more intensively or to sell off part of it in order to reduce the tax burden.

As shown earlier, farm size distribution in Bangladesh is less unequal than in many developing countries. Still with a large and rapidly growing population on limited land, it is difficult to visualise how a development strategy purported to achieve output and employment growth with equity can avoid land redistribution.

Discussion of the Paper by
S. R. Bose

The admirable paper by Dr Bose is divided into two parts, one of which is concerned with growth and the other with income distribution. As regards growth, there can be little disagreement that the 2·5 per cent average rate of expansion of the agricultural sector represents relative stagnation if not decline. One issue is whether Bangladesh can move away from dependence on one or two crops toward a more diversified crop structure. I hope the country can shift from rice to jute and to other crops, e.g. vegetables and fruit.

One area of priority is the realignment of the irrigation system. There is an obvious area for expansion in boro (winter) irrigation. Productivity per acre is twice as high in the boro season as in the aus and aman seasons. It may be possible to increase the amount of irrigation by planning water management jointly with India.

The pricing system in agriculture merits considerable attention. It is alleged that there may be a tendency for a scissors crisis to develop. In my opinion this is unlikely because of the natural sympathies for the peasantry as a whole on the part of the government. Because of the concern of the government for the welfare of the rural population it is doubtful that the terms of trade would be radically turned against agriculture.

One of the exogenous factors operating on agricultural prices in Bangladesh is the trend of prices in India. Rising prices across the border will tend to pull up prices here, and the government must be careful not to allow the prices of local foodgrains to rise unduly. Similarly, a viable export sector, which in Bangladesh means jute, requires low prices. For this reason, the government should not jack up jute prices to the Indian level, unless it is able to engage in joint planning of the jute industry with India.

I do not agree with Bose about the importance of introducing structural changes, especially land reforms, in the agricultural sector. I doubt that the structure of land distribution is violently inequitable. Certainly land is not as unequally distributed here as in India. Moreover, even if one were to have a radical land reform there would not be much land available for redistribution. A radical reform would require that land be taken from those with 5–12 acres, and this can't be done given the level of poverty in the country. A radical reform would create instability in the countryside and perhaps would disturb the tempo of production.

It might be possible, however, to move gradually towards the development of service co-operatives in providing credit, seeds, irrigation and modest mechanisation which is not labour displacing. This would enable some economies of scale to be exploited and would bring about more equality than a land reform. Meanwhile, the state should establish a public foodgrain distribution system in rural areas for the benefit of landless labourers and small farmers in the slack season. Ultimately, as output rises, the benefits of growth will percolate downwards to small farmers.

Bose does not refer explicitly to the problem of capital accumulation in agriculture. There is no surplus that could be transferred from industry to agriculture. Therefore agriculture must be self-reliant. The government should tax the bigger holdings if it is politically possible to do so. Perhaps it may be possible to squeeze some surplus in this way. In addition, labour must be mobilised, as suggested by Anisur Rahman. The great problem is one of leadership.

I attach critical importance to primary education. Mass education is essential in order, first, to make farmers receptive to technical change, second, to enable them to understand what development involves and, third, to inform them of their rights, to help them to assert their rights and thereby to avoid exploitation.

COMMENTS ON THE PAPER BY MICHAEL LIPTON

Dr Bose begins with a succinct and informative account of agriculture in Bangladesh, and I would question only four points. (*a*) His estimate of safely available surface water exceeds the usual figure (80,000 cusecs, implying 40,000 low-lift pumps, though pump (and tubewell) expansion is indeed limited by shortages of administrators and mechanics – perhaps a third of tubewells are out of action, and command areas on the rest are low, partly because field channels are not dug or maintained. (*b*) As in most less developed countries, the aggregate estimates of tenancy and of inequality of landholding are well below data in comprehensive micro-surveys, though as Dr Bose says, inequality is less than elsewhere in Asia. (*c*) The rural credit situation is indeed unsatisfactory, but perhaps half the 86 per cent of credit that was non-institutional in 1966 came from friends and relatives at low or zero interest, and other institutional sources are less 'big-farm-oriented' than the Agricultural Development Bank. (*d*) The favourable view taken of the Comilla experiment strikes me as correct but for the wrong reasons. It has produced cadres of 'model farmers' who are highly efficient extension workers, has developed a fully committed yet honestly self-critical group of rural researchers, and has undertaken a variety of social experiments that fully justify its cost; but one would doubt its replicability on a large scale. The farmers' organisations took many years to develop, required huge subsidies, left out the poorer half of farmers (and all tenants), and enhanced net private farm income – as compared with neighbouring Chandina – by disappointingly small sums.

Passing from description to strategy, Bangladesh is seeking to build a socialist agricultural sector in the framework of a socialist economy. Several countries have tried this, and Bangladesh is to be congratulated on emulating Chile's attempt to do so in the context of free enquiry and criticism. We must not conceal the fact that in the U.S.S.R. massive transfer of forced savings and cheap food from agriculture to finance urban investment, together with forced collectivisation, attracted Soviet policy-makers because agriculture was private while industry was socialised and hence represents a similar temptation to Bangladesh. This strategy impeded the growth of an efficient agricultural sector in the U.S.S.R. while contributing to the development of the industrial sector.

The example of the temptation to 'squeeze' private agriculture to finance socialist industry is crucial. The share of resources for agriculture – administrative and educational as well as conventionally investible – is the central strategic issue facing Bangladesh. 'Top priority for agriculture' is hardly compatible with plans to invest only 20–35 per cent of public capital in that sector, especially since agricultural investment is likely to be 2–3 times as productive as non-farm investment. It is even self-defeating to force wage goods out of agriculture too cheaply, and to use its savings to fuel off-farm investment; such a policy deprives farmers of both incentive and capital to increase the future supply of wage goods.

How can a socialist Bangladesh tolerate the reinvestment of sums far in excess of the agricultural savings surplus in agriculture itself? Here land reform is an essential part of the strategy. If agriculture is non-exploitative, its support through massive inputs becomes acceptable to socialists. I applaud Dr Bose's logical arguments in favour of redistributing land to small farmers. He rightly refuses to pretend that the evidence supports collective or co-operative farming, with its proven bad record in Asia for production and equity, its high administrative costs and its encouragement of labour-replacing and import-using techniques. Nor does the evidence provide an argument for 'land to the landless'. Perhaps due to the impact of part-time farming, the link between per-acre employment (and yield) and falling size of farm ceases to hold below 0·5–1 acre. Moreover, the landless have by definition no experience of farming, and a ceiling even as low as 10 acres would release too little land (about 2·3 million acres) to give enough land to support a family of five (say, 2 acres) to more than an arbitrary minority of Bangladesh's 2½ million landless farming families. Thus, of the three ways to use surplus land – collective/co-operative farming, distribution to landless and mini-farmers, distribution to farmers with 0·5 to one acre – the last seems a more efficient way to create viable holdings. However, to be acceptable such a reform must be accompanied by a massive rural works programme to provide a 'right to work' to the landless and the mini-farmers.

Dr Bose describes the problems of supporting services, which will need alignment to whatever sort of new farm units it is eventually decided to create. There is a contradiction between increasing quantity and quality of extension workers. To my mind quality matters much more, and might be assisted through performance bonuses, better pay relative to clerical and Dacca-based officers, and a much less classroom oriented approach to training. Credit, like extension, needs to be concentrated where it has something to support; rural credit in Bangladesh is under-administered and over-defaulted and to try to expand it everywhere would be administratively self-defeating. This applies even more to input supply, probably the crucial constraint on agricultural development. Unavailability of improved seeds in several districts, scarcity (and smuggling into India) of fertiliser, and failure to maintain minor irrigation works are the main problems. In all departments, a region's or agency's right to expand might well be made conditional on its efficiency in utilising existing facilities. Duplication among and even within public distribution agencies, especially in irrigation, is a major problem.

Scarce and underpaid administrators constitute a powerful argument for price policy, as against physical controls. Dr Bose's case for incentives through price stabilisation rather than price distortion is well argued, especially in view of the high cross-elasticity of supply of jute in response to rice prices and the low direct rice price elasticity. Major price distortions are difficult to sustain because of the ease with which goods can be smuggled into India. The halving of fertiliser subsidies was a step in the right direction, given the huge excess demand, but urea prices are still 20 takas per maund as compared to an unofficial market price of 60 takas and an Indian price of 40 rupees. Hence farmers find urea scarcer than necessary, and constant and costly inspection is needed to prevent corruption by those who administer the subsidy and allocate the fertiliser. Moreover, pesticides remain free, and improved seeds heavily subsidised, though both are in excess demand. The situation is further complicated by the fact that the taka is worth much less in unofficial markets than its official value of one Indian rupee.

It is especially important not to subsidise labour replacing inputs such as tractors. One of the most plausible short-run aims of planning in Bangladesh is to raise employment levels; yet one is struck by the decline of traditional irrigation, notably by the silting-up and covering with water hyacinth of minor channels whose clearance needs little but labour and is normal practice in neighbouring West Bengal.

The other plausible short-run goal for Bangladesh is foodgrain self-sufficiency. This seems odd at first sight; unit production costs of jute are lower in Bangladesh than elsewhere, while the reverse is true of rice. Certainly an agreement incorporating jute quotas for India and Bangladesh, and a kenaf quota for Thailand, should be actively sought. Nevertheless, a purely comparative-advantage appraisal of the jute-rice choice would be unduly static. Jute has poor market prospects; much faster technical improvement is possible for rice; and a socialist agricultural economy is naturally unwilling to rely on non-socialist foodgrain suppliers indefinitely. But a thrust towards rapid foodgrain self-sufficiency has strict implications for other aims. To meet its heavy costs, projects with long gestation periods such as flood control and higher education will have to be delayed or given lower priority. Similarly, there may be a conflict with regional equity.

Bangladesh has enormous potential for agricultural development, and a properly defined socialist transformation could help the process greatly. There are great technical possibilities, a not-too-unequal income and land distribution to start with, and still some momentum in the independence movement. But if this potential is to be realised two things are needed soon: political decisions and controls and incentives permitting planners to monitor a properly co-ordinated system to deliver rural inputs. Dr Bose has provided a valuable guide to the initial situation and some of the areas where strategic decisions are needed.

DISCUSSION

The discussion centred on the desirability of land reform, the possibility of achieving high rates of growth of output, the ease with which technical changes could be introduced and additional inputs supplied, appropriate price policies and the objective of self-sufficiency in foodgrains.

There was no unanimity on the importance of land tenure in fostering development nor on the urgency of land reform. Several participants thought it was more important to increase the supply of inputs than to change existing agrarian institutions. *Akira Takahashi* noted that the low proportion of land under tenancy was a conspicuous feature of the agricultural sector of Bangladesh. This, evidently, was an advantage, but it also raised problems. For example, in most countries with tenant farmers, the large landlords play a leading role in agricultural development. Who will play that role here? Can we rely on the initiative of small farmers? Assuming agriculture does develop rapidly, will this not lead to a less equal distribution of land in the future? In Bangladesh there are no farmers' organisations which can be used to accelerate initiative and innovation. In other Asian nations, farmers' associations and anti-landlord movements have created solidarity within the mass of the rural community. These peasant associations and movements have tended to be anti-government and have been an indispensable part of agrarian progress.

Branko Horvat argued that land redistribution creates antagonisms within the village community; the object of policy should be to make everyone better off. Only land which is being rented out should be redistributed. Land should not be confiscated as this would create bad feeling and dampen enthusiasm. Land should be paid for at a self-assessed value in bonds over, say, twenty years. Expropriated land should continue to be farmed by tenants, who now sharecrop with the government rather than with the former owners. This would make it possible both to lower rents and increase government revenue. Instead of expropriating land in large quantities he advocated expropriating the differential rent through taxation.

Keith Griffin suggested that the problems Bangladesh confronts in the agricultural sector are, first, how to ensure equity within a socialist framework while achieving a high rate of accumulation and, second, how to overcome the difficulties of the transition toward socialism. In his opinion these problems can be resolved by introducing the following three measures: (1) the immediate acquisition by the state, without compensation, of all land owned in excess of 5 acres; (2) the imposition of a 100 per cent tax on land upon the death of the current owner; and (3) the prohibition of the sale, but not the renting in or renting out of land.

The first measure would fall on only 13 per cent of the rural population and would result in the acquisition by the state of approximately 5 million acres. The three measures combined would ensure that the state slowly would become the owner of all agricultural land in the country. As the owner of the land the state would be entitled to rent and this rent would form the base of a broad and equitable system of resource accumulation.

The land owned by the state, in other words, should be rented out or leased, preferably to the highest bidder, without prejudice to the system of farm management proposed by the leaseholders, be it family farms, co-operatives, joint farming schemes, etc. This scheme, thus, would lead to the elimination of inequality in the distribution of landed wealth and to the socialisation of the most important means of production in the country. It would contribute to greater equality of income and it would result in higher output and efficiency. At the same time, it would permit a decentralised and flexible system of land management consistent with a variety of tenure forms.

The rents received by the state, a part of which could be allocated to local or village authorities, could be paid either in cash or in kind, whichever is more convenient to the cultivator. These rent payments would create a marketable surplus and would provide the wage goods for a massive programme of labour-intensive capital accumulation in rural areas. Such a scheme is one way, perhaps the only way, of quickly reversing the downward trend in the productivity of labour in rural Bangladesh.

Even in the first phase of the scheme, when only the first of the recommended measures is operative, a substantial investment fund would be generated. This can be demonstrated quite easily. The rental price of land can be as high as takas 900 per acre per annum, but let us assume that the state rent on average is only takas 200 per acre. This rental applied to the 'surplus' 5 million acres would yield takas 1000 million a year, i.e. 40 per cent as much as the total revenue from all sources received by the government in 1969/70 (takas 2,396 million) and seven times the yield of the land tax of that year (takas 13·5 million) which, unfortunately, has recently been abolished. If the government is determined to follow a socialist pattern of society and wants to improve the level and rate of increase of the well-being of the mass of the population, some scheme such as this – or an equivalent in terms of land taxation – must be introduced. Resources *must* be mobilised from agriculture; they *ought* also to be largely reinvested there.

Horvat thought that part of the additional output generated in the agricultural sector could be transferred to non-agriculture. This could be achieved by paying slightly lower prices for farm products while charging slightly higher prices for the products farmers buy. It would be sufficient if 0·5 per cent of the agricultural growth were transferred to the non-agricultural sectors.

Nurul Islam asked whether it was realistic to plan for a 6 per cent annual rate of growth of rice output. Could technical improvements be introduced fast enough? Most participants agreed with *Takahashi* and *Horvat* that Asian farmers were not resistant to change, provided of course that they benefit from change. *Mahfuzul Huq* thought *Bose* was a bit too optimistic about the possibilities for rapid technical innovation. The villagers would need considerable encouragement, guidance and perhaps a bit of regimentation. It was unlikely that the introduction of high-yielding varieties of rice would increase labour utilisation by as much as 65–70 per cent as was claimed. The main constraint, however, was the probable nonavailability of sufficient tubewell water.

S. D. Chowdhury said no breakthrough in crop production is possible unless winter irrigation can be substantially increased. Given correct price incentives, farmers can grow almost any crop, but this can be done only in the winter season, from November to March. In the summer and during the monsoon it is possible to grow only three or four types of crops. Thus the hope for the future is that the number of tubewells will greatly increase and thereby permit a switch of the main growing season to winter cultivation. This being so, *Esra Bennathan* enquired whether it would not be best for the next 3–4 years for the government to limit its activity to supplying water. *Abdullah Farouq* replied that the possibilities for unlimited irrigation are greatly exaggerated. Additional irrigation will be helpful only in the winter crop, which at present is small. Better drainage is even more important than irrigation. The existing irrigation facilities are not fully used because of the need to level the land and consolidate small holdings. Instead of irrigation plus land redistribution, the government should concentrate on land consolidation and levelling.

Turning to prices, *Mitra* asserted that a planned economy should plan its own structure of relative prices. At present, relative prices in Bangladesh are determined by India's prices. *Dr R. H. Khondker* was concerned that the price of rice was lower in Bangladesh than in India, while the prices of many other commodities were higher. In consequence rice was smuggled in exchange for other goods. If this continued, Bangladesh would have to produce enough rice to satisfy not only internal demand but the demand in India as well. *Gustav Ranis* said there was no need to be disturbed by this since Bangladesh and India were, in essence, engaging in mutually profitable trade. *Nurul Islam* pointed out that eventually relative prices would change. Yes, said *Khondker*, but this will lead to a higher price of wage goods here and a higher level of prices in general. The real issue, replied *Islam*, is whether Bangladesh can have a radically different set of relative prices from India. *Farouq* argued that agricultural prices in Bangladesh were too low, partly because the exchange rate was overvalued and partly because imports of free wheat under the P.L. 480 scheme has depressed foodgrain prices. The government should try to raise agricultural prices in order to provide an incentive to farmers.

Horvat was confident it would be possible to increase the rate of agricultural growth to 6 per cent by the end of a five-year plan, and in eight years it should be possible to cover the present rice deficit. *René Dumont* said it was wrong to concentrate exclusively on rice because rice cultivation provides less employment and nutrition per cubic metre of water, the scarce input. More attention should be devoted to vegetables, as in China. In addition, sugar was becoming scarce on the world market and prices should rise. This could be an attractive crop for Bangladesh, and the left over cane makes good fodder. *Chowdhury* added that the cultivation of high-yielding varieties of rice on a wide scale could lead to disaster if a single disease or pest were to wipe out the crop over a vast area. *Farouq* asked why the government concentrated so much on rice, since already per capita production of rice in Bangladesh was as high as in Japan. We should be searching for other crops. *Bennathan* agreed. If the transport network were much better, if the ports were improved, if the internal distribution system were better, it is unlikely that the government would be wise to aim for self-sufficiency of the most ambitious kind. Should we not prepare to move incentives in favour of jute, oilseeds fruits and vegetables? It might be better to think not in terms of food self-sufficiency but in terms of an annual rice deficit of, say, one million tons.

Responding to the general discussion, *Bose* said that if we are to be honest in our socialist protestations we must do something about land distribution. Furthermore, the evidence suggests that a redistribution of land would raise production – both now and in the future. This is especially true since the high-yielding varieties are neutral to scale. We can be confident, therefore, that family based small farms can produce rapid growth. Socially, the 2·5–7·5 acre farmers have considerable prestige. These middle peasants are a potent force in the social structure of the village. There are no large landlords or zamindars in Bangladesh; they disappeared around 1950, and that change in land relations was the most important social change in the last twenty-five years. What is required today is a ceiling of 10 or 12·5 acres or, alternatively, a steeply progressive land tax. He is confident this would raise output and create a productive family-based farming system.

Co-operatives could be used as an institution for introducing small irrigation facilities. He is not suggesting joint farming, however, as that would probably result in a fall in output. The historical experience of the socialist countries does not show that collective farms perform better than small farms. Indeed, Poland's experience shows how successful small farms can be.

Money-lenders have disappeared from the villages of Bangladesh and the larger farmers have partially filled the gap left by their departure. Large farmers often act as traders and money-lenders. Thus, even though land is not as unequally distributed as in India, to strengthen family farms it is necessary to free small peasants from the grip of the larger landowner-cum-trader.

Irrigation clearly deserves high priority, but irrigation without credit will not suffice. As regards the cropping pattern, he would not advocate an increase in jute production at the expense of self-sufficiency in food-grains.

6 The Institutional Framework of Agricultural Development in Bangladesh

S. A. Rahim and M. Shamsul Islam

PLANNING COMMISSION, GOVERNMENT OF BANGLADESH [1]

I. INTRODUCTION

Bangladesh is a land of small family farms. There are about seven million farms, of which 92 per cent are less than 7·5 acres in size, accounting for about 70 per cent of the total farm area. More than half of the farms are owner-farms, the rest are owner-cum-tenant farms except a small percentage of pure tenant farms. About 25 per cent of the estimated 10 million rural households possess little or no land, depending primarily on wages earned from agricultural work.

The total cultivated area in Bangladesh is 22·5 million acres. Out of a total cropped area of 32 million acres, rice is grown on about 25 million acres. The most important commercial crop, jute, is grown on only 2·5 million acres. The agriculture is primarily dependent on monsoon rains, and frequently affected by floods. The average farm family depends heavily on traditional modes of production. More than 80 per cent of the total assets of an average farm family is in the form of land. The agricultural operations are labour intensive. Bullocks are the only source of power. Most of the farm inputs are supplied from the home. About 10–15 per cent of the produce is marketed. The farmer's relationship with the urban and industrial centres is marginal. Within the rural area, the small farmer's economic life is controlled by a small number of surplus farmers, money-lenders and traders.

Although the value added to the gross domestic product by agricultural production is about 60 per cent, the public investment in the rural sector in the past never exceeded 10 per cent of the total value of agricultural output. The major investments in the past were in rural works programmes, subsidies to modern inputs (fertilisers, insecticides and mechanised irrigation) and institutional farm credit.

[1] The authors are Section Chief and Division Chief respectively in the Rural Institutions Division of the Planning Commission of the Government of Bangladesh. The views they express in this paper are not in their official capacity.

The introduction of new agricultural technology in Bangladesh is a recent phenomenon. Chemical fertilisers and power irrigation were first introduced on commercial scales in the mid-fifties. But the spread of those innovations was slow until a decade later when high yielding varieties of rice seeds were introduced and new institutions were developed. The rate of diffusion of innovations can be judged from the following figures: the annual consumption of chemical fertilisers increased from 66,000 tons in 1960–1 to 375,000 tons in 1970–1; the area irrigated by low-lift pumps and tubewells increased from 62,000 acres in 1960–1 to 785,000 acres in 1970–1; the percentage of total irrigated area under high yielding varieties of rice increased from 38 per cent in 1968–9 to 70 per cent in 1970–1.

The rate of diffusion of new technology is sharply increasing, but the total coverage is still small. At present roughly 10 per cent of all farmers in Bangladesh are using some combination of the new inputs (fertilisers, H.Y.V. seeds and irrigation). The total area under the Package-inputs is about 5 per cent of the total cultivated area.

II. INSTITUTIONAL DEVELOPMENT IN THE PAST

Modern institution building foı agricultural development in Bangladesh began in the late fifties. The Water and Power Development Authority was established in 1959 and the Academy for Rural Development began functioning in the same year. The Agricultural Development Corporation was established in 1962 to ensure expeditious supply of new agricultural inputs. The national Community Development Programme (known as the Village Aid Programme) reached its peak operation in the late fifties. This programme however, was abandoned in 1960. The Academy for Ruıal Development began a series of pilot experiments on rural institutions in the early sixties. The pilot experiments produced encouraging results leading to the formulation of such national programmes as the Rural Works Programme, the Thana Irrigation Programme, and the Integrated Rural Development Programme. The academy's experiments provided some models of the essential rural components of the agricultural development institutions.

(*a*) *The Rural Works Programme* was designed to mobilise the rural population for infrastructure development and to generate employment in the rural areas. The programme was implemented through the local government councils. The rural people and their elected representatives, with the assistance of government officials, prepared schemes for building linkroads, bridges and culverts, irrigation and drainage channels and community centres. Funds generated through the P.L. 480 programme were made available to the local councils for execution of the scheme. Between 1962 and 1967 takas 710 million were allocated for different construction works. About 75 per cent of the total allocation was for road construction and maintenance. It is estimated that the rural works programme provided, on an average, about 170,000 man-years of employment annually during the period 1962–7.

During the initial years the performance of the works programme was good, and local participation was encouraging. However, at a later date the government in power began to manipulate the programme so as to get votes from the members of the local government councils who constituted the electoral college. As a result, the local councils lost the confidence of the people. Control over the project works and over funds became weak. At present the R.W.P. is in a poor state as a consequence of the absence of a local government constitution.

(*b*) The *Thana Irrigation Programme* began in 1966–7 as a pilot project in ten thanas. In 1967–8 the programme was extended over the whole country. The team of officers of various government agencies at the thana and district level and the local government councils were responsible for implementation of this programme. The farmers were organised around low-lift pumps for growing, an irrigated boro rice crop. The leaders of the irrigation groups received training at the thana training development centre. Agricultural credit, fertilisers, insecticides and high yielding varieties of seeds were supplied to the irrigation groups.

The Thana Irrigation Programme made a significant impact on the agriculture of Bangladesh. In 1970–1 the programme covered 352 thanas and organised 800,000 farmers in 20,000 irrigation groups. An area of 785,000 acres was irrigated by low-lift pumps and tubewells for growing the boro rice crop. About 72 per cent of the total irrigated area was under high-yielding varieties of rice. It is estimated that the programme generated an additional 100,000 man-years of employment in 1970–1.

The co-operative department registered about 70 per cent of the irrigation groups as agricultural co-operative societies. About 40 per cent of the total members of the irrigation groups joined the co-operatives. About 70 per cent of the co-operative members received short-term loans at the rate of takas 215 per loanee. The total amount of loan distributed by the co-operative department was takas 28 million.

The Thana Irrigation Programme is founded on a temporary organisational structure. The team of officers at the thana and the irrigation groups or co-operatives at the villages are organised around a single purpose, to raise an irrigated boro rice crop. The organised groups remain active for a period of 4–5 months in a year. Every year groups are organised afresh and the membership composition changes significantly. Owing to the temporary character of the organisation and the changing composition of membership it becomes difficult to develop an effective system of continuous training, supervised credit, timely realisation of water charges and loans, and proper planning of long-term improved agricultural operations.

(*c*) *The Integrated Rural Development Programme* (*I.R.D.P.*) was designed on the basis of a pilot project on a two-tier system of co-operatives in Comilla Kotwali Thana. The Academy for Rural Development began this experimental project in 1960 with a view to finding a suitable rural institutional framework for rural development. Under this project multipurpose co-operatives are organised at the village level, and village co-operatives are federated into a thana central co-operative association. The village and the thana associations are managed by elected representatives of the members. An initial grant, loan funds and trained project officers are provided to the thana central association by the government. Much emphasis is laid on proper training of the project officers and the leaders of the village co-operatives. Officers are trained at B.A.R.D. Comilla, where both the theoretical and practical aspects of rural development are studied in the context of Bangladesh. The managers, model farmers and other functionaries of the village co-operatives attend weekly training classes at the thana training and development centre. The thana level government officials conduct the training classes. The village leaders, in their turn, act as teachers when they attend the weekly meetings of the village co-operatives. Thus a two step system of communication is established between the village co-operatives and the thana central association. The co-operative members are required to follow certain disciplines such as attending weekly meetings, building up capital through thrift deposits, adopting improved agricultural practices and utilising credit according to the production plan prepared by the co-operative society.

The expansion of the Comilla-type two-tier system of multipurpose co-operatives began in 1965 on an experimental basis. In 1971–2 the government decided to undertake a national programme of expansion. So the Integrated Rural Development Programme was launched. The progress of this by July 1972 is as follows: thana central co-operative associations (T.C.C.A.) have been established in 33 thanas. A total number of 5,118 primary village co-operatives have been organised under the T.C.C.A.s. The total membership of the primary co-operatives is 124,041 farmers. The members have accumulated takas 10·35 million as savings and shares. The cumulative amount of loans so far issued to the members is takas 59·02 million. Of this the members have already repaid takas 27·82 million. The overall rate of overdue loan is 25 per cent.

The two-tier system of multipurpose co-operatives is considered a significant improvement over the traditional type of co-operative system. In Comilla Kotwali Thana (where this system has been in operation for the last ten years) evaluation studies have been carried out to measure the impact of the programme on the individual member-families. A panel of co-operative members studied in 1963 and again in 1969 shows the following results:

(1) the average production of paddy per family increased from 49 mds in 1963 to 95 mds in 1969; this increase was exclusively due to higher intensity of land use and better yield per acre of land cultivated; mechanised irrigation and high-yielding varieties of rice contributed to higher intensity and higher yield;

(2) the amount of paddy sold per year per family expressed as percentage of total paddy produced increased from 11 per cent in 1963 to 25 per cent in 1969;

(3) the average annual cash farm-expenditure per acre of land under cultivation increased from takas 111 in 1963 to takas 393 in 1969; the increase is primarily due to the cost of additional labour and new inputs;

(4) the average amount of outstanding loans per family increased from takas 697 in 1963 to takas 1,700 in 1969; the increase is primarily due to loans received from the co-operative societies;

(5) the average amount of liquid assets owned per family increased from takas 281 in 1963 to takas 1,412 in 1969; about one-fifth of the increase in the liquid assets is due to farmer's savings and shares with the co-operative society.

All the three programmes discussed above are included in the first annual development programme of the Government of Bangladesh. These programmes account for about 10 per cent of the total allocation in the A.D.P. of 1972–3.

III. INSTITUTIONAL DEVELOPMENTS AND PROBLEMS DURING THE FIRST PLAN PERIOD: LAND REFORM

Any serious discussion on institutional development cannot ignore the man–land relationship, which in many respects is the most fundamental factor determining agricultural development. In most countries of the world the first decisive step towards new institution building has been a reform of the traditional land tenure system. In traditional agriculture land is the most important means of production. Significant change in the modes of agricultural production is conditioned by the cultivators' economic, social and psychological relations with land. Thus agricultural development becomes extremely difficult without first changing those relationships which operate as constraints.

The East Bengal Estate Acquisition and Tenancy Act of 1950 abolished the rights of all intermediaries between the state and the tenants. The tenants were given the right to use land in any manner they like subject to payment of revenue to the state. Sub-letting of land was not permitted, but no restriction was imposed on sharecropping. A ceiling on land holding at 100 standard bighas[1] per family was imposed. But in 1959 the ceiling was raised to 375 bighas per family. The Government of Bangladesh took certain land reform measures immediately after independence. The ceiling was refixed at 100 bighas per family. Farmers owning less than 25 bighas of land were exempted from payment of land revenue. The government also announced its intention to distribute excess land among the landless cultivators.

The traditional system of share-cropping is in fact a special form of separation of ownership from cultivation. The agricultural census data of 1960 shows that share cropping accounts for roughly one-third of the total number of farmers. As the result of widespread share-cropping the inequality in the distribution in the farm income due to inequality in the distribution of ownership is significantly reduced. But this takes place at a substantial social cost. The large farmer, finding investment in traditional farming risky and uneconomic, seeks an easy alternative by renting out land to the poor landless cultivator. He earns an easy income without any investment or work. His attention is shifted from agricultural and rural areas to other occupations and urban areas. The poor cultivator on the other hand works very hard on rented land to meet his own requirements and to pay high rent to the landowner. But he does not make any capital investment, because he has neither the means nor the necessary incentive. Thus technological change in agriculture is rendered difficult.

The extent to which the farm size and tenure system affects adoption of technological innovations can be roughly examined by relating available data on farm size and land tenure to cropping

---

[1] 100 bighas = $33\frac{1}{3}$ acres.

intensity, land-use intensity, and the use of power-pump irrigation, H.Y.V. seeds and chemical fertilisers. An analysis shows that the farm size is inversely related to land-use and cropping intensity. The small and medium farmers are more receptive to labour-intensive innovations than the large farmers. Similarly it is found that the owner-farmers are more receptive to those innovations than the tenant-farmers. These findings seem to indicate that large farm-size and share-cropping practices tend to put constraints over the spread of innovations currently encouraged. It may be noted that the innovation package, consisting of irrigation, H.Y.V. seeds and fertilisers, requires labour-intensive methods of cultivation, because mechanised cultivation transplantation and harvesting are not in-cluded in the innovation package. If mechanisation in a broader sense was introduced along with H.Y.V. seeds and chemicals the large farmers would probably respond more than the small farmers. But in that case the problem of unemployment and income inequality would become much more serious.

The present policy of fixing a land ceiling at 100 bighas, remission of land revenue up to 25 bighas, and re-distribution of a few lakhs of acres of land can be best regarded as preliminary efforts at land reform in the new state of Bangladesh. Much more has to be done in this area, and programmes have to be formulated as soon as possible. To determine an effective strategy, satisfactory statistics on distribu-tion of income from land should be collected immediately. Statistics collected on a sample survey basis will serve the purpose of strategy formulation; later a detailed census will be needed for the purpose of land administration. The present ceiling on land holding will probably have to be reduced considerably in order to make a land redistribution programme meaningful. The present policy of land distribution to individual landless labourers will need careful examination, because distribution of very small parcels of land to a very large number of cultivators may add to the problems rather than solve them. The efficacy of alternative methods, such as distribution of a reasonable quantity of land to co-operatives of landless labourers, may be examined.

The traditional share-cropping practice is economically and socially undesirable. An effective land redistribution programme will reduce the incidence of share-cropping. However, improvement in the existing tenure legislation and system of land tenure will be needed to eliminate share-cropping practice. The problem of consolidating scattered holdings will also have to be tackled along with other measures of land reform.

The implementation of any land reform programme in Bangladesh will require tremendous efforts. The existing land administration structure is grossly inadequate to meet the demands. Improvement in land administration is needed. But, in course of administration of a land reform programme, assistance of local government bodies and peasants' organisations will be crucially important. The land reform programme will need full support from the major political parties. Considering the urgency of the problem it may be necessary to accept a rough-and-ready execution of the programme. Such a method will hurt a small number of people, but the overwhelming majority of the cultivators will greatly benefit.

IV. FARMERS' ORGANISATION

The farmers' organisation is an essential component in any institutional framework for agricultural development. In the process of development, the individual farmers need to establish new linkages with people and agencies outside the village community. Frequently the farmers are required to make decisions in units larger than the family farm. The adoption and management of innovations require collective action in the field for both economic and social reasons. The establishment of new norms of behaviour necessitates firm control over the behaviour of individuals involved in the process of change. It becomes essential to change the traditional system of services, especially credit, supply and marketing, so that the control of those services is transferred from the private money-lenders and traders to the collectivity of the farmers. Moreover, the farmers are required to shoulder more responsibilities, become less dependent on the government bureaucracy, and increasingly become more effective in participating, influencing and assisting decision making at regional and national levels. All these changes are required to be made effectively and quickly. Hence, the need for new organisations and leadership.

In Bangladesh, out of about 7 million farmers about one million are at present associated with some kind of organisation or group for developmental activities. About 800,000 farmers are members of the groups under the Thana Irrigation Programme; but less than half of them have so far joined farmers' co-operatives organised by the department of co-operatives. The total membership of village co-operative societies under the Integrated Rural Development Programme is about 125,000. In addition to these there are another 100,000 farmers associated with co-operatives under the programmes of the Water Development Board and privately organised co-operatives.

The government of Bangladesh is committed to a rapid expansion of farmers' co-operatives during the first plan period. The two-tier system of multipurpose co-operative, first developed in Comilla, has been accepted as the basic model, which will be introduced through the Integrated Rural Development Programme. It is envisaged that, by the end of the first plan period, primary co-operatives will be formed in most of the villages in Bangladesh. These co-operatives will be supported by the Thana Central Co-operative Association in each thana. At the district level co-operative unions will be organised for co-ordination and supervision of activities of T.C.C.A.s. The national organisation of I.R.D.P. will execute the programme. A national Rural Development Board will deal with matters relating to policy formulation and co-ordination. The co-operatives will be managed by elected managing committees. The government will provide initial grants, loan funds and trained officials to the thana association.

The implementation of I.R.D.P. will present a number of logistic problems. A large number of project officers will have to be trained. For this purpose the present training facilities will have to be extended and strengthened. In organising village co-operatives collective efforts by various government agencies and local government council will be required. To make the Thana Federation an effective body, active support from the thana level officers of other government departments will be essential. All these actions will be possible if the ministries responsible for agricultural and rural development accept I.R.D.P. as the basic programme for institutional development. At present such a concensus seems to be lacking.

Besides these problems there are a number of other issues which have emerged recently from field experience in areas where Comilla-type co-operatives are in operation. The village co-operatives generally exclude the landless labourers from membership. Thus a vast section of the agricultural labour force actually engaged in field-work remains unorganised and therefore cannot participate in the decision-making process. Even the small farmers can not exert sufficient control over the management of the co-operatives. In most cases the large and medium farmers become the members of the managing committee. The distribution of power and authority within the co-operative is greatly influenced by the traditional power structure in the village community.

The village co-operatives tend to grow around existing factions within the villages. Since new technology often increases tension and conflict in the villages, the members try to maintain cohesion and discipline by keeping the membership confined among persons of similar interest, opinion and attitude. Such a process improves group solidarity and cohesion, but the co-operative fails to become a socially and economically viable unit. It becomes more and more dependent on the Thana Central Co-operative Association. As a result the T.C.C.A. gets involved in many activities that should have been taken care of by the village co-operatives.

The solution to these problems probably lies in allowing the small cohesive groups to operate informally, but combining them into a formal structure of primary co-operative society. In this structure a particular person can become member of more than one small group, if required.

V. AGRICULTURAL CREDIT

The diffusion of new technology in a subsistence agriculture depends among other things on availability of farm credit. Dependable estimates of credit requirement are not available. The total annual requirement probably lies between takas 1,000 and 3,000 million. At present 10–15 per cent of the total credit requirement is met by the institutional sources of credit. The Agricultural Development Bank of Bangladesh and the National Co-operative Bank are the two main credit institutions. During the period 1960–1 to 1969–70 the A.D.B.B. distributed takas 54·2 million, and the Co-operative Bank distributed takas 44 million. In addition an amount of takas 21·8 million was distributed as government Tacavi loans. The A.D.B. loans are mostly medium- and long-term loans, primarily meeting the needs of medium and large farmers and tea plantations. The Co-operative Bank's loans are short-term loans meeting the need of farmers, fishermen and weavers.

Recent experience suggests that institutional credit primarily serves the surplus farmers. This happens partly because of short supply and partly due to poor distribution arrangements. The small farmer cannot compete with the surplus farmer because he cannot easily reach the sources of institutional credit and he is less creditworthy than the surplus farmer. If the volume of credit supply is increased, the existing institutions will not be able to cope with the situation. Obviously, the institutions will have to be expanded and strengthened. But at the same time it will be necessary to involve the local farmers' organisations in the distribution and realisation of loans. The co-operatives can perform these functions only if they are socially and economically viable. Therefore, it seems that the problem of agricultural credit is closely linked with the problem of farmers' organisation at the village level. The Integrated Rural Development Programme is expected to handle a large amount of institutional credit. Its success in this respect will depend on how I.R.D.P. is supported by the Agricultural Development Bank and the national Co-operative Bank. It will be necessary to work out clearly the relationship between these organisations.

VI. INPUT SUPPLY AND AGRICULTURAL EXTENSION

The Bangladesh Agricultural Development Corporation is responsible for the procurement and distribution of modern agricultural inputs. The corporation has a network of establishments for import and supply of inputs to the country. The efficiency of B.A.D.C.'s supply function depends considerably on advance information about local demands and on the performance of local dealers who carry the inputs from the warehouses to the villages. At present only crude estimates of local demands are available. The local dealers' handling of the supply is not very efficient. The situation can be much improved if the local supply channels are linked with the co-operatives when they are organised under I.R.D.P.

As regards agricultural extension there are two different views about what system should be developed. The Ministry of Agriculture proposes that the existing extension system should be strengthened. The number of trained extension workers should be increased so that one worker can be placed for each 500 acres of cultivated area where modern inputs are introduced. The extension workers should be given proper training for which a large number of training institutions should be established. The extension workers will generally contact individual farmers and advise them about proper use of the new inputs. They will also organise local demonstrations. The effectiveness of the extension worker will be greatly improved if his area of operation is kept small and adequate facilities are available for his training. The other view emphasises group extension work and training of farmers as local extension agents. Each village co-operative should select one 'model farmer' as local extension worker. This person should be trained continuously at the thana centre. The training facilities of the thana should be improved by posting qualified agricultural technicians as teachers of the local extension agents. The 'model farmer' will work in his own village through the village co-operative meetings every week. His own farm will be a demonstration credit in the village. He will carry individual farmer's problems to the thana centre for consultation with the agricultural technicians and bring back their recommendations.

The 'model farmer' approach to extension can be made highly effective if adequate training and advisory services at the thana centre are ensured and if proper selection of the 'model farmer' is made by the village co-operative. In a country where there are seven million farmers to be served by a relatively small number of trained extension personnel (expansion in their number will not only be time-consuming but also disproportionately expensive), the second approach seems to be much more realistic.

VII. LOCAL PLANNING AND MOBILISATION OF RESOURCES

The Government of Bangladesh will soon introduce a strong local government institutional system in the country. This system will have tiers at the district, thana and union levels. Elected representatives of the people will govern these institutions. They will be required to perform many development functions. It is expected that the local councils will prepare development plans and mobilise local resources for their implementation. Financial and technical support will be provided by the national government. The details of the local government institutional system have not yet been worked out. But some issues can be raised here for discussion. If the local government institutions prepare local development plans, then a system will have to be developed for co-ordination and integration of local plans into regional and national plans. Similarly, the implementation programmes will have to be co-ordinated and integrated. The relationship between administrative, professional and technical agencies of the national government and the elected representatives of the local government organisation will have to be defined in clear terms. The scope, functions and responsibilities of the co-operative institution *vis-à-vis* the local councils will have to be defined. The institutional framework for agricultural and rural development will have to be so laid out as to assign distinct but mutually supporting roles and functions to the government bureaucracy, the co-operatives and the local government institutions.

Discussion of the Paper by
S. A. Rahim and M. Shamsul Islam

COMMENTS ON THE PAPER BY RENÉ DUMONT

The most important thing to bear in mind is that the 'surplus' farmers of Bangladesh control the small farmers and the rural community as a whole. Unless the small farmer is liberated it will not be possible to achieve the planned rate of growth of agricultural output of six per cent per annum. This is our point of departure.

Let us consider briefly the experience of other countries. In China, phase one of the land reform consisted of a reduction in land rent and in interest paid to the money-lender. In Sri Lanka a paddy land act was passed but not implemented. What was lacking was a committee of peasants and agricultural workers in every village. The villagers need to acquire economic and legal power. A census should be administered in each village.

What are the options open to Bangladesh? One could follow the Chinese path of violent struggle and confiscation of land from 'surplus' farmers, but I do not believe this is possible in Bangladesh today. Alternatively, one could adopt a reformist solution, as in Japan and Taiwan, and impose a land ceiling, paying compensation for any land expropriated above the ceiling. This solution is not possible here, however, because if compensation were paid there would be no money left over to finance agricultural development.

I would like to put forward the following tentative solution for consideration by our Bangladeshi friends. All land given in share-cropping or cultivated with hired labour should be expropriated without compensation, i.e. confiscated. The ownership of such land would then be vested in the village. Peasants could cultivate this land on payment of a fixed rent. The rent might be equivalent to a quarter of the crop, instead of the current half, and would be paid to the village. In cases where the landowner now receives one-third of the crop, the rent might be reduced to, say, one-fifth. I prefer to give the rent to the village, not to the central government. The system I advocate would provide strong incentives to the cultivator to increase output, particularly if the rent were fixed for an extended period of, say, five years. At the same time, the village would receive resources which would enable it to finance rural works – water control schemes, drainage, tubewells – and thereby reduce rural unemployment. At the present rate of population growth, unemployment will be tremendous by the end of the century.

Each village should become a small focal point for development. Canals and irrigation ditches should be maintained by the village. The village should provide credit to every small farmer through the organisation of a multi-purpose village co-operative. Since village money would be at stake, I think we can rely on the villagers putting pressure on defaulters to repay their loans.

Much can be learned from the experience of Denmark. There primary and secondary school became compulsory relatively early. The co-operatives were formed thirty years after this. They were purely voluntary; the state did nothing to promote them. This experience underlines the importance of having literate poor peasants. Massive functional education is a vital prerequisite for the success of co-operatives, the green revolution and land reform. The villagers must become educated in order to become aware of the wider world and to increase their understanding of their own economic and political problems.

If you want to build socialism in Bangladesh you must eliminate corruption and nepotism and liberate the women. At present we are trying to build socialism at the planning commission level! This is not possible. Socialism can be built only at the village level. Part of the land of the nation should be owned by the village and this could become part of the self-managed public sector. The village should keep the land rent, but it should not charge an excessive amount. The Japanese after 1869 imposed a high tax on land, but it was not so high that a good farmer could not easily pay it. The Japanese example would be a good one to remember here.

Let me conclude with a few scattered remarks about the problems of developing a more intensive farming system. Everyone speaks of miracle rice and miracle wheat. In primitive agricultural systems cereals predominate, but as agriculture develops the importance of cereals declines. Moreover, some crops are much more labour-intensive than cereals. What is needed is 5000 people from South China to show the farmers how to grow Chinese vegetables. In China they cut the green peas after 21 days – and obtain more protein than we get after three months. Again, there is more protein in banana leaves than in rice. Has anyone considered the mulberry silk worm and natural silk instead of artificial fibres? The future of jute is not as bright as the future of silk. The essential point is that you must get away from a cereal monoculture.

DISCUSSION

The discussion focused on two issues. The first, a continuation from the previous session, was whether land reform was complementary to or in conflict with measures to raise production. The second issue was the establishment of institutions of local government and the problem of organising the peasantry.

A. F. A. Hussain said that the government should try not to introduce too many social changes right away. These might disrupt production, particularly the supply of foodgrains, and produce a social crisis. The immediate priorities were to provide a minimum nutritional level for the population and create employment and income for the three million households who are landless. At the moment the economy is incapable of sustaining even the present level of consumption without foreign assistance. *Dr Chowdhury* said the country is now in a position to achieve a technological breakthrough with I.R.R.I. rice and no steps must be taken which might disrupt that. We should concentrate on strengthening institutions to supply credit, extension and perhaps marketing services; other institutional changes could wait until these priority needs were met. Tubewell co-operatives could be formed once tubewells had been installed, but the investment must come first.

Daniel Thorner pointed out that the present land ceiling is 33⅓ irrigated acres. Given the size distribution of land holdings, this in effect was no ceiling at all. *Michael Lipton* agreed and argued that if one doesn't have a land reform now, the green revolution will strengthen the rich classes and make it more difficult to have a land reform later. The ceiling of 5 acres advocated by some participants probably was too low, however. He preferred a 10-acre ceiling on the grounds that a lower ceiling would encounter strong political resistance. A 5-acre as compared to a 10-acre ceiling increased the amount of land available for redistribution by 100 per cent but multiplied the number of people who would lose some land by 300 per cent.

Nurul Islam asked whether a programme to increase food production by saturating certain areas with free inputs would increase inequality. If so, could one compensate for this with a land reform or would a reform hamper in the short term a massive input policy? *Dumont* replied that under his scheme, share-cropped land would be expropriated but the share-cropper would continue to cultivate it. So there need be no disruption of production. *Rehman Sobhan* said that an argument against Dumont's scheme is that sometimes it is very poor people who rent out their land and then work elsewhere.

Gustav Ranis assumed there would be no major social revolution and no major improvement in administrative capacity. Under these circumstances the government should concentrate on supplying inputs to family farms and get development going in the rural areas. *Jaroslav Vanek* disagreed. The political obstacles were clear, but tenure changes were needed quickly. Moreover, a switch from share-cropping to a fixed rent system would alter the incentive system in a way favourable to higher output. *Branko Horvat* also thought a land reform would result in higher output.

Jozef Pajestka argued that people develop their capacities, learn new skills – both technically and administratively, in the course of doing new things. Seen from a narrow point of view, land reform may present problems, but from a larger perspective a land reform would help to develop capacities. Unless Bangladesh is ambitious, the initial impetus of independence will be lost.

The key role of agrarian reform in the overall development process was emphasised by *Ilya Redko*. Reform implies not only a redistribution of land ownership but also a deep and complex series of social changes. In the first stage of the reform ceilings should be introduced and land redistributed to small peasants. Later the more mature stage of collective farming will be necessary in order to overcome the forces restricting output. Meanwhile, experimental state farms could be created in order to develop the most suitable technology. It is important to forbid the sale of land in order to prevent the growth of kulaks; the peasantry – especially landless workers and small peasants – should be helped to become well organised and politically conscious. An agrarian reform can succeed if it goes through democratic channels, with the support and action of the peasantry itself.

In the various stages of the reform, however, the constellation of class forces will change. Land reform is not a once-and-for-all affair. This view was strongly supported by *Vladimar Kondratiev.*

Ashok Mitra argued that to push through a land reform one needed an effective political organisation. This was certainly supported by the Indian experience in West Bengal. *Anisur Rahman* asked whether it was possible for such a political movement to emerge from a Western parliamentary system. He feared the answer was no, in which case another social revolution was the only solution. In the absence of a land reform the green revolution would create intolerable social tensions and these tensions, in turn, would sabotage the green revolution itself. *Swadesh Bose* did not agree with *Rahman.* A democratic framework is essential for creating and focusing pressure from rural areas for institutional change. There was no reason to believe that in Bangladesh the mass of the rural population would vote in accordance with the wishes of 'surplus' farmers.

Rehman Sobhan observed that the Ayub system of Basic Democracies was designed to insulate rural society from the progressive urban forces and to strengthen the existing social order within the villages. In the last thirty years the major social changes – the money-lenders act and the land reform of 1950 – were achieved because the dominant political forces were essentially urban middle class. Today, Parliament will be essentially urban and middle class and thus the abolition of share-cropping is a possibility. Moreover, only a land reform can bring democracy to the villages quickly.

Akiri Takahashi advocated forming village land committees. Land reform changes not only the distribution of land but psychological and sociological relations as well. In Asia land reforms have succeeded only where power has been in the hands of the villagers. Naturally, bureaucrats in the central government are reluctant to give power to illiterate country folk, but if villagers are given executive power, it has been shown that as long as they receive legal and moral support from the government they will demonstrate competence. Japan is a case in point. Village land committees were organised in each village, which on average contained 300–800 households. These committees were given full power to carry out reforms. The committee included members from the landowning class, tenants and neutrals. The important point was that each member had detailed knowledge of village conditions and thus the peasants were able to ward off counter-attacks from landowners.

Previous attempts to organise the peasantry in Bangladesh had not been very successful, however. *Daniel Thorner*, and others, drew attention to the fact that small farmers were controlled by a small number of 'surplus' farmers who dominated not only the land but credit and marketing as well. This remained true even in Comilla. Landless workers were excluded from the co-operatives and the influence of small farmers was slight. The managing committee of the co-operatives reflected the traditional power structure of the village. The report on the Comilla scheme of December 1970–January 1971 by its founder Akhtar Hameed Khan reads like a Chinese-style confession before a People's Court. Even the rural public works scheme is doing poorly after a good start. Now the central government has announced that it will introduce strong local government institutions. How will such a programme avoid the fate of the Comilla scheme as described by A. H. Khan? The local base of the Awami League is the small number of locally powerful 'surplus' farmers. Does the government really intend to break their control?

Even if the control of the local notables were broken, this would not ensure the success of socialism. *Anisur Rahman* stressed that socialism consists of much more than the elimination of exploitation. It implies planned economic development, and in an economy composed of millions of small farms and enterprises planning is impossible. We must form political and economic institutions which will enable us to plan, to take collective decisions and assume collective responsibilities.

Dr Rahim replied by saying the intention was to have local government institutions at the union, thana and village level. The people would elect their representatives directly and be given responsibility for local planning, implementation and resource mobilisation. Government officials will be under the control of local institutions, not the other way round.

As regards land reform, we all agree that it is necessary in the long run, but some have doubts about its immediate priority. Political and administrative capacity are constraints. It is essential to introduce institutional change, especially to organise the farmers, but even the organisation of co-operatives – as in Comilla – has increased inequality. Perhaps for the time being the composition of the co-operatives should reflect the social composition of the rural community. Land reform can come a little later.

7 Nationalisation of Industries in Bangladesh: Background and Problems

Rehman Sobhan[1]

PLANNING COMMISSION, DACCA

I. THE SCOPE OF THE NATIONALISED SECTOR

As of today, 620 enterprises with assets valued at takas 3774 million are under state ownership or control.

These enterprises are distributed as follows:

TABLE 7.1

	No. of enterprises	Value of fixed assets (takas million)
A. Corporations		
1. Jute mills (B.J.M.C.)	76	1784·00 (for 73 units)
2. Textile mills (B.T.M.C.)	52	391·70 (for 45 units)
3. Sugar mills (B.S.M.C.)	15	235·30
4. Steel (B.S.C.)	8	473·74
5. Engineering (B.E.S.C.)	17	26·48 (for 7 units)
6. Fertilisers, chemicals and pharmaceutical (B.F.C.P.C.)	9	56·64
7. Food and allied (B.F.A.P.C.) products	16	38·56
8. Paper and Board (B.P.B.C.)	10	489·60
9. Oil, gas and minerals (B.O.G.M.C.)	6	28·30 (for 5 units)
10. Forest industries (B.F.I.D.C.)	6	35·90
11. Tanneries (B.T.C.)	30	10·00
B. Foundations		
1. Sena Kalyan Samitha	20	22·40
2. Freedom fighters foundation	15	11·30
C. Disinvestment Board	340	170·00 (approx.)
D. Total	620	3773·92

By contemporary standards this implies a degree of public ownership of industry which is to be found in few countries outside the socialist world. It has consequently imposed a major responsibility on the government to ensure the efficient management of these

---

[1] The author is a Member of Planning Commission, Government of Bangladesh. The views expressed in this paper are however purely in his personal capacity and do not reflect the view of the Government of Bangladesh.

enterprises. Any serious deficiences in the organisation and management of the state sector in Bangladesh would have inevitable repercussions on the modern industrial output. Given the sensitive position of the industrial sector in the economy the consequences of any failure would perforce affect a much wider area of the economy than the 7·2 per cent contributed by modern industry. For this reason the policy-makers were particularly aware of the need to make appropriate institutional arrangements which would permit the efficient performance of the nationalised sector.

II. THE BACKGROUND TO NATIONALISATION

To understand the nature of the institutions that have been set up to manage the industrial sector and the problems faced in working these institutions requires some understanding of the background and circumstances under which nationalisation took place. The objective conditions prevailing at liberation were themselves a critical factor in guiding decisions both for strategy and for implementation.

At the time of liberation the industrial sector still accounted for only 7·2 per cent of the G.N.P. of Bangladesh, and of this the modern large-scale industrial sector covered 4·4 per cent. Compared with the situation in 1949–50, when modern industry accounted for only 0·06 per cent of G.N.P. in Bangladesh, the modern industrial sector had recorded significant strides. Growth of industrial output averaged 6·6 per cent per annum as between 1949–50 and 1969–70. This growth was, however, still small compared with West Pakistan which had been the main beneficiary of investment in the industrial sector during the last two decades. Even in 1969–70 value-added from large-scale modern industry in Bangladesh accounted for only 24 per cent of value-added for the whole of Pakistan.

Within Bangladesh public sector industrialisation had come to bulk large because of the poor performance of the private sector. Industrial enterprises under the then state-owned East Pakistan Industrial Corporation (E.P.I.D.C., or B.I.D.C. as it came to be named after liberation) accounted for 36 per cent of fixed assets in the modern industrial sector in Bangladesh. Privately-owned industrial enterprises at liberation accounted for assets worth takas 3000 million. This may be contrasted with investment of takas 1700 million in the public industrial sector.

III. THE CHARACTER OF BENGALI CAPITALISM

The low level of private enterprise in Bangladesh concealed the more significant fact that a major segment of industrial assets in the private sector was owned or controlled by West Pakistanis. It is reckoned that 53 per cent of fixed assets in the private sector were owned by non-indigenous elements.

Large-scale Bengali entrepreneurship was largely confined to the jute and cotton textile industry. In jute, 34 enterprises with assets worth takas 600 million were owned by Bengalis. These accounted for 34 per cent of fixed assets in the jute industry.

In cotton textiles, Bengalis accounted for 24 enterprises with assets worth takas 210 million, that is 53 per cent of fixed assets in the textile sector.

Outside of jute and cotton, it appears that there were only 6 Bengali owned enterprises with assets above takas 2·5 million. This gives some idea of the dominance of Bengali industry by West Pakistanis and the character of Bengali entrepreneurship.

Bengali entrepreneurs, it appears, were inclined to restrict themselves to small and medium industries with assets below takas 2·5 million. Even here fixed assets attributable to Bengali ownership in the modern industrial sector accounted for only 20 per cent of fixed assets. The expansion into larger business ventures associated with jute and cotton was itself a recent phenomenon. Of the 34 jute mills owned by Bengalis at liberation, 28 had gone into production in the last five years.

This move into large-scale business was itself the result of special financing arrangements specifically designed to promote private entrepreneurship amongst Bengalis. Twenty out of these enterprises were in fact set up in collaboration with the E.P.I.D.C. This meant that part of the equity was subscribed by E.P.I.D.C. who made arrangements for providing the foreign exchange and took care of the various administrative problems involved in setting up a mill. Apart from E.P.I.D.C. equity, it was possible to raise equity finance from the Equity Participation Fund and the National Investment Trust (N.I.T.). These funds were supplemented by loan financing from the two financing agencies, the Industrial Credit Corporation and the Industrial Development Bank. If we take all Bengali-owned mills, only 24 per cent of the investment cost of the project came from the sponsors. The balance of 19 per cent came from public equity and 58 per cent from public loan finance.

This in fact meant that in some cases the Bengali entrepreneur had to put up as little as takas 2·8 million, or 10 per cent, as his share of the finances needed to set up a jute mill with assets worth takas 25·8 million. The precise situation naturally varied as between enterprises, depending on the personal resources and enterprise of the particular Bengali entrepreneur.

These figures themselves conceal the fact that many Bengali

entrepreneurs required much less than the sponsor's share as usually recorded, to set up a jute mill. Many borrowed their share of the equity from the commercial banks by pledging fictitious or over-valued assets with the ready connivance of the banks. These quasi-legal transactions were done largely for personal considerations but seemed commercially secure since it was known that the entrepreneur in question would soon have control of valuable assets with a high repayment potential.

Many such entrepreneurs quickly liquidated these private loans by various expedients of established efficacy in Pakistan of those days. Given the over-valuation of the rupee, foreign exchange sold at a premium in the decade before liberation, the 1960s. As a result of association in a jute mill venture a Bengali entrepreneur was given access to foreign exchange for import of machinery. In most cases machinery imports were over-invoiced, so that against them letters of credit for more than the full value of machinery were opened. The balance was left abroad. Whilst a part of this was kept as a safe nest-egg for darker days and swelled the sizeable hoards of Pakistan and now Bengali foreign exchange resources cached abroad, the residual was brought back into the country unofficially and converted into local currency at the rate of foreign exchange. This could finance a substantial part of the sponsor's share or retire his bank overdraft. In principle it means that a penniless entrepreneur with good connections in the administration could acquire control of assets worth takas 30/40 million.

In the case of cotton textiles, less reliance on public resources was apparent than for jute, in that E.P.I.D.C. equity participation was not forthcoming. Otherwise there were still a variety of sources for securing public money to finance a cotton textile mill, so that an average sponsor's contribution accounted for 41 per cent of investment. Though even here there were cases of Bengali mill-owners setting up a 12,500 spindle mill with assets of takas 8·3 million by putting up only takas 1·4 million, or 17 per cent as their share. These equity investments of sponsors were, however, funded by the same expedients deployed by the jute entrepreneurs.

Whatever be our view of the social ethics of these arrangements, there is no doubt that in the last five years a new class of Bengali capitalists controlling sizeable assets at home and abroad had begun to emerge. Quite a few of them had demonstrated enterprise in exploiting the opportunities provided by the Ayub raj and some were developing as perfectly competent managers.

In the history of capitalist development, there is nothing unique about these aids to private enterprise. Indeed in its early years Pakistan capitalism was itself the creation of state patronage. The distinguishing feature of the Bengali *haute bourgeoisie* at the time of liberation was therefore their relatively recent ascent to the upper reaches of the capitalist ladder. This implied, in many cases, only a recent acquaintance with industry. Few Bengali jute mill owners in fact had actually even owned or run an industry before they moved into the jute industry. This factor tended to reduce the confidence which goes with long access to wealth of this class and made them a highly insecure social group in the fluid social milieu of post-liberation Bangladesh.

IV. THE OBJECTIVE CONDITIONS IN BANGLADESH

The social background of the Bengali capitalist emerged as a particularly relevant factor in determining the strategy towards industry taken up by the government in the post-liberation phase. It was clearly recognised that there was no really established class of Bengali entrepreneurs, with the exception of the handful of sponsored capitalists in jute and cotton, on which to build an industrial base. What there was of Bengali capitalism would have to be nurtured by the state through liberal provision of equity and loan capital, subsidised land, controlled labour, protection from competition and liberal tax self-sustaining dynamism which could make them the mainstay of an industrialisation programme.

The *zeitgeist* of post-liberation Bangladesh did not easily lend itself to such policies. The liberation war had been fought largely by workers, peasants and students. The bulk of human and material sacrifices had been borne by the lowest income groups. It was the Bengali mill-owners, motivated by profit as much as fear of the Pakistani army, who tried to keep their mills working to provide exports and foreign exchange for the Pakistani military machine. It was this class, albeit living in a state of fear and insecurity under Pakistan occupation, who experienced no material hardships. In contrast it was their workers who obeyed the call of the Bangladesh Government to deny their labour to the Pakistani regime and who consequently had to face the insecurity of joblessness during the liberation struggle. Many of them took up arms to fight, and many were killed in the industrial areas of Bangladesh merely for being a source of support for the liberation struggle. With this background it would have been difficult for any government to start patronising a small class in order to give them the necessary stature to sustain the industrialisation of Bangladesh. It was this awareness which interacted with another significant consequence of the liberation struggle to give direction to the government's industrial strategy.

As the liberation struggle during 1971 intensified many of the

Pakistani entrepreneurs in Bangladesh began to see the writing on
the wall and began pulling out of Bangladesh. Whilst it was difficult
to carry away their machinery and plant, they began during 1971 to
export financial assets to West Pakistan. Where there were cash
resources, these were transferred west. To build up cash, inventories
were depleted and very few imports or replacements brought in, so
that at liberation inventories of raw materials and spares in most
factories were at an all-time low. Where liquidity was low, over-
drafts were extracted from West-Pakistan-owned banks and were
transferred to accounts in the west. As a result, most enterprises
carried heavy financial liabilities at the time of liberation.

By the time Bangladesh was liberated on 16 December 1971,
virtually all Pakistani owners of industries in Bangladesh had moved
west themselves to join their families and what assets they had
transferred from Bangladesh. The Government of Bangladesh on
liberation consequently found itself responsible for no less than 544
abandoned enterprises.

These enterprises were at a standstill. Ownership and middle-
echelon managers, and in some cases skilled workers, had disappeared. Inventories of spares and raw materials were low. In some
cases inventories of unexported finished goods had piled up. At
liberation, the jute industry carried stocks of 42,000 tons of jute
goods. Heavy liabilities lay on the books of their bankers. Power
supplies were uncertain because of damage to transmission lines.
Marketing and movement of goods was disrupted by the closure of
the main ports through mines and wrecks, the damage to road and
rail bridges, and the damage or disappearance of a sizeable segment
of the country's transport capacity.

The immediate task at liberation in the industrial sector was one of
getting the factories working again to provide employment and
income to the workers, some goods and services to domestic consumers, and access to foreign exchange to finance the import bill.
In the absence of any management in the enterprises abandoned by
absentee owners, the government took over the management of these
enterprises. In the initial stage a management board was set up under
the chairmanship of various officials of the Ministry of Industries.
This was tending to seriously overstrain the meagre administrative
resources of the government and these boards were in practice replaced by administrators specially appointed to manage these enterprises.

V. THE NATIONALISATION PROGRAMME

On 26 March 1972, the government formally took over the ownership of all assets belonging to Pakistani nationals. While this sorted

out the juridical status of these enterprises, the management position remained tenuous. Administrators were an essentially *ad hoc* expedient. Whilst many were qualified managers or professionals, in most cases from the enterprise itself, a number of outsiders were also included as administrators, not all of whom had the necessary competence required for the job. With 544 enterprises to administer this managerial vacuum was hardly surprising, given the historical background to entrepreneurship in Bangladesh and the dislocations of the liberation war. In not a few cases the factory workers themselves took over the management of the enterprises with varying degrees of success.

After the initial six weeks of *ad hoc* management the need for a durable institutional and policy framework to cope with these enterprises became manifest. The government had the option of handing these enterprises over to what there was of the private sector in Bangladesh; alternatively it could nationalise them in all or part and run the enterprises as part of the public sector.

Any policy measure of such far-reaching consequences could only be made within the context of the government's own social commitments. This had anticipated the goal of a socialist economic system in the government party's election manifesto, where it committed itself to nationalise large-scale industry, including jute but not cotton textiles or sugar.

This commitment seems to have been given a sense of specific urgency in the aftermath of the liberation struggle. The social forces sustaining the struggle and the underdeveloped character of the Bengali *bourgeois* conspired to make an expanded public sector as much a functional as a social imperative. The government therefore found no real uncertainty in giving its industrial policy a socialist basis.

This, however, still left a number of options. Whilst there was no question of wholesale disinvestment of Pakistani enterprises there was an awareness of the hazards of assuming managerial responsibility for 544 enterprises with assets varying from takas 10,000 to takas 50 million. It was accepted that the larger enterprises should be taken over. But it became a moot point where the line should be drawn and what should be done with units below the takeover line.

More important was the question of Bengali-owned enterprises. Liberation had sudenly enlarged the public sector out of all proportion to the ambitions and current capabilities of the government. According to the manifesto, only jute and large-scale industry were committed for nationalisation, but there was some uncertainty as to whether these should be defined to exclude Bengali units, because of the large managerial burden already vested with the government.

According to the manifesto there was no question of taking over cotton textiles, even though enterprises had been vested in public ownership through the departure of their owners.

Whilst there was an awareness of the hazards of too rapid an advance towards public ownership, the social background as much as apprehension for the future was matter for consideration. Jute and cotton textiles contained what little there was of a Bengali *haute bourgeoisie* or big capitalist class. To let them survive, grow and prosper would be building the foundations of a virile and indigenous class who in years to come could acquire far greater durability than the expatriate capitalists from West Pakistan. The political environment was certainly appropriate for any such radical move and the people were thought to be willing to face any temporary dislocations which might accompany the move towards socialism. The rather disorganised and demoralised state of the Bengali *bourgeois* in the post-liberation period precluded any serious opposition to radical measures.

As a consequence of this interaction of considerations, the Prime Minister, in his speech on the first anniversary of the declaration of independence, 26 March 1972, declared that the following sectors of the economy were henceforth to be nationalised: Jute; Cotton Textiles; Banking; Insurance.

Along with these, 111 enterprises abandoned by their Pakistani owners, all with assets above takas 1·5 million and with an aggregate of assets of takas 1600 million, were also formally nationalised.

As of 26 March 1972, the public sector was made up of the following corporate sources:

TABLE 7.2

Name of source	No. of enterprises (including under construction)	Value of fixed assets (takas million)	Share of fixed assets in %
1. Formerly under E.P.I.D.C./ B.I.D.C.	53	1700	48
2. Abandoned by Pakistanis	111	1047	29
3. Jute and cotton mills owned by Bengalis	75	810	23
4. Total	239	3557	
5. Abandoned units under takas 1·5 million	400	214	

It may be seen from the above table that, with the nationalisation of the larger abandoned enterprises, 77 per cent of assets in the modern industrial sector were already under public ownership. The Bengali enterprises added another takas 810 million of assets to the public sector and these in turn accounted for only 23 per cent of public sector industrial assets. In perspective, the takeover of Bengali-owned enterprises therefore was an act of marginal significance once the basic nationalisation decision had been taken. The Bengali enterprises in fact accounted for only 34 per cent of fixed assets in the jute sector and 53 per cent of fixed assets in the cotton textile sector.

As part of the nationalisation proclamation, the government set up the first 10 sector corporations indicated in Table 7.1, under whom were distributed the 238 enterprises taken over from the sources identified in Table 7.1. This explicitly implied the demise of E.P.I.D.C./B.I.D.C., whose enterprises were to be distributed amongst the corporations along with the assets and staff of the B.I.D.C. head office.

The 433 abandoned enterprises with assets under takas 1·5 million were to be disinvested. First preference was, however, to be given to workers' co-operatives. The task of valuation and sale was entrusted to a Disinvestment Board under the Ministry of Industries.

In actual practice it took a while for the board to be set up and start disinvestment procedures. In the interim period there was further enlargement of the public sector. In August 1972 all of 30 abandoned tanneries were taken out from the purview of the board, even though the assets of none of these units exceeded takas 1·5 million, and they were declared to be nationalised. They were henceforth placed under a Tanneries Corporation. The main considerations here were the virtual standstill in production in the abandoned tanneries and the vacuum in Bengali entrepreneurship in this sector. Traditionally this industry in Bangladesh had been dominated by the Chiniotis, a community from West Pakistan, and all abandoned enterprises were in fact owned by this community.

Two welfare foundations set up by the government also made inroads into the disinvestment list. The Sena Kalyan Samitha was a successor organisation to the Fauji Foundation, in turn inheritor to the British post-war resettlement fund for ex-army personnel. This foundation already owned four enterprises but has since been given nineteen abandoned enterprises from the Disinvestment Board.

A new foundation, the Freedom Fighters Foundation, set up for rehabilitation of the freedom fighters in the liberation war and war victims, has been given ownership and control of another fifteen enterprises. Both the foundations control a medley of industries with little in common except a potential for generating income.

A number of units with assets below takas 1·5 million have been taken over by the corporations as part of a balancing programme. For instance, the re-rolling mills have been taken over by the Steel Corporation, a flour mill by Food and Allied Products, and a number of other such units have been put under the corporations.

As of today no unit has actually been sold to the private sector, so that encroachments of the public sector are by no means at an end. It remains to be seen how many workers' co-operatives appear, to constitute yet another segment of the public sector. A number have been constituted since the principles for disinvesting abandoned units were publicised. The policy here is to let workers in the units form co-operatives involving at least 80 per cent of the workers of the enterprise, when they will be sold the unit against a 15 per cent down payment against the value of the assets of the unit.

Once this process works itself out, the residual will be sold to private parties. Here it is hoped that expatriate Bengalis may take up some units on payment of foreign exchange, for which some incentives have been provided.

VI. INSTITUTIONAL FRAMEWORK FOR THE PUBLIC SECTOR

As it stands then, the public or social sector in industry covers the 280 enterprises controlled by sector corporations, the foundations and eventually some co-operatives. Of these, for purposes of analysing management practices and problems, it is most relevant to look at the corporations which account for over 95 per cent of fixed assets in the public sector.

When it became apparent that the social strategy of the government was going to invest the state with responsibility for such a large number of enterprises as compared with the 53 managed by E P.I.D.C./B.I.D.C., the need for working out an institutional framework which could guarantee efficient management became paramount in policy planning.

Bangladesh's experience with the public sector had previously been limited to industries run by E.P.I.D.C. Pre-liberation experience indicated that the investment of takas 1700 million financed through B.I.D.C. was generating a very low rate of return. Many of the 53 units were in fact running at a loss.

The problems of E.P.I.D.C. had been subject to scrutiny in a number of studies. All these, in the light of their assessment of the organisation, had made recommendations for change. To enunciate and discuss the points raised in these reports would be outside the purview of this paper. It may merely be mentioned that all studies found a consensus in suggesting:

(1) the need to break away from the over-centralised and bureaucracy-dominated structure represented by B.I.D.C.;
(2) the need for professional management with clearly defined lines of responsibility;

(3) the need for creating conditions where the enterprises could function with sufficient freedom to be able to secure their own commercial viability.

The consequences arising from these disabilities were very apparent to the government, who did not need much convincing about the need to redefine the institutional arrangements for the public sector in the post-nationalisation period.

The first decision, which previous administrations in Pakistan had been playing around with for a decade, was the break up of the B.I.D.C. conglomerate structure. In its place came the ten new corporations. The corporations were defined by the technical similarity of products and processes of the enterprises grouped under them.

There may have been some scope for increasing the number of corporations where the range of products became too wide or the ambit of responsibility too large. But here, as in other cases, the awareness of scarce managerial talent tended to inhibit proliferation. Obviously as the public sector grows and management resources expand, new corporations may be carved out of the existing ones or built up to accommodate new industries, as was done with the Tanneries Corporation, set up five months after the others.

VII. THE ASSUMPTIONS UNDERLYING THE FRAMEWORK

Whilst the corporation in practice became the focal point of management in the nationalised sector, the *inter-se* relations between the various tiers responsible for the nationalised sector needed definition. The original policy conception sought to make all enterprises the primary base for the public sector. These were to be left free to manage their enterprises on a commercial basis, with a view to attaining their commercial viability through freedom to buy, sell, hire, fire and raise funds from the now state-owned banking system. The chief executive has, however, to be responsible to the corporation which retained the authority to appoint him.

The corporation was thus cast as a supervisory organisation, to evaluate the performance of the enterprises, co-ordinate personnel, finances and commercial policies where deemed necessary, and to solve specific problems which were beyond the capacity of the individual enterprise.

The corporation was in turn to be responsible to the government for the efficient performance of the enterprises under it. The immediate problem became one of defining the relations as between corporation and government. As conceived, the chairmen were to be directly responsible to the Minister for Industries and would, in effect, function as his secretariat in all matters pertaining to their respective industries.

The minister was to be served by a small secretariat of his own in the Ministry of Industries, to be known as the Nationalised Industries Division (N.I.D.), under a secretary. This was to be staffed by a small body of professionals designed to provide specific technical assistance to the minister in dealing with the corporation's diverse problems. The relation with the minister was envisaged as a lateral one rather than as a tier between the corporations and the minister.

The guiding idea remained to free corporations from the nagging interference of the secretariat bureaucracy which had characterised and bedevilled E.P.I.D.C.'s role in the government. The principle of accountability on which the system was to rest demanded this freedom of action for chairmen. In order to get people who were worthy of this responsibility and could fit into the concept of a commercially oriented public sector, it was aimed to recruit professionally competent executives with a background of commercial and managerial experience. This again was dictated by the experiences of E.P.I.D.C., which between 1965 and 1972 had seven chairmen all of whom were permanent civil servants. For them the assignment was either a purgatory for past failures or a staging post to higher office, so that they had neither the commitment nor could acquire the experience to make a success of their assignments.

VIII. WORKERS' PARTICIPATION

A further departure from past practice was visualised in the need to involve workers in the affairs of the nationalised sector. In a capitalist dominated society the basic contradictions between labour and capital had carried over to the public sector where workers tended to see public sector managers as another part of the traditional instruments of exploitation. Labour relations were thus as taut in the public sector as elsewhere, and perhaps more so, given the difficulty for public managers to buy off corrupt trade union leaders.

As part of this same commitment to create a socialist and democratic society the concept of workers' participation in the affairs of the enterprise was seen as a means of transcending the traditional dichotomy between worker and management.

Policy in this direction evolved from a committee set up by the Planning Commission. This recommended that two elected representatives of the workers sit on the five-member management boards of all enterprises and workers participate equally in the factory workers' committees. To give workers a stake in the performance as much as in the affairs of the enterprise, the report recommended that they should also be given a share in the profits.

Workers' participation was seen in the interim phase as being functionally necessary to compensate for the lack of trained socialist cadres who could help in motivating workers in the enterprises. Till such time as such cadres were placed in the enterprises much greater reliance, it was felt, had to be placed on purely traditional motivations of responsibility and material gain. This was in fact seen also as the basis on which the top professional management had to be recruited and retained, since few from amongst this class were expected to have the requisite political commitment to the building up of a socialist economy.

IX. THE PROBLEMS FACED BY THE NATIONALISED SECTOR

It is only nine months since the nationalisation decrees were enunciated, and by any standards it is too early to make a definitive evaluation of the validity of the original conception on which nationalisation was to function or to evaluate realistically the actual performance of the public sector.

Personnel problems. The objective of building up the nationalised sector through professional managers was realised in the appointment of the corporation chairmen. Of the nine chairmen initially appointed, three were brought in straight from the private sector where they had established reputations for entrepreneurial ability. Two others were outstanding professionals in their field who had started their careers in P.I.D.C., where they had played seminal roles but had currently moved to the private sector. Three had been public sector managers and executives with excellent reputations in their respective areas of responsibility. One was a civil servant but with a background in economics who had been in E.P.I.D.C. for some years as a director. Two recent appointments have been from the finance service.

As part of this practice, directors of the corporations have also tended to be professionals either with a private sector background or a long association with public sector industry in their professional capacity.

At the enterprise level the task has been made more difficult by the entrepreneurial vacuum created by the departure of the Pakistanis and the general shortage of trained management. This gap was partially bridged by persuading Bengali owners of the nationalised enterprises in jute and cotton mills to stay on and serve the public sector. These accounted for seventy-five units; a sudden vacuum could have had serious effects on production in these enterprises. Under the nationalisation order boards of directoıs of these particular enterprises were asked, until further notice, to continue to discharge their managerial functions, albeit under the supervision of the corporations. The original idea had here been to dissolve these boards immediately and simply ask the chief executive of the enterprise to stay on as the chief executive for the public sector enterprise. His board was to be supplemented by a corporation nominee, a representative of a publicly-owned financing institution, and two elected representatives of the workers.

It was recognised that this expedient of retaining former owners might create suspicion in the minds of the workers about the socialist intentions of the government and that former owners might give currency to these apprehensions by using their position to siphon off resources from the enterprises into their own pockets. This was again seen as a necessary price to pay for preventing any consequential dislocation in production.

All these expectations were in effect realised over these nine months. Workers' suspicions were aroused, some speculation did take place, but production in these units went up rather than down in the post-nationalisation period.

Over the past two months the boards of directors in jute and cotton have been gradually dissolved. In the case of jute this was done at one stroke in November 1972, but for cotton the process has been more gradual. As planned, most of the old chief executives have been asked to stay on but, based on their performances since March, a number of them are being deliberately excluded from this invitation.

The biggest problem had been faced in the abandoned units. In former B.I.D.C.-owned units or Bengali private sector units lines of management were available. In this area the corporations merely inherited the *ad hoc* administrators appointed by the government immediately after liberation. Some had done a good job, in many cases supported by responsible participation by workers in the management.

In others, the inherited problems and general scarcities had proved too much for inexperienced administrators operating without supervision, in a policy vacuum. In others, these circumstances had been exploited, occasionally in connivance with some trade unionists, to milk the enterprise systematically of whatever resources it could yield up. Here the corporation inherited moribund units with empty coffers, warehouses and inventories and depleted assets. A large number of these administrators have now been either fired or relocated in less sensitive jobs. More may follow once the full audit of all enterprises by their respective corporations has been completed.

Problems of production. Whilst manpower scarcities persist, an unresolved problem still remains in the rewards structure for the nationalised sector. The original intention of giving both workers and managers a stake in performance persists. This will remove the image of salaried state functionaries running the public sector and apply commercial standards to remuneration practices. This may generate some tension from the inevitable inequalities which must emerge within and between enterprises. Incomes and fiscal policy measures may partially cope with this, but the inequalities must persist albeit on a more just basis, if the incentive system is to serve any purpose.

In practice no incomes policy for the nationalised sector has as yet emerged. A pay commission is evaluating fixed remunerations but an effective incentive system still needs to be worked out. A Yugoslav team has examined this and a further study may be forthcoming as a basis for policy.

At the base the managerial problems are compounded by the general state of the economic infrastructure. Persistent scarcity of spare-parts and raw materials has perhaps been the critical constraint in virtually all units. The need to rebuild very low inventories required a crash import programme. In the initial months, lack of foreign exchange resources delayed issue of import licences till May 1972. Since then a higher rate of licensing has been offset by the tardiness not just of import procedures but of programming and eventual despatch of the imports. Consequently most units continue to operate well below capacity. Inadequacies in transport, power, banking and finance remain, independent of institutional change or managerial resources. Improvements over time have in turn been reflected in improved performances. For example, the opening of Chittagong and Chalna ports had a dramatic impact on jute goods exports and production.

Labour problems. Whilst all these problems are a function of time, the crisis on the labour front remains more persistent. In spite of the proclaimed commitment to workers' participation, all enterprises have been chronically plagued with labour unrest. This takes the form of various demands for material and other benefits which are put forward through the medium of the 'gherao', a more militant version of the traditional strike where managers are surrounded and confined until demands have been conceded. As a result large sums have been extracted by the workers, either as *ad hoc* benefits or in terms of higher wages and benefits. Managers complain that this situation is compounded by increases in workers' indiscipline and reduced efficiency on the part of the workers.

There is no doubt that liberation found workers in a much stronger position in society than ever before. They had been in the vanguard of the liberation struggle both in terms of sacrifice and resistance. They had a long history of exploitation and neglect in the capitalist-oriented Pakistan of Ayub and Yahiya Khan. In the heady atmosphere of liberation it was widely expected that not only would past neglect be compensated but workers would be singled out as special beneficiaries of the new order.

These hopes were disappointed by the sheer dimension of the general economic crisis. Whatever was extracted as increased wages and benefits was threatened by the price inflation which followed liberation. Devaluation of the taka, along with scarcities in all basic wage goods, was matched by a downward redistribution by incomes where labour were beneficiaries. In spite of the fact that most workers got rations of foodgrains, kerosine and edible oils at controlled prices, inflation eroded much of the newly secured benefits for the workers because of price rises in the unprotected areas of the market.

This disappointment was fuelled by the failure of expectations. Rival trade unions promised everything from complete workers' ownership of all industries to a demand for a major share of profits and complete control over management.

The concentrated character of the urban working class and their higher level of political consciousness which had grown out of their long history of political struggle heightened the militancy of the workers. Trade unions increased greatly in numbers between liberation and the end of October 1972.

This multiplication of unions was a progressive development in that it brought a much larger segment of the labour force within the ambit of organisational control. This factor was, however, neutralised by the fact that unions were not linked by craft, industry or any community of economic interests, but by political, regional and personal affiliations. Various federations which cut across the industrial sector were loyal to diverse political parties. Others were welded together by a powerful personality who might be motivated by political or personal loyalties. These federations cut across industries and regions so that within the same industry multiple unions of varying strength might operate within different enterprises in different regions.

Under these circumstances labour unrest became, in many cases, a function of the power struggle between different unions who competed for the loyalty of workers in outbidding each other in their promises to the workers and the militancy with which they could make good their promises.

Such a development not only threatened effective revival of

production but struck at the very roots of workers' participation. Where multiple unions operated in an essentially competitive framework, the concept of workers' representatives becoming an organic part of the management process was seriously prejudiced. Inter-union dialectics threatened to replace the traditional contradiction between labour and management. The elected workers' representatives were likely to be faced with pressures from defeated union rivals which could force them to become spokesmen of the management board or simply bargaining agents for workers on the board.

In a multi-party system committed to democratic processes it appears that this crisis can only be resolved by a general political consensus which is secured by massive political authority of the government. As yet this has not been forthcoming. It remains to be seen whether the post-election period permits the post-election government to make the necessary political effort to secure a consensus amongst all the various unions and political groups in support of workers' participation.

If they succeed, then the new order will have to be secured by a major effort in training workers to their new responsibilities. Hence the whole question of management training for the public sector is under review and policy measures in this direction should be forthcoming shortly when a Planning Commission committee submits its recommendations.

The institutional format. Whilst the critical problems remain at the enterprise level, the overall institutional format remains of considerable consequence to the performance of the nationalised sector. To assess this one has to evaluate the position of the corporations in the current administrative framework.

As yet no rules of business, defining relations between the various tiers of the nationalised sector, have been forthcoming. Whilst basic principles defining these relations had been enunciated in the policy paper on which nationalisation had been enacted, it was felt that such rules should only be formalised after professional evaluation of the nationalised sector's role. A leading firm of management consultants from the United Kingdom were employed for this task.

They have presented the first part of their report recently defining the relationship between the corporation and government.

In their task they have been guided by the experience of the corporations in the last nine months, which appears to have sustained the validity of the original assumptions on which nationalisation was based. Their proposals have therefore been only marginally different from the original conception of the policy planners. They basically support the principle of a direct relationship between the minister and the corporations who they argue should be given both the status and responsibility analogous to that of a secretary of government. They vest co-ordination and policy-making in a board made up of the chairman under the minister but aided by special advisers for different problems. N.I.D. is to be reconstructed, with the secretary replaced by a co-ordination secretary with a status subordinate to the chairman. He will perform purely secretariat functions to the board and advisory functions to the minister.

These recommendations have emerged out of the working problems of the corporations. In the absence of any formalised rules of business, the relations between N.I.D. and the corporations have been largely on an *ad hoc* basis. This has led to occasional difficulties.

Problems have arisen out of policies of purchase, out of selling policies, and out of the traditional dependence on planning and finance ministries for release of investment funds and foreign exchange. Budgetary constraints are likely to retain this dependence on planning authorities for external funding. But for local resources, more reliance is sought to be placed on bilateral dealings between corporations and the state-owned financing institutions. Similarly, centralised purchases are being reduced. For example, imports vested with the state trading corporations are being passed back to the industrial corporations and enterprises. Jute export sales are being transacted by enterprises, though under reference to the corporation.

Pricing problems. As part of this same policy of decentralisation and emphasis on commercial criteria, pricing policy is being revised. Fixation of prices is as far as possible being made the responsibility of the corporation and enterprises. Here they are guided by market and profit considerations. They have, however, tended to discipline themselves in the scarcity market of post-liberation Bangladesh by keeping ex-factory prices below the equilibrium price. This was designed as a benefit to the consumer and an anti-inflationary devise. In practice, however, the premium has been absorbed by middlemen without any real benefit to consumers. It appears that where scarcities persist any attempt to enforce price control in the public sector at the enterprise level will have to be matched with government intervention in the marketing sector.

Price-formation of certain key products, such as sugar, fertilisers, newsprint, produced by a state-owned monopoly still remains centrally determined. For historical as much as social reasons these have been priced below cost to the enterprise, which has been forced to incur heavy losses. Whilst conceding the need to keep some control over prices of such items, the new policy aims at nationalising the subsidy element to the consumers. Rather than pass the burden of the subsidy on to the producer the objective will be to fix his price at a level where some profit is possible. The distributing agency which pays this price may then sell to the end-user at a loss which will be reflected in the annual budget. As a result the social cost of subsidies will be more clearly evaluated whilst state enterprises will be evaluated on their ability to earn higher profits by cutting costs rather than be left to take refuge behind enforced losses.

X. THE PROBLEMS OF TRANSITION

Most of the problems enunciated above remain problems of an economy and society in transition. Problems of inventories, marketing and communications will improve and are already doing so. The jute industry is producing at 88 per cent of the efficiency realised in the pre-liberation period 1969–70. Cotton textiles have already reached this level. The Chittagong steel plant, the largest unit in Bangladesh and chronically sick, has in most shops reached record output. In virtually all enterprises, production during July–October 1972 has shown a substantially higher average level compared with the January–June 1972 average. In most cases production is approaching the 1969–70 levels and will reach and surpass these by mid 1973, the end of the financial year. A number of units remain closed or sick largely due to the material constraints spelt out above. Their specific problems are in process of solution and one has regularly received reports of idle units reactivated by the corporation concerned.

This is not to say that the corporations own administrative weaknesses have not slowed down recovery. But the very fact that a number of agencies, equipped with some of the best professionals in the country, have been made directly responsible for the performance of all 284 units has generated great pressure at the base to get output moving. The sheer dimensions of the problems in relation to human and material resources at hand would have acted as its own constraint. But the fact that this has been carried through following the traumatic impact of rationalisation as well as nationalisation speaks well of what has been achieved to date.

XI. THE FUTURE

Whatever successes are recorded, certain fundamental problems will require solution within a wider perspective. Labour problems are certainly beyond the realm of mere policy planning and require political solution on the ground. The commitment to operate a multi-party system within a democratic framework will generate a variety of pressures on the public sector which may militate against the most indicated latitude for action required by the public sector. Institutional safeguards may be evolved, but again the basic problems demand a political solution. The awareness that the efficient performance of the large public sector is now of critical significance, not just for the economy but as a demonstration of the validity of the nation's social goals, greatly improves the prospects for confronting these problems in the days ahead.

8 Planning for Industrialisation of Bangladesh

Muzaffar Ahmad[1]

BANGLADESH PLANNING COMMISSION

I. THE BACKGROUND

It is necessary to begin by understanding the setting in which planning for industrialisation of Bangladesh is being discussed. Bangladesh is one of the smallest countries in the world, with 55 thousand square miles of area of which 35 thousand square miles are agricultural land including fallows, 8·6 thousand square miles are forest, 10 thousand square miles are non-cultivable land including rivers and urban areas. It has to support a population of some 74 millions, the eighth largest in the world. Density per square mile averages 1342, one of the highest. But population is not evenly distributed and the density varies from about 400 to 2000 per square mile. The annual rate of population growth is estimated at about 3 per cent.

Conventionally measured, income per head for 1972–3 is estimated to have been takas 425 at 1969–70 prices and in terms of 'normal' per capita income (defined as the level that would be expected under average conditions, apart from post-war dislocations, and without any further capital investment). At current 'normal' prices (defined to exclude current scarcity effects on prices) income per head is estimated to be takas 584, or only about $75.

As is to be expected, agriculture is the predominant occupation, providing activity for over 80 per cent of the civilian labour force which is now estimated at 25 million. Agriculture contributes about 55·3 per cent of G.D.P., which at 1969–70 prices is estimated at takas 43,210 million. Basically, a single-cropping pattern prevails and output per acre is deplorably low (i.e. rice 1039 lbs. per acre, jute 1200 lb., sugarcane 18 tons, tobacco 805 lb., tea 627 lb.). The emphasis of agricultural production is on four major crops – rice (11·7 m. tons), jute (7 m. bales), tea (67 m. lb.) and sugarcane (7·48 m. tons). Other crops are potatoes (9 m. tons), tobacco

---

[1] The author is chief of the Industries Division of the Planning Commission of the Government of the People's Republic of Bangladesh. The views expressed in this paper represent the author's own viewpoint and do not necessarily reflect the views of the Agency to which he belongs.

(85 m. lb.), pulses (0·24 m. tons), fruits and vegetables. Of rice there are three principal varieties. In recent years high-yielding varieties have been introduced. Double cropping has made certain headway. Use of improved inputs are limited (176 thousand tons of urea, 65 thousand tons of T.S.P., 15 thousand tons of potash, 3 thousand tubewells, some 8 thousand extension workers, 23 thousand tons of improved seed).

The pattern of landholding is inequitable. Of the total holdings of agricultural land in 1960, 52 per cent were of less than 2·5 acres, 45 per cent were between 2·5 and 12·5 acres and only 3 per cent were more than 12·5 acres. About 23 per cent of the rural population constitute landless labourers and 15 per cent do not possess more than 1 acre of land.

Foodgrains provide 77 per cent of the calorie intake of the population. Per capita availability of foodgrains, including grain used for other inputs, in 1969–70 was a little over 16 oz. per day. There has been an annual average deficit of about 3 m. tons of food grains in normal years, despite a barely subsistence level of income. Per capita consumption of meat is 6 lb.; of fish 20·6 lb.; of tea 0·23 lb.; of pulses 6·68 lb. per annum.

It has been estimated that the economy of Bangladesh grew at about 4·4 per cent per annum during the period 1965–70. This rate of growth has been chiefly determined by the conditions in agriculture. Naturally, a year of better agricultural performance was also a better year for the economy as a whole. Agriculture on average grew at about 3·3 per cent a year, whereas large-scale industry grew at 16·1 per cent and utilities at 11·2 per cent. During this period the net investment/G.D.P. ratio stood at about 5 per cent. (Total net investment in the public and private sectors during the five years was takas 4544 million whereas G.D.P. for the five years was takas 89,500 million). The marginal saving rate was estimated at 10 per cent and it may have been lower.

Literacy today stands at around 17 per cent. Educational facilities are meagre; only 53·42 per cent of the children in the age group 6–11 go to school; in the secondary level (12–16) only 23·47 per cent of male and 7·11 per cent of female are enrolled; at the higher level, including vocational education, only 3·15 per cent of the population in that age group (17–22) avail themselves of the existing opportunities. At the higher education level, around 87 per cent go for general education and only 13 per cent for technical and vocational education.

Physical housing conditions are deplorable. The average number of rooms per household is 1·78 in the rural areas and 1·83 in the urban areas. The average number of persons per room is estimated at 3·01 in the rural and 3·11 in the urban areas. In the rural areas only 1·8 per cent of the houses are permanent or semi-permanent; 77·1 per cent are temporary and 21·1 per cent unclassified. In the urban areas, only 27·6 per cent are in the permanent or semi-permanent category.

Life expectancy is low, and infant mortality high. Incidence of malaria, tuberculosis, gastro-enteritis is high. But medical facilities are limited. There are 40 government hospitals and 8 medical institutes. There is about 1 doctor per 6200 persons and the situation is further aggravated by uneven geographical distribution of medical facilities. There is only one hospital bed per 10,000 persons.

The national railways, with about 1770 route-mileage, play an important role in the transport sector supported by 2398 miles of metalled roads and 4995 miles of river-ways. There were an estimated 65,000 motor vehicles in 1969 of which 5500 were buses and 8900 trucks. The railways with 18,000 wagons, carried about 1·29 million tons of cargo in 1968–9; their 1208 coaches carried some 73 million passengers. The river-ways carried 2·73 million tons of cargo in the mechanised fleet; there is no estimate available for cargoes carried by country boats. They also carried 26·5 million passengers in mechanised carriers; again no estimate for country boats is available.

In the energy sector, the total installed capacity in 1969 was 488 mW; consumption per head was 13 kWh and the total number of consumers stood around 213,000. Rural electrification was available to 250 villages only.

The trade balance of Bangladesh has been negative for some time past. The deficit reached its peak in 1968–9 when it amounted to takas 822 million. Imports, analysed by economic category, in 1969/70 amounted to 27·69 per cent for consumer goods (takas 502 m.), raw materials for consumer goods 20·96 per cent (takas 380 m.), raw material for capital goods 9·04 per cent (takas 164 m.) and capital goods 42·31 per cent (takas 767 m.), with a total import of takas 1813 m. Foodgrain import during the same period amounted to 505,000 tons of rice and 1·1 million tons of wheat. Of a total 1642 million takas of exports from Bangladesh in 1969/70, raw jute accounted for takas 762 million (46·41 per cent), jute manufactures for takas 768 million (46·77 per cent); other important exports were hides and skins, tea, paper and matches; the last three items went wholly to Pakistan.

II. INDUSTRIAL DEVELOPMENT BEFORE 1970

In contrast to 1947, when the part of the world that now constitutes Bangladesh could boast of only a handful of industrial units – a few textile and sugar mills and some jute bailing presses – we begin today with a larger industrial base. Measured at 1964–5 factor cost, the manufacturing sector in 1969–70 contributed 2128 million rupees to a total G.D.P. of 24,536 million rupees. Of this, 1422 million rupees was contributed by large-scale industries and 691 million rupees by small-scale industries. The annual compound growth rate of the large-scale industries in the five-year period from 1964–5 to 1969–70 was 16·1 per cent, in contrast to a 9·3 per cent growth in the preceding five-year period. Small-scale industries exhibited a growth rate of 2·7 per cent in both these five-year periods.

The number of registered factories in Bangladesh in 1968–9 was 3130, of which 791 were in the textile sector, 576 in the chemical sector, 406 in the food manufacturing sector, 257 in the metal products sector, 207 in the sector of footwear, wearing apparel and made-up textiles, 149 in leather and leather products, and 143 in printing, publishing and allied industries. There are a large number of small non-registered units as well. These industries in 1966–7 employed 229,235 persons. In terms of gross value added in 1966–7, manufacture in Bangladesh contributed a total of 1257 million rupees. Of this, textiles contributed 431 million rupees, food manufacturing 301 million, tobacco 183 million, chemicals and chemical products 121 million. Electrical and other machinery, apparatus, appliances, etc., contributed only 71 million. The total value of fixed assets in industry in 1965–6 was 1769 million rupees, of which textiles accounted for 776 million, food products 261 million, chemical and chemical products 231 million, and paper and paper products 211 million.

By 1969–70, the jute industry produced 593 thousand tons of jute goods; cotton textiles produced 105 million lb. of cotton yarn and 69 million yards of cotton cloth. The sugar industry produced 88 thousand tons of sugar (with a capacity for 169,000); cement industry produced 64 thousand tons of cement (with a capacity for 150,000). The fertiliser industry produced 94 thousand tons of urea (with a capacity for 406 thousand). The paper industry produced 75 thousand tons of paper (with a capacity for 84 thousand).

Much of this growth of the period 1965–70 had been stimulated either by sponsored association with the public sector, or by deliberate concessions, or by public sector development. In jute many of the mills were established in association with P.I.D.C./E.P.I.D.C. In sugar and paper almost all the plants were built by P.I.D.C./ E.P.I.D.C., as also in fertiliser, cement, and other instances. The private sector was predominant in cotton, in other textiles, in leather, tobacco, pharmaceuticals, in other chemicals, in tea, food, and beverages. Heavy industries such as the steel mill, and shipbuilding, were in the public sector, while lighter engineering and electric accessories were in the private sector.

In this process of growth, participation of the so-called non-locals was substantial, as was to be evidenced by the number of units taken over as abandoned units by the Bangladesh government. The non-locals not only invested their money and took advantage of the opportunities, privileges and patronage available under the system that then existed, but also provided substantial managerial skill in almost all sectors, including textile and tea. The only sizeable local managerial class was that which was growing under the supervision of the public sector during the later stages of E.P.I.D.C.-sponsored enterprises. In many cases the so-called non-locals provided the skilled workers and in certain cases the unskilled labour as well.

Though the Industrial Development Corporation helped the growth of large-scale industrial units, the public sector ownership was limited to the heavy engineering and chemical industries, to the paper, cement and steel industries, where the numbers of units were few, and to sugar where the public sector had a virtual monopoly. Attempts were made to disinvest many of these units on the accepted principle of a mixed economy in which the public sector was to supplement and not to supplant the private sector.

III. CHANGES WITH THE EMERGENCE OF BANGLADESH

The emergence of Bangladesh radically changed the whole framework of industrial ownership and policy. The government took over all units owned by non-locals as abandoned units and then proceeded to nationalise all units in the jute, textile and sugar sectors and to establish corporations for jute, textiles, sugar, engineering and shipbuilding, steel, paper and board, chemicals, fertilisers and pharmaceuticals, food and allied products, gas, oil and minerals, and tanneries, in addition to a fisheries, forest products and small industries corporation. A cottage industries corporation is still in the offing. The government has brought nearly 250 enterprises with 89 per cent of all industrial fixed assets under public ownership.

Further, the government has proceeded to affirm repeatedly that socialism is one of the four basic principles of this state policy. The term socialism has as yet not been defined either in philosophic or concrete terms. Certain clarifications are, however, available. The constitution allows private property within limits and co-operative ownership within the legal framework of the country. The industrial policy aims to encourage the private sector within limits set in terms of fixed assets for any single unit of enterprise. The same policy will allow foreign private investment as a minority shareholder in association with a public corporation. Moreover the government will undertake promotional and investment activities in the small industries sector. The full implications for income, pricing and taxation policies, in the context of the socialist objectives of the government, have not yet been worked out in detail, though it is expected that this will soon be done.

In this changed context, the government has deliberately taken over a major responsibility for running a large number of enterprises efficiently, not only in the interest of the enterprises themselves but also in the interest of economy, with the intention to generate surplus, to take advantage of external economics, and to exploit to the greatest possible extent the opportunities for growth and employment, in the general context of the national policy. This is not easy when a trained managerial class is lacking, general efficiency is low, commitment to 'ideology' is weak, the level of literacy is poor. Further, the conflict between self- and social-interest, between labour and capital, between management and bureaucracy, and between various socio-political pressure groups make the inherent contradictions more involved and complicated than they would be in a monolithic, autocratic or regimented society.

Though the Presidential Order setting up sector corporations was published on the 26 March 1972, the sector corporations were unable to start functioning even at a minimum level before May, and in most cases not before the end of June or early July, when the Industrial Development Corporation was allowed to disintegrate. It is thus too early to judge the performance of the nationalised sectors. It will be realised that most of them have still to set up their head offices; furthermore, the regulations governing their conduct have yet to be published.

However inadequate the basis for assessment, it is of interest to record the performance of the nationalised industries since January and to observe how far the various sectors have recovered from their war-time difficulties. In most cases, data for a period later than October are not yet available and hence assessment of the performance since nationalisation is a little preliminary. Most of the corporations have been busy taking over their units, streamlining administration, meeting immediate needs for material and working capital, and in facing demands from labour. In part the aggregate figures for January to June are misleading because in the initial months production was virtually at a standstill and it was only in the latter part of the period that production picked up. This is particularly true for jute and cotton textiles.

Performance in the jute manufacturing sector has been picking up

steadily since March. The monthly average production for January–
June 1972 was 28,740 tons; it rose to 42,540 for July–October. The
average monthly production in 1969–70 had been 48,956 tons. This
is a remarkable achievement since in other socialist countries
institutional changes of this magnitude have, in the short run,
tended seriously to disrupt production. As things stand, the latest
production figures for October are now up to 87 per cent of the
1969–70 monthly average for the industry. Full recovery is expected
to have been achieved by the end of the year. There is, however,
still much ground to make up in this case since in pre-liberation days
the efficiency of the industry was still well below its rated capacity,
averaging about 60 per cent compared with the 80 per cent achieved
by the Indian jute industry. Much ground still has to be made up
under nationalisation to realise the full potential of the industry.

Cotton textiles have performed equally well since nationalisation.
From a virtual standstill, monthly average production has increased
from 4·4 million lb. of yarn in January–June to a monthly average
of 7·3 million lb. in July–October 1972; the monthly average of
1969–70 was 8·8 million lb. Cloth production has fared even better,
and production has risen from a monthly average of 2·2 million yds.
in January–June to 4·9 million yds. for July–October 1972. This
may with satisfaction be compared with the monthly average of
cloth production in 1969–70, which stood also at 4·9 million yds. If
one allows for the critical situation with regard to raw cotton supply,
the spate of labour unrest in the industry, the upheaval caused by
nationalisation and the abandonment of many units by their
erstwhile owners, this is a record to reckon with.

The chemical sector has been functioning much below capacity.
Fertiliser plants have yet to achieve 50 per cent of potential capacity
because of lack of proper maintenance, labour trouble and shortage
of spares. The Ghorasal urea plant was not functioning till mid-
August and two T.S.P. plants have yet to start production. Even
thus production has increased from a monthly average of 354 tons
in January–June to 13,658 tons in July–October. Other chemical
plants have suffered from shortage of material and also lack of
working capital but their production has again picked up in recent
months. Pharmaceuticals have also registered low production due
to non-availability of materials and to labour problems in the early
months of the year, but they report rather better production in
July–October. They expect much better production in future when
raw materials inventories have been fully rebuilt.

The engineering and shipbuilding sector has inherited a number of
poorly conceived projects from B.I.D.C. It is now suffering from the
loss of markets in Pakistan and inadequate local demand. But steps

TABLE 8.1

CAPACITY UTILISATION IN PUBLIC SECTOR PROJECTS
(January–June 1972 and July–October 1972)

Sl. No.	Group of industries	No. of Units	Capacity monthly average	Monthly average production		Percentage of capacity utilised (monthly average)		Average monthly production 1969–70	Remarks
				Jan.–June 1972	July–Oct. 1972	Jan.–June 1972	July–Oct. 1972		
(1)	(2)	(3)	(4)	(5)	(6)	(7)	(8)	(9)	(10)
1.	Jute (thousand tons)	73	66·0	28·7	42·5	44	64	49·0	Production for October not available
2.	Cotton	43							
	Yarn (m. lbs.)		11·2	4·4	7·3	39	65	8·8	–
	Cloth (m. yds.)		10·1	2·2	4·9	22	49	4·9	–
3.	Sugar (thousand tons)	15	28·0	7·9	–	28	–	15·6	Because of seasonality, there is no sugar production April–Oct
4.	Steel (1 steel mill) (thousand tons)		53·6	9·4	12·6	17	24	10·8	October production not available
5.	Basic metals (thousand tons)	8	8·6	1·0	1·1	12	13	2·8	–
6.	Engineering industries								
	Diesel plant (engines)	1	250	111	166	44	66	106	
	Shipbuilding (million takas)	1	1·60	–	0·91	–	57	0·80	(Naravangonj dockyard only)
	Other engineering units	6	–	–	–	from 2% to 30%	from 13% to 73%	15% to 80% of capacity utilised	Production values not available; in different units for different products; the capacity utilisation

8.	Oil products (tons)	3	576	380	473	66	82	892	Includes oil and vegetable ghee
9.	Beverages (thousand bottles)	1	793	180	201	23	25	793	
10.	Fertiliser (thousand tons)	2	37·2	0·4	13·7	9	36	8·0	No production at Ghorasal in 1969–70
11.	Pharmaceutical	2							
	(a) tablets (millions)		27·34	—	7·1	—	26	27·2	Production figures for Squbb of Bangladesh not available
	(b) injections (thousand ampules)		382	—	116	—	30	382	
	(c) others		—	—	—	—	40	—	
12.	Chemicals (tons)	5	2,502	602	825	24	33	—	
13.	Glass (thousand sq. ft)	1	531	—	631	—	119	—	
14.	Paper and board (tons)	4	7,219	3,481	4,332	47	60	7,747	Excludes 1 unit for which information was not available
15.	Wood processing and wood products	2							
	Processed wood (c. ft)		4,312	788	756	17	17	4,312	
	Wood products (sq. ft)		2,819	2,866	6,171	10	20	2,819	

are being taken to gear up administration, to discover markets and to step up production. The shipbuilding sector has picked up production with the recovery of steel plants and the reconstruction and expansion of the river transport activities. The same is the case with the diesel plant in which diesel engines for irrigation are produced. The steel sector inherited the Chittagong steel mill which was B.I.D.C.'s biggest loser. It has had to face serious labour problems, shortages of skill, inadequate supply of materials, an irrational import policy and lack of working capital. Actual production has in the past been much below capacity; the steel mill was only operating one furnace instead of four. In spite of these problems production in the steel mill is now picking up, and is beginning to feed the shipbuilding industry. Attempts to rationalise the capacity and to integrate it with re-rolling mills are under way. Outside the steel mill a number of component units in this sector are moving towards normalcy.

The food sector has been operating below capacity for such varied reasons as non-availability of crude soya bean oil, smuggling of shrimps, inadequate supplies of tobacco and of cigarette paper. Here again the sector is slowly picking up and can expect to exceed its pre-war performance. Sugar production is at a standstill due to non-availability of cane and will only be marginal in the current season.

The forest industries sector is the one area of unrelieved gloom. Most industries are at a standstill. Since liberation no full-time chairman has been appointed and in its orphaned state this industry is heading for total collapse. The paper and board sector is also suffering from the loss of markets in Pakistan on the one hand and from inadequate supply of chemicals on the other. It is a major casualty of past pricing policy but has hopes of picking up production on the basis of exports to India and other countries.

The minerals sector registers for the time being, low offtake of gas by industrial consumers, problems with supply of crude oil to the refinery, and inadequate supply of raw material for cement and ceramic units. Chattak has produced 20,000 tons of cement in place of 43,000 tons in pre-liberation days. This picture will be radically transformed once the Kanerreh limestone from across the border reaches the crushers at Chattak and the full potential can be realised.

Actual production in each sector is given in the table on pp. 208–9.

Man, machine and material working in harmony is necessary to ensure efficiency in industrial production. Materials are either imported or available locally. Formerly a large part of the locally available industrial intermediates in the form of materials came from Pakistan and thus were not on the foreign import list. In addition, some of the locally available materials had substantial import content. The stocks of these with manufacturing units were soon depleted. Until May, commercial import licences for these materials were not given; this led to strain on the local availability of materials. From a survey carried out by the Planning Commission, it seems that importers were slow in utilising import permits for the following reasons:

   (i) non-availability of finance;
  (ii) non-functioning of local agency offices of importers who were co-operating with the licence holders;
 (iii) inexperience of new administrators;
 (iv) inexperience of small units which had depended on local markets or supply from Pakistan and now needed a licence to get the supply; their needs had to be assessed by the Directorate of Industry before they could get a commercial licence.

For these reasons the shortage of materials continues. It may improve with the arrival of the programmed imports between now and the end of the year.

Machines need maintenance – both preventive and routine. During the nine months of the struggle some machines were dismantled and others were closed down. In many cases in small units proper care was not taken. Many technicians were non-locals whose services ceased to be available; this gap has yet to be filled. The new owners and administrators have found difficulty in identifying the exact specification and actual requirements of spares and components. As a result machinery has not been in working order.

Man is the second crucial factor. In the absence of a well-defined and enforceable labour policy it has not been possible to make the best use of labour, who in many cases have misunderstood the concept of nationalisation.

Administrators chosen in haste have also done considerable damage in some cases. Those interested in making quick money for themselves have tended to deplete stocks or sell off machines. Such behaviour has also created financial problems since units with depleted stocks and deficient machinery are now prevented from raising working capital from the banks. Adequately trained manpower at all levels has been a critical constraint.

Finance is a complicated problem. Banks have excess liquidity and they should be eager to make their money work. Creditworthiness of the units or of the persons involved is a major question. Some units are already burdened with past debts; some units have become a liability because of the role played by the new class of administrators. Moreover, the industrial climate does not look attractive at the moment. Foreign exchange availability is also a vexing question. To the extent that licences are issued, that necessary provisions are made in the foreign exchange budget, and that the parties are able to find the cash cover to utilise foreign exchange, there is no problem. But problems may have arisen because, as a result of the impact of devaluation, of price escalation, or for other reasons, the increase in cost of imports in foreign currency and takas has not been properly allowed for by the responsible administration. There is also in some cases a shortage of demand. Some products had their principal market in Pakistan and thus their capacity cannot be utilised unless export is possible to new markets or until local demand expands. There also seems to be a shortage of demand for 'non-essential items' (or items whose demand can be postponed) because of the shrinkage in the real income of the fixed-income group who ordinarily have a very high propensity to spend money. This shortage can only be cured by a return of buoyancy in the economy.

The available data on the basis of which the extent of the nationalised sector was estimated indicate that what remains of the indigenous private sector in Bangladesh constitutes enterprises with assets worth approximately takas 340 million. It is evident that today, with the nationalisation of the jute and cotton textile industries, there is very little left of large-scale Bengali-owned private industry. Such as survive could not be classified as key industries whose ownership status would significantly affect the social order or working of the economy. Given this dispersal of indigenous capitalism, it is clear that the growth potential of Bengali capitalism is limited to the scope this and successive administrations may give them. Of their own initiative these existing enterprises have limited growth potential in a regulated economy and may be expected to retain the status of medium-sized enterprises for some time to come. By the time any of these enterprises generate sufficient surplus to move to a higher level of capitalist enterprise the transition stage towards socialism is likely to be drawing to its close. To the extent that returns are quick and the financial involvement small, non-abandoned industrial units in the private sector have made the best of a scarcity situation unless they have been held back by non-availability of materials or spares.

IV. THE IMPLICATIONS FOR INDUSTRIAL POLICY

Deductions from the above discussion are fairly obvious. The pressure of population on land is too high to be allowed to deteriorate any further. This calls not only for a vigorous effort to halt the growth of population, which is likely to be more successful with better economic living conditions, but also for release of pressure on land through creation of employment opportunities elsewhere.

Since agriculture cannot offer much scope for employment when there is idle labour already existing in that sector, employment of surplus labour is one of the objectives to be seriously considered as a criterion in the choice of sectors for development in industry. In considering this, however, we should always value efficiency over any other criterion. Surplus generated from efficient units can be used to create employment elsewhere; but losses sustained in an inefficient labour-intensive unit take us nowhere. There is apparently a conflict here.

Neither agriculture nor industry nor any other sector is inherently efficient in the sense that it is possible to increase productivity without discipline, organisation or improved practices. In the agricultural sector efficiency is imperative in the interest of attaining self-sufficiency in food, of making the jute industry more viable economically, of rehabilitating the sugar, tea and tobacco industries. Industry can play the important role of supplier of inputs for higher production in agriculture.

Industries based on agricultural raw materials need to be sustained, made efficient and wherever possible expanded as a corollary to efficient agriculture because of the complementary relations that exist in these.

Provided that agriculture and industry generate a surplus, government will be in a position to sustain a large investment in social and physical infrastructure which alone can generate external economies for the benefit of other sectors. However, investment in social and physical infrastructure cannot wait for generation of surplus and this equation of resource balance should be viewed in the long-run and dynamic context. The social infrastructure sector also provides an excellent field in which surplus manpower, adequately trained, may be absorbed.

Consumption per head is today at a low level. With greater generation of income and redistribution of it, the demand for such basic facilities as food, shelter, health, clothing, education and transport will expand. A carefully worked out balance of growth provides in effect for enough scope for industrial development ranging from food and beverages to steel and plastics, from furniture and textiles to pharmaceuticals and packing, from timber and cement to paper, from light engineering to heavy industries like shipbuilding.

The resource base of Bangladesh is still narrow – jute, hides and skins, and natural gas. Jute in the past has provided the leading sector for growth, but its rate of expansion both physically and employment wise will in future be limited. Hides and skins offer only a limited prospect both because the base is small and also because of the distance from market. Hence we are left with only natural gas of which judicious exploitation can do no more than accelerate the pace of development in future.

A labour surplus economy could benefit most in converting this apparent liability into an asset if skill could be introduced appropriately and exploited quickly. The ultimate objective is to export skill even when the material on which it works has to be imported, as is the case with Japan. The immediate scope for such a policy is limited; but there may be no escape from making a determined effort in this direction. It has to be recognised that with a limited material base, man is the resource to be developed.

The technological base of Bangladesh is very limited. It has mostly been imported and its application has not been as efficient as in the countries from which it has been brought. Either as the result of deliberate price intervention or because of other natural advantages, some of these units have managed to survive. But in the long run social benefit cannot be maximised unless the requisite efficiency is achieved or a technology suitable for the conditions of Bangladesh is developed.

Underutilisation of capacity has not only existed in the difficult days following liberation; it has been chronic even earlier. Unless the unit is basically 'undesirable' or has been ill-planned and ill-executed (over-capitalised in many cases) there exists a case for making a sustained effort for utilisation of capacity. If under-utilisation was the result of deliberate government policy these policies need to be modified. But this begs the question whether a unit, which would impose high cost inputs on other sectors, should be encouraged to operate at capacity. The answer may not be a simple one, though the sunken fixed cost may be valued at zero to avoid extreme distortion.

V. THE JUTE INDUSTRY

Against this background may I review the possibility of investment in various sub-sectors? I shall begin with jute. Jute is vital to the economy of Bangladesh, as more than 95 per cent of all foreign exchange earnings come from export of raw jute and jute manufactures. In 1947, though Bangladesh produced 90 per cent of all Indian jute, it had no jute mill of any size. The first jute mill was built in 1952 and by 1959–60 there were 8000 looms installed, producing 256,280 tons of jute goods. By December 1970, the number of installed looms had risen to 25,084 and projects under implementation were designed to increase the capacity to 25,923 looms by June 1973. This clearly demonstrates the rapid growth of the jute sector in Bangladesh. The I.B.R.D. report on industrialisation of Pakistan of March 1970[1] noted the possibility of further profitable investment in the jute sector [8]. But the position of the jute industry has significantly changed during the past two years when synthetics have made significant headway in the absence of the normal supply of jute from Bangladesh and with the high prices charged by India.

The Bangladesh jute industry, in order to retain its position, must be able to provide a steady supply of jute products at a competitive price. Unless this can be assured, further expansion of the jute sector will be impossible and it may even be difficult to operate the existing mills at capacity. Since raw material cost is the single important cost it is necessary to reduce the cost of raw jute. But this has to be done without imposing on the income opportunities of the farmer. This is only possible if the per acre yield can be raised considerably more than proportionately to the cost of improved inputs. Further, because of the emphasis on foodgrain self-sufficiency, prices have moved in favour of rice; and because of illicit trade with India, the possibility of the rice price going down seems to be small. Under the circumstances, it would indeed be difficult to hold down jute prices and at the same time expect a reasonably good supply to feed our overseas markets at a price that will compete with the synthetics. This possibility opens the question of the valuation of our currency; this is, perhaps, not the place to deliberate on it. In passing it may be noted that a recent study shows that the cost of producing raw jute is about takas 40 per maund; assuming that the average rice price is takas 70 per maund, if we take a 1:1 ratio (rather than the 2:1 traditionally assumed), then the jute price ought to be takas 70. The government has fixed it at takas 50.

In the cost of conversion, wages and salaries, overheads, depreciation and power costs represent the four major items. In recent years wages have gone up but output per unit of labour has not shown any improvement. In fact if we compare actual output with the machine-rated capacity, our production comes to only about 45 per cent of that. Frequent power failures have been reported and a study by the jute mills corporation shows that due to power failure they have lost about takas 120 millions worth of production. Armitage and Norton, a British consulting firm, had pointed out that at least 50 per cent of the loss of time had been due to bad maintenance of machinery and lack of proper management [10]. This has been further aggravated by depletion of the managerial class as many of them

[1] For this and other references see p. 230.

were non-locals. A recent survey shows that many important managerial positions in the jute industry cannot be filled or can only be filled by inadequately trained personnel. This is largely the result of dependence on Dundee for training and of failure to exploit the full potential of the Bangladesh Textile Institute.

Last, but not the least, the high cost of machinery and spares, increases of duties and taxes, higher rate of interest and depreciation, have all contributed to increase investment and operating costs over the years, while the price of the finished product has increased only at a slower pace in the face of the threat from synthetics, the development of alternative fibres as well as the manufacturing capacities in many competing countries. In addition, there does not seem to have been any concerted research in jute cultivation or product development. Certain inconclusive work has been done on woollenisation and cottonisation, but it was shelved as problems of bleaching and of removal of brittles could not be solved. Rayonisation is technically possible, but it will be uneconomic unless the cost of raw material can be brought down. The same is true of pulping, though jute can produce high grade pulp of which the world has a shortage.

At the present level of efficiency the mills can produce 690 thousand tons of jute goods a year. If we reduce the current idle looms from 15 per cent to the normal $2\frac{1}{2}$ per cent by the end of 1977–8, and operate either a third shift or two longer shifts making a total of 21 hours a day, and increase efficiency from 45 per cent to about 60 per cent of the rated efficiency, Bangladesh jute mills can produce over 1 million tons of jute goods a year, provided, of course, that the world can provide a market for it. At this level, according to an F.A.O. forecast, there would be surplus production in the world.

These facts serve to indicate that the jute industry does not offer scope for expansion in the near future. There seems to be an obvious case for using the existing capacity more efficiently, and if necessary more intensively. Increased employment will come only if the sector makes intensive use of existing looms through operating a third shift. The survival of the industry depends on a concerted effort to reduce raw material cost, to improve the performance of labour, to reduce waste time due to stoppages arising from power failures or bad maintenance, and to improve quickly managerial skill. The possibilities of reviewing taxation policy and even exchange rate policy cannot be totally ruled out.

VI. COTTON TEXTILES

Though cotton textiles had a head start over jute (as the first mill was built in 1908), development of this sector has been less phenomenal. In 1947–8 there were 10 mills with 109 thousand spindles and 2·7 thousand looms. In 1959–60, the numbers rose to 359 thousand spindles and 3·4 thousand looms. By 1968–9 they had reached 731 thousand spindles and 7 thousand looms. In addition there are about 400 thousand hand-looms. But the power-looms operated at a maximum of 52 per cent of rated capacity in 1968–9 and the hand-looms at 51 per cent of capacity in that year. Availability of cloth, including imports from Pakistan and elsewhere, was estimated to be 7·68 yards per capita per annum. Imports from Pakistan ranged between 22–30 per cent of total availability.

The demand for cloth on the basis of 10 yards per capita and a population of 75 millions growing at 3 per cent a year, comes to about 870 million yards, which would need about 570 thousand bales of yarn. On this basis, there will have to be at least 1400 thousand spindles by 1977–8 and 14·5 thousand looms which, together with existing hand-loom capacity, will process nearly 900 thousand bales of cotton or artificial fibres.

The problems that confront the cotton textile industry are very similar to those discussed in respect of jute, ranging from loss of working hours due to power failure and management lapses to comparative inefficiency measured in terms of labour output. They range from high cost of raw materials to high cost of investment due to increasing machinery prices, and to high cost also of conversion. The distinctive feature, in contrast to jute, is that raw materials are imported. Before December 1971, cotton used to come from Pakistan at a relatively cheap price, with no duty to be paid on it, and at a reasonable transportation cost. Now that cotton has to come from elsewhere, not only are prices much higher but duty is payable and the transportation cost in addition makes the total cost of raw materials to the mills very high as compared with that of pre-liberation days. As a consequence, yarn prices to the weavers have gone up. Bangladesh used to get raw cotton from Pakistan at takas 700 per bale as against present prices of takas 1900. This has increased ex-mill prices of cotton yarn. For example, pre-liberation the ex-mill price per lb. of 20 count cotton yarn was takas 51. The price today is takas 79, and the free-market price is much higher. In turn this has increased the price of textiles to the consumer, to whom if the scarcity premium is excluded, the prices of imported textiles are less than those of Bangladesh-made textile products.

There has been talk of making Bangladesh self-sufficient in cotton. West Bengal is making plans to grow cotton in Sundarbans. Even if it proved feasible, it probably has to wait since priority goes to self-sufficiency in foodgrains. Alternatives lie in developing synthetic fibres. Given our resources, the possibilities are nylon 66 from the pith of bagasse and polyester from a naphtha base, polyvinyl-acetate and polyacrylonitrile from natural gas, and rayon from bamboo pulp. Technological reasons limit our choice to the last three and consumer preference to the last two. While rayon can displace an equal amount of cotton, inaccessibility of bamboo forest makes its availability only limited. Hence, the textile industry may have to depend on a blended fibre and make its best efforts to use a 1–2 dernier type of MN blended with rayon and/or cotton. In terms of cost this may not mean a large advantage to mills, but it would certainly save foreign exchange and thus ensure a more steady supply.

While due to the supply gap, the textile sector offers good possibility of expansion and is likely to play the role that jute played in earlier years in generating income and employment, it will in effect have limited possibilities unless better management practices, labour discipline, and a steady and reasonably priced source of raw materials can be established quickly. In the interest of consumer preference, aesthetics and employment, it is much to be desired that the hand-loom sector can operate profitably. This has not been the case recently due to shortage of yarn, lack of spares and dyestuffs, lack of finance and marketing facilities. The recent shortage of yarn and the unsatisfactory system of yarn distribution has hit the small weavers hard. Weavers' co-operatives have been suggested as a remedy, but they are yet to prove beneficial. Hand-looms have successfully catered for the needs of Bangladesh consumers of saris, lungis, dhotis, and the like. These requirements may continue to be met by hand-looms. But in the modern textile sector we must have efficient production units, otherwise the social cost may prove too high, even though we may succeed in creating some employment.

VII. OTHER SECTORS

Sugar was one of the sectors that grew rapidly in the early years of industrialisation under the Pakistan regime. Installed capacity in 1947 was 39,000 tons; it remained at that level until 1956–7, after which it increased to 74,000 tons in 1959–60 and to 169,000 tons by 1969–70; another 10,000 tons of capacity is in the offing. The maximum production of sugar was 112,000 tons in 1966–7. The cost of sugar production has increased over the years partly due to deteriorating of quality and a low recovery rate but also due to a limited availability of cane. The government attempted to fix both the price of sugar cane and the price of sugar for the government quota, which represented at least 75 per cent of the output. In addition it subjected the mills to an injudicious tax policy based on capacity. The result has been operation at a loss and heavy financial liabilities for each of the mills.

The salvation of the industry must lie in introducing a better variety of cane, which will give higher recovery, and improved farm practices to increase per acre yield. Without this not only will sugar cane cultivation contract but also the cost of its raw material to the industry will not be maintained at a reasonable level. The industry does not offer any scope for expansion at the moment and social returns from new investment are negative.

Molasses have not found any productive outlet in Bangladesh. In some years these have been exported. There has been some production of spirit. Large-scale utilisation for production of yeast, cattle feed and spirit need to be explored. This may turn the sick sugar industry into a viable one. Cattle-feed could generate external economics for meat and for the leather industry. The absence of dairy firms for the moment limits this possible market.

Even before 1947, North Bangladesh, and particularly Rangpur, was an important *tobacco* producing area. In 1947–8, 131 thousand acres were under tobacco, with a crop yield of 44·5 thousand tons. The average area cultivated has subsequently declined and fluctuated between 100 and 112 thousand acres, producing a total crop of 28 to 40 thousand tons. Thus in the agricultural sector tobacco has not done well. In the industrial sector there has been an impressive growth of manufacturing capacity. There are 17 units with a capacity to produce 13 thousand million cigarettes, actual production being around 9·7 thousand million a year. They produce low-priced cheap-quality cigarettes from locally produced tobacco, blended with imported tobacco. These serve as a substitute for the bidi which used to be manufactured in cottage industries for local consumption. Import of high-quality cigarettes from Pakistan (now from elsewhere) suggests the possibility of expansion of this sector. In such a case it will have to be an import-substitution industry, based on imported tobacco and materials. Apart from creating employment and generating revenue for the government, the tobacco industry may not have any high claim for priority.

Bangladesh, because of its rivers, is comparatively rich in *fish*, though no survey worth its name has been made. There have not been strenuous enough endeavours to promote development of fisheries, fish-culture, or fish preservation and processing. It is estimated that in 1968–9 the total catch of freshwater fish was 741 thousand tons and of marine fish 42 thousand tons. There are a few ice plants, 3 freezing plants for shrimps and frog-legs and a small canning plant. With the recent addition of trawlers, the catch, particularly of marine fish, is likely to increase manyfold. A projection forecasts it to be 131,000 tons. This opens up possibilities of investment in ice plants, and in a fish preservation and fish processing unit. Fish has a possibility of becoming a reasonably good foreign exchange earner and it can supplement the protein sources so badly needed by the people of Bangladesh.

Horticulture has hardly claimed any attention either from the agriculture sector or from the industrial sector. There have been some feeble attempts to go in for commercial cultivation of such fruits such as pineapples, mangoes, cashew-nuts, bananas. No investment designed to improve their quality has been made. The same is true of vegetables other than potatoes. It is believed that concentration of production would make possible the operation of a few economic units for, say, mango pulp, canned pineapple, guava jelly, the dehydration of bananas. Preservation facilities, if established, would also reduce wastage and increase the value of the product. This is also an area where geographical dispersal of investments both in agriculture and industry could be profitably applied. The bottleneck seems to be lack of proper packaging units. It is claimed that nearly 1·6 million tons of fruit and 2·6 million tons of vegetables are grown in Bangladesh. Of these between 10 and 25 per cent are wasted. There are only 8 fruit processing units producing jam, syrup, vinegar, pickles, tomato sauce, squash and the like. None of them produce a quality product at a price that can compete in the world market.

The *edible oil* industry has seen considerable expansion. In 1947 there were 5 mills in addition to numerous indigenous ghanis. Today there are about 60 large and small edible oil units with a capacity of 800 thousand maunds a year; the production recorded in 1968–9 was only about 40 thousand maunds. They suffer from lack of raw materials as these have to be imported. One large unit set up in the public sector to process groundnuts has never operated and is likely to face chronic shortage of raw materials. It also suffers from over-capitalisation, since the total infrastructure had to be built, including housing facilities in the out of the way place selected for it in the name of decentralisation of industrial units.

Bangladesh has a large *livestock* population, which forms almost a part of the household population. There are a few poultry and dairy farms. Land for pasture is expensive. Care of cattle is far from satisfactory. Thus, it is not surprising that very few commercial ventures have made headway in this sphere. Even so, Bangladesh on an average produces 2·8 million cowhides and 7 million goatskins annually. In 1947 there were hardly any *tanning* facilities apart from a few cottage units. Today there are 206 tanneries, of which 124 are recognised by the Directorate of Industry; 70 of these are mechanised. They have a capacity to process 30 million square feet of upper leather and 6 million lb. of sole leather. But the export consists mainly of blue leather with hardly any finished leather. There is a problem of quality but even so goatskins from Bangladesh are among the best in the world. After liberation the tanneries faced problems as many units were abandoned by non-locals; these now form the core of the tannery corporation. No research into product development or preservation has ever been undertaken. The technical institute has fallen apart. There is no large unit producing leather goods except for Bata and E.P.S.I. Since leather and leather goods show promise of export potential, it is necessary to exploit it by improving the quality of leather and finding markets for finished leather instead of wet blue.

Bangladesh is fortunate in having a reasonably rich forest area. Production of *timber and firewood* from homesteads and forests has been 35 million cubic feet and 40 million cubic feet respectively. There has been production of 2 million tons of bamboo in addition to other products like gol-patta. Forest resources have made possible the newsprint mill based on gewa wood, a hardboard mill based on sundari firewood, a paper and rayon mill based on bamboo, and timber and plywood factories. A new mill to use reed grass for kraft paper is in the offing. A rubber plantation has already started to supply the market. In spite of all these, it has to be noted that no scientific forest management seems to be practised; nor has there been any marked progress with systematic exploitation of forests. As a result timber production has not grown and the possibility of exporting timber and timber products has not been explored except for a few consignment sales of plywood chests to Hong Kong. Bangladesh has still to develop a wood-substitute industry, such as particle board from jute sticks, chipboard from sawdust. There are proposals to use anhydrite to produce gypsum board and to use leather waste to make chipboard. These in fact economise the demand for timber which can find markets abroad.

We have discussed thus far the possibilities of industries based on agricultural products. Let us now turn to consider what industries can be developed to supply *inputs to agriculture*. It will be recalled that a big drive in agriculture is being planned with a primary emphasis on reaching self-sufficiency in foodgrains. This involves a 49 per cent increase in output over five years on the benchmark production of 11·4 million tons of rice. Since land availability is limited and no increase in net area is envisaged, the entire emphasis is on improved inputs such as fertiliser, pesticides, irrigation, seeds, credit facilities and the like.

The first *fertiliser* plant, at Fenchugonj, was planned in the mid-fifties and went into production in 1961. It has a capacity to produce 116,000 tons of urea and in one year it reached a maximum of 110,000 tons, but it normally produces between 80,000 and 90,000 tons. Recently it has run into trouble since it needs replacements of its generating sets. Its cost of production, before recent escalation of prices, was around $100 at the official rates of exchange prevailing before December 1971. Since then, despite the increased cost of consumables and spares and increases in wages and salaries, its cost of production remains about $100 a ton at current rates of exchange. But this means a substantial increase in the taka cost, and hence a demand for refixation of the price. The new urea factory at Ghorasal has a capacity of 340,000 tons and it enjoyed the advantages both of a technological breakthrough and of economies of scale. Even at 80 per cent of its capacity, its cost of production is estimated at $80. Both plants use indigenous natural gas as a raw material and are in a position to supply 350,000 tons of urea.

In 1968–9, 196 thousand tons of urea were distributed to farmers. Taking the production target of rice by 1977–8 and the area expected to be under high yield varieties, the demand for urea in 1977–8 is estimated at 700,000 tons. This does not include demand from other crops. This level of demand justifies another urea plant of the capacity of 340 to 450 thousand tons. This unit is envisaged as a part of a petrochemical complex. Moreover, India and China may be regarded as urea-short countries. The possibilities of exporting urea need to be explored, since with a standard size of urea plant it is possible in Bangladesh to produce urea at world market price.

Bangladesh has not been so fortunate in phosphatic fertilisers. It has no deposit of phosphate rock, nor does it have any indigenous source of sulphur. In order to meet the needs of agriculture, P.I.D.C. originally planned to produce 32,000 tons of single-superphosphate, and later hurriedly converted the project to triple-superphosphate. The scheme has gestated for nearly six years and it has yet to produce any T.S.P. The second unit in the T.S.P. complex at Chittagong has a capacity of 120,000 tons. The idea of having a domestic source of supply blinded other considerations, since it was quite clear that the two projects do not represent meaningful import substitution. Imported T.S.P. would be cheaper than any produced in these plants. Only part of the difference of cost is to be explained by over-capitalisation and expenditure on infrastructural facilities. There has since been a technological breakthrough, and T.S.P. plants can now be based on phosphoric acid. This brightens the chance for setting up new capacity. In 1968–9, T.S.P. distributed was 65·5 thousand tons. Making similar calculations to those in the case of urea, demand in 1977–8 for rice alone is likely to increase to 560,000 tons. If they can satisfy economic tests, there is room for establishing 2–3 plants of the size of the second unit. Ammonium sulphate has been used mostly in the tea gardens. The current capacity is about 12,000 tons. The demand is likely to go up to 32,000 tons, which would allow a unit which could fit conveniently in the petrochemical complex.

To turn next to *pesticides and insecticides*, it is estimated that the Bangladesh economy suffers from a loss of takas 1500 millions worth of crops every year caused by pests and diseases; this estimate claims that a third of the yield is destroyed or damaged by pests or insects. If this estimate is to be believed, the crop availability would change dramatically if selective application of pesticides and insecticides could be ensured. It is also believed that increased use of fertiliser is likely to necessitate increased use of pesticides. In 1969–70 Bangladesh used 5132 tons of pesticides to cover about 20 per cent of the cropped area. In 1972–3 the total area under crop cultivation is estimated at 32·36 million acres. A rate of 2 sprays for traditional varieties of rice and 10 for high-yield varieties, of 2 for local varieties of wheat, and 3 for Mexican wheats, of 2 for jute, 3 for sugar-cane, 10 for tea and 2 for other crops, would give 94·23 million spray-acres. If we assume the recommended 265·2 tons per million spray-acres, the demand for pesticide comes to the staggering figure of 25,000 tons. This estimate is reported to stress the fact that the demand for pesticides and insecticides offers a possibility to set up a pesticides manufacturing unit as an import-substitution possibility. Here, as in the case of pharmaceuticals, the ingredients are patented and must be imported from collaborating foreign firms. Hence, the cost of imports and the terms and conditions of their collaboration will be the determining factors in judging the social benefit of setting up what may be 'highly desirable' import-based units. At present there is only one plant which has the capacity to produce 1282 tons of organic phosphoric pesticides.

Next among agricultural inputs comes *agricultural implements*, including pumps and pipes for irrigation, tools, tackle, tillers, sprayers and certain simple equipment such as grinding machinery. These are currently imported, but the nucleus of an import-substitution industry based on imported inputs has been just around the corner. There exists capacity to assemble 300 diesel engines per year on one shift, or twice that number on two shifts. It cannot go far towards actual manufacture since the mother forge and foundry in its sister plant is yet to come into operation. There is pump manufacturing capacity in a specialised plant in the machine tools factory operated by the Dockyards and Shipyards. Limitations of managerial

capacity and technical knowledge, limitations resulting from
inadequate supply of imported materials, components and parts,
the high cost of power, competition from similar equipment provided
under international aid, together with shortages of skilled workers,
have all served to inhibit the growth of both large and small units.
The government has failed to standardise units for installation and
has contributed to the distortion of cost structures by imposing
discriminating import surcharges [I.B.R.D.]. Nor has it attempted
to impose quality control, to improve management techniques or to
import technological assistance through an organised institute.
Moreover forge and foundry facilities are still limited and make any
effective progress difficult. The only enterprise in *steel making* and
processing in the pre-liberation days was in the public sector. It
started operation with an annual capacity of 150,000 tons and later
added another 100,000. Its products have included plates, rods and
sheets. There have been some 40 re-rolling mills in the private sector,
with a capacity to produce 200,000 tons of rods from billets. The
steel mill has used scrap with a limited addition of ore as inputs and
has never operated at capacity. Its maximum production has been
56,000 tons. Complaints of imbalance, lack of proper management,
absence of technological ability at higher levels, inadequate provision
of foreign exchange have all been cited as reasons for the poor
utilisation of capacity. Moreover, import of steel products has made
its operation unprofitable since its costs have been much higher
than the international price. Steel being a basic material for construction and manufacture, the high price of steel products was spread
to other sectors of the economy. The current shortage of steel is
helping the steel mill, and in addition shortage of supply of plates for
the shipyards is increasing the utilisation of its capacity. But it is
certainly not an attractive project from the point of view of social
cost criteria. There is large idle capacity not only in the steel mill
but also in the re-rolling mills, and it is possible to increase effective
capacity and diversify the products by regrouping the mills and putting the four electric arc furnaces under one control.

There is a nucleus of an *engineering industry*. A *machine tools*
factory was planned as a mother unit in which forge and foundry
capacity will be available and castings will be produced not only for
the factory itself but for other units as well. Its completion has been
delayed and ill-planned, and in consequence the plant that was to
come into operation by 1972 may not be ready till 1976. This in
itself will impede the growth of the engineering industries. It was the
intention that these, besides producing agricultural machinery and
machine tools for industrial workshops, should also serve the power
sector by production of electrical equipment and accessories and

produce spare parts and components for textile machinery and for transport vehicles. They were also to produce precision products such as clocks, typewriters, calculating machines and the like. There already exist shipbuilding and ship-repair facilities. Provided that inputs are available at world prices, these yards can produce craft and boats at a competitive price and they provide much-needed repair facilities. The complaints against them are of delays due to non-availability of spares which is in turn the result of non-standardisation of engines. The consequences have been the serious underutilisation of capacity and high repair charges.

Bangladesh has a proven reserve of 9 trillion cubic feet of *natural gas* which contains 98 per cent or more of methane. So far the only uses of this have been to produce urea, to help to generate electricity, and to substitute for other fuels in industries and households. Even so the offtake is small. One reason for this, of course, is that gas is available through the distribution lines only in limited places. Once the distribution network is expanded, the offtake is likely to increase. Bangladesh has for long hoped to use gas as an industrial raw material, since such use adds more to value in the shape of the final product. There have been as many as ten studies and appraisals of projects to establish an *industrial chemical complex*. There is general agreement in Bangladesh that three main products are desirable – urea, fibres, and P.V.C. Urea and fibres have been discussed in earlier paragraphs. Urea has never been in doubt. In the changes circumstances, fibre is also making its claim firmer. As for P.V.C., it is not that one does not desire it as a product. It is that the quantum of it needed is a function of the other end-use facilities that are to be developed. At present this potential offtake is low; a study puts it between 6 and 12 thousand tons. Hence efforts to develop end-use facilities both in the private sector, in the form of small industrial units, and in the public sector need to grow simultaneously. As a by-product of the complex, we should get products such as bleaching powder, caustic soda and soda ash, methanol, acetone in quantities whose absorption will not pose much of a problem. Development of formalin and other similar products may also deserve consideration.

The *pharmaceutical industry* has grown in the past mostly as a tableting and phialing business without being concerned with basic manufacture. The foreign partners have used this marginal investment to protect their markets and reportedly have remitted high profile. Though this arrangement has ensured quality, it has inhibited any growth of production of the basic ingredients. With the population of Bangladesh and with incidence of disease very high, even if medical attention reaches no more than the 25 per cent claimed by the public health department, it should be possible to manufacture the essential basic drugs for the most common diseases and to sell these by generic name rather than trade name. There may well be resistance from the established manufacturers.

Cement is a basic need. Even before independence a factory based on Meghalaya limestone was operating at Chattak. In 1965 when the supply was interrupted, quarrying was started at Takerghat. The costs started mounting as underground mining proved necessary. But recent negotiations with India have shown that the price of limestone from across the border will not be as cheap as had been expected. If in addition the present import duty and sales tax have to be paid, India is likely to prove a more expensive source. The demand for cement will certainly grow and is estimated at 2 million tons by 1977–8. The project report for a limestone and cement works at Jaipurhat prepared since liberation shows the project to be attractive both financially and commercially. Under certain assumptions the social rate of return is estimated to be less than 10 per cent, but this neglects the external economies and the impact on the development of North Bengal.

Small industry is not to be confused with cottage industry. Small industry need not be primitive. An undertaking employs few workers and requires limited investment. Cost considerations should never be overlooked. We want efficient small units which will be commercially viable, economically paying and normally competitive. Small industries can make low-cost low-quality products for a local protected market. But the national industrialisation effort can not be served by such units apart from their limited contributions to the employment objective. The small industry sector can stimulate development of modern industry and of traditional products which offer possibilities of modernisation and semi-mass production under quality control. Examples are hand-looms, woodworking, metalworks, ceramics, cane and bamboo products. But in any case the development of traditional small industries should not imply the neglect of modern small industry designed to satisfy local demands and which is thereby protected against low-cost, large-scale manufacturing.

Pragmatically, the policy towards *foreign private investment* should be guided by the gap in resources and the gap in technology and skill. The wider is the gap, the less stringent should be the terms. This gap is also a function of the rate of growth that is envisaged, of the amount of foreign aid and of the macro-economic policies. Only in the light of these will the picture be clear. Politically, however, it must be determined by taking a stand consistent with the political principles of the state. The rival claims of political stand

and of economic necessity must again be decided on the political plane.

The development objectives of the government often diverge from other socio-political objectives, and at times from other economic policies. The extent of divergence is not only not constant, but often erratic. This creates not only a problem for planning but also for the execution of the plan itself. No attempt in harmonisation has had much success in the past.

VIII. THE GEOGRAPHICAL DISTRIBUTION OF BENEFITS

The geographical location of industries is important. Bangladesh has suffered as a whole from a sense of deprivation and it is necessary to guard against such a stiuation within Bangladesh. Much of the industrial development in Bangladesh has centred around Dacca, Chittagong and Khulna. This, unfortunately, has also restricted the employment effects to certain zones. Industrial locations can, however, only be selected within certain constraints. For example, fertiliser plants cannot be located in North Bengal as location either depends on natural gas or on imported sulphur and rock phosphate. Similarly the sugar industry could not be located in South Bengal. The jute industry might have been more diversified but its location depended mostly on the sponsors and their associates. The same is true of cotton. In future, it may be possible to diversify the location of new cotton mills within the hand-loom belt of Bangladesh. Since jute is not due for much expansion, it does not offer any scope for great diversification. Nor does sugar. Some diversification of livestock-based industries may be possible within the so-called milk zone extending from Savar to Pabna/Bogra. Implementation of the Jaipurhat project may open up new industrial possibilities in North Bengal, including the mining of hardrock and coal. Tobacco curing offers limited possibilities in some of the under-industrialised areas. Poultry farming can be tried. Utilisation of molasses and pith from bagasse offers certain possibilities for North Bengal. South Bengal may have to depend on a fish-processing industry, on import-based units and export-oriented industry. The natural gas belt of Eastern Bangladesh can profitably develop gas-based industries whereas North Bengal may be expected to develop mineral-based industries. The building materials complex can be diversified to some extent. Depending on their raw materials, the consumer-goods industries may also be diversified so as to be close to points of consumption.

IX. GENERAL CONCLUSIONS

The deductions that may be drawn from the above discussion of the present conditions, possibilities and problems of the various sub-sectors of economy seem to be these. First, jute, the leading sector in the past history of industrial growth, offers limited scope for expansion and its future can only be ensured through making it available at a competitive price. This in turn is possible only if the raw jute cost can be lowered through a more than proportionate increase in yield and through increase in the efficiency of labour and management. A case for the more intensive utilisation of manufacturing machinery has been made.

In the absence of jute to serve as the leading growth sector, we may have to turn to the textile sector as a natural alternative. This is an import-substitution sector initially based on an imported raw material; it is only in the long run that a part of the raw materials may be substituted by locally produced synthetics such as rayon, P.A.C.N. and even polyester. Since there is a large unsatisfied demand, it will be possible to exploit economics of scale and also to disperse units geographically.

Apart from jute, the other export possibilities lie in leather, fish and tea. In magnitude none of them are likely to be as large as jute. The outlook for leather exports can possibly be brightened if more dairy farms are in existence and if we can sell more leather, and particularly more finished leather. Expansion of the livestock sector is likely, however, to clash with that of foodgrains and to be less attractive as it is more capital-intensive. Fish exports offer new possibilities but their impact remains to be seen. They cannot grow without complementary facilities. The future of tea depends on producing at a competitive price in the face of the expansion of tea production in Africa. Further expansion in this sector is unlikely.

The only other major resource is natural gas, the exploitation of which has so far remained limited. The possibility of expanding fertiliser capacity together with production of P.V.C. and synthetic fibres offers a real chance of changing the face of this region, not only because of the magnitude of the investment but also because it offers a chance to reduce import-dependence and the possibility of setting up many small labour-intensive units, to the considerable benefit of employment and of the small industries sector. Limestone deposits also claim certain attention.

The engineering industries have a future so far as linkage effects create demand for spares and components, or for agricultural tools and irrigation equipment, or for components for transport vehicles, or for electrical accessories or equipment. The demands seem to be sizeable but to require an intelligent import policy, limiting foreign credit for such products. But success depends on the development of skills.

The need is to create efficient industry. Capital-intensity and labour-intensity are secondary criteria. Only an efficient industry will generate surplus, other things being equal. This surplus can be used to create employment. Since it is not certain whether the effective labour cost in our industry is low, the emphasis on labour-intensive technology may beg a lot of questions. Moreover, even when the basic core of industry is capital-intensive, many other industries may grow which are labour-intensive in character. Again, does not the fact of state ownership of capital provide an additional argument in favour of less labour-intensive techniques because of the income-distribution effect of investment? Further, is not the extent of labour-intensive investment limited by the possibility of increasing availability of wage-goods?

The main bottlenecks, in present circumstances, seem to be lack of labour discipline, lack of managerial ability and lack of trained manpower. In fact, industrialisation on the scale that is now being talked of, may find this shortage of technical manpower the single major constraint. This is not only true of the industrial sector but also of other sectors as well. The story of the last two decades is that of investment in industry outpacing investment in the development of skilled manpower and in the development of managerial skill. This has become a principal bottleneck to efficient utilisation of investment.

Lastly, it is far from clear what purpose the criteria for investment and the ranking of projects really serves. A project may score high/ low, positive/negative marks if we take each one of the various criteria and judge them. Better, we can so rank them. A composite picture of all possible projects in terms of all possible criteria will give us a ranking that is more relevant for selection than speaking vaguely of these criteria. Of course, one can speak of applying social rates of return. But to make it applicable, much basic work needs to be done. In the final analysis, the choice of strategy in the industrial field lies in utilising the existing capacity (unless it was so thoroughly ill-conceived as not even to allow operation at marginal cost) and utilising domestic resources so that, through linkage effects and by balancing requirements, there is generated from other sectors as well as the industries sector the power to develop capital goods industries and intermediate goods industries, as well as engineering industries.

BIBLIOGRAPHY

[1] *Statistical Digest of Bangladesh,* No. 7, 1970–71; Bangladesh Bureau of Statistics, Dacca.
[2] B.I.D.C. figures, compiled and published by the Planning Division of B.I.D.C.
[3] *Economic Survey of East Pakistan,* 1969–70, Government of East Pakistan, Planning Department.
[4] *The Fourth Five Year Plan 1970–75,* Planning Commission, Government of Pakistan.
[5] *Strategies and Programme for the Fourth Five Year Plan, 1970–75 for East Pakistan,* Planning Board, Government of East Pakistan (June 1970).
[6] *Policy for Land Reform,* Planning Commission, Government of Bangladesh (mimeo).
[7] *Industrial Policy,* Planning Commission, Government of the People's Republic of Bangladesh.
[8] *Industrialisation of Pakistan: The Record, The Problems and The Prospects* vol. I, II and III: International Bank for Reconstruction and Development (March 1970).
[9] *Economic and Engineering Feasibility Study on Alternate uses of Jute,* B.I.D.C. (Jan. 1972).
[10] *Investigation of Productivity and Costs in Member Mills;* (by Armitage & Norton); Pakistan Jute Mills Association (June 1968).

Discussion of Papers by
Rehman Sobhan and Muzaffar Ahmad

The session was opened by *Rehman Sobhan* who explained the purposes behind that day's (8 January 1973) policy announcement. Industrial activities are to be divided vertically, i.e. certain activities will be reserved for the public sector, others will remain in the private sector, and still others will contain both state and private firms. The ultimate objective, however, is for the state to acquire control over the means of production; this will be done gradually over time. Today's policy puts a limit of 2·5 takas million to fixed investment in the private sector. The few private firms above this limit will be taken over. In return, the government guarantees that no other firms will be nationalised within the next ten years.

The private sector will in effect be limited to small enterprises. By imposing a ceiling on capital assets businessmen should be induced to search for labour-intensive techniques of production. Incentives to expand should be strong since the private firms will be allowed to increase the size of their fixed assets by up to takas 1 million through the reinvestment of profits.

Foreign investment would be expected to enter into partnership with the government, and the government would hold at least 51 per cent of the equity of such joint ventures. Foreign capital would not be allowed to form partnerships with private Bengali capitalists. On the other hand, foreign investors would be guaranteed against nationalisation for ten years, in the same manner as the private Bengali sector. Furthermore, foreign firms might be offered management contracts or concessions of various sorts in order to encourage them to invest in Bangladesh.

COMMENTS ON THE PAPERS BY JOZEF PAJESTKA

The immediate problems of the country are urgent, but some consideration of longer run issues is necessary. It is possible to devise an industrial strategy for Bangladesh on the assumption of a per capita income of about $400. This would permit the country to have a viable and diversified industrial structure. Individual projects should be viewed in this context and the time horizon should be ten or fifteen years.

I assume that the per capita income today is $150, not $75 as commonly claimed. My guess is that the purchasing power parity of the currency is two times the actual exchange rate. Given this starting point, $400 per head can be achieved in ten to fifteen years. To do this, typical industrial programming methods should be adopted. The crucial problem is the transition to an income of $400 per capita.

Let us consider the immediate short-run strategy. We need, first, to identify the main limiting factors to growth and, second, to have clear in our minds the basic concept of industrial structure. Now, as regards constraints, in the very short run the main limiting factors are human factors, management skills and organisation. Shortage of capital is not the main problem. Hence we need to ask ourselves why is the discussion of the role of the private sector only in terms of the maximum size it will be allowed to achieve. In the Polish economy we believe that the private sector should be protected, as long as it contributes to the economy.

Especially in the short run, industry should be looked upon primarily in terms of its links with other sectors – agriculture, transport, etc. The share of industry in output is less important than its structure and its links with the rest of the economy. Care should be taken that industry doesn't develop as an isolated sector.

The number one problems today are why industrial capacity is not fully utilised and why the nationalised industries are not profitable. Many explanations have been given to us, but it is clear that we economists should pay less attention to macro-economic questions and more attention to these specific issues of the firm. It is not enough to nationalise; one must profit from the nationalisation – by increasing efficiency, by merging and forming stronger enterprises. If not, inefficiency may arise. There are very many inefficient nationalised industries in the world – in the Third World, very many indeed. A national objective should be full capacity utilisation and profitability of all nationalised industries. This could be achieved in two or three years, and all firms could be operating more than one shift.

There are ample opportunities to develop industries based on the existing resource endowment: jute, fish, natural gas, hides and skins, etc. There are many countries which would willingly help Bangladesh increase capacity in these fields. In addition, building materials and power are crucial and deserve high priority. I do not see any particular reason for expanding capacity in cotton textiles. There is much unused capacity here and abroad, and raw materials must be imported. Thus this industry has few links with other sectors. Instead I would look to agriculture and transport-related industries: shipbuilding perhaps and certainly modernisation of water transport. The technology used in these industries is not too sophisticated and these activities represent potential exports. Similar opportunities exist in agriculture, e.g. irrigation pumps.

COMMENTS ON THE PAPERS BY GUSTAV RANIS

I have been very impressed with both the papers. They lay out the recent history and current problems faced by the planners of Bangladesh with respect to the industrial sector clearly and fully. I shall have a number of comments to make on the papers themselves, but shall use them in the main for a more general comment on the role of the non-agricultural sector in the future development of Bangladesh.

This conference deals with the economic development of Bangladesh within the framework of a socialist economy. But regardless of the choice of development model that Bangladesh has made, or will make, addressing the economic problems and furthering the broadened objectives of this society requires a realistic assessment of the resources available to it and as careful a husbanding of these resources as possible. No matter what social system Bangladesh will ultimately follow, in fact, policy-makers will have to remember that this is an economy unusually dependent on agriculture, that it is short of capital, short of entrepreneurs and managers, in and outside of government. They will have to remember that the non-agricultural sector which we are talking about in this session is really a very small sector and that the large-scale industrial sector to which one of the two papers is wholly devoted comprises less than 6 or 7 per cent of the value added in the economy, and probably less than 4 or 5 per cent of the employed labour force. Thus, at this point, and for some time to come, output and employment will have to be generated in the rural areas of Bangladesh, mostly in terms of traditional agricultural activities and in terms of non-traditional rural activities. That is to say, the future of Bangladesh is intimately bound up with her success, or lack of it, in increasing her rice production, the success she has in multiple and secondary crops, and the success she has in initiating small-scale rural industry – which comes closer to the heart of the topic of this session.

Nevertheless the two papers before us are much more concerned with the large-scale and the small-scale urban industrial sectors. The relevant political decisions have now been taken, in part during the course of this conference, to the effect that large-scale industry shall remain in public hands and that small-scale industry, i.e. anything below takas 2·5 million, shall remain in the private sector for at least a ten-year period. Given these decisions, the problem of policy divides itself into at least three component parts: first, how can Bangladesh ensure the maximum efficiency of its public sector industries, mostly abandoned Pakistan companies taken over by the government; second, what should be the future development of the overall industrial sector in terms of both output and employment maximisation objectives; and third, what should be the longer-term future division between the public and private sectors.

With respect to the first of these issues, Nurul Islam asked us the other day to focus on the optimum extent of decentralisation towards which the government should work, on the nature of the incentive system to be used, if any, and on the role of markets and prices that should be permitted. Rehman Sobhan's paper contains a sobering realisation of the large number of difficulties with the existing public sector industries and a realisation that the government cannot afford to subsidise them indefinitely. While their expropriation was politically easy, very much like post-partition land reform, the problem now is one of trying to ensure that these firms yield a surplus rather than constitute a continuous drain on the exchequer.

On questions concerning how best to ensure an efficient public sector, I frankly would have liked to hear more from our socialist friends, for they have presumably much more experience in this area. I can only offer our hosts some rather conventional wisdom here, i.e. to go for as much decentralisation as possible, as far as the span of control permits, permitting subunits to compete as much as possible with each other. For example, the ten existing corporations might be broken down further into smaller subunits of management, with each responsible for its own books and abiding by some agreed-on norms of profitability. Secondly, all special pricing in intermediate and primary inputs in the public sector, including the pricing of imports through the state trading corporation, should be discouraged; otherwise indirect or invisible deficits will be just as heavy a drain on the economy as direct and visible ones. Third, where possible, management contracts should be used to provide an incentive for better than average managers competing with each other. Profit or surplus sharing by both managers and workers is much to be preferred at this stage to a Yugoslav-type worker participation scheme for which, in my view, Bangladesh is not ready.

While it may be interesting and fascinating to talk about the large-scale sector, and ways and means of increasing its productive efficiency, the heart of the problem lies with the non-agricultural activity reserved for the private sector, at least for the next ten years. This means that in addition to assuring a sustained increase in agricultural productivity at its source, the success of Bangladesh will rest, in my view, on the generation of a balanced, domestically oriented growth, leaning heavily on the development of small rural industries producing for the domestic market, a market simultaneously generated by a sustained increase in agricultural productivity – both in the primary crops and in such secondary crops as vegetables, fish and fruit. I do not agree with Dr Ahmad that industrial packages of natural gas, fertiliser, and P.V.C. synthetic fibers can ever change 'the face of this region'. It is tantalising to think so but also dangerous because, if we do care, with Professor Horvat, about the present generation of peasants, the answer must lie in mass participation in a large number of non-spectacular rural activities – not in focusing on a few items of capital-intensive, modern growth.

If balanced, small-scale, domestically oriented growth is to be the main direction of pay-off over the next decade or two, this is not far removed from the conventional wisdom of Nurkse, Lewis and others, involving not 'investment without savings', but rather the simultaneous generation of savings and investment without the need for much financial intermediation. How to do it is still the question. One suggestion that has been made here is to channel existing revolutionary enthusiasm by collectivising agriculture and taking over the industrial sector *in toto*. In fact, according to Dr Anisur Rahman, the private industrial sector is less capable than the public both of absorbing labour and of improving the lot of the individual worker through wage increases. Dr Ahmad in his paper also asks the (rhetorical) question of whether state ownership of capital does not argue for a lesser need to be labour-intensive and to have to worry about income distribution effects. I wonder. There are no magic wands and no way I know of legislating against the endowment. No matter what system is chosen, care must be taken to ensure that output and employment are made as complementary as possible; the wrong signals given to either the public or the private sectors can inhibit the growth of vital small-scale non-agricultural activity and ensure the persistence of conflicts between the main development objectives of employment, income distribution and output.

Luckily a firm decision has now been taken with respect to small-scale and rural industry, at least for the next ten years. This should give a chance for light engineering, metalworking, ceramics, leather goods, textiles, tobacco curing, silk, wood, wood processing, fish, fish products, and others, all industries which are likely to be dispersed in a large number of small hands, to make a substantial contribution. But we are by no means out of the wood because, if I understand Rehman Sobhan correctly, he views this decision as a temporary and unpleasant palliative, and would like the state to nationalise the entire industrial sector just as soon as possible. If that view – even if administratively impractical – is conveyed to the small and medium-scale entrepreneurs, actual and potential, Bangladesh is likely to get the worst of both worlds. If the private sector in this area is really to have a chance to show what it can do in a favourable environment over the next ten years, then a (strongly implied) policy setting which will discriminate against it, in terms of access to credit, to imports, etc., would be extremely harmful to its performance and thus to the chances of the system as a whole to become viable. A much more sensible policy might be to have government, especially local government, focus on the critical rural infrastructure, plus making sure that those new small industrial entrepreneurs who up to now have not had access to the necessary inputs at reasonable prices are no longer discriminated against. This means fair access to credit, imports, etc., even if this means somewhat higher interest rates and foreign exchange costs. Moreover, rural electrification, better roads and marketing facilities are required for the kind of rural agricultural/industrial interaction I've described to take place – and only government can provide those. It would indeed be very costly if, at this late stage of our understanding of development, Bangladesh imitated the Indian programme of the fifties which subsidised khadi industry, at one extreme, and heavy industry, at the other, while discriminating against medium- and small-scale non-agricultural activities in the middle. It is in these very areas that a lot of domestic ingenuity is likely to be found, just as labour-using technological change was discovered to have a substantial potential in agriculture proper, as the Bose paper indicates.

Whatever international comparative evidence we have indicates that medium- and small-scale industrial activity is likely to be most efficient in the use of the scarce factors, i.e. capital and possibly skilled labour. It is this portion of the non-agricultural sector which must bear the heaviest burden of supporting a balanced, domestically oriented growth over the next two decades in Bangladesh. The government does not have enough 'fingers' to do this job – under present realistic assumptions. It must therefore depend on the human resources it has elsewhere at its disposal and encourage and activate them. Agricultural productivity increase along with the domestically oriented non-agricultural production of wage goods for the domestic markets must be the first priority. Labour-intensive industrial exports can play an increasing role over time. But, in my view, the physical and human infrastructure must have been prepared before such exports can become significant, and the best preparation for this later phase is to permit the domestically oriented development process to move forward, with full participation of the economy's hitherto neglected actors

DISCUSSION

The discussion was concerned primarily with the organisation of industry and the role of prices and performance indicators. *Konstantin Gabrovski* stressed the importance of the public ownership of the means of production and the necessity for the private sector to be regulated and under the control of the state. *Alexsander Bajt* claimed that sooner or later state corporations would become progressively bureaucratised and their efficiency would decline. He suggested that when this begins to occur, the corporations should be disbanded and voluntary associations of enterprises should be encouraged. He would allow ownership of individual enterprises by workers, if that is what they want. Any monopoly profits that arise could be siphoned away by taxation. At present in Bangladesh, workers' representatives account for 2 of the 5 members of the board of management of state enterprises. This system is unlikely to work well, given the multi-union and multi-party system in the country; the representatives will become political leaders.

A. R. Khan pointed out that about 40 per cent of the assets in industry still are privately owned, although the average size of private firms is very small. The ceiling of takas 2·5 million is quite high, and implies that 100 people could be employed by a private firm. That is, private and public sectors are not coterminous with small and large industry. Moreover, projects larger than takas 2·5 million are not likely to be socially profitable, because they are likely to be capital-intensive, and thus if it is insisted that public sector enterprises must be at least takas 2·5 million in size, there might not be much left for the public sector to do. Hence, there must be no floor to the size of public sector enterprises.

Branko Horvat suggested that foreign trade (exports as well as imports) be centralised in one corporation. In addition, whenever an activity is risky, it should be centralised, and whenever the government is in doubt, centralise. The nationalised industries should be grouped into two categories. First, dependent public enterprises consisting of new firms, newly nationalised firms and unprofitable firms which need help. These should be run in an administrative way and not launched into the market orbit until they have been properly organised and ceased to be infants. Second, the remaining independent public enterprises should be market orientated, free to compete for labour and inputs and to engage in active competition. The ministry need only provide general supervision for these firms.

Performance indicators for the nationalised sector were considered by *Jan Lipinski*. He argued that industry could be divided into two zones: Zone 1 containing industries producing exportables and Zone 2 industries producing largely for the home market. The prices of raw materials and of the output of industries in Zone 1 should correspond to world prices. The performance indicator should be profits, although this might have to be modified, e.g. by subsidising employment of unskilled labour. The pricing rule for products produced in Zone 2 was difficult to determine and depended on national objectives; profits are not a good performance indicator for goods produced in this zone. *A. R. Khan* said that the suggestion that world prices be used rests on the assumption that the rate of exchange is, in some sense, correct. Moreover, profits are not a good guide to performance in those industries, e.g. paper, which were unwisely established in the past. In such cases, public enterprises should be allowed to write-off past investment. A similar procedure should be followed in cases in which tied aid financed projects suffer from excess costs.

Esra Bennathan said prices determine not only how goods will be produced but also what industries will be undertaken. Price signals regulate short-term behaviour but, perhaps more important, the level and pattern of investment. Prices also have a major influence on the pattern of foreign trade. In discussing prices one cannot, for instance, avoid considering the nature of interchange with India. Linkages are not just internal but also external. Lastly, the pattern of output is a major determinant of the distribution of income.

Saburo Okita, Austin Robinson and others emphasised the importance of modern, power-using, small industries such as bicycles, repair shops, small boats, sewing machines, pumps and motors. Bangladesh should look for the accumulation of many small accomplishments. *Muzaffar Ahmad*, however, questioned the reliability of data which suggested small-scale industry is more efficient than large. He hoped to change the face of the land by concentrating on large firms in industrial complexes, e.g. petrochemicals, plastics and synthetic fibres.

9 Employment in Bangladesh: Problems and Prospects

Iftikhar Ahmed[1]
UNIVERSITY OF DACCA

I. INTRODUCTION

The purpose of this paper is to review briefly the nature and magnitude of unemployment and underemployment as they exist in Bangladesh today. An attempt is made to investigate some of the major causes of the high unemployment rate. Finally this paper focuses on identifying and recommending policy measures which would help create job opportunities.

It is essential to recognise that if policy-making is to be relevant to this crucial problem of Bangladesh today, at least an approximation of the general nature and magnitude of unemployment and underemployment has to be made. The problem is far too vital for the nation – socially, politically and economically – to permit postponement of an assessment of the problem until precise statistics are available to us.

II. AVAILABLE CENSUS DATA

According to the census definition of 1961 the unemployed labour force of Bangladesh was found to be a meagre 0·49 per cent of the total labour force [6].[2] The significance of this figure as a measure of overall unemployment and underemployment is of course very limited, given that the data on employment conceal a considerable measure of underemployment. In a basically agrarian economy like that of Bangladesh underemployment is more rampant than unemployment. The notion of 'looking for work' is subject to considerable misinterpretation. Independent workers or self-employed and unpaid family workers do not consider themselves unemployed even if they are working only a few hours a week. In fact cultivators do not

[1] The author, who was formerly Post-Doctoral Associate, Iowa State University, U.S.A., is currently Assistant Professor of Economics, University of Dacca. He is deeply indebted to Dr Erik Thorbecke, Professor of Economics at the Iowa State University, U.S.A., and currently Director, World Employment Programme, International Labour Organisation, Geneva, for useful comments offered during his recent visit to Dacca. The author alone is responsible for any errors.

[2] References in square brackets are to the bibliography on pp. 258-9.

regard themselves as unemployed if their families have land and they are supported by the general activity of the household. According to the *Quarterly National Sample Survey* [10], the proportion of such self-employed and unpaid family workers amounted to nearly 70 per cent of the total labour force in 1967–8 [10, p. 33]. It is little wonder that an extremely small proportion of workers were recorded as looking for work.

Such a definition of unemployment, which includes only people who are voluntarily unemployed, naturally leads to a very low unemployment level, especially in view of the fact that the level of skills is extremely low in Bangladesh,[1] compared with the relatively high skill requirements to qualify for the available jobs. It is obvious that, if the notion of 'seeking work' is not interpreted broadly, the under-reporting of female labour-force participants is inevitable, particularly in developing countries where economic conditions restrict the number of so-called 'suitable jobs'. In a traditional society, generally men are preferred to women in most jobs. Owing to the high rate of unemployment and underemployment (to be discussed subsequently), it can easily be visualised that fewer job opportunities are left for females – a deterrent factor in reporting of females as even looking for work.[2]

III. UNEMPLOYMENT EQUIVALENT IN AGRICULTURE

One way to determine the unemployment equivalent of the under-employed would be to express the labour force in man-year (or man-hour units) and then examine the man-years of employment that can be provided in cultivating the available land and in livestock and fisheries activities. On the basis of the cropping pattern and the required man-hours per acre derived from farm management studies, Stern [21] estimates that one acre of land can provide 650 man-hours of employment. In addition, the labour force employed in animal husbandry and fisheries is one-third of the man-hours employed on crops. A full year's equivalent of employment is 2200 man-hours for farmers working on agricultural crops of Bangladesh. Account has to be taken of the changes in labour requirements resulting from changes in cropping patterns and practices.

[1] Out of the total employed labour force, the proportion of professional, technical and related workers amounted to only 1·64 per cent in 1967–8 and the proportion of administrative, executive and managerial workers was 0·27 per cent in the same year [10, table 25, p. 13]. These two categories together constitute 'high level manpower'.

[2] A complete analysis of the limitations of the national census data is presented in [1, pp. 38–43].

TABLE 9.1

LABOUR INPUTS FOR MAJOR CROPS IN BANGLADESH[a]

Item	1960–1 Acreage (million acres)	Man-days per acre	Million man-days	1964–5 Acreage (million acres)	Man-days per acre	Million man-days	1969–70 Acreage (million acres)	Man-days per acre	Million man-days
Crop									
Aus	6·30	41	258	6·65	50	332	8·25	55	454
Aman	14·58	52	758	15·11	58	876	15·00	60	900
Boro	1·01	64	65	1·05	65	68	2·30	75	172
Jute	1·52	98	149	1·66	98	163	2·25	98	221
Mustard	0·56	40	22	0·46	40	18	0·55	40	22
Total	23·97		1,252	24·93		1,457	28·35		1,769
Man-days/acre			522			585			624

[a] Source: [21, p. 6].

Note: This Table covers major crops only and the cropped acreage for these crops is appreciably less than the total cropped acreage shown in Table 9.2.

Using the factors mentioned above together with information compiled in Table 9.1, agricultural employment in Bangladesh is computed and presented in Table 9.2.

TABLE 9.2

AGRICULTURAL EMPLOYMENT AND UNEMPLOYMENT IN BANGLADESH[a]

	1960–1	1964–5	1969–70
Average hours/man-year	2,200	2,200	2,200
Cropped acreage (m. acres)	27·50	28·54	30·00
Average hours/cropped acre	650	728	775
Employment on crops (m. man-years)	8·15	9·44	10·57
Livestock and fishing (m. man-years) (= $\frac{1}{3}$ of Row 4)	2·71	3·11	3·50
Total agriculture employment (m. man-years)	10·86	12·55	14·07
Total agricultural labour force (m. man-years)	16·46	18·13	20·82
Unemployment (m. man-years)	5·60	5·58	6·75
Per cent unemployed	34·0%	30·8%	32·4%

[a] Source: [21, p. 7].

Seasonal characteristics. Agricultural underemployment may be conceived as having two distinct components [23, p. 50]. The first component is structural underemployment, which represents a measure of the total labour force which is truly 'surplus' even when labour requirements are at the seasonal peaks. By definition, therefore, this part of the labour force could be removed from agriculture without reducing total output at any time of the year. The second component is the seasonal underemployment and consists of that part of the peak labour force which is not required during off-peak periods.

Information on labour availability and its use is available from a survey conducted in a village of Noakhali district of Bangladesh [12]. Information on labour utilisation in man-days (one man-day constituting 8 hours of work) on a week-by-week basis was collected for the whole year consisting of 52 weeks. For the purpose of investigating the magnitude of agricultural underemployment (both structural and seasonal) these 52 weeks are grouped into 13 equal four-week periods.

Thus, more rigorously, let

P = peak four-week period
d_m = the four-week labour requirement in man-days
$m = 1, 2, 3, \ldots p, \ldots, 13$

s_m = supply of labour in the four-week period, m
S = total labour force in agriculture in man-days in a year and
D = total labour employed in agriculture in the same year
    expressed in man-days.

There are variations in the four-weekly labour supply (in man-days)
due to geographical migration as evidenced by the fact that about
one-third of the active adults engaged in farm work at one time or
another migrate to other areas of Bangladesh and India; leaving
their families in the village, in search of mainly urban jobs such as
cooks, domestic servants, office peons, taxi drivers, bus conductors,
brick-layers, painters, police constables, porters, cart pullers,
dock workers, etc.; among other jobs they work as mill hands,
bamboo and sugar cane cutters, crew in river crafts, seamen in
ocean-going vessels and so on [12, p. 10].

The ratio of underemployment – that is, the excess of total labour
availability over and above total labour requirements expressed as a
percentage of the former is $S - D/S$. This ratio can be split up and
expressed as shown below [23, pp. 50–1].

$$S = \sum_{m=1}^{13} s_m = 40619, \quad m = 1, 2, \ldots, 13.$$

$$D = \sum_{\substack{\text{for } m \neq pm = 1}}^{13} dm = 19714 \cdot 5, \, m = 1, 2, \ldots, p, \ldots, 13 \text{ and } d_p > dm$$

$$d_p = 2710.$$

Now we can show that

$$\frac{S - D}{S} = \frac{S - 13d_p}{S} + \frac{13dp - D}{S}, \text{ or}$$

$$51 \cdot 5\% = 13 \cdot 3\% + 38 \cdot 2\%.$$

Underemployment rate = Structural underemployment rate +
                        Seasonal underemployment rate.

It is interesting to note that during the peak season in agriculture,
the man-days engaged in non-farm work is a minimum (the twelfth
period in Table 9·3) while during the slack season man-days of
employment in non-farm jobs is the highest. These non-farm jobs,
both self-employed and wage-paid, include jobs like felling trees,
dressing fuel, sawing wood, making and repairing houses and furniture, brick-laying, boat-building, boat-plying, carting, etc., and
trade activities such as trade in fruits, betel nut, coconut, paddy,
vegetables, tobacco leaf, stationery, grocery, etc. [12, pp. 17–18].

TABLE 9.3

SEASONAL PATTERN OF EMPLOYMENT:
TOTAL MAN-DAYS USED, BY FOUR-WEEK PERIODS; VILLAGE SABILPUR, NOAKHALI, EAST PAKISTAN[a]

Utilisation of labour supply	Four-week periods[b]											(peak period)		Total for whole year
	(1)	(2)	(3)	(4)	(5)	(6)	(7)	(8)	(9)	(10)	(11)	(12)	(13)	
Total agricultural work (self and wage employment)	1,116·0 (37·0)	1,326·0 (42·0)	911·0 (29·4)	593·0 (19·0)	484·0 (15·4)	1,258·0 (40·7)	1,210·0 (40·0)	1,044·0 (34·4)	1,120·5 (37·1)	1,318·0 (43·4)	2,027·0 (64·2)	2,710·0 (81·0)	1,762·0 (51·4)	16,879·5 (44·6)
Garden work (self and wage employment)	133·0	26·0	65·0	154·5	320·5	82·5	108·5	298·5	471·5	661·5	358·0	–	155·5	2,835·0
Total farm work dm	1,249·0 (41·0)	1,352·0 (43·7)	976·0 (31·5)	747·5 (24·0)	804·5 (25·7)	1,340·5 (45·4)	1,318·5 (43·6)	1,342·5 (44·1)	1,592·0 (52·7)	1,979·5 (65·2)	2,385·0 (75·5)	2,710·0 (81·0)	1,917·5 (55·9)	19,714·5 (48·5)
Total non-farm work	736·5 (24·0)	567·0 (18·3)	694·0 (22·4)	758·5 (24·3)	692·5 (22·2)	616·0 (19·9)	643·5 (21·5)	730·0 (24·0)	674·0 (22·3)	535·0 (17·6)	487·0 (15·5)	311·5 (9·3)	595·0 (17·4)	8,040·5 (19·80)
Total gainful employment	1,985·5 (65·0)	1,919·0 (61·9)	1,670·0 (53·9)	1,506·0 (48·3)	1,497·0 (47·8)	1,956·5 (63·3)	1,962·0 (64·9)	2,072·5 (68·2)	2,066·0 (75·0)	2,514·0 (82·8)	2,872·0 (91·0)	3,021·5 (90·0)	2,512·5 (73·3)	27,755 (68·3)
Not available for work (due to rains, socials, etc.)	270·0 (8·9)	342·0 (11·0)	218·5 (7·0)	191·5 (6·1)	169·5 (5·4)	181·5 (5·9)	102·0 (3·4)	152·0 (5·0)	222·5 (7·4)	111·0 (3·7)	86·0 (2·7)	290·5 (8·7)	200·0 (5·4)	2,536 (6·2)
No work found	767·5 (26·1)	833·0 (27·1)	1,210·5 (39·1)	1,416·5 (45·6)	1,466·5 (46·8)	954·0 (30·8)	960·0 (31·7)	813·5 (26·8)	534·5 (17·6)	412·5 (13·5)	199·0 (6·3)	44·0 (1·3)	715·5 (21·3)	10,328 (25·4)
Overtime work (more than 8 hours a day)	–	4·5	–	–	–	–	–	3·5	18·5	45	86·5	527·5	12·5	698·0
Total labour supply (100·0)	3,023	3,094	3,099	3,114	3,133	3,092	3,024	3,038	3,023	3,038	3,157	3,356	3,428	40,619

[a] Sources: [12, p. 73, Appendix C-1; 14a, p. 251, Table II].
[b] Figures in parentheses are percentages.

The shortage of labour during the peak season is also indicated by a rise in wages of hired labour in this period, which go up by about 50 per cent.

IV. NON-AGRICULTURAL EMPLOYMENT

Taking the changes in labour productivity into account, Wouter Tims [25 and 26] derives the employment elasticities relating sectoral employment changes to changes in sectoral value added. The relevant employment elasticities and the changes in employment and value-added by sectors are shown in Table 9.4. The implicit rate of change

TABLE 9.4

EMPLOYMENT ELASTICITY, PERCENTAGE CHANGES IN VALUE-ADDED AND EMPLOYMENT IN BANGLADESH [a]

Sector	Employment elasticity	Percentage change	
		Value-added	Employment
Manufacturing:			
1960–1 to 1964–5	0·46	21·5	10
1964–5 to 1969–70	0·50	58·3	29
Other sectors:			
1960–1 to 1964–5	0·80	19·4	16
1964–5 to 1969–70	0·82	26·4	22

[a] Source: Employment elasticities from Tims [25] and the remainder from Stern [20].

in the sectoral labour productivity underlying the estimates of sectoral employment as computed by Joseph J. Stern [21] are shown in Table 9.5. Using these estimates the non-agricultural employment in Bangladesh is derived as presented in Table 9.6.

TABLE 9.5

COMPOUND RATE OF GROWTH IN OUTPUT/WORKER IN BANGLADESH [a]

Year	Agriculture	Mining and manufacturing
1960–1 to 1964–5	– 1·5%	2·4%
1964–5 to 1969–70	– 0·2%	4·0%

[a] Value-added in constant 1959–60 prices.

TABLE 9.6

NON-AGRICULTURAL EMPLOYMENT IN BANGLADESH (1960–1 to 1969–70)

Year	1960–1	1964–5	1969–70
Labour Force	2·68	3·13	3·90
Employment	2·51	2·89	3·60
Unemployment	0·17	0·24	0·30

Table 9.7 summarises briefly the employment picture in Bangladesh during the last twenty years; Table 9.8 presents the same set of information in the form of proportions. From these tables we can draw certain broad conclusions:

(i) Nearly one-third of the entire Bangalee human resources have remained completely utilised during the last two decades.

(ii) Agricultural unemployment as a proportion of agricultural labour force was 31·29 per cent in 1950. Throughout the last two decades it showed no sign of any improvement. In 1969–70 over 32 per cent of the agricultural workers remained unemployed.

(iii) Unemployment among non-agricultural workers showed some degree of improvement during the last two decades.

(iv) Out of every 100 unemployed Bangalee workers 93 have always been agricultural workers.

The above picture of unemployment in both the agricultural and the non-agricultural sectors of Bangladesh must be viewed in the light of the fact that more than 82 per cent of the total Bangalee labour force has always been and still is agricultural.

TABLE 9.7

LABOUR FORCE AND EMPLOYMENT IN BANGLADESH
1950–1 to 1969–70[a]
(million man-years)

	1950–1	1954–5	1960–1	1964–5	1969–70
Total labour force	15·60	17·00	19·14	21·26	24·72
Agriculture	13·10	14·00	16·46	18·13	20·82
Non-agriculture	2·50	3·00	2·68	3·13	3·90
Total employment	11·20	12·10	13·37	15·44	17·67
Agriculture	9·00	9·30	10·86	12·55	14·07
Non-agriculture	2·20	2·80	2·51	2·89	3·60
Total unemployment	4·40	4·90	5·77	5·82	7·05
Agriculture	4·10	4·70	5·60	5·58	6·75
Non-agriculture	0·30	0·20	0·17	0·24	0·30

[a] Sources: [25, p. 12, Table II; 21, App. Table 1].

V. URBAN UNEMPLOYMENT

A census of private industrial establishments was carried out, mostly in the mid 1960s, covering eight principal cities of Bangladesh. This census provides information on employment in private industrial establishments for each of these cities and all establishments engaged in any kind of economic activity were enumerated in the census; specifically it included, (i) manufacturing establishments,

TABLE 9.8

UNEMPLOYMENT IN BANGLADESH BY ECONOMIC SECTORS 1950–1 TO 1969–70

Labour Force
(percentage of total labour force)

Sector	1950–1	1954–5	1960–1	1964–5	1969–70
Agriculture	83·97	82·29	86·0	85·3	84·2
Non-agriculture	16·03	17·71	14·0	14·7	15·80
Total	100·00	100·00	100·00	100·00	100·00

Unemployment
(percentage of sector)

	1950–1	1954–5	1960–1	1964–5	1969–70
Agriculture	31·29	33·60	34·02	30·80	32·42
Non-agriculture	12·00	6·65	6·34	7·70	7·69
Total	28·20	28·20	30·15	27·58	28·52

Proportion of
(percentage of total labour force)

	1950–1	1954–5	1960–1	1964–5	1969–70
Agriculture	26·28	27·65	29·26	26·24	27·31
Non-agriculture	1·92	1·18	0·87	1·13	1·21
Total	28·20	28·20	30·15	27·38	28·52

Unemployment
(percentage of total unemployment)

	1950–1	1954–5	1960–1	1964–5	1969–70
Agriculture	93·18	95·92	97·05	95·88	96·74
Non-agriculture	6·82	4·80	2·95	4·12	4·26
Total	100·00	100·00	100·00	100·00	100·00

Computed from sources: [21, p. 12, App. Table 1, and 25, p. 12, Table II].

(ii) commercial establishments including banks, insurance companies and wholesale and retail trade, (iii) service establishments including offices of lawyers, doctors, schools and colleges run on a commercial basis, hotels and restaurants, cinema houses and repair shops. Those excluded from the census were: (i) all government and semi-government institutions, (ii) trade associations and unions, etc., (iii) non-profitable charitable institutions and (iv) vendors, hawkers, pedlars, etc.

Population estimates for each of these cities are provided in this census report for the various years the census was conducted. Applying the labour force participation rates as obtained in the 1961 population census for each of these cities to the prevailing population figure[1] we obtain the total labour force for each city in the relevant year. In Table 9.9 is shown the total labour force obtained

TABLE 9.9

LABOUR FORCE AND EMPLOYMENT IN THE PRINCIPAL
CITIES OF BANGLADESH[a]

City[b]	Year	Labour force	Employment in private industrial establishments	Employment in government sector	Total employment	Employment as % of total labour force
Chittagong	1964	179420	84197	59807	144004	80·26
Khulna	1964	90526	26955	30175	57130	63·20
Saidpur	1965	18611	3541	6204	9745	52·36
Rajshahi	1965	17786	6113	5929	12042	67·70
Mymensingh	1965	24649	5232	8213	13445	54·56
Barisal	1965	24564	5988	8188	14176	57·71
Comilla	1965	16488	7030	5496	12526	75·97

[a] Computed from sources [9, pp. 8–9, Table nos. 1 and 2; 6, pp. 35–8, Table 2].

[b] Dacca and Narayanganj cities are excluded because the present assumption of the government sector employing one-third of the total labour force (as against less than one-third of the total *employed* labour force in reality) gives obviously exaggerated employment figures.

on this basis as well as the total employment for all establishments as obtained for each city under the survey. Except for the cities of Dacca and Narayanganj it is found that these private industrial establishments provide employment at most for 40 per cent of the city's labour force. In some cities employment from these sources is as low as 17 to 20 per cent. As government and semi-government establishments are excluded from this census, employment figures for these sectors are not available. However, it is known that the

[1] The population projections have been made on the basis of 1951–61 intercensal net growth rate for various cities/towns as yielded by the censal data [9, p. 8].

government sector employs less than one-third of the employed labour force [12, p. 2, section II]. On this basis, probably exaggerating a little, let us assume that the government sector employs one-third of the total labour force in each city. The government employment, thus obtained, together with the employment in private industrial establishments gives us the size of aggregate employment for each of these cities. Total employment therefore ranges from 52 per cent to 80 per cent of the total labour force in these cities as shown in Table 9.9. Possibly a part of the remainder of the labour force is self-employed or ends up as street vendors, hawkers, pedlars, and the like – the sector which is believed to perform the role of mopping up the residual labour force.

Even if we are not prepared to acknowledge that all of the remaining labour force whose employment status cannot be explained, is unemployed, these figures at least indicate that even if some fraction of this remaining labour force is employed, the unemployment situation in cities is grave.

VI. SOME MAJOR CAUSES OF UNEMPLOYMENT

Rapid growth of population and labour force. The first major cause of unemployment in Bangladesh is, of course, the high rate of growth of the population. The echo of the population explosion of the post-British period is increasingly being heard as an explosion in the labour force today. During 1951 through 1961 the population of Bangladesh grew at the compound annual rate of 2·5 per cent. Such a rapid growth in population is being closely followed by a rapid increase in the labour force with a lag of ten years. A surviving child born in year t, joins the labour force in year $(t +10)$.[1] Among the various estimates currently available, one reasonable estimate shows that Bangalee population grew at the compound annual rate of 3·3 per cent during the sixties (1961 to 1968). The estimate made by the O.E.C.D. [16, p. 24] on the basis of a B.I.D.E. projection of population [2] assumed that two-thirds of the family planning programme as laid down in the Third Five Year Plan was fulfilled. The labour force during 1961–8 grew at the compound annual rate of 3·3 per cent.

Capital intensity in Bangladesh industries. The Bangladesh economy is characterised by an abundance of labour and scarcity of capital. The principle of comparative advantage dictates the adoption of labour-intensive techniques of production. But if we analyse the technology of the Bangladesh industries, it is most perplexing to note that most of them are of a highly capital-intensive

[1] The age limit for inclusion into the labour force in Bangladesh is ten years.

nature. One way to judge whether Bangladesh industries are unduly capital-intensive is to compare the capital-intensities of the Bangladesh industries with those prevailing in countries whose economies are characterised by labour scarcity and capital abundance. For our purpose, we choose the United States, which compared with Bangladesh is extremely capital rich (labour-scarce). We also extend our comparison to Japan, which compared with Bangladesh has a relatively abundant supply of capital and scarcity of labour. For our evaluation capital-intensity is defined as the value of fixed assets per man-year of employment, that is the capital–labour ratio.[1]

Table 9.10 presents the capital-intensities of a number of industries in Bangladesh, Japan and the U.S.A. The Bangladesh values are set at unity; the Japanese and United States values are deviations from unity. Certain startling conclusions are immediately revealed by this comparison:

(1) Industries in Bangladesh are more capital-intensive than those in Japan. The only exception is the basic metals. This conclusion is further strengthened by the fact that even the Bangladesh cotton textiles industry for which a considerable amount of inter-country product similarity is believed to exist, the technology is more capital-intensive than that of the Japanese textiles.

(2) Many of Bangladesh industries are as capital-intensive as U.S. industries. What is more surprising is that capital-intensity in the paper industry in Bangladesh exceeds the capital-intensity of the paper industry in the U.S.A.[2]

[1] The following comments drawn from Khan [17] are presented to emphasise the point.

The bulk of the fixed assets consists of machines and equipment imported primarily from Japan and the U.S. and these assets are evaluated at the official rate of exchange when entered into the accounts. As nearly two-thirds of the total machinery and equipment come from these two countries, there certainly exists comparability of these assets used in Bangalee, Japanese and U.S. industries. Yet international comparability of the value of capital is made difficult by its inherent heterogeneous characteristics. The question of whether inter-country product homogeneity exists would also arise.

It is indeed possible that if the above factors could be taken into account the values of the capital-intensity could change. But in so far as we are concerned with certain broad qualitative conclusions, any change in the value of capital-intensity arising from the above correction is most unlikely to be so drastic as to render our conclusions invalid.

[2] Gerard K. Boon [3, p. 213] performs a similar test for the efficiency of Mexican industries. Using the capital–output ratio as the index of capital-intensity, Boon compares the indices between Mexico, U.S.A. and the U.K. for various industries. Except for basic metals and machinery and metal products industries all other Mexican industries were found to be less capital-intensive than those in the U.K. and U.S.A.

(3) That capital-intensity in the Bangladesh industries does not reflect the relative scarcity (abundance) of capital (labour) is further demonstrated through a comparison of capital-intensities between the Japanese and U.S. industries. Compared with the United States, Japan is a relatively labour-abundant (capital-scarce) economy. In keeping with the factor endowments, industries in Japan are consistently less capital-intensive than those in the U.S.A.

It is rather perplexing to note that in spite of a high level of unemployment in the country, the industries tended to be relatively capital-intensive. An investigation is made to determine the causes of such a paradox.

A phenomenon observable in Bangladesh is the existence of a whole set of biases and distortions affecting factor prices. Such price distortions have led to a reduction in the price of capital below its equilibrium level (that is its marginal value product) while forcing the price of labour above its equilibrium. As a direct consequence of such factor price distortions, industries in Bangladesh naturally tend to take advantage of the relatively cheap factor (i.e. capital) and economise on the relatively more expensive one (i.e. labour).

Several factors tended to reduce the price of capital. The maintenance of an overvalued exchange rate thus provided incentives to the industrialists to import capital goods at a relatively low price. During 1948–9 through 1964–5, according to one estimate, the rate of overvaluation ranged between 80 per cent to 210 per cent [14a]. The interest rate structure is kept artificially low which does not

TABLE 9.10

CAPITAL–LABOUR RATIOS IN MANUFACTURING INDUSTRIES: BANGLADESH, JAPAN AND THE U.S.A.[a]

Sector	Bangladesh	Japan	U.S.A.
Cotton textiles	1·00	0·38	2·18
Jute textiles	1·00	–	–
Paper	1·00	0·07	0·85
Leather goods	1·00	0·59	1·40
Rubber goods	1·00	0·32	4·43
Fertiliser	1·00	–	–
Other chemicals	1·00	–	–
All chemicals	1·00	0·33	2·49
Basic metals	1·00	4·04	13·60
Machinery	1·00	0·20	1·96
Wood products	1·00	0·40	–

[a] Computed from Azizur Rahman Khan [17, p. 261, Table VIII] in terms of values of fixed assets in U.S. dollars per worker, after correcting for devaluation of the Bangladesh currency following liberation of Bangladesh.

reflect the scarcity of capital. The rate at which funds have been borrowed has varied between 3 per cent to 7·5 per cent during the last two decades. The interest rate on saving was generally 2–3 per cent annum around 1960 wheareas the price rise during the same period averaged about 14 per cent per annum, yielding a negative return to the saver.

Moreover, numerous policies were adopted by the government to promote industrialisation which discriminated in favour of capital. The provision of accelerated depreciation allowance was a common feature. The cumulative effect of such allowances has been that 39 to 44 per cent of the fixed capital costs could be recovered in the very first year, 70 to 89 per cent of the total and 78 to 89 per cent of the machine cost part of the total, gets recovered through these allowances within the first five years. The investment control system which virtually functioned as the foreign exchange control system for the import of capital goods into the private sector, provided imported capital goods to those who received sanctions of licences at low prices. Around 5 per cent of the capital cost of investment projects was exempt from tax (tax holiday) for the first five years of its life.[1] This in short was the effect of the type of economic policies followed during the days of Pakistani rule.

A number of factors tended to raise the price of labour in Bangladesh. The minimum wages are fixed by the government and have often been revised upwards.[2] Cost of living allowance, paid leave, free housing or low-cost housing (in 1969 the government contributed takas 100 million towards the construction of housing for workers) are provided to employees. The power of labour unions is on the increase and demand for increased wages often bear no relation to corresponding increase in labour productivity.

Rural urban migration and urban unemployment. While the bulk of the Bangalee population reside in rural areas, there is a persistent trend towards urbanisation and more recently this phenomenon has accelerated. During the intercensal period (1951–61), while Bangladesh's total and rural population increased by 21·0 and 19·8 per cent respectively, the urban population increased by 43·2 per cent [7]. During the same period the populations of the principal cities of Bangladesh – Chittagong, Dacca, Khulna and Narayanganj – have increased by 25·6, 65·7, 209·0 and 137·0 per cent respectively [19].

This rapid increase in urban population is a function of the rate of natural increase and of migration. As shown by the 1961 Census, 'a number of urban areas have been gaining in population far beyond what might have been expected from natural increase alone,

---

[1] Dealt at length in Rab [20].
[2] Following liberation the minimum wages have been fixed at takas 150.

whereas not a few rural areas have been losing population more or less consistently' [7, p. 13]. Moreover demographers believe that in the case of Bangladesh the natural rate of increase in the population of urban areas is lower than that of the rural population [19, p. 31, 3].

A National Quarterly Sample Survey conducted by the Central Statistical Office of the erstwhile Government of Pakistan in 1967–8 revealed that 5·97 per cent of the total urban Bangalee population of age 10 years and above had migrated within the preceding one year. The migrants of such age groups clearly represent a new addition to the already large pool of urban labour force.

Information on the reasons which motivated such rural to urban migration were also collected by this survey. The findings are summarised in Table 9.11.

TABLE 9.11

REASONS GIVEN BY RURAL POPULATION[a] WHO HAVE MIGRATED TO THE URBAN AREAS: 1967–8

Reasons for rural–urban migration	Proportion of total migrants of age 10 and above
To seek job	39·37
To set up industry or business	4·07
To study	0·90
To marry	10·41
Others	45·25
Total	100·00

Source: [10, p. 46, Table no. 31].
[a] Population of age 10 years and above.

It is clear from the survey that in Bangladesh almost two-fifths of the total migrants of age 10 and above who migrated into the urban areas from the rural areas were looking for work.

Such a rapid rural–urban migration could be directly attributed to the 'push' effect commonly believed to be arising out of the growing population pressure on land (worsening land–man ratio), increase in rural debt, unemployment and underemployment in agriculture, lack of rural industries to provide alternative sources of employment and income to the villagers and of course low incomes and wages. It is found that for Bangladesh, the monthly urban wage rate exceeds the rural wage rate by 69 per cent [1, p. 148]. Moreover the rural–urban per capita income differential is found to be quite high. According to a computation by Bose [4, p. 455] per capita rural income was only 32 per cent of the urban per capita income in 1963–4 (takas 755 versus takas 279).

There is also the 'pull' effect forcing such high rates of urbanisation in Bangladesh. Urban–rural wage and income differential is indeed one of the main factors contributing to it, but such other factors as the 'city lights' or 'quality of city life' which obviously include the public amenities and certain types of urban services also lure people into the urban areas from rural life. It is obvious from Table 9.11 that those migrants whose reasons for migrating into the urban areas are categorised under 'others' may rightly be presumed to contain a great many of such individuals migrating on account of the 'pull' effect.

VII. IMPACT OF WAR OF LIBERATION

Effects on the productive capacity of the economy.[1] The actions of the Pakistan Army resulted in massive destruction of properties and massacre of the people of Bangladesh during the nine-month-long war of liberation. The all-out war of December 1971 led to further human and material losses. In addition, 10 million people were driven out of Bangladesh. Following liberation they returned to find their meagre assets, including their dwellings, bullocks and ploughs completely destroyed. In agriculture, productive capacity was reduced due to the loss of cattle, ploughs and other farming implements. Around takas 100 millions worth of assets of the manufacturing industries were destroyed and about 3 per cent of the installed plant and machinery of the large-scale manufacturing industries have been lost.

The hardest hit were the vital economic overheads – transport, communication and power transmission in particular – and to some extent the sea ports. Two hundred and eighty-seven large and small railway bridges were damaged and some of the largest will require considerable time before they can be fully repaired.

To give some idea of the extent of the drop in output resulting from this devastation to the economy a comparison of the level of post-liberation output is made with the level of the output of the pre-liberation period in Table 9.12. It is apparent that jute textiles, matches, steel, petroleum products and cement have made noteworthy recovery. Paper and fertiliser have made steady progress though incomplete recovery. However, progress has been slowest in cotton textiles, the second largest industry. Among the small-scale industries, cotton hand-loom weaving (the biggest of them all) produced only one-fifth of what would have been normal output during January to May 1970.

[1] This section draws heavily from the Annual Plan, 1972–73 of Bangladesh [11, pp. 2–6].

TABLE 9.12

PRODUCTION IN SELECTED INDUSTRIES OF
BANGLADESH IN THE POST-LIBERATION PERIOD [a]

Name of industry	Unit of output	Monthly average output in 1969–70	Output and time period	Recent monthly output as index of 1969–70 monthly output
Jute textiles	thousand tons	48·3	40·9 (May 1972)	85
Newsprint	tons	2978	1985 (May 1972)	67
Paper	tons	3518	1568 (May 1972)	45
Petroleum products	thousand tons	99·1 (Jan 1971)	75·8 (May 1972)	76
Cement	tons	4417	3238 (av. Apr–May 1972)	73
Fertiliser	thousand tons	7·9	3806 (av. Mar–May 1972)	42
Steel mill	metric tons	3238 (Jan 1971)	500 (est. av. Jan–May 1972)	118
Cotton cloth	thousand yards	4929	2800 (est. av. Jan–May 1972)	10
Cotton yarn	thousand pounds	8808	1059 (est. av. May 1972)	32
Matches	thousand gross boxes	1080		98

[a] Source: [11, p. 6, Table 1].

The primary reason for reviewing the impact of the war of liberation is to form some idea of the possible extent of loss in employment resulting from such low levels of production in these various
industries. Apart from this, the freedom fighters who fought bravely
to liberate Bangladesh have returned to civilian life and many of
them need to be provided with employment. There are in addition
400,000 Bangalees stranded in Pakistan; even if we assume that
50 per cent of them are dependent women and children, 200,000
jobs will have to be provided when they are repatriated to Bangladesh.

VIII. POLICIES AND MEASURES TO PROMOTE EMPLOYMENT IN BANGLADESH

I shall now attempt to suggest certain policies and measures which would help alleviate if, not eliminate, the unemployment problem in Bangladesh. In this section, various new measures and policies, together with changes in current policies, are identified and recommended which would help increase job opportunities, both in the modern and the agricultural sectors.

Population control policy. In the face of the rapidly growing population and labour force, with its adverse impact on employment, population control measures under government auspices began to receive serious attention from the government only from the start of the 1960s. The family planning programme corresponding to the Third Five Year Plan (1965–70) was the first comprehensive scheme adopted. The objective of the programme was to reduce the birth rate from 50 per 1000 population to 40 per 1000 population.

The government claimed that the birth rate had been reduced to 41·15 per 1000 population. Many have, however, called in question the credibility of these figures. The shortcomings associated with the family planning programme in Bangladesh have included lack of adequately trained workers, inadequate leadership provided by family planning officers, and the placing of emphasis on initial acceptance alone, without adequate steps towards subsequent continuation [1a].

Removal of factor price distortions. As the existence of factor price distortions have led to the adoption of capital-intensive techniques, current policies which have contributed to such distortion should be discontinued. Decision to devalue was postponed by the government in the belief that the demand for jute exports was inelastic and that the prices of imported foodstuffs would increase. Taxes from profits earned by importers could – it was argued – be collected with greater ease.

Current policies, such as the provision of the accelerated depreciation allowance, the investment control system and the tax holiday, all of which are designed to promote industrialisation and which discriminate in favour of capital, have to be revised or discontinued.

The government will have seriously to consider the effect of patronising labour (that is it should take into account the impacts of revising upward of minimum wages, the provision of social welfare benefits, and similar policies on employment).

More rural jobs through works programmes. At the start of the 1960s a Rural Works Programme was initiated in Bangladesh with a view to providing employment for the unskilled rural labour force

TABLE 9.13

SUMMARY OF ACHIEVEMENTS OF THE RURAL WORKS
PROGRAMME: 1962–8 [a]
(totals during period 1962–8)

	New	Repaired
Hard surface roads (miles)	90	3,160
Dirt surface roads (miles)	20,925	115,211
Embankments (miles)	3,743	7,595
Drainages irrigation canals (miles)	9,031	9,966
Acres benefited by above (000's)	7,191	
Community buildings	9,584	
Employment created (000 man-days)	172,958	
Total allocation (takas millions)	925	

[a] Source: [23, p. 23, Table 4].

in the construction of embankments for flood-control, drainage
canals, rural roads, schools, community houses, markets, drinking-
water supplies, graveyards, dispensaries and a few local government
buildings. The increased availability of such facilities and the
emerging rural economic infrastructure was not only expected to
boost agricultural productivity but also to provide employment for
the large body of unemployed and underemployed agricultural
workers.

The physical achievements of the programme are summarised in
Table 9.13. The following three features deserve our attention.

(1) During the period 1962 to 1968 almost 173 million man-days
of employment were created. It is estimated that on an average
40 million man-days of employment were created annually
[21, p. 22]. As the seasonal underemployment rate in Bangladesh is over 38 per cent of the agricultural labour force
[1, p. 82] the rural works programme should be conducted at a
time to coincide with the slack season in agriculture.

(2) In the late 1950s and early 1960s the average wages paid to
unskilled rural workers during the slack season amounted to
taka 0·75 per day – an amount which could barely provide
subsistence to the workers. At the inception of the works
programme, wage rates were fixed at takas 1·50 to takas 2·00
per day and by 1967 the wage rate ranged between takas 2·00
to takas 2·50 per day for unskilled workers. The non-works
programme job wage rates also went up to between takas 1·75
and takas 2·25, thereby implying that a demand for agricultural workers was created during the slack season in agriculture. The raising of rural wages through the works programme
helps to check or reduce the speed of rural–urban migration
by reducing the rural–urban wage differential. Moreover, the

influence of the 'push effect' on the rural-to-urban migrants is dampened by the works programme not only through the alternative non-agricultural job opportunities available, but also through agricultural productivity being enhanced by the resulting infrastructure.

Output and employment with new improved seed varieties. Currently information is beginning to be available about yield, employment and profitability of cultivating the new improved varieties as compared with the local native varieties of rice grown in the irrigated areas of the Comilla district of Bangladesh during the winter. Taipei-177 and I.R.R.I.-8 are the two new improved varieties of rice imported from Taiwan and the Philippines (the International Rice Research Institute near Manila); Shaitta and Boro are the two local native varieties of rice grown in the Comilla area.

On an average for four years (1966–9) Taipei-177 yielded 96 per cent more than the local Shaitta variety and 86 per cent more than the local Boro rice. The I.R.R.I.-8 output per acre exceeded that of Shaitta by 125 per cent and that of Boro by 113 per cent on an average during the period 1967–9 [1, p. 173].

With respect to labour requirements under the new varieties as compared to the 'desi' (local) varieties, certain facts emerged:

(1) overall labour requirements per acre under Taipei-177 were found to be on average for the four years 78 per cent higher than under the Shaitta rice and 28 per cent higher than under the Boro rice;

(2) for I.R.R.I.-8, labour requirement per acre on an average for the three years exceeded the Shaitta labour requirement per acre by 92 per cent and that for Boro by 38 per cent.

(3) For every acre brought under cultivation with Taipei-177 29·9 man-days of additional employment was created as compared with that with Shaitta rice and 14·8 additional man-days of employment over that with Boro.

(4) every additional acre brought under I.R.R.I.-8 provided 35·5 additional man-days of employment as compared with Shaitta and 20·4 additional man-days as compared with Boro [1, pp. 173–5].

According to the findings of the Comilla Academy for Rural Development Survey [14] the returns to investment (1967–9 average) were 31 per cent for the local varieties and 116 per cent for I.R.R.I.-8 both in terms of net income,[1] and 77 per cent for the local

$$^1 \text{ Net income} = \frac{\text{Gross return} - \text{Total cost}}{\text{Total cost}}$$

varieties and 116 per cent for I.R.R.I.-8 in terms of family income.[1]
Thus we note that the new varieties are more profitable than the
traditional varieties of rice in Comilla and that this alone should
provide adequate incentives to the farmers to adopt the new
varieties.

Evidence is further available from other areas of Bangladesh.
Information obtained from the Gumai Bil area [18] indicates that
the labour requirements for the growing of I.R.R.I.-8 rice is double
that required for growing local varieties. At the same time, the yield
of I.R.R.I.-8 rice is three times that of the local varieties. Other
evidence also indicates that under the new varieties a doubling of
yield results and labour requirements increase by about 65 per cent
over that of the local varieties [17].

Thus, it is abundantly clear that the increased and wider use of
the new varieties of seed will lead to increased employment, higher
yields, increased productivity and income in agriculture,

REFERENCES

[1] Iftikhar Ahmed, 'Unemployment and Underemployment in Pakistan' (and
Bangladesh), unpublished Ph.D. Dissertation, Iowa State University, 1972.

[1a] Lee L. Bean, *Pakistan's Population in the 1970s: certainties and uncertainties*
(New York, N.Y., The Population Council, 1971).

[2] Lee L. Bean, Masihur Rahman Khan and A. Razzaque Rukanuddin,
Population Projections for Pakistan: 1960-2000 (Karachi, Pakistan Institute
of Development Economics, 1968).

[3] Gerard K. Boon, 'Factor Intensities in Mexico with special reference to
manufacturing', in H. C. Bos (ed.), *Towards Balanced International Growth*,
pp. 201-18 (Amsterdam, Holland, North-Holland publishing Co. 1969).

[4] Swadesh R. Bose, 'Trend of real income of the rural poor in East Pakistan,
1949-66, *Pakistan Development Review*, 8: pp. 452-84 (Autumn 1968).

[5] John C. H. Fei and Gustav Ranis, *Development of the Labour Surplus Economy: theory and policy* (Homewood, Illinois, R. B. Irwin, 1964).

[6] Government of Pakistan: *Population Census of Pakistan, 1961: economic
characteristics* (Karachi, Office of the Census Commissioner, Census,
Bulletin No. 5, 1963).

[7] ——, *Population Census of Pakistan, 1961: Sexes, urban and rural* (Census
Bulletin No. 2, 1962).

[8] ——, *Report of the Advisory Panel for the Fourth Five Year Plan, 1970-75*,
vol. 1 (Karachi, Pakistan Planning Commission, July 1970).

[9] ——, *Summary Findings of the Census of Establishments in Selected Cities,
1962-66.* (Karachi, Central Statistical Office, Dec. 24, 1968).

[10] ——, *Summary Report, Population and Labour Force, 1967-68* (Karachi,
Central Statistical Office, 1969).

[1] Family Income $= \dfrac{\text{Gross return} - \text{Cash cost}}{\text{Total cost}} \times 100.$

[11] Government of the People's Republic of Bangladesh, *The Annual Plan 1972–73* (Planning Commission, Dacca, 1972).

[12] M. T. Habibullah, *The Pattern of Agricultural Unemployment* (Dacca, Paramount Press, 1962).

[13] Mahbubul Haq, 'Rationale of Government Controls and Policies in Pakistan', *Pakistan Economic Journal, 9* (Mar 1963).

[14] Anwarul Haque, *Cost and Return: a Study of Irrigated Winter Crops* (Comilla, Pakistan Academy for Rural Development, 1969).

[14a] A. I. Aminul Islam, 'An Estimation of the Extent of Overvaluation of the domestic currency in Pakistan at the official rate of exchange, 1948/49—1964/65, *Pakistan Development Review 10*, pp. 50–9, (Spring 1970).

[15] Nurul Islam, 'Concepts and Measurement of Unemployment and Underemployment in Developing Countries,' *International Labour Review*, 89: pp. 244–55 (Mar 1964).

[16] F. R. Kahnert, H. Stier Carmignani, and P. Thomopoulos, *Agriculture and Related Industries in Pakistan* (Paris, France, Organization for Economic Cooperation and Development, Development Center, 1970).

[17] A. R. Khan, 'Capital Intensity and the Efficiency of Factor Use: a comparative study of the observed capital labour ratios of Pakistani industries', *Pakistan Development Review*, 10: pp. 232–63 (Summer 1970).

[18] John W. Mellor and M. Raquibuzzaman, *Generating Employment in Bangladesh: Some Special Problems and their Possible Solutions* (Department of Agricultural Economics, Cornell University, Mar 1972).

[19] Mian M. Nazeer, 'Urban Growth in Pakistan', *Asian Survey 6:* pp. 310–18 June 1966).

[20] A. Rab, 'Income Taxation in Pakistan', unpublished Ph.D. thesis. Cambridge, Mass., Library, Harvard University, 1968.

[21] Joseph J. Stern, *Employment by Regions and Sectors: 1960–1975.* (Cambridge Mass., Harvard University, Dec 8, 1969).

[22] John W. Thomas, 'Agricultural Production, Equity and Rural Organization in East Pakistan', Mimeographed paper presented at the Pakistan Rural Development Workshop, East Lansing, Michigan, June 21, July 28, 1971. Asian Studies Center, Michigan State University, 1971.

[23] John W. Thomas, 'Rural Public Works and East Pakistan's Development', mimeographed paper presented at the Development Advisory Service Conference held at Sorrento, Italy, September 5–18, 1968. Harvard University Center for International Affairs, Economic Development Report No. 112, 1968.

[24] Erik Thorbecke and Ardy Stoutjesdijk, *A Methodology to Estimate the Relationship between Present and Future Output and Employment, applied to Peru and Guatemala.* (Paris, France, Organization for Economic Cooperation and Development, Development Center, Oct 1970).

[25] Wouter Tims, 'Employment by Regions and Sectors: 1950–1985', memorandum to perspective planning section of the Planning Commission, Government of Pakistan, June 11, 1965.

[26] ——, 'Memorandum to Dr. Mahbub ul Haq', Cambridge, Mass., Harvard University, June 11, 1965.

10 Population Policy in Bangladesh

Badrud Duza

UNIVERSITY OF CHITTAGONG

I. INTRODUCTION

Modern developing countries are faced by an enormous challenge of
rapid economic development and vast societal transformation. The
developmental framework has to take into cognisance a complex
and tense background of:

(a) the emergence of new social philosophies and dynamics of
varied economic forces involving national and international
politics of development;

(b) inhibited development under colonialism and imperialism,
side-by-side with new socio-economic and political alternatives
envisaged;

(c) conspicuous differences in life conditions among various strata
of the same society and between what have been called the rich
nations and the poor nations;

(d) incredible achievements in modern communications, helping
instant diffusion of cultural traits, organisations, new ideolo-
gies, and technological innovations in a quickly shrinking
world;

(e) partly as a corollary, a nearly endemic feature of intra- as well
as international demonstration effects leading to rising expectations and rising frustrations, a strikingly new awareness
of wants and poverty, and a desparate feeling of relative
deprivations around the world.[1]

---

[1] It is neither possible nor appropriate to list here the vast area of research
and publications in the field. Among a host of others, some relatively important
ones are: B. F. Hoselitz, *Sociological Aspects of Economic Growth* (Glencoe,
Ill.: Free Press, 1960); R. Braibanti and J. J. Spengler (ed.), *Tradition, Values, and
Socio-economic Development* (Durham, N.C.: Duke University Press, 1961);
Karl Marx, *A Contribution to the Critique of Political Economy* (New York:
International Library, 1904); Richard T. Gill, *Economic Development: Past and
Present* (Englewood Cliffs, N.J.: Prentice-Hall, Inc., 1963); David E. Apter, *The
Politics of Modernization* (Chicago: The University of Chicago Press, 1965);
Barbara Ward, *The Rich Nations and the Poor Nations* (New York: W. W.
Norton & Co., Inc., 1962); Gunar Myrdal, *Asian Drama: An Inquiry into the
Poverty of Nations*, 3 vols (New York: Pantheon, 1968).

The above observations are equally true of population issues in contemporary developing societies. Most of these issues are typically modern – intricately related to the complex process of modernisation itself in terms of both antecedents and consequences. And although at a micro-level they involve individuals and individual families, at a micro-level such issues are not only national but international, generating widespread debate, concern and inhibitions at various levels in modernising as well as modernised societies.

As will be shown in detail later, the population question in its current perspective arises as one of the early impacts of modernisation. We may, indeed, characterise the phenomenon as the modernisation of mortality rates, i.e. considerable decline in hitherto existing death rates as a result of marked improvements in the areas of public health and sanitation. The consequent increase in population growth, often referred to as population explosion, leads to the problem of effecting a corresponding modernisation of fertility rates, i.e. reduction in traditional high birth rates. This is a goal which, even if pursued, is not easy to reach. Although widely attempted in recent times, so far this objective has not been attained in any society that has not made substantial headway into modernisation.

This poses a paradox. While the new mortality situation is clearly a consequence of early stages of modernisation, the resulting growth of population becomes a serious impediment to further modernisation of developing societies, and contributes to the vicious circle of poverty and population growth where the two phenomena generate and tend to perpetuate each other. Scarce but considerable resources have to be diverted to the maintenance of a fast-expanding population at the cost of sacrificing productive investment requirements.

The problem becomes further complicated because of: (*a*) a continual threat of inflation and hunger; (*b*) the rapidly increasing size and proportion of potentially unemployed and politically virile young population; and (*c*) conflicting economic, political, ethical and ideological positions on the pertinent issues. Indeed, on these latter factors depend how a society would view the population problems and what approach would be taken to their resolution.

Issues concerning population in contemporary Bangladesh can be adequately understood only in the broad developmental frame of reference outlined above. The present paper examines the population problems in this new-born nation by analysing the implications of the current growth trends for the social and economic programmes the government has worked out, as well as by addressing itself to an appraisal of the efforts directed so far toward solving the population problems.

II. MAJOR POPULATION TRENDS[1]

Table 10.1 reflects the trend of population growth in the area, presently comprising Bangladesh, since the beginning of the century. A progressive expansion of the population throughout this period can be easily marked. While figures relating to the present population size will remain conjectural until the next census, an estimated 75 million may not be far from reality.[2]

TABLE 10.1

POPULATION GROWTH IN BANGLADESH
1901 to 1961
(millions)

Year	Population
1901	28·9
1911	31·6
1921	33·3
1931	35·6
1941	42·0
1951	42·1
1961	50·8

Source: *Census of Pakistan*, 1961, Bulletin 2, p. 7.

The recent acceleration of growth can be appreciated against a background of the historical growth of the population. As M. R. Khan points out, whereas it took over two-hundred years to double its size between the middle of the seventeenth and nineteenth centuries, it took only eighty years to double in the next period, ending 1940.[3] Similarly, as the above figures indicate, during the first six decades of the century the population failed even to double itself. As a conspicuous contrast, it is now ready to double every two decades or five times in a century. This would result from an estimated growth rate of 3·3 per cent – based on assumed crude birth and death rates of 50 and 18 respectively, and allowing only twenty-one years for the population to double.[4]

[1] This and certain other portions of the following presentation are partly based on a recent paper of the author entitled, 'National Policy for Bangladesh', presented at the Bangladesh National Family Planning Seminar, Dacca, Nov 21–5, 1972.

[2] M. R. Khan estimates a population size of 73·9 million as of Jan 1, 1973, assuming a net emigration of one million during the past decade. See Masihur Rahman Khan, *Bangladesh Population during the First Five Year Plan Period, 1972–77* (Dacca: Bangladesh Institute of Development Economics, Oct 1972).

[3] M. R. Khan 'Demographic Profile of Bangladesh', paper presented at the Bangladesh National Family Planning Seminar, Dacca, Nov 21–5, 1972.

[4] 1971 – World Population Data Sheet, Population Reference Bureau, Inc., Washington, D.C., August 1971. We assume the same rates for Bangladesh as that of the total of former Pakistan, given in this document.

It is well known that such a phenomenal increase in population is the inevitable consequence of the familiar combination of a pre-modern birth rate and a modern death rate. As suggested earlier, major improvements in medicine and public health measures have contributed to revolutionary declines in mortality. The high fertility norm and practice, previously indispensable for societal survival in a high mortality context, however, still outlive such needs. This is clearly revealed in Table 10.2. While the birth rate has remained fairly stable at a high level of around 50 since the beginning of the century, the death rate has registered a sharp decline – from a high level of approximating 50 to a fairly low level of less than 20.

TABLE 10.2

ESTIMATED BIRTH AND DEATH RATES AND NATURAL RATE OF POPULATION GROWTH IN BANGLADESH, 1901–65

Period	Birth rate (per 1,000 per year)	Death rate (per 1,000 per year)	Natural rate of population growth (per cent per year)
1901–11	54	46	0·82
1911–21	53	47	0·56
1921–31	50	42	0·87
1931–41	53	38	1·49
1941–51	49	40	0·91
1951–61	51	30	2·16
1962–65	50	19	3·15

Source: M. R. Khan, 'Demographic Profile of Bangladesh', op. cit.

That there exist considerable potentials for further gains in mortality decline – with obvious consequence for the growth rate – could be easily visualised if we took into account the current mortality rates not only in the economically developed countries today but also in some of the modern developing countries, such as Ceylon and Egypt.[1] As pointed out by Robinson:

... the death rate has fallen in the last decade because of an inter-related complex of socio-economic and medico-environmental causes; that increases in per capita income and the more general availability of modern drugs in the market have been at least as important as disease-specific public health programmes by government. We would argue further that when the now-planned extensions of the rural public health programmes and water supply and sanitation improvement schemes become realities the death

[1] 1971—World Population Data Sheet.

rate can be expected to fall even more sharply, most particularly in the younger ages which are affected most severely by gastro-enteric disorders, pneumonia and other such ailments.[1]

Such a trend will be further accentuated by prospects of the eventual success of various comprehensive measures introduced in the health sector since the liberation of the country.

III. IMPLICATIONS OF POPULATION TRENDS

One can speculate that if the growth rate remains unabated, Bangladesh can attain a population exceeding 200 million before A.D. 2000. In the course of only three-quarters of a century, its population may equal that of present China; and in slightly more than a century, it can exceed the total world population today. It needs no great imagination to appreciate that sharp Malthusian checks will precede and preclude such impossible and improbable population size for the country. At the same time, it cannot be taken for granted that the

DIAGRAM 10.1

PROBLEM OF POPULATION DENSITY IN BANGLADESH

Total land 55,126 square miles. Population in 1961 50·8 million.
Average land share of a family of six persons 4·10 acres.

1961   0·40 acre major river
2·5 acre available cultivable land
0·64 acre forest
0·60 acre land not available for cultivation

This man/land ratio is going to shrink drastically by the year 1980 if the present rate of population growth continues and the rural–urban distribution is maintained as may be seen below.

1980   0·22 acre major river
1·09 acre available cultivable land
0·35 acre forest
0·60 acre land not available for cultivation (i.e.
homesteads, roads, forests and cities, etc.)

It is unthinkable that a family of six persons can be sustained out of the agricultural produce of one acre (much less in practice) even if the best methods and techniques hitherto developed are applied.

Source: Urban Development Directorate, former Government East Pakistan. Cited in *Report of the Governor's Committee for Evaluation of the Family Planning Programme* in the then East Pakistan (June 1970), p. 2.

[1] Warren C. Robinson, 'Recent Mortality Trends in Pakistan', in Robinson (ed.), *Studies in the Demography of Pakistan* (Karachi: Pakistan Institute of Development Economics, 1967), p. 38.

decision-makers concerned are necessarily aware of the country's growth potential and its socio-economic and political implications, and are prepared to adopt measures timely and adequately so as to avert a Malthusian crisis.

Colonially exploited for a quarter of a century even after the British left the subcontinent and devastated by the war of liberation, Bangladesh represents an essentially pre-modern, rural, agricultural, near-subsistence economy, further accentuated by the problems outlined above. Her population density – around 1350 per square mile – is certainly the highest among countries at a similar level of development. This is more revealing when we consider that: 'For every person depending on land as a source of living the available cultivable acreage is only 0·43 on the average. This means that a family of 5 persons has to eke out a living from a farm of just over two acres only.'[1] That the problem is going to be accentuated in the coming years is clearly brought out in Diagram 10.1.

TABLE 10.3

POPULATION COMPOSITION OF BANGLADESH (1961 CENSUS)

Characteristics	Level
Percentage urban	5·2
Percentage literate	21·5
Percentage dependants under 10 years	37·0
Percentage non-agricultural labour force	14·7
Percentage males single at 45	1·0
Percentage females single at 45	0·0
Age at marriage (rural females)	13·8
Age at marriage (urban females)	15·9

Source: Badrud Duza, 'Differential Fertility in Pakistan', unpublished M.A. thesis, Cornell University, 1964, pp. 33–60.

Tables 10.3 and 10.4 elaborate further on some additional socio-demographic indices of under-development, such as low literacy and urbanization, and high dependency ratio as well as preponderance of agricultural labour force.

One can easily visualise the planners' nightmare in such a desperate milieu – problems of human miseries demanding fast economic development, gains of which are continually nullified by a fast-increasing population. The social transformation to be achieved in the future will also be limited by the constraints we are considering.

Myrdal has presented a revealing analysis of this problem as it

---

[1] A. R. Khan, 'The Cost of Population Growth', paper presented at the Bangladesh National Family Planning Seminar, Dacca, Nov 21–5, 1972.

TABLE 10.4

PERCENTAGE OF POPULATION BY SEX AND ECONOMIC
CATEGORY FOR BANGLADESH (1961 CENSUS)

Economic categories	All	Males	Females
Population 10 years and over	63·0	64·1	61·8
Civilian labour force	34·3	56·2	10·8
Not in civilian labour force	28·7	8·0	51·1
Dependants below 10 years	37·0	35·9	38·2

Source: *Census of Pakistan*, 1961, Bulletin 5, pp. ii–iii.

affects various countries of South Asia.[1] Even the socialistic countries today have begun to recognise that development is retarded by
the current lag between fertility and mortality levels, and are
evolving programmes of fertility control designed to restore and
maintain the ecological balance.

An appraisal of the former First Five Year Plan (1955–60) can
speak for itself:

Against the Plan expectation of 15 per cent increase in national
income, the actual achievement will be of the order of 11 per cent.
Because of the increase in population, however, the rise in *per
capita* income is unlikely to exceed 3 per cent, compared with the
increase of 7 per cent envisaged in the Plan.[2]

Similarly, the Second Five Year Plan (1960–5) aimed at increasing
national income by 20 per cent, but 'in view of the anticipated
increase in population of about 9 per cent', this would mean 'an
increase of about 10 per cent in *per capita* income'.[3] By and large, a
similar trend is likely also to hold true for subsequent plans.

This would appear obvious if the capacity of an economy to
absorb additional growth in population is kept in view. There exists
considerable agreement on the assumption that the ratio between
new capital investment and added income flow in the developing
countries may be as low as 3:1. That is to say, it would require a
9 per cent capital investment to produce the 3 per cent increase of
income that could simply maintain at the existing level of income per
head a population growing at a rate of 3 per cent.[4]

[1] Op. cit., vol. II, pp. 1387–1529. On socialistic countries, see, for example:
ibid.; also: *Population Trends in Eastern Europe, the U.S.S.R. and Mainland
China* (New York: Milbank Memorial Fund, 1960).

[2] Government of Pakistan: Planning Commission, *The Second Five Year Plan*
(1960–65), (Karachi: Government of Pakistan Press, June 1960), p. 3.

[3] Ibid., pp. 4–5.

[4] Findings of the Phelps–Stokes Intercollegiate Assembly, *A Report on the
Population Dilemma* (New York: The Phelps–Stokes Fund, 1965), p. 9.

As Notestein calculates:

> ... If this is the situation, the investment of 9 % of the national income would add 3 % to the annual national income. ...
>
> A 3 % increase in the national income will bring no improvement in living conditions if the population grows at the same rate. A 4 % growth in national income will bring only a 1 % gain in per capita income if the population is growing by 3 %. Indeed, national income increasing at the annual rate of 4 % for a population growing at 3 % requires about 70 years for a doubling of per capita income because, meanwhile, the poulation increases by more than eight-fold. Alternatively, the same rate of economic growth would yield a sixteen-fold increase in per capita income to a stable population. ...
>
> ... Even rather notable success in promoting economic development yields glacial rates of improvement in living conditions and the ability to lift the rate of savings and investment.[1]

Criticisms have been levelled against such models, reasoning in terms of investment, output, and the capital–output ratio, investment regularly and almost entirely being assumed to be physical investment rather than human, social and organisational – the latter variables manipulated more prominently in socialistic planning. Speaking in methodological as well as substantive terms in one of his recent writings, Myrdal argues:

> ... The model pretends to demonstrate in a simple way the adverse effect of population increase and even to measure it in terms of what is sometimes called the purely 'demographic investment' needed to prevent a decrease of average incomes. ...
>
> This kind of mechanistic and schematic analysis gives the appearance of knowledge where none exists, and gives an illusion of precision to that pretended knowledge.[2]

Among other things, such models also do not take into account such basic factors as nature of age-structure of the population, and size and nature of the labour force – factors to be considered later in our analysis. Notwithstanding such shortcomings, however, the basic trend noted in such models should be of general validity and should offer reasonable guidelines to planners and policy-makers.

This was apparent in our brief reference to the difficulties faced by

[1] Frank W. Notestein, 'Some Economic Aspects of Population Change in the Developing Countries', in J. Mayone Stycos and Jorge Arles, *Population Dilemma in Latin America* (Washington, D.C.: Potomac Books, 1966), pp. 93–94.
[2] Gunar Myrdal, *The Challenge of World Poverty* (Middlesex, England and Victoria, Australia: Penguin Books, 1970), p. 153.

the previous Five Year Plans. That such tendencies are pertinent for Bangladesh can be deduced also from the following observations of Said Hasan made in the Pakistani context:

> ... with the rates of population growth of the order under consideration, Pakistan would need to invest between 6% and 9% of its national income just to hold its own after it has reduced death rates. All gains in per capita income must come from still higher levels of investment. Few under-developed countries have a net savings rate in excess of 10% of national income. In fact, the domestic savings rate in Pakistan has been estimated to be barely 6% to 7% at present. This is a reflection of the low margin between income and consumption in the country, which makes the capacity for savings practically non-existent.[1]

In a recent analysis of the Bangladesh economy, A. R. Khan makes a relatively liberal assumption of 2·25:1 'incremental capital–output ratio' and a modest 2 per cent of national income to be required as replacement of depreciation, and insists, along similar themes noted above, that about 9 per cent of national income will have to be invested merely to 'keep the dismally low current standard of living unchanged'. He further elaborates:

> ... It is well known that in the recent past the rate of investment in Bangladesh rarely exceeded 9 per cent by a significant margin. The current year's development plan, excluding the reconstruction and relief components, is no greater than the indicated level. It is thus quite clear that all the ordinary investment effort will be completely eaten up by the normal growth in population. To obtain any improvement in the standard of living at all, extra-ordinary effort must be made and the elbow room in this direction is rather narrow.[2]

Problems of social and political demography arising out of such factors in national economy and a consequent threat of perpetual dependence on foreign aid will, thus, continue to strain national decision makers.[3] Such problems assume special significance in view of the socialistic goals set forth in the country's development plans.

---

[1] Said Hasan, 'Address at the Conference on the World Population Crisis', New York, May 11, 1961, in Stuart Mudd (ed.), *The Population Crisis and the Use of World Resources* (The Hague: W. Junk, 1964), p. 165.

[2] Op. cit.

[3] See: Myron Weiner, 'Political Demography: An Inquiry into the Political Consequences of Population Change', in National Academy of Sciences, *Rapid Population Growth: Consequences and Policy Implications* (Baltimore & London: The Johns Hopkins Press, 1971), pp. 567–617.

IV. *POSSIBLE ALTERNATIVES OF POPULATION POLICY*

It is against such a background of rapid population growth impinging on national development – perhaps, national existence under certain circumstances – that we have to view the philosophy, evolution and logistics of population policy in Bangladesh. The government has apparently recognised that a positive population policy is imperative if social or economic progress is to be ensured. But is enough being done in the required direction? What could be some reasonable alternatives of a national population policy? Does the government really have any choice? Or is some given alternative a must? These are some of the questions that will be dealt with in the remaining presentation.

In reviewing various possible courses of events or actions that demand attention in formulating a population policy, Sauvy[1] has outlined four broad possibilities, which singly or in varying combinations can change a situation arising out of rapid growth. These are:

(1) A return to an *increased death rate*.
(2) A *geographical solution* in the form of emigration to other lands.
(3) An *economic solution* in the form of progress in production.
(4) And, finally, a *demographic solution* in the form of reduction of the birth rate.

He further insists:

> Many writers try to escape from this prison of facts and figures by suggesting solutions which appear to be quite different concerning the political regime, the spiritual state, imponderables, etc. This attempt at evasion is only an illusion. All suggestions ... must in the end be reduced to figures which bring us back to one of the above possibilities. It is always a question of knowing *which of the four parameters will be set in motion: death, emigration, economic level and birth*.[2]

While the feasibility of having an increased death rate as an element of deliberate population policy would be ethically untenable and politically suicidal on the part of any government, the eventual prospect of increased mortality as a dominant Malthusian factor in the demographic equation should not be taken lightly. The scope of any major emigration as a solution to the population

---

[1] Alfred Sauvy, *Fertility and Survival: Population Problems from Malthus to Mao Tse-Tung* (New York: Criterion Books, 1961), p. 86.
[2] Ibid., pp. 86–87.

pressure is also out of the question at the present stage. Myrdal's elaboration in this area is relevant for the present context:

> We must conclude that the various South Asian populations will have to remain within the lands of their birth. There is no practical possibility of migration of any demographic significance, either within the region or beyond it. To put it more generally, we have come to the end of an era. Peaceful migration of poor people will play an ever smaller role in adjusting economic conditions, except for some movements between countries in Western Europe – where few people are really poor – and, perhaps, in Latin America. The borders of the rich countries began to close with the First World War; the poor countries themselves followed; and the newly independent under-developed nations in South Asia have aligned their policies with this world-wide trend.[1]

Of the remaining two approaches, 'economic' and 'demographic', in Sauvy's outline, the former has often received a disproportionate emphasis, as if this alone would be a panacea. Clearly, as shown in the foregoing analysis, economic development itself is jeopardised by rapid population growth. In other words, of the two ultimate 'Malthusian' variables of population dynamics, we are left only with one, i.e. fertility, and the population policy, is forced to be neo-Malthusian.[2]

That such a policy is economically beneficial has been indicated earlier. While the size of the labour force will remain unaffected for at least a generation – since the potential labour force should already have been born – lower fertility will facilitate economic progress by reducing the size of consumers as well as the dependency ratio in the immediate future. Thus Coale and Hoover indicate:

> ... a 50 per cent linear reduction in fertility in twenty-five years provides in 3 decades an income per consumer 38–50 per cent higher than would occur with sustained fertility. In 25 more years, reduced fertility would yield an income per consumer about twice as high as with continued high fertility. If one takes account of the favourable effects of technological change and of the stimulus provided by higher consumption on the one hand, and of limits imposed by pressure on land and other resources on the other, these estimates of the gains obtained from reduced fertility appear conservative.[3]

[1] *Asian Drama*, op cit., p. 1500.　　　　　[2] Ibid., p. 1462.
[3] Ansley J. Coale and Edgar M. Hoover, *Population Growth and Economic Development in Low-Income Countries* (Princeton, N.J.: Princeton University Press, 1958), pp. 334–335.

And as they show, the differential advantage to be gained from reduced fertility is in the same general range whatever the size of a country; whatever its stage of modernisation of mortality rate; whether it is relatively self-sufficient or heavily engaged in trade; and whether development is following a capitalistic or socialistic model.[1]

In a recent exercise based on data relating to Bangladesh economy, A. R. Khan attempts to demonstrate that the social cost of preventing a birth is a small fraction of the social benefit of doing so. Arriving at a social cost of a birth as takas 1918·00 and calculating the cost of birth-prevention as takas 133·5 and takas 119·2 respectively, by condoms and oral pills, as examples, he indicates resulting benefit–cost ratios as high as 14:1 and 16:1 for the two methods. Even accepting his apology for the rudimentary data for such calculations, the direction and magnitude of benefits to be accrued from investments in government programmes of fertility reduction would appear obvious.[2]

V. APPRAISAL OF THE PAST POLICY[3]

It will be useful at this point to attempt a brief appraisal of the adequacy of the past family planning programme as part of a national policy of fertility decline. In the absence of vital statistics in the country, coupled with recent mass movements of population and destruction, it would be impossible to measure the exact impact of the family planning programme on the nation's fertility level. However, available reports[4] reveal that, in spite of a fairly positive attitude to family planning and some awareness about methods of family limitation on the part of the adult population of the country, the extent of actual practice of family planning is so far negligible.

This has been attributed, among other things to:

(a) an irrational system of targets of potential family planning clients tied up with an equally irrational system of monetary incentives;

(b) lack of any comprehensive arrangement for training of concerned personnel, especially at the advanced leadership levels;

(c) careless expansion of programmes virtually without any field-experimentation;

(d) various problems relating to research, evaluation and programme administration; and so on.

[1] Ibid., p. 320. [2] Op. cit.

[3] This and the following analyses are heavily based on my recent paper on population policy of Bangladesh, referred to earlier.

[4] See, for example: *Report of the Committee for Evaluation of the Family Planning Programme in Bangladesh*, June 1970.

It would be important to find out how far family planning programmes today are being restructured in the light of the earlier programme critiques. While it is necessary that improvements shall be made on the basis of the past experiences, it is in particular indispensable that, unlike in the past, major blunders shall be avoided by desisting from implementation of innovative mass programmes without positive field-testing, whether they relate to contraceptive methods or areas of programme administration or any other basic area. It is also to be noted that if the helplessness of the Pakistani planners at the end of the former government's Third Five Year Plan is to be avoided by our planners after five years of experience, immediate concrete steps must ensue for the collection of dependable benchmark evaluation data, preferably some form of vital statistics. Only this will show the relative success or failure of the programme from time to time.

The report under reference also reveals serious shortfalls in the needed priority for the programme as well as in the level and quality of personnel, especially at the cadre of professional leadership. It pleads for a stronger programme, backed by higher priority, and calls for expansion of the ertswhile narrow approach in family planning. To quote a few words from its conclusion:

> Family Planning, as a critical operational programme, must not only be continued but considerably strengthened, with top priority assigned to it. It must be appreciated by our planners and national élites that the success of this programme would be crucial for the social, economic, and political stability of the province, in particular, and the country, in general. Responsibilities in this important national problem should not be limited, as in the past, only to functionaries officially serving the Programme but should be taken up by élites in the bureaucratic, educational, medical and legal professions, and they must all be made involved at the national, regional, and local levels of programme planning and implementation.[1]

In practice, little has so far been done in this latter area of enhancing the viability of the programme by involving the élites of the country – a question examined in detail by the author in a study conducted in the mid-sixties.[2] It is pertinent here to mention a few

[1] *Report of the Committee for Evaluation of the Family Planning Programme in Bangladesh*, p. 166.

[2] M. Badrud Duza, 'Attitudes of Pakistani Élites toward Population Problems and Population Policy: A Study of Professors, Lawyers, Doctors and Government Officers', unpublished Ph.D. dissertation in Sociology (Ithaca, N.Y.: Cornell University, 1967).

findings of the study, which could be utilised for generating public support for the programme and at the same time removing whatever complicated ignorance still prevails among the élite in their own thinking on the vital issue of population. The study included a sample of 1170 members of four groups of professional élite in Bangladesh – doctors, lawyers, professors and government officers. It is reassuring to note that, even seven years ago, they were generally aware of the rapid population growth in the country; viewed such growth with concern; and offered reasonable suggestions for a population policy. To cite a few salient points:

(*a*) As many as 87 per cent of the respondents rated population growth of the then East Pakistan as rapid or very rapid (contrasted to the rating of such growth in then West Pakistan by 55 per cent of the samples).[1]

(*b*) As many as 86 per cent of the sample rated population growth as bad or very bad (compared to only 69 per cent in the sample from the then West Pakistan who considered so).[2]

(*c*) Rationale expressed in an open-ended question for the above rating by the sample from Bangladesh included problems relating to – economic development (70 per cent); food (45 per cent); standard of living (23 per cent); housing (21 per cent); health (12 per cent); education (6 per cent); and others (22 per cent).[3]

(*d*) Only 6 per cent of the pertinent sample saw no population problem; 14 per cent treated the problem as not so serious; and as many as 80 per cent considered the population problem as serious or very serious.[4]

(*e*) Suggestions on solution to the population problem given in an open-ended question included family planning (65 per cent); economic development (40 per cent); and education (33 per cent),[5] Between economic development and population control, as means to solve the population problem, the response categories included – economic development to be more important (20 per cent); both equally important (72 per cent); and population control to be more important (7 per cent).[6] On the other hand, persons approving family planning as a means of limiting family size represented 91 per cent, while those considering family planning necessary as a solution to the population problem was 87 per cent of the sample.[7]

[1] Ibid., p. 99.   [2] Ibid., p. 172.   [3] Ibid., p. 175.
[4] Ibid., p. 182.   [5] Ibid., p. 194.   [6] Ibid., p. 196.
[7] Ibid., p. 214.

It is also interesting to note a few comments, quoted verbatim from the respondents on the population problem. In spite of some fatalistic expressions, the statements reflect a wide range of issues relating to population. Thus:

Population is growing according to Allah's will. So I should not comment on the matter. It is Allah's will. He knows what is good or what is bad. I don't like to give opinion against Allah. So I have no judgment in this matter. (Lawyer)[1]

When it is not so serious, the question of checking does not come. Had it been serious, means and methods could be found out to check this population growth. Moreover, a catastrophes and calamities have gone a long way to check East Pakistan's population. It is only He who can check it. (Professor)[2]

Atom bomb! There should be famine, war, and other destructions. Causes of destructions are wars, famines, and diseases. This will tackle the problem, but man has tackled the problem (by reducing mortality, etc.), and the (population) problem has come up. Therefore, sterilize man. Man is more dangerous. Therefore, sterilize him. After every three pregnancies, he should be sterilized. (Doctor)[3]

Our nation is a poor country with limited sources of production. If the growth of population continues to rise in the same way, then a day will come when people will either starve or they will kill others to fill their stomach. (Professor)[4]

By propagating the ideas of family planning through all media and publicity. Converting religious leaders and persuading them to propagate the same idea. (Professor)[5]

Forced vasectomy and ligation after the birth of 2 or 3 children. (Government Officer)[6]

Legislation to the effect that unless a person is able to maintain a family, he won't be allowed to marry; that unless he is able to maintain children, he won't be allowed to give birth to children. (Lawyer)[7]

If you don't believe in socialism, there must be family planning. And if you believe, there would be no problem. (Professor)[8]

Answer to this question depends on what facilities have been provided by the government to convert each man and woman into

[1] 'Attitudes of Pakistani Élites toward Population Problems and Population Policy: A Study of Professors, Lawyers, Doctors and Government Officers', p. 216.   [2] Ibid., p. 217.   [3] Ibid., p. 218.
[4] Ibid., p. 176.   [5] Ibid., p. 223.   [6] Ibid., p. 225.
[7] Ibid., p. 223.   [8] Ibid., p. 220.

a real asset for the state. In East Pakistan, such facilities are awfully lacking. In East Pakistan, government spends 600 rupees against 6000 in West Pakistan (per capita?). ... The problem of population in Pakistan can be tackled properly only when the government understands that the real human energy is the best resource of the country, and spends money accordingly – not jute or coal is important but human energy. ... Concentration of wealth must go. Equitable distribution of the total wealth of the society among the whole population. There must be sufficiency before superiority for some. (Professor)[1]

As contended earlier, findings of the sort mentioned above could be utilised in the process of formulation as well as implementation of a strong population policy.

VI. DIFFICULTIES OF A POPULATION PROGRAMME

Even conceding that the family planning programme were made free from major abuses and given a top priority, appropriate contraceptive technology, and organisational as well as professional leadership – goals not easy to achieve – how well could we expect to tackle the problem of population growth in Bangladesh?

One has to bear in mind that the greatest obstacles in this matter are not primarily technological but sociological. For, reproductive norms have deep roots in the social and cultural systems, and careless ways of handling them might result in costly implications for the latter. In examining problems of implementing an anti-natalist policy, Notestein observes: 'Populations whose social institutions and personal aspirations are those developed in high mortality cultures are little interested in contraception and will not make effective use of the methods normally at their disposal. ...'[2] The situation is further complicated by a fatalistic attitude and problems of social security, often typical in a subsistence society. As Stycos puts it:

... in a society where progress seems impossible for a family, where advancement may in fact depend more on luck or connections than on hard work or sacrifice – in such a society it may be by no means clear why there should be any particular advantage in having three or four children rather than six or seven. In

[1] Ibid.
[2] Frank W. Notestein, 'Problems of Policy in Relation to Areas of Heavy Population Pressure', in Joseph J. Spengler and Otis Dudley Duncan (eds.), *Population Theory and Policy* (Glencoe: The Free Press, 1963), p. 478.

short, it is unrealistic to expect strong motivation for family
Planning to develop without social change which will place
economic and social penalties on large families.[1]

It can be reasonably assumed that the attainment of socialistic goals
in future will facilitate the diffusion of the small family norm among
the people by removing some of the difficulties mentioned above.

It is important to note that the population problem involves
innumerable factors interrelated through complex mechanisms,
and as such, tendencies to provide simplistic answers to this must be
avoided. In a recent paper[2] Berelson provides a thoughtful taxonomy
suggesting a sixteen-fold problem-area for population policy. The
cross-tabulation of four demographic factors (size, rates, distribution and composition) with four behavioural categories (economic,
political, ecological/environmental, and social) would yield sixteen
cells of interrelations, and thus, sixteen sets of potential policy
problems:

DIAGRAM 10.2

TAXONOMY OF POTENTIAL POPULATION POLICY
PROBLEMS

	Size	*Rates*	*Population distribution*	*Composition*
1. Economic	S_1	R_1	D_1	C_1
2. Political	S_2	R_2	D_2	C_2
3. Ecological/ Environmental	S_3	R_3	D_3	C_3
4. Social	S_4	R_4	D_4	C_4

Source: Bernard Berelson, ibid., p. 176.

It is clear that the demographic as well as behavioural categories
could work as determinants and consequences to each other. From
the top down is indicated the effects of demographic factors on the
other variables, while from the side across the tabulation, the causes
of demographic change.

When one thinks of many possible sub-categories within each
set of variables outlined above, the multiplication of the number of
cells, indeed, becomes overwhelming. In short, 'population policy,
since it deals with people, potentially covers an extremely large and
complex range of reality',[3] so that amateurish or pseudo-expert
handling of population issues almost always would result in con-

[1] J. Mayone Stycos, 'Population and Family Planning Programs in Newly
Developing Countries', in Ronald Freedman (ed.), *Population: The Vital
Revolution* (Garden City, N.Y.: Doubleday, 1964), p. 168.
[2] Bernard Berelson, 'Population Policy: Personal Notes', *Population Studies*,
25 (2) (July 1971), pp. 173–82.
[3] Ibid., p. 176.

fusion and might end up in blunders. It is important that pertinent care should be taken in the formulation and execution of the population policy for Bangladesh. The point will be taken up once more in the next section.

VII. ADEQUACY OF THE CURRENT POLICY

Among various difficulties encountered in a policy of population control, one has to appreciate in particular that the control of fertility is a much more difficult problem than the control of mortality. As discussed elsewhere,[1] longevity and good health are eminently desirable goals for man and are accepted by him without reluctance and debate. Also, public health measures in these fields are not likely to require the consent and motivation of an individual. Limitation of fertility, on the other hand, requires strong and sustained motivation, long-range planning, and institution of a number of restraints, inconveniences, and efforts on the part of individuals. This is true whether one conceives of delayed marriage, continence within marriage, use of contraceptives, abortion or sterilisation as a means of limiting fertility.[2]

For the sake of clarity, I shall take the liberty of quoting here a few paragraphs from an earlier paper[3] in order to focus on certain additional problems from which the current population policy of Bangladesh might badly suffer. These observations are of critical significance so far as they relate to policy decisions of far-reaching importance. Authorities in the field are demonstrating the total absence of any example of appreciable reduction of births without pertinent social and economic pre-conditions preceding it. As bluntly put by Davis in a classic article:

> ... the conditions that cause births to be wanted or unwanted are beyond the control of family planning, hence beyond the control of any nation which relies on family planning alone as its population policy.[4]

The statement indicates how Davis has changed his own position taken two decades previously regarding the prospect of family planning. Thus, earlier he said:

> It (birth control as opposed to death control) involves the management of only one type of germ and only one kind of contagion, as against hundreds of types of health work. It involves

[1] Duza, 'Population Policy . . .', op. cit.   [2] Cf. Stycos, loc. cit.
[3] Duza, 'Population Policy . . .', op. cit.
[4] Kingsley Davis, 'Population Policy: Will Current Programs Succeed?' *Science*, 158 (November, 1967), p. 734.

only one period of life, as against all periods subject to disease; and only one type of medical specialist, as against dozens in fighting sickness. It involves relatively simple and easy principles that the layman can grasp, as against complicated ones that he cannot grasp in general medicine. The money it requires cannot compare to that required for other kinds of medical attention. Indeed, . . . it is absurd to think that science, which has accomplished so much in so many more complex matters, cannot find suitable techniques for accomplishing this goal. In fact, we know that when there is a will to limit family size, even crude techniques will greatly reduce fertility.[1]

Apart from the distinction between birth and death control philosophy and motivation that we drew earlier, the emphasis on 'will to limit family size' in the above statement deserves particular attention. This indicates how the present population problem is to be treated essentially as a social and economic problem, and its solution also must be approached from the social structural view point. My purpose is by no means to enter into undue controversy as to whether family planning is to be dominated by the social scientists or by the medical experts. Nevertheless, it is my professional responsibility to draw the attention of our decision-makers to issues of great moment:

> . . . family planners tend to ignore the power and complexity of social life. . . .
> Designation of population control as a medical or public health task leads to . . . evasion. This categorization assures popular support because it puts population policy in the hands of respected medical personnel, but, by the same token, it gives responsibility for leadership to people who think in terms of clinics and patients, of pills and IUD's, and who bring to the handling of economic and social phenomena a self-confident naiveté. The study of social organization is a technical field: an action programme based on intuition is no more apt to succeed in the control of human beings than it is in the area of bacterial or viral control. . . .[2]

I am afraid that in the present state of reorganisation of the family planning programme in Bangladesh we may be in the process of confusion and consequent error pointed out above. In a milieu where even death control – in relation to smallpox and cholera, for

---

[1] Kingsley Davis, *The Population of India and Pakistan* (Princeton, N.J.: Princeton University Press, 1951), p. 226.
[2] Davis, 'Population Policy . . .', op. cit., p. 733.

example – is more a cultural than a technical or essentially medical problem, it is difficult to appreciate how far the family planning programme is capable of being integrated with the traditional death control mechanisms. Even if organisationally feasible – which itself is an open question – how well could the former, directed towards decrease of population, be merged with the latter, directed towards increase of population?

This by no means indicates that I am against a comprehensive approach in the area. In fact, I am all for it. The question is – integration with what and and at what level? When the entire social, economic, political and ideological fabric is at stake because of the population problem, can we afford to remain complacent with the present narrow approach? How could we integrate the population programme with a mere part – whatever its importance – at the cost of sacrificing the whole?

To alleviate any scope of misgivings relating to undue professional jealousy and fear of loss of importance on the part of physicians, it is necessary to emphasise that they would, of course, play an indispensable and vital role in the nation's efforts towards population control. Certainly the clinical aspects could be handled only by them, and the country could ill afford to continue with their erstwhile isolation from the official programme. Family planning as a modernisation effort needs all the priority and adequate collaboration and interaction with all agencies concerned with societal transformation of Bangladesh today. Unless we are determined to make the task of national planners unduly strenuous five years hence, it is imperative that we make the necessary rethinking and reorganisation without any loss of time, and broaden our population perspective as an integral part of the total plan for social and economic transformation.

Before I conclude, it is necessary to point out that today mature family planners themselves are already thinking beyond family planning.[1] That current family planning efforts by themselves could achieve only limited success has already been pointed out. A single-factor family-planning approach has its inherent limitations. It might result in the postponement of effective steps to tackle the population problem. That is to say:

> . . . To continue to offer a remedy as a cure long after it has been shown merely to ameliorate the disease is either quackery or wishful thinking, and it thrives most where the need is greatest. Today the desire to solve the population problem is so intense that

[1] For an adequate elaboration of this theme, see: Bernard Berelson, 'Beyond Family Planning', in Nafis Sadik, *et al.* (eds.), *Population Control: Implications, Trends and Prospects* (Islamabad: Pakistan Family Planning Council, 1969), pp. 67–97.

we are all ready to embrace any 'action programme' that promises itself. But postponement of effective measures allows the situation to worsen.[1]

Among others, the new approach distinguishes between the concepts of 'conception control' – primarily constituting the present family planning efforts, and 'fertility control'[2] – so far ignored in the population policies of developing countries. The latter would call for the prevention of births through some form of careful abortion, after conception has taken place, and could be a second and surer line of defence against population growth. This is not to say that the present author is necessarily subscribing to such a viewpoint. None the less, it is essential to bear in mind that without such an approach substantially supplementing the traditional family planning orientation, the goal of population control will be difficult to attain – at least within the time-scale we have in view. As Hauser insists, 'no matter what the posture of a given country may be in respect of abortion, a complete birth control programme, as distinguished from a conception control programme, is not possible without it'.[3] There is, of course, no debate that 'as contraception becomes customary, the incidence of abortion recedes even without its being banned'.[4]

Some of the Malthusian preventive checks like postponement of marriage will also form part of contemporary thinking beyond family planning.[5] That such measures could be both legislative as well as institutional is obvious. Similar other areas need careful consideration in the formulation of a systematic scheme of incentives and disincentives in the promotion of the small family norm in Bangladesh. In short, the present neo-Malthusian preoccupations must be supplemented with 'some' Malthusian as well as non-Malthusian approaches to the problem of population growth in order to avert an ultimate Malthusian débâcle.

VIII. CONCLUSION

The foregoing discussion reveals the nature of the population problems that confront Bangladesh today; their short- and long-range implications; the difficulties, strengths and weaknesses of possible

[1] Davis, 'Population Policy . . .', op. cit., p. 737.
[2] Ibid., pp. 730–3.
[3] Philip M. Hauser, 'Non-Family Planning Methods of Population Control', in Nafis Sadik, *et al.* (eds.), op. cit., p. 64.
[4] Davis, ' Population Policy . . .', op. cit., p. 733.
[5] See: Hauser, op. cit., pp. 58–66; Berelson, loc. cit.

alternatives in a national population policy; the social, economic and political consequences of timely action or its failure for the whole future course of national development. That a correct population policy is imperative in order to attain national goals of economic development and social transformation has been sufficiently demonstrated. It is important that the issues under review shall receive attention and due consideration from decision-makers at the national level.

There is no room for complacence. The present unprecedented problems can be tackled only by an unprecedented scale and level of efforts. Even decisions in the form of methods that may currently be considered drastic or unethical may have to be accepted in order to preserve greater and highly cherised values of human life and prosperity, that could be seriously at stake during the next few decades.

Hitherto, however, budgetary, institutional and leadership priorities attached to the vital problem of population have been lamentably disproportionate to the huge task to be performed. While necessary steps should be taken in these areas, some specific points need emphasis.

Without any suggestion to build up a top-heavy organisation for family planning – which in future may preferably be called population planning – I would suggest the immediate establishment of a National Population Commission or Council, headed by the top national leadership, preferably by the Prime Minister himself, and involving top planners and professionals.

A National Population Centre also must be established without any delay. The purpose of such a centre would be to examine major population issues; to formulate answers to them; and to develop expertise in various specialisations in population investigations – as contrasted with the immediate research and training needs of the official population programmes, which will continue to be carried out by the latter. There would be increasing need for professionalisation in population planning, and care should be taken to avoid taking major decisions except with assistance from experts in all the relevant fields of specialisation within population studies.

As emphasised earlier, the present programme-base will have to be substantially broadened. Co-ordination between the various departments of government concerned in matters of population programmes must be sought at all the various levels in order to ensure maximisation of national goals in the field of population. The creation of a co-ordinating Ministry of Population Planning or some sort of a substitute may be taken up for consideration. Finally, the erstwhile narrow family planning approach should give way to new frontiers where we can think and act beyond clinics and beyond family planning, with concerted action also from persons outside the cadre of family planning functionaries proper.

In short, major rethinking must ensue in order to determine viable strategies in one of the most serious problems confronting Bangladesh, and on which will significantly depend the future course of the nation's social, economic and political history. Only with determined efforts, backed by sound planning, can one expect to avert an otherwise imminent population crisis.

Discussion of the Papers by
Iftikhar Ahmed and Badrud Duza

COMMENTS ON IFTIKHAR AHMED'S PAPER BY
AMBIKA GHOSH

I shall limit my remarks to the interesting paper by Iftikhar Ahmed. Any analysis of the employment problem in Bangladesh confronts a serious obstacle: inadequate data. There is no information on the post-liberation period and data from the earlier period are fragmentary and rather unreliable. Be that as it may, it is clear that unemployment in an absolute sense is less important than underemployment, and most of the latter is located in rural areas.

Employment, of course, is not an end in itself. The ultimate objective of economic policy is to raise output, not employment, and any jobs created should be viable in the long run. This is not to deny that the employment problem has great social significance – obviously it does – but the creation of employment should follow as a consequence of decisions taken in the fields of agriculture, industry, infrastructure, etc. It must be recognised, however, that in practice the need to provide more employment imposes severe constraints on the path of development of most countries, including Bangladesh.

We can consider the employment problem in two stages: the long range and the short range. In the long run it is obvious that for Bangladesh rather more than for most other countries it is essential to follow an effective population control policy with an equally urgent industrialisation policy. The new industries, however, need not necessarily be large-scale enterprises. No amount of reform can alter the fact that Bangladesh has a very adverse man–land ratio and that it will become rapidly worse unless energetic steps are taken to decrease the rate of demographic increase and transfer some of the population from agricultural to industrial activities.

Turning to the short run, the options open in the urban areas also are fairly straightforward. For the next two or three years, attention should be concentrated on fully utilising the existing excess capacity in industry. Next, small entrepreneurs should be encouraged to go into business to produce a very large number of goods which are badly needed. State banks or similar financial institutions should be able to provide assistance. In addition, some training facilities may be needed. In India there are a large number of small engineering industries and one-man shops which absorb much labour and produce useful products. The dimension of the urban unemployment problem in Bangladesh is not as great as in India, and there is no problem of the educated unemployed. What is needed here is the development of skills which at the moment are absent. These skills often are rather simple, but if they were available they would permit the country to establish small firms producing bicycles, plastic goods, toys, sporting equipment, etc., as one can find, for example, in Calcutta.

It is in the rural areas that the problem of unemployment and underemployment becomes much more complex and the solution becomes linked to the highly controversial social and economic programmes we have discussed in the last few days. It is evident that the kind of land reform that is implemented will have a considerable impact on employment. For instance, if all land that cannot be cultivated by family labour directly is redistributed, the labour market for rural workers may be destroyed and those still left with little or no land will be forced to seek work elsewhere.

One solution which has been suggested is to diversify farm activities by introducing ancillary occupations, e.g. poultry, dairy products, bee-keeping, silk, tobacco curing. These new activities would require credit and marketing facilities. A far-flung system of rural banks would have to be created and officials prepared to live and work in rural areas would have to be found. One of the biggest difficulties would be to find a large number of people with the necessary banking and promotional skills willing to do this work. The unemployed youth often are unwilling to go into the villages. Even sons of cultivators, once they have been educated, are reluctant to return to the village.

Social conscription, analogous to military conscription in the Western countries, may have to be introduced. This would break a major administrative bottleneck. Capital for small rural industries is not the main problem because these industries are not very capital-intensive. Skills are lacking and raw materials must be supplied deep into the interior. This cannot be organised from Dacca; it must be done from within the interior itself, and this requires that skilled personnel be located in the rural areas. It has also been suggested that much of the surplus rural labour could be used to build up rural capital and infrastructure. Many highly useful rural activities are in fact of a type which needs very little equipment, but the kind of assets and outputs that can be created without any capital at all is strictly limited. Many labour-using rural works programmes are characterised by extremely low productivity of labour. We should move away from some of the early experiments toward slightly more complex activities. The Chinese experiment with backyard furnaces, although not successful, points in the right direction. There is much more to be done than making roads with bare hands. What is needed is simple rural industries using new technology and producing new outputs.

COMMENTS ON DR DUZA'S PAPER BY DANIEL THORNER

I have been asked to comment on the paper by Dr Duza. It is a clear, representative example of crisis thinking. The author claims the population is likely to launch us into a disaster; it may even bring into question the existence of Bangladesh as a nation. The author is a strong advocate of birth control as one, important, policy operating within a broad framework. Indeed he sees the population problem as being essentially socio-economic in nature and argues that its solution must be approached from a social structural viewpoint. There is in the paper an undercurrent of anxiety, strain and stress to avoid a Malthusian débâcle. In the face of what is thought to be a huge task, efforts of an unprecedented scale are required and drastic methods of control are not ruled out.

We have seen too many examples of the use of drastic and unethical methods by governments – right in this area of the world and not so long ago. Dr Duza's institutional proposals are for the creation of yet another Ministry and a National Population Council. Both would be located in Dacca, no doubt.

To my knowledge, the words 'woman' or 'women' do not appear once in the paper. Nothing at all is said about women's liberation. It is a pity the paper wasn't co-authored by a woman.

The crisis thinking represented in this paper is what we have been getting for quite a few years. Yet we have gone for over a century without encountering the catastrophe predicted by Malthus. This crisis thinking has been much influenced by the two great private U.S. foundations. The paper reflects this thinking: there are no new ideas; no allowance is made for innovation; no confidence is expressed in his own people – in their capacity to face and overcome their own problems.

A series of studies on leaf protein has been conducted in Calcutta. Other studies have been made of the nutritive value of water lettuce, water lilies and hyacinth. Professor Dumont has mentioned the potential of the banana leaf as an example. I happen to have with me five ordinary weeds which research has shown to be edible. In dehydrated form they can be stored for a long time. Under cultivation, 1·4 tons of protein per acre can be obtained. This research is part of the liberation process from dependence on cereals. If the pressure of population on food became anywhere near as great as the paper suggests, these opportunities would be grasped.

The impending disasters Dr Duza fears have not appeared. The reason is that food is essentially a perishable commodity. There is seldom more around than is needed. But it usually is possible to increase supply in response to greater need.

It is instructive to consider the role of foreign aid and foreign advisers since 1947. Rockefeller, for example, have never supported an advanced technology centre for industry, although they have supported population and agricultural research centres. The implicit and often explicit judgement or presupposition or prejudice is that really modern advanced industry should be left to the West, and to Japan of course. When I think of the history of Pakistan from 1947 to 1971, and of the part played by foreign aid, I wonder whether it would not be worth while for the Planning Commission of this country to examine what would be the cost of zero foreign aid. I'm not sure that a refusal to accept foreign aid and foreign advisers would be harmful.

DISCUSSION

There was a lively debate about the seriousness of rapid population growth and what steps, if any, should be taken to control it. There was less disagreement about appropriate employment policies.

A. R. Khan, referring to Table 10.2 of Duza's paper, questioned the reliability of the population growth rate for 1962–5. Unlike the estimates for earlier periods, the figures of 3·15 per cent per annum is not based on census data. The 1971 census in India showed that demographers over-estimated the population growth rate in that country. In Bangladesh a large amount of survey data shows demographic growth rates of 2·0–2·6 per cent a year. Obviously, we need to examine the facts again. Even if the growth rate is 2·5 per cent, however, this does not mean that the problem is less urgent; that is still a very fast rate of population growth. *Michael Lipton* remarked that surveys in Comilla in three recent years indicate the population is expanding 3·08 per cent per annum.

Whatever the present rate of demographic expansion, *Austin Robinson* asked whether we can take Thorner seriously. Are there in fact new possibilities for feeding the human race? The potato – an exotic plant brought into Europe – was enormously important in solving Europe's food problem at one stage. Clearly, we should promote all possible research into nutrition. But is Thorner right in his history? We have been living with Malthus for 175 years, but the problem of steeply falling mortality is a relatively recent phenomenon; it is very largely a phenomenon of the last 30 or 40 years.

Moreover, rising population does not create just a food problem. Duza's paper was realistic on the economic side. Many countries are virtually standing still in per capita terms because of rapidly expanding population. In a great many countries of Asia, capital per head is tending to decline rather than to grow. If we look at the consequences in terms of the cost of the number of jobs that must be created year by year, then it is very serious, and makes technical progress much more difficult. The population problem is almost the central problem and its solution will determine whether Asian standards of life can be raised to a tolerable level within 50 or 500 years.

Thorner replied that his reference to the Malthusian menace was to the ideology of development. The West is concerned about the rising tide of humanity, particularly non-white humanity. East Bengal has always been more prosperous than the regions of West Bengal where the rivers have been dying. Consider, too, what the Japanese have done with the rocks which constitute their soil. The problem is not so much a shortage of capital as of using unutilised resources, especially labour, to increase output. This is largely a problem of organisation.

Ghosh agreed that there is no end to the things we can eat – slugs, rats, etc. – but the objective is not merely to enable the people to survive but to improve their diet.

The role of the prophet, according to *Paul Streeten*, is not to be right but to exhort us to mend our ways. This is the role of Thorner. Some of the conventional views on the consequences of population growth for capital formation and savings also have been questioned by Goran Ohlin. We really must think again about population, but it is not crystal clear what exactly it is on which we should focus attention. Perhaps a major question is what are the implications for income distribution.

Lipton was not convinced and suggested it might be possible to help change family size norms by linking population control to agrarian reform. For example, land might be distributed to families with more than two children only if the father agreed to undergo a vasectomy. *Alexander Bajt*, on the other hand, supported Thorner.

Ashok Mitra said let us assume the Club of Rome is right and that Thorner is a false prophet. We know that foreign agencies are more willing to give money to restrict population growth than to set up fertiliser plants. But what happens to this money? Surveys suggest that except in Singapore, Hong Kong and Taiwan, there is no evidence that birth control measures have had any impact on reducing demographic expansion. Investment in capital equipment will yield 35 takas for every 100 takas invested. Expenditure on population control, in contrast, will give a very uncertain return. Moreover, even if population growth is high and foodgrains are limited, a lot can be done if the distribution of income is equitable. This would be true even in Bangladesh. It would be instructive to know more about what is happening in China. It seems that population policy there operates largely through social pressure encouraging people to delay the age of marriage.

Réné Dumont said the Chinese encourage not only late marriage but also birth control. In addition, the third and subsequent children of a household are not entitled to a clothing ration. Public opinion in the villages is strongly opposed to a family having more than two children. *Swadesh Bose* said the drive for smaller families must become part of a wider social movement in Bangladesh if it is to be successful. Women's liberation is needed. Mothers must be allowed to decide the number of children they wish to bear; they must have freedom of choice.

Dr Duza, replying to the discussion, said that issues related to population in Bangladesh are complex and sensitive; much confusion exists and the evidence is conflicting. In his paper he was concerned with broad policies, not specific programmes. The predictions of possible future population size was indicative of the unprecedented efforts that will be required to solve the problems facing the country. Present policies, carried over from the past, are inadequate. What is needed are non-family planning methods to go beyond the family planning programmes.

An anti-natality programme would include 'intercourse variables', e.g. raising the age of marriage; 'conception variables', e.g. supplying contraceptives; and 'gestation variables', e.g. abortion. The present policy contains few programmes relating to intercourse variables and gestation variables. Abortion, for instance, must be considered seriously by the government. Similarly, legislation raising the age of marriage or increasing the length of the education period could be considered. The current tendency in Bangladesh is to ignore the social and economic dimensions of the population problem and view it as a medical problem. A clinical approach is inadequate, however. This has become apparent in a recent report evaluating the family planning programme – which the government so far has failed to publish. The report was very critical of existing programmes and showed that the statistical information collected in the course of the programmes was unreliable. For example, the number of vasectomies was overstated. We need much better data on vital statistics and it was partly for this reason that he suggested forming a new ministry or coordinating council.

Turning to employment policies, *Streeten* said there is general agreement that small-scale enterprises and firms with low capital–labour ratios should be encouraged. But the requirements of these enterprises for working capital sometimes is quite high, so that the overall capital–output ratio may be high. We should not concentrate on *fixed* capital alone. Moreover, small firms may use the scarce factor of organisational and administrative talent. Lastly, large firms – even with high capital–labour ratios – may result in more output and hence more employment in the future.

These sophisticated arguments of *Streeten*, according to *Gustav Ranis*, tip the balance in the wrong direction. We must keep wages down and establish a good set of price signals. If this is done there will be no danger of small industries petering out, as Ghosh seems to fear. The petering-out problem arises when new, subsidised, capital-intensive industries are allowed to destroy small- and medium-scale industries. *Alexander Bajt*, however, claimed he did not see the point of encouraging labour-intensive industries. Activities should be chosen on the basis of comparative advantage and this usually implied using the most modern and advanced technology.

Jan Lipinski, in contrast, was concerned whether the present price structure makes it more difficult to promote labour-intensive industry. The rate of exchange is overvalued, but for the time being it may be difficult for political reasons to change it. One solution could be to introduce tariffs on imported capital goods and subsidise value-added of exportable products. A tax on capital could be implemented in order to compensate for the excessively low rate of interest. There are also wage distortions in the labour market. The solution is difficult because the shadow price of unskilled labour would be close to zero. Unskilled labour could be subsidised. This won't solve all problems, but it might help.

René Dumont said we must also take technical change into account. The 'green revolution' may lead to a decline in employment in the long run because it reduces labour input per unit of cereal output. Hence he stressed the need to expand market gardening, vegetable cultivation, etc. *Esra Bennathan* noted that in a period of drought and when no fertiliser is applied at all, the yield of chandina (a new rice variety) was higher rather than lower than the yield of unimproved local varieties. This is a remarkable finding. Moreover, in the short run, the introduction of high-yielding varieties of cereals raises employment, although in the long run they may reduce it as Dumont says.

Iftikar Ahmed concluded the discussion by noting that the government is concerned with the employment problem in part because its solution would help to improve the distribution of income. There is also a political dimension: urban unemployment may contribute to political instability which, in turn, would affect the level and rate of growth of output.

11 Some Aspects of the Foreign Trade Policies of Bangladesh

K. H. Imam

PLANNING COMMISSION AND BANGLADESH INSTITUTE OF
DEVELOPMENT ECONOMICS

I. INTRODUCTION

It would be useful to distinguish between the two sets of problems – the short run and the long run – that have beset the formulation of foreign trade policies for Bangladesh since liberation. The short-run problems relate to readjustments in the domestic arrangements to changed sources of supply and demand for tradeable commodities, changed price relationships both because of devaluation and protective duties and other barriers against all importables from non-Pakistan sources, the necessity of creating suitable new trading institutions, and so on. The long-run problems relate to resolving such questions as what constitutes the optimal trade pattern for the economy, and the exchange rate policy and the investment policy that need to be pursued to this end. The distinction is essentially artificial, made in the interest of descriptive and analytical convenience, for it is easy to see that the two sets of problems and their policy solutions have common elements. For example, the abolition of the common external tariff with Pakistan against the rest of the world necessitates adjustments in the pattern of tradeables. These adjustments necessitate both short-run decisions to maintain domestic activity and consumption levels as well as long-term investment choices so that the evolving production and trade pattern could gravitate towards what could be described as normatively optimal.

II. THE BACKGROUND OF PAST EXPERIENCE

It may be useful to recall some of the structural inheritance of Bangladesh's foreign trade in order to provide a perspective of the problems involved. As can be seen from Table 11.1, roughly one-third of the export trade and half the import trade were with Pakistan. As regards the balance of trade, Bangladesh had a consistent deficit with Pakistan, while only in more recent years (i.e. 1968–9) had it developed a deficit with the rest of the world. In other words Bangladesh's surplus with the rest of the world had until 1968–9 been

TABLE 11.1

PRE-INDEPENDENCE STRUCTURE OF FOREIGN TRADE OF BANGLADESH
(crores of takas at current prices)

Years	Exports to			Imports from			Balance of trade		
	Pakistan	Rest	Total	Pakistan	Rest	Total	Pakistan	Rest	Total
1965–6	65·18	157·41	222·59	120·86	132·81	253·67	−55·68	+24·60	−31·08
1966–7	73·89	166·70	240·59	132·48	156·66	289·14	−58·59	+10·04	−48·55
1967–8	78·49	147·98	226·47	123·32	132·75	256·07	−44·83	+15·23	−29·65
1968–9	87·13	153·99	241·12	138·53	182·34	320·87	−51·40	−28·35	−79·75
1969–70	92·34	167·01	259·35	166·69	181·31	348·00	−74·35	−14·30	−88·65

Source: Bangladesh Bureau of Statistics, Dacca.

Note: 1. The figures exclude air-borne trade due to non-availability of data.
2. No adjustments have been made on account of currency over-valuation.
3. 1 crore = 10 million.

financing part of her deficit with Pakistan, the rest being accounted for by invisibles and capital movements. These two aspects of the pre-independence foreign trade of Bangladesh illustrate the now famous resource transfer syndrome of Pakistan's inter-regional patterns of growth and foreign trade.[1]

As regards the commodity-composition of trade (Table 11.2), the predominance of intermediates (mainly raw jute and jute products) is

TABLE 11.2

COMMODITY COMPOSITION OF FOREIGN TRADE OF
BANGLADESH, 1965–6/1969–70
(percentages of total)

	Exports		Imports	
	to Pakistan (%)	to Rest (%)	from Pakistan (%)	from Rest (%)
Consumer goods	16·41	0·56	18·23	13·89
Intermediate goods	7·39	63·50	15·40	17·09
Capital goods	–	–	2·05	17·25
Miscellaneous	9·58	2·56	10·76	5·33
Total	33·38	66·62	46·44	53·56

Source: Bangladesh Bureau of Statistics, Dacca.

Note: A hybrid category called 'miscellaneous' has been introduced in the above classification because of the non-availability of more detailed commodity-composition of the trade with Pakistan. This category should, in principle, be divisible between the three preceding categories.

well known. The marketability of this product category is not liable to cause any serious problem except in relation to the pricing policy, a range of problems to which we will return later. As regards consumer goods, the structural transition whereby these can be marketed abroad will not be easy to achieve because of the inadequate product specification of many of the commodities in this category (matches for example), moreover rather difficult export problems now face these commodities since most of the consumer goods exports are predominantly of semi-processed agricultural commodities. Such problems of marketing will, of course, ease if trade relations are resumed with Pakistan, but problems of transition will still remain. For example, in the past Bangladesh has had access to the sheltered market of Pakistan for the disposal of her exportable surplus in tea. Resumptions of trade relations with Pakistan will not, however, mean that tea can now be exported to Pakistan at pre-independence prices, roughly one and a half times the current export price level of

[1] For detailed documentation see *Report of the Panel of Economists* on the *Fourth Five Year Plan*, May 1970 (Government of Pakistan, Planning Commission).

takas 2·00 per lb. As can be seen from Table 11.2, Bangladesh exports no capital goods and no possibilities of this are being aired at the moment in relation to the First Five Year Plan.

May we next consider the commodity-composition of Bangladesh's import trade? As regards capital goods, it is obvious from Table 11.2, that the problems of switchover from Pakistan to non-Pakistan sources of supply will be minimal in the light of the fact that both Pakistan and Bangladesh were significant net importers of capital goods. The situation with regard to consumer and intermediate goods is, however, not so obvious. At the moment, Bangladesh lacks substitutive productive capacity in either – problems which are worse confounded by the low level of utilisation of such productive capacity as the economy has in these areas and which have largely contributed to the recent price-spiral. Needless to say, capacity can be created in these areas, although the all important question to ask is what should be the dimensions of the import-substituting capacity-creation in all the three product categories. If the current rate-structure of customs tariff is anything to go by and if the private sector is allowed some play in investment, then almost certainly there will be additional capacity-creation for consumer goods. Similarly, additional capacity-creation is also likely in the intermediate and capital goods sectors, largely dictated by the public sector investment policy. The basic question here is whether the experience of Pakistan's industrialisation will be repeated, with consequent implications for foreign trade policies, or whether such experiences have been meaningful for the evolution of Bangladesh's industrialisation and foreign trade structures. In a later section we shall discuss some of the relevant aspects of this question.

It will be pertinent in the present context to review the roles the previously existing regime of an over-valued exchange rate and other barriers to trade played in the evolution of the foreign trade of Bangladesh. Currency over-valuation during the period of association with Pakistan was at around 50 per cent.[1] While the disincentive effects of such over-valuation had been partially offset by the provision of a higher exchange rate on exports of jute goods, it had a particularly disastrous impact on the export of raw jute, as yet the mainstay of Bangladesh's export trade. While on the one hand, the over-valued exchange rate provided increasing disincentives to growers of jute in the face of rising prices of the alternative crop, rice, it at the same time kept the foreign exchange price of raw jute artificially high, thereby leading to large-scale product substitution

[1] Nurul Islam; 'Comparative costs, Factor Proportions and Industrial Efficiency in Pakistan', *Pakistan Development Review* (summer 1967).

in the end-use market of raw jute. While the higher exchange rate for jute products could compensate this drift, in practice the benefit of the differential did not get passed on to the export market so as to offset the rapidly improving price-advantage of substitute products such as woven polypropylene. The end result has been a virtual stagnation in the export trade of Bangladesh to the rest of the world.

On the exports to Pakistan the effect was, however, asymmetrical. The over-valued exchange rate, the high common external tariff and other barriers to trade necessitated a certain amount of trade diversion to Pakistan. Thus while around 29 per cent of total export trade went to Pakistan in 1965–6, the ratio was 36 per cent in 1969–70 (Table 11.1). The main commodities which used to be exported to Pakistan were tea, matches, jute textiles, paper and newsprint, on all of which there were direct barriers to import from the rest of the world or high external tariffs or both. The existence of this high common external tariff and other barriers to trade did not, however, mean that the exchange rates which Bangladesh received on her exports to Pakistan were necessarily more favourable for all products than could be obtained under free trade. For example, the ban on imports of tea except for a small amount for blending was associated with a ban on exports, and the latter had tended to offset the scarcity premia caused by the former. Indeed, the scarcity premia, as calculated by Soligo and Stern,[1] had been less than the currency over-valuation of around 50 per cent suggested above. On jute textiles, matches, paper and newsprint the excess of the scarcity premia resulting from barriers to external imports was, however, significantly positive and could thus be credited with having encouraged the exports of Bangladesh. Unfortunately, this relative profitability of marketing in Pakistan has not exactly been an unmitigated blessing. For example, in paper and newsprint the advantage of the sheltered market in Pakistan had led to such over-capitalisation that the social rate of return in this product has been calculated to have been negative.[2] And if current indications on the export marketing of matches are any guide, similar judgement on it would also be justified.

As regards the import trade, the currency over-valuation and high cost of importables from Pakistan may be regarded as having encouraged imports from the rest of the world. However, here again, tariffs and other barriers to trade had caused a diversion in favour of imports from Pakistan. These imports have been mostly of

[1] R. Soligo and J. Stern, 'Tariff Protection, Import Substitution and Investment Efficiency', *Pakistan Development Review*, (summer 1965).

[2] A. R. Khan, *The Economy of Bangladesh*, ch. 10, p. 125 (London: Macmillan, 1972).

consumer and intermediate goods, scarcity premia on which, because of the barriers to trade, have been highest. Since such barriers to external trade were also associated with direct restrictions on investment on these goods in Bangladesh, there had in consequence been very little investment in import substitutive productive capacity. With the termination of trading relations with Pakistan, together with devaluation and virtually similar trade barriers to those of the past, the scarcity premia have persisted, providing import-substitutive investment incentives for such investment. As has been already suggested, this has implications for the evolving trade and industrialisation pattern, a question to which we will return shortly.

III. THE EFFECTS OF DEVALUATION: EXPORTS

One of the first decisions undertaken by the Government of Bangladesh was to fix the sterling parity of the currency, the taka, at 18·97 to the pound. In terms of the sterling parity of its currency predecessor, the rupee, this amounted to a devaluation of around 66 per cent. The important question which should be asked is whether this has been enough to give the much needed boost to exports. The current unofficial sterling parity is around takas 35. Part of the excess over the official parity is certainly the risk premium of unofficial and illegal dealing and part of it is probably due to the relative inactivity of domestic producing capacity. It is conceivable that in spite of these two factors the sterling parity of the taka might be even lower than has been suggested above. However, it would be still too premature to guess at the true sterling parity. For this, some time must still elapse to let the economy adjust to the new set of relative prices.

However, the lingering discomfort is due to the fact that, despite a devaluation of 66 per cent, none of the benefit seems to have been passed on to the export market. To take the export prices of the two major export goods (raw jute and jute goods), it seems that for raw jute the current f.o.b. price per ton of B.W.D. grade (£112) is virtually the same as the average 1970–1 price (£113)[1] while for jute goods[2] the average July–October 1972 price is £184 per ton as compared with £143 per ton during 1970–1. And this has happened in the face of the worsening competitive position of these commodities. Thus the fundamental rationale for devaluation that it allows the domestic cost-price structure to adjust from a fundamental disequi-

[1] Jute Directorate, Government of Bangladesh.
[2] *Monthly Statistical Bulletin of Bangladesh*, table VIII–2, for average 1970–1 prices while for July–October 1972 price, the source is *Trade Statistics* (Advance Release) Oct 1972, ibid.

librium, seems to have been entirely lost. What the new exchange rate has allowed the government to do is to provide a better exchange rate for the growers of raw jute. The statutory minimum price for raw jute has been revised upwards from takas 35 per maund[1] to takas 50 per maund in October 1972. While this was essential to maintain jute acreage in view of high prices of rice, the alternative crop, one cannot help a feeling that this was somewhat overdone. The average harvest price of medium grade rice in 1971–2 was around takas 48·00[2] while the harvest price of average grade of jute (i.e. comparable to B.W.D. export grade) was around takas 35·00, thereby yielding a ratio of 0·73 of the latter to the former. However, if we consider that the current harvest price of rice is around takas 60 per maund, the relevant jute–rice price ratio becomes close to 0·83, a 14 per cent increase in the relative price in favour of jute. The increase in the price advantage of jute, however, is somewhat illusory if one considers the fact that the net acre–yield ratio has altered in favour of rice because of the planting of high-yielding varieties of rice. While a farmer's judgement with regard to relative acreage may be favourably influenced by the current price advantage of jute, it may at the same time be adversely influenced by jute's disadvantage in terms of the net acre–yield ratio. The effect to be expected on the jute acreage is, however, difficult to establish for various reasons, including the uneven incidence of the high-yielding varieties of rice in competing jute-growing areas, the uncertainty with regard to the provision of input-service for high-yielding varieties of rice in potential jute-growing areas, and so on.

Undoubtedly, the need to maintain jute acreage makes it difficult to reduce the foreign exchange price of jute with the current exchange rate. But the home truth needs to be realised that given the current foreign exchange price of raw jute (£112 per ton of B.W.D. grade) its competitive position cannot be sustained and that it will progressively lose out to synthetic substitutes. Similar comments also apply to jute products. The current competitive position of raw jute has been variously quoted within a range of £80–£105 per ton of B.W.D. grade while for hessian the quotations are between £185–£202 per ton. The seriousness of the situation has impelled a certain amount of research on our part and hopefully, the results will be available shortly. Ultimately what happens to raw jute and jute products will determine what the exchange rate for Bangladesh will be and there

---

[1] 82·29 pounds.

[2] Assuming that there is a difference of around takas 5·00 per maund between the harvest price and the wholesale price (see *Monthly Statistical Bulletin of Bangladesh*, table V–1). For harvest price of jute see Sep 1971 price in table V–2 in the same source.

should be no hesitation in going over to a new exchange rate if that is in the interest of pursuing an optimal price policy for raw jute and jute goods exports.

IV. THE EFFECTS OF DEVALUATION: IMPORTS

What has been the role of the new exchange rate with regard to the imports? Consider first the effect on goods previously imported from the rest of the world. On these, the effect of devaluation as such has been to raise the taka cost. However, such escalation has been prevented in general by a proportionate reduction in customs duties. Previously, there existed a three-tier import licensing system bonus, cash-cum-bonus, and cash licensing. The implicit exchange rates were progressively lower for the above three methods of import licensing given the over-valuation of the currency. The strategy which has been followed in revising the tariff schedule is that the duty-paid value of imports under each of the above three licensing bases would remain at their pre-liberation levels; in other words, the relative price structure of the imported commodities should remain the same as in the pre-liberation days. Quite clearly, this has serious implications for the production and trade strategy to be followed by the country. However, in fairness to the government it may be said that the revision carried out was done only in view of the immediate necessity of having such a revision, given the abolition of the bonus and cash-cum-bonus system of licensing and the retention of only the cash licensing basis. The detailed work necessary for revising the tariff schedule to conform to what one could regard as an optimum tariff schedule could not be carried out within the given time constraint. This work is now in progress and the Planning Commission, at some stage in the future, will be able to make the necessary policy recommendations. My own view here is that in this matter one should be guided by the consideration of equalising the 'effective' rates of protection for the goods producible and devise the tariff schedule – the nominal statutory rates – accordingly.

The basic argument here is the well-known consideration of not interfering with the pattern of incentives for resource-allocation— that is to say to use tariffs not in their resource-allocative function but only in their revenue-generative function. Using this argument as the point of departure one may, however, readily concede the need to provide an additional degree of protection to industries which are eligible for infant-industry protection from the view-point of externalities. The solution for nominal rates of tariff would, consequently, have to be obtained subject to the above constraint. One could similarly build in such additional constraints as the need to obtain postulated revenues, the need to have prohibitory nominal rates of tariff on some items due to socio-political considerations, and so on.

As regards the effect of devaluation and cessation of trade with Pakistan on commodities which were previously imported from Pakistan, the effect has been asymmetrical. The largest item of import was cotton textiles, representing close to 13 per cent of total imports from Pakistan in 1969–70.[1] On these the scarcity premium on account of the common external tariff was around 152 per cent.[2] The taka cost, therefore, consequent on devaluation would thus be comparatively less. Similarly on oil seeds the average landed cost in Chittagong of a ton of mustard/rape seed in 1969–70 was around takas 1466.[3] On current quotations, the landed cost per unit is around takas 1086.[4] On raw cotton, however, the situation has been different. The average landed cost of a ton of raw cotton in Chittagong in 1969–70 was around takas 2326 per ton. For current arrivals, the price (c.i.f. basis) is takas 6164 per ton.[5] Admittedly, part of the increment in cost may be due to an already tight market situation in April–May 1972 (when contracts for the current arrivals were drawn); however, the current price quotations are close to takas 5000, still a substantial increment in cost.

V. STATE TRADING

One of the major innovations with regard to foreign trade has been the introduction of state trading agencies. In export trade, the coverage is almost total since the specialised state trading corporations like Jute Export Corporation and the Jute Mills Corporation have the monopoly of exports of raw jute and jute goods respectively. On import trade also the government share is the dominant one. Thus, of the total licensed imports of takas 85·45 crores during January–June 1972 the share of the public sector has been takas 43·92 crores. The ratio would be considerably higher if one takes account of the fact that a very large part of the remaining imports were, in fact, made by the different nationalised sector corporations as part of their import entitlement. With regard to the non-licensable imports the government agencies have the monopoly. Thus foodgrains, the dominant product in this category, is imported exclusively by the Food Ministry.

The economic reasons behind the introduction of the state trading

[1] *Monthly Statistical Bulletin of Bangladesh* (Apr 1972), table VIII–6.
[2] R. Soligo and J. Stern, op. cit.
[3] *Monthly Statistical Bulletin of Bangladesh*, table VIII. 6, op. cit.
[4] *Trade Statistics* (Advance Release) (Nov 1972).
[5] Ibid.

agencies in export and import trade are different. For export trade, the argument is basically one of greater ease of pursuing determinate export price/volume policies and absorption of trading profits by the public sector, thereby helping public sector resource mobilisation. For import trade, the main argument is that it would facilitate import programming and would probably result in better terms of trade on the basis of the bilateral monopoly argument. As against this, it is being suggested that, since the trading corporation of Bangladesh, for example, imports only in bulk, such imports are often not consistent with the demand for goods requiring varying product specifications. In this regard one may report that a policy of allowing the holders of import entitlements for raw materials already in the public sector, in practice the overwhelming mass of such entitlement holders, to import directly while limiting public sector trading agencies to bulk consumer goods is being urged on the government.

An equally forceful argument for introducing gradual state monopoly would be that, given the current over-valued exchange rate regime, the allocation of foreign exchange to the private sector amounts to the latter being awarded income subsidies financed by an implicit taxation on the exporters. While abstracting from the issue of whether or not the importers as a class deserve such income-subsidies in the interest of maximisation of social welfare, the private sector import-licensing system must be a rather inefficient method of providing such income-subsidies because of the indeterminate patterns of administrative procedure involved and market arbitrage. A conceptually better method would be to let the public sector absorb the scarcity premia through its pricing policy and thus finance any direct public income-subsidy programme, if necessary. Alternatively, such import licences could be auctioned off so that the government could absorb the resulting scarcity premia and thus finance any desired expenditure programme.

VI. LICENSING POLICIES

With regard to the import trade policies it may be said that while the import-licensing system has been retained with all its attendant inefficiencies, the trend has been towards significant liberalisation. Thus in the import policy for July–December 1972, only a few non-essential industries like cosmetics were given import licences at less than 100 per cent of their entitlement for import of raw materials and spares. The import allocations against the entitlements have since then been raised to a uniform 100 per cent during January–June 1973 period. In addition, certain industries have been included in a relative novelty, the raw material replenishment scheme, whereby the exporting industries would be allowed varying percentages of their f.o.b. export values as additional import allocations.

The basic rationale behind this liberal industrial licensing policy as part of the import policy has been a simplistic but a compelling one – that domestic manufacturing levels have to be maximised in view of the rather tight situation with regard to domestic availabilities in these products as well as for employment considerations. Similarly, with regard to consumer goods imports, allocations have been made such that at least 1969–70 real availabilities will be maintained. In many cases, the 1969–70 levels have been sought to be improved upon because of incremental demand considerations. And in any case, greater capacity utilisation in the import-substitutive industries would improve upon such availabilities.

It will be readily admitted that the industrial licensing policy may have been somewhat indiscriminate because for some of the industries which have been licensed the social marginal productivities may be negative (for example, paper) and for some it is fairly low (for example, rubber).[1] However, as has been stated earlier, the rationale for this policy has been based on current considerations such as regeneration of employment and relieving domestic scarcities in consumables. More long-range considerations, such as readjustments in the production and trade structures to conform to something approximating to what may be regarded as optimal, have been temporarily shelved, but should be taken into consideration in formulating government policies once the current reconstruction phase is over.

VII. CURRENT TRADE FLOWS

It is pertinent to look at the trade flows of the country for this, after all, is one sure test of the efficiency of trade policies. It has been a difficult task to assemble the necessary data and large anomalies still remain. The data in Table 11.3 are thus extremely tentative and refer only to sea-borne trade.[2]

While we have almost a complete coverage with respect to export trade, since land-borne and air-borne export trade had been minimal, the same is not true with respect to the import-trade figures. First, the import-trade figures exclude all land-borne trade and a large part of the air-borne trade. Secondly, even for sea-borne trade, a large part of the relief arrivals have been excluded from the figures pending customs declarations as to their value to be given by the

---

[1] See A. R. Khan, *The Economy of Bangladesh*, p. 125.

[2] By some quirk of the data collection machinery this includes a small part of the air-borne trade.

TABLE 11.3

MERCHANDISE TRADE FLOWS IN BANGLADESH, 1972
(in crores of takas)

Months	Imports	Exports
January	2·27	3·46
February	2·49	5·92
March	9·84	18·57
April	3·42	22·46
May	9·69	26·06
June	7·29	31·11
July	11·93	21·58
August	5·32	22·40
September	6·02	22·65
October	16·03	24·04

Source: *Trade Statistics* (Advance Release) (Oct 1972),
Bangladesh Bureau of Statistics, Dacca.

relief agencies. These anomalies are being sorted out, but it will be some months before the customs authorities will be able to provide figures with anything resembling a complete coverage.

In analysing the trade figures, apart from the limitations cited above, one must also remember that 'normal' trade activities did not really start till July 1972. The trading institutions were in considerable disarray during the first half of the year. Similarly, port facilities and internal transport facilities had only a fraction of their normal capacity. This, however, is not to suggest that these hindrances have disappeared by July 1972, so that date must be regarded as somewhat arbitrary. However, using it as the point of departure, one can see that the average monthly level of exports (takas 22·8 crores) has already exceeded the figure postulated in the *Annual Plan for 1972–73*.[1] In all probability, the monthly export trade figure will rise above the October 1972 level of takas 24·03 crores and merchandise export earnings of around takas 300·00 crores may be regarded as very much within the realm of possibility for the year 1972–3.

On the face of it, and despite the reservations already expressed with regard to them, the import trade figures may be regarded as rather disappointing. Thus the average monthly level of non-food imports during July–October, 1972, has been around takas 7·86 crores, whereas in the projections of imports made during the formulation of the Annual Plan the required monthly level of imports of this category was assumed to be takas 47·83 crores, implying

[1] The export projection for 1972–3 was takas 260·00 crores yielding a monthly figure of takas 21·66 crores; see *Annual Plan, 1972–73* (Government of Bangladesh, Dacca).

around takas 485·00 crores for the whole year 1972–3. The import-trade figures for the July–October 1972 period do not reflect, of course, the import allocations made during the July–December 1972 period but the allocations made during January–June. The disloca-tion of trade links, the creation of new trading institutions, together with a more egalitarian system of distribution of import licences to the private sector have lengthened the usual three-month gap between the issuing and retirement of letters of credit against licences into something close to a six-month gap. Although this gap is closing it seems at this stage almost inevitable that a large part of the goods to be imported against the allocations made during 1972–3 will be carried over into 1973–4. While the import flow in October 1972 is considerably higher than in July, it is unlikely that it will rise enough to yield a monthly average of takas 47·83 crores for non-food im-ports for the year 1972–3.

VIII. LONG-TERM FOREIGN TRADE POLICIES

Finally, we come to some considerations which should influence the long-term foreign trade policies of Bangladesh. The evolution of the foreign trade structure of a country is inextricably linked with its investment policy, while both are in turn influenced by such factors as the exchange rate and various barriers to trade. My views on the exchange rate and such barriers to trade as the tariff structure have already been indicated in a preceding section. The objective now should be to devise an investment policy that is consistent with the resource endowment of the economy so that the economy may be on an efficient investment time-path, thereby yielding an efficient time-path in tradeables. The relevant considerations are well known and the general principles are usually accepted.

Having made these almost valedictory statements, what conclu-sions can we draw from them? If the trade structure is to be consis-tent with the comparative cost pattern of the economy, one must identify the latter on which the investment pattern is to be based. On this aspect, there already exists a general equilibrium model prepared by Mirrlees and Khan and briefly reported in the book by the latter on the Bangladesh economy cited earlier.[1] Briefly, the model provides a programming solution for obtaining accounting prices over a 29 sector breakdown of the economy and suggests a comparative cost pattern on the basis of appropriate 'border' prices. Admittedly, the model does not take account of externalities and uses 'border' prices instead of long-run equilibrium international prices for the tradeables to identify the comparative cost pattern.

[1] A. R. Khan; *The Economy of Bangladesh*, ch. 10.

Subject to these limitations, the model provides a useful guide to practical policy decisions with respect to the investment pattern. Of the twenty-two tradeable sectors, the model identifies four as potentially exportables, ten as import-substitutables but not profitable enough to export, and the remaining as importables. These results are not startling. In all those sectors which have been identified as exportable Bangladesh has been known to have advantages in terms of factor endowments. Among these which have been marked as importables are sugar and cigarettes. While the former has very great disadvantages in terms of the productivity of competing crops, the latter is a highly capital-intensive industry based on imported raw materials. As regards the intermediate category – goods which are producible but not profitable enough to export – the results are interesting. In this category such sectors as metal products and machinery appear. The intra-sectoral product composition for these products is biased towards relatively labour-intensive metal fabrications, light machinery and spares. Similarly, textiles are also included in this sector and import-substitutive capacity creation can be pursued in these industries. Clearly, the model could be improved to obtain a more detailed sector breakdown, by using more recent inter-sectoral cost information,[1] and an additional algorithm for, possibly, generation of long-term equilibrium prices and by identifying externalities. The main contribution of the model, however, is that it provides a useful point of departure for the determination of inter-sectoral priorities for investment, and thereby of the trade pattern.

The preliminary ideas which are being adumbrated in the Planning Commission about sectoral priorities for investment have a certain amount of consistency with the results of the above model. For example, major import-substitutive capacity expansion in rice is being thought of. Similarly, capacity expansions are also being considered for raw jute, jute textiles, fisheries and leather. With the resumption of trade relations with India and given the relative cost-structures for the production of raw jute, efforts should be made to persuade India gradually to move out of her costly trade-diversion from import of Bangladesh jute, in the mutual interest of both countries. A competitive pricing policy in this area would certainly help. An extension of similar pricing policies would also help in jute textiles and other exportables.

It should be borne in mind that short-run balance of payments considerations may make it necessary to persist with domestic activities which, in terms of the solutions of the model referred to above, should be regarded as importables. A rationalisation for this

[1] The current input matrix dates to 1962–3.

approach may be offered in the following form, since, in general, the replacement value of the capital stock in such activities will be approximately zero: only the current costs of such activities need to be evaluated at appropriate prices and the continuation of activity levels in these sectors may be justified accordingly. An adverse judgement will be applicable only to incremental capacity.

Discussion of the Paper by K. H. Imam

COMMENTS ON THE PAPER BY PAUL STREETEN

My task is easy and I shall be brief. The paper contains a full and lucid presentation of the trade problems of Bangladesh and some of the answers. The main issues can be grouped conveniently under two headings: on the one hand there are the short-term difficulties with which the government is immediately confronted, while, on the other hand, there are the medium- and longer-term trends and policies.

There are two major problems the government must face in the short term. First, the production bottlenecks and remaining transport shortages, which arose as a result of the war for independence, must be eased. Second, the historical heritage of trade between the East and West wings of Pakistan must be replaced. New sources of supply may have to be found for some commodities, such as cotton, and new markets will have to be found for others, such as tea. There is no reason to fear that tea production cannot be made more competitive or that with an appropriate marketing effort the supply cannot be sold.

Let us turn to some of the medium- and long-term problems. Dr Imam's paper includes an extremely interesting sociological and political analysis of the past bias in favour of jute manufactures as against exports of raw jute. This discrimination has now been removed. The effective subsidy of manufactures before independence, however, was much higher than the apparent subsidy and this encouraged the growth of the Bangladesh jute manufacturing industry at the expense of India. The question today is whether the reversal of policy will lead to a reversal of past trends and, specifically, to a reduction of jute acreage in India. What are the social returns to exports of jute manufacture? Some economists have claimed they are negative. Clearly it is important to find out. Another high priority item should be the negotiation with the E.E.C. of the Community's duties on processed jute products. A 30 per cent reduction of jute prices in Europe is necessary if jute products are to compete effectively with other substitutes.

We need to know much more about the long-term prospects for jute. Technical revolutions in transport and cargo handling may have led to growing inelasticity in the demand for some jute products. Several of the changes which have occurred may not be reversible. On the other hand, the demand for substitutes for jute bags is likely to be elastic. Jute producers may be able to undercut the price of bags made of plastic film, for instance. Evidently, it would be in the interests of both countries if Bangladesh and India could work out a common policy and programme for jute. One area for joint effort would be in research: at present, research on jute represents only 0·5 per cent of turnover whereas research on plastics is equivalent to 20 per cent of turnover.

An important issue of policy is whether, at the margin, Bangladesh should attempt to be self-sufficient in rice at the expense of jute. There may be a conflict between self-sufficiency and self-reliance and it is not clear what is Dr Imam's position on this. Of course, it is generally agreed that Bangladesh must increase exports of products additional to jute, e.g. leather goods, hides and skins.

The paper before us is pretty neo-classical, although it is rather subtle. It raises the question whether there is such a thing as a socialist foreign trade policy. On the face of it, the answer would appear to be 'no', but I think there is more to it than that. Much has been written recently on the pros and cons of outward-looking and inward-looking policies. The real issues, however, are *where* do you look and for *what* do you look. We tend nowadays to ignore the effects of foreign trade on attitudes and institutions. J. S. Mill thought these effects were very important and were a major contribution of trade towards encouraging development. It is possible, however, to stand Mill on his head and say that a country which relies excessively on foreign trade tends to adopt inappropriate technologies, create inappropriate institutions and produce and consume inappropriate products. Some products, for example, 'over-kill' the needs they are intended to meet, to satisfy the wants of high-income groups and leave nothing for the rest of the population. It is not enough to say get the income distribution right and all will be well because trade and income distribution interact and it may not always be possible to alter income distribution as much as one would want.

It is often argued that at full employment there is no need to protect industry. But if one accepts the educational, institutional and technological argument I have been advancing, then we should examine whether we should look for trade and exchange with countries in a similar position and try not to stir up demand for the wrong goods, wrong technologies and wrong institutions. Bangladesh can learn much from the mistakes of Pakistan. I am a bit sceptical about relying entirely on international prices: what is at stake is not just which prices will be used for accounting purposes but which style of development will be pursued.

DISCUSSION

The discussion centred on three broad topics: outward- versus inward-looking strategies of development, state trading and ways of integrating foreign trade policy into the planning procedures.

Gustav Ranis claimed that timing was of considerable importance in choosing when to adopt an outward-oriented and when an inward-oriented strategy. Bangladesh, for the foreseeable future, will have to do the best it can both to promote exports and encourage import-substitution while concentrating on achieving balanced growth. Eventually industrial exports will emerge, but this cannot occur for some time unless they are heavily subsidised. He did not know what Streeten meant by a socialist foreign trade policy. Basically, Bangladesh must play the foreign trade game under the existing rules. This does not imply free trade. Revenue tariffs and protection of infant industries were desirable, but the tariffs must not be too high, otherwise smuggling would be encouraged.

In phase one, the country should conserve foreign exchange by imposing high tariffs on luxury commodities and be satisfied with domestic production of lower quality substitutes. He suggested that foreign exchange restrictions be liberalised in order to help the private sector to grow; experience in Pakistan indicates that direct controls on foreign trade do not work well. Phase two would be an outward-looking phase. During this phase Bangladesh should make a major effort to expand exports to other countries of the region and encourage more trade among Asian nations.

The special problems that arise with India were raised by *Esra Bennathan*. At present Bangladesh is a reasonably open economy, as the unimpeded movement of rice across the border to India indicates. In exchange for smuggled rice, Bangladesh presumably is obtaining manufactured goods. The existence of this trade is important and, indeed, however low is the ratio of total foreign trade to G.N.P., international commerce has a vital role to play in the development of the country. In particular, it follows that any plan for developing manufactures in Bangladesh must bear in mind the price structure in India. This problem must be tackled directly, preferably by making special trading agreements with India.

An implication of Bennathan's argument is that tariffs on trade with India must be fairly low. *A. R. Khan* suggested that the tariff rate should be equivalent approximately to India's rate of indirect taxation of manufactured goods, i.e. about 20 per cent. One could have relatively higher tariffs on items in which India does not have a comparative advantage. The thrust of policy should be to promote a pattern of trade that would result from free trade. *Jaroslav Vanek* was in favour of much higher tariffs, say of 100 per cent, because it is essential to raise revenue in order to finance a high rate of accumulation. The basic tariff rate should be high and then selectively lowered on goods coming from India in order to inhibit smuggling. *Ranis* said that 90 per cent of all commodities would fall in the second category. Perhaps, replied *Swadesh Bose*, but the tariff on trade with India probably need not be as low as 20 per cent, since smuggling entails a cost too.

Nurul Islam then reminded the conference that foreign commerce in Bangladesh was organised under a system of state trading. In this institutional context, what is the role of tariffs and other conventional instruments of trade regulation? State trading is a system of direct controls taken to its logical conclusion. Socialist trade is state trading. In Bangladesh 70 per cent of the import trade is in the hands of the government, including food (rice, wheat, edible oils, sugar), imports for the nationalised industries, bulk items of consumer goods and barter trade with the socialist countries. There is little scope for the private sector in importing. Similarly, 80 per cent of exports consists of jute and jute manufactures, so here too only a small amount of exporting can be done by the private sector.

Streeten did not agree that state trading is *ipso facto* socialism; it is equivalent to quantitative controls or a licensing system. The question is who gets the scarcity value. It need not necessarily be the state; it could be local businessmen or even foreign suppliers. Certainly the existence of a State Trading Corporation does not imply that the composition of imports would be the same as in a fully socialist country. *Vanek* found it impossible to believe that a state trading corporation in Bangladesh would not distribute the scarcity rents to the private sector in some form or other. *Khondker*, on the other hand, said much depends on whether the trading corporation acts merely as a buying and selling agent or as an institution for determining the quantity and pattern of trade.

It is government policy that a private sector will be permitted to exist, at least for ten years, and presumably, said *Ranis*, the government wants it to flourish. In fact, in his opinion it will become a major source of strength to the economy. This can occur, however, only if the sector can acquire foreign inputs and is forced to use them efficiently. He suggested that one way of allowing new businessmen to become established and new firms to be created would be for the state trading corporation to auction imported goods.

This suggestion raised the issue of how trade policy was to be integrated into the planning system. *Austin Robinson* noted that foreign trade has two functions. First, it enables a country to obtain food, materials, and other things which it does not possess or in which it does not have a comparative advantage. Second, almost as important, it enables a country to overcome short-period bottlenecks resulting from failure of production or exports to develop as planned. In India, whenever there is a failure of anything, they run into balance of payments difficulties. It is important not to repeat this mistake in Bangladesh by planning too tightly. The 'braver' the plan, the more important it is to reserve part of the foreign exchange earnings, say 5–10 per cent, to deal with emergencies.

Branko Horvat said one would expect foreign trade would be linked closely to the plan. This could be done by using a simple approach. We assume that in a planned economy the most important bottleneck is the foreign exchange bottleneck. The objective of planning, hence, should be to maximise foreign exchange subject to the constraint of the largest trade deficit that can be tolerated. In this way output would be maximised.

The correct principle, according to *Jozef Pajestka*, is that foreign trade should be functional or instrumental in supporting an active internal development policy. The more active is internal policy, the more institutions will be necessary to control foreign trade; a *very* active policy may require a monopoly of foreign trade. The important point is that the country should not allow undesirable external factors or forces to disturb its internal policy. Considerable experimentation with a variety of trading institutions has been done in Poland. It has become clear that the trading organisations must play according to the rules of the game established by organisations concerned with internal development. Yet the central authorities cannot take all decisions on exporting and importing; if they try they will make many, many mistakes. Poland now has differentiated exchange rates and special export and import taxes. These have worked quite well and may be useful in Bangladesh. There must not be too many different prices, however, or the system becomes unmanageable.

A. R. Khan agreed that there is a case for multiple exchange rates when the inherited structure of capacity is not optimal, as in Bangladesh.

Would it not be far easier, however, to allow unprofitable nationalised industries to write off the value of their capital? The problem with multiple exchange rates is that they influence investment decisions as well as trade and create a system of inefficient and incorrect investment signals. *Pajestka* replied that in Poland the 'basic exchange ratio' was used for all development decisions; the so-called 'marginal exchange ratios' are never used in making investment decisions.

There was much discussion of the possible advantages, inefficiencies and complexities of a multiple exchange rate system. *Rehman Sobhan* said that firms which run into trouble could be given a 'marginal exchange rate'; alternatively, they could receive a subsidy or be allowed to run at a loss. It is not clear which is the better signal to the planners that something is wrong. *Alexander Bajt* remarked that in Yugoslavia there is a uniform rate of exchange and each enterprise engages in free foreign trade; barter trade agreements have practically disappeared. *Vladimir Kondratiev*, on the other hand, informed us that in the U.S.S.R. foreign trade is a state monopoly; trade is largely based on barter deals.

Konstantin Kolev said production cannot be separated from trade. What is the link, in Bangladesh, between the enterprise and the State Trading Corporation? *Dr Imam* replied that in the case of jute manufactures, for example, the producing agency is also responsible for exports. Raw jute, in contrast, is procured from the growers by the government at an announced price and part of this jute is exported, the rest being retained for domestic processing. As regards imports, there seems to be a tendency to give enterprises greater freedom to determine their import needs. If this tendency continues, the tariff structure will become very important in influencing investment decisions.

12 Social Infrastructure and Bangladesh Development

A. F. A. Husain[1]

BANGLADESH PLANNING COMMISSION

I. INTRODUCTION

Although much has been written in recent years about social development and the need for integrating social planning in the overall development planning, in the context of the Bangladesh situation such an approach will remain an ideal for some time. For the present it seems inevitable that social planning relating to the First Five Year Plan of Bangladesh will consist of a sectoral approach, i.e. planning of individual sectors which have so far been labelled as social. Even though consistency with the overall objectives and other sectors may be attempted the approach is necessarily fragmented. Unfortunately, as much of the thinking relating to the social sectors has still to crystallise in a reasonably workable form, this paper instead of attempting a detailed discussion of the problems and policies in these sectors will mainly highlight the issues on which answers are to be sought.

With the adoption of the new constitution in Bangladesh which lays down a number of important social objectives as fundamental principles of state policy, the role of the social sectors is to be greatly emphasised. However, investment in social infrastructure is to be planned not on the consideration of 'human rights and social amelioration' points of view alone. Such investment quite definitely contributes to economic development after a period and the externalities of such investment (skill formation, better productive capacity through improved health and peace of mind) may be considerable. However, statistical studies on cost–benefit ratios or rates of return on investment of the so-called social type which have been made by a large number of writers do not provide adequate guidance for investment in the social sectors.

---

[1] The views expressed in this paper are strictly those of the author although these reflect much of the thinking on the subject within the technical sections of the Planning Commission. He is deeply indebted to Chiefs, Education and Health, Family Planning and Social Welfare of the Commission for the material presented in this paper.

II. EDUCATION

In the field of education it is impossible to lay down any satisfactory criteria of the total investment that should be made. Investment as a proportion of the total development plan is a matter of judgement. A better guideline may be total expenditure as a proportion of the G.N.P. Currently in Bangladesh expenditure on education and training forms only 1·5 per cent of G.N.P., one of the lowest among developing countries. It is a matter for consideration whether this should be stepped up to 4–5 per cent of G.N.P. as recommended by the UNESCO Conference of Ministers a few years ago. A target may be set in this respect for each plan period.

Within the field of education it is important to fix priorities. The rate of literacy in Bangladesh has remained constant over the last twenty-five years at 20 per cent or so. The rate of growth of enrolment at the primary stage has been much slower than growth at the secondary and higher levels of education. However, the pay-off on investment is undoubtedly highest for primary education apart from the constitutional obligation to provide mass-oriented and universal education at the earliest date.

The implications of providing facilities for universal primary education, i.e. for the 5 + to 10 age group in the population by the end of the first plan period through conventional methods is staggering. The cost may amount to takas 2000 million. If the goal is more modest – i.e. it is aimed to raise enrolment from the present figure of 58 per cent to 78 per cent of the relevant age group of the population by the end of the first plan period – this will involve (on the assumption of 1 : 50 teacher student ratio) hiring 59,250 additional teachers – i.e. increasing the number by 51 per cent and increasing the number of schools by 15,400, i.e. by 50 per cent. If the cost of books and equipment is to be taken into account the total additional cost of primary education (developmental and recurring) amount to over takas 1000 million on a very tentative basis. This excludes cost of teacher training. It has been estimated that by making maximum utilisation of 48 existing primary teacher training institutes and setting up 15 new ones it may be possible to raise the number of trained primary teachers from the present 66 per cent to 74 per cent of the total by the end of the plan period.

The point at issue is what unconventional methods may be used to raise the percentage of enrolment at the primary stage while keeping the financial implications low. Among the possibilities are use of school rooms for double shift, introducing an element of compulsion to secure services of young matriculates as teachers for limited periods, setting up a National Service Corps for literacy, introducing condensed programmes of teacher training, etc.

For an effective primary education programme the problem of dropouts must be tackled seriously. Only 38 per cent of the children enrolled in primary schools complete the primary stage, the rate of dropouts being higher for girls. An effective strategy for checking dropouts must be devised without which investment in primary education will yield poor returns.

The rate of illiteracy being as high as it is, in order to remove it within the shortest possible time, it is essential to have a mass literacy programme to supplement the primary education programme. Here again conventional methods have serious financial implications. A mass literacy programme which makes use of Comilla-type co-operatives under the Integrated Rural Development Programme and aims at linking literacy efforts with various production and service-oriented activities has been tentatively drawn up by the Rural Development and Co-operative Division. An essential feature of the programme is the use of a National Literacy Corps comprised of draftees made to work on a nominal allowance. A five-year adult literacy programme is expected to cost tentatively takas 600 million. A great many details of this programme and also some of the basic concepts need to be articulated before it may be considered worth undertaking.

If the problem of primary education is tackled effectively, secondary education will present less difficulty. A planned expansion of enrolment at the secondary stage is to be made. The implications of increasing enrolment from 17 per cent to 24 per cent of the 10+ to 15 age group of the population by 1972–8 – i.e. by 1,020,000 – are: (*a*) upgrading 1811 existing junior high schools so as to increase enrolment from the present 115 to 300 students on an average; (*b*) expansion of 2000 high schools so as to increase enrolment from 309 to 600 on an average; (*c*) hiring 36,700 additional teachers (on the assumption of a teacher–pupil ratio of 1:30). At the secondary stage, intensive use of schools and other facilities will be more feasible than at the primary stage. Training of teachers will be extremely important at the secondary stage as at present only 27 per cent of the necessary teachers are trained. The number of trained teachers can be increased substantially by increasing the capacity of the existing training institutions, upgrading the junior training colleges and introducing condensed courses.

An important policy issue to be determined is how far a vocational bias is to be given to schools at the primary and the secondary stage. Opinion is divided as to the desirability of providing a vocational bias at the primary stage. But at the secondary stage there is a growing thinking that craft courses catering to agriculture, industry and services may form part of a school curriculum. Already programmes on these lines have been introduced in some schools. An issue is whether such courses are to be provided to all on a compulsory or optional basis. Successful completion of a vocational course may lead to issue of a special certificate which will help those who regard the secondary stage as a terminal education to secure employment.

At the college and university level it is obviously important to plan production of high-level manpower to manpower requirements and employment opportunities as higher education is particularly costly. The strategy at this level should be consolidation and maximum utilisation of existing facilities and further expansion must be made cautiously. This means that standards of admission are to be raised and selectivity in admission is to be introduced. In view of the larger social demand for higher education it remains to be seen how far such a decision will be taken politically. If such a decision cannot be taken, higher education will pre-empt a large part of the financial resources to the detriment of primary and secondary education and contribute to the pool of the unemployed. The major effort during the plan period should be directed towards raising standards and the output of research activities and the improvement of facilities in scientific and technological fields.

Manpower and employment studies are extremely important for planning education and training facilities in spite of the considerable imperfections of such studies. One such study was carried out by the planning department of the erstwhile Government of East Pakistan.[1] On the basis of projections of growth rates and marginal investment–employment ratio for specific occupations, the demand for skilled manpower of certain types was estimated for 1975 (the terminal year of Pakistan's Five Year Plan), 1980 and 1985. Similarly, supply was also projected for these years, on the basis of the planned facilities and certain assumed pass ratios. Although in the present context the results are not relevant there is obviously a need for carrying out similar studies in the changed circumstances. Some of the findings of the previous study are quite interesting. For example, in the case of engineering personnel in 1980, on the basis of one projection while supply at the degree level was expected to exceed demand by 15 per cent, at the diploma level it was expected to exceed by only 2·5 per cent. However, at the certificate or skilled craftsmen level supply was expected to meet only a seventh part of

[1] Government of East Pakistan, Planning Department, 'Manpower Planning in East Pakistan' (1969) and 'Education and Employment in East Pakistan' (1971).

demand in 1980. For natural scientists supply was expected to exceed demand by more than 30 per cent by 1980. For medical personnel at all levels demand was expected to outstrip supply.

Even if a new study is made, it will no doubt reveal a critical shortage of certificate level technicians and health personnel at all levels, particularly of para-medical staff. It is necessary to go for a large increase of output of technical high schools, on-the-job training schemes and so on. It is likely that at the low level of development of Bangladesh, saturation point in demand is reached rapidly in the case of high-level personnel like engineers and scientists. If this is true, a major emphasis on scientific and technological education as is often advocated in popular discussion may lead to serious maladjustment between demand and supply of highly trained manpower in these fields with a consequent serious wastage of resources. It has been suggested that if on political or other considerations an undue expansion of higher education cannot be averted it may be better to permit a large expansion of enrolment in the humanities courses rather than an undue expansion in scientific and technological education.

III. HEALTH

Both on social as well as economic considerations a large investment in the health sector is called for, much larger than what was spent in erstwhile East Pakistan. Our health programme has of necessity to be preventive biased as most of the mortality and morbidity in our country is due to preventible diseases, and per capita expenditure for effective preventive programmes is much less than for curative programmes and prevention of morbidity may be expected to enhance the quality and quantity of work of the labour force. However, on social considerations curative programmes cannot be neglected and a balance has to be struck between the preventive and curative programmes. The success of a health programme depends on co-ordinated efforts in allied sectors, viz., housing, environmental sanitation including potable water supply and hygienic night soil disposal, food and agriculture, transport and communications, education and social welfare, etc.

Some of the major deficiencies of the health programme so far have been the neglect of the rural areas, lack of co-ordination between health and family planning programmes and the failure to integrate a number of preventive programmes running independently.

To remove these drawbacks it will be necessary to integrate all vertical projects concerned with communicable diseases (including malaria, tuberculosis, leprosy, smallpox and cholera), with provision of supervision of all activities in the field. The services so integrated with the general health services will have its base at the rural health centres at the thana and union level. The most important development in the health sector is likely to be the establishment of a basic health infrastructure at the grass-roots level which has been lacking so far. The rural health complex is visualised as the unit organisation for providing integrated and comprehensive health care to the rural population. Each rural health complex will have two components:

(1) Rural health centres at the thana level and sub-centres at the union level.
(2) A small hospital (25–50 bedded) at the thana level.

One rural health centre will be created in each rural thana headquarters with sub-centres at the union level. Each rural health centre and union sub-centre will give coverage to a population of approximately 15–20,000. Each complex will not only administer the preventive programme but will provide usual health services, family planning service and contain a maternity and child health unit. Altogether 356 rural health centres and 3698 union health centres will have to be established. There are at present only 150 rural health centres in existence. It is proposed to establish all the 356 thana health complexes (Thana health centre and 25 bedded hospital) in the first plan period, while the 3698 union sub-centres will have to be spread over three plan periods.

Other important programmes in the health sector are: raising the number of hospital beds, manpower training, introduction of health programmes for industrial work, improvement of drug control, drug research and distribution.

A takas 2500–3000 million programme, comprising $7–7\frac{1}{2}$ per cent of the possible planned outlay, will make it possible to implement the essentials of the health sector programme. However, there is a critical shortage of trained personnel. The total number of qualified doctors inside the country does not exceed 7000, giving a doctor-population ratio of 1:10,000. If we consider the loss of doctors due to death, retirement and migration and take into account the additional requirement of doctors due to population increase, at least 600 doctors annually have to be produced even to maintain the existing doctor-population ratio. The current production of doctors is half this figure. The target can be met by completing the on-going institutions, expanding one and establishing two new medical colleges. However, effective measures will have to be taken to ensure complete absorption of the doctors so produced in programmes for which they are urgently required and to prevent or reduce considerably the existing migration of doctors to foreign countries. In particular it is necessary to formulate and implement appropriate measures to attract doctors to villages by providing incentives for rural jobs.

There is a great dearth of nurses and para-medical personnel in Bangladesh. We have a peculiar ratio of 1 nurse per 10 doctors as compared with 2–5 nurses to 1 doctor in any developed country. Further, while in a developed country there are 6 to 10 para-medical workers to each qualified doctor, in Bangladesh the total number of para-medical personnel is less than the total number of qualified doctors. This imbalance has to be corrected through appropriate programmes and policy measures.

Certain major policy issues relevant for health sector planning may be stated. Tentative suggestions made below to meet the problems reflect the thinking of the relevant technical section in the Planning Commission.

(i) Production of manpower will be planned on the basis of complete utilisation of all available medical, nursing and para-medical personnel. No qualified person will be allowed to remain unemployed so as to avoid unnecessary investment in manpower production.

(ii) Growth of medical specialities should be channelled in the desired directions depending on the requirements to support the national health programmes and not on the basis of individual preferences.

(iii) All doctors, nurses and para-medical personnel after qualifying from national training institutions must serve compulsorily for a period, say five years, in the national health programmes. After this he or she may be free to choose his or her own career.

(iv) All doctors after qualifying must compulsorily serve in a national health programme in the rural areas for at least two years. Suitable residential accommodation should, however, be provided for the doctors in the rural areas.

IV. FAMILY PLANNING

The Family Planning Programme was first initiated under the erstwhile East Pakistan Health Department during the plan period of 1955–60 with a modest budget. However, it gained momentum and in 1965 the programme was revitalised by establishing the Family Planning Board, an autonomous body with an elaborate staffing pattern from the headquarters at Dacca to the village level. Unfortunately, the action programme was weak as the basic workers for motivational work and for providing supplies of non-clinical methods or guiding clients to clinics were 'dais' (midwives) or 'chief male organisers' who were invariably illiterate with a nominal salary. The clinical methods were provided through female workers whose responsibility was to insert I.U.D., and part-time medical doctors who performed vasectomy. The supervision of workers was poor. The programme adopted a controversial strategy in providing monetary incentives to clients, field workers, doctors and even to the midwives. In terms of actual achievement – i.e. control of population – the programme was extremely discouraging although there is evidence that it succeeded in creating awareness about family planning among the population to a considerable degree.

Although the current concept of population control is much wider than that of family planning and it is realised that a successful population control policy will need action on a wide front, it is not proposed to set up a new elaborate organisation for population control at this stage. It is proposed to strengthen the existing organisation of family planning and give it a new direction and establish close co-ordination with the health programme which has been lacking in the past. In other words, as at present there will be two Divisions under the Minister for Health and Family Planning – viz., a Health Division and a Family Planning Division – with a Secretary in charge of each or both Divisions. Maximum co-ordination will be provided at the thana level through the thana health complex where the thana administrator will be in charge of health as well as family planning. There will be a National Board for Family Planning with the Minister, Health and Family Planning as Chairman to provide overall policy guidance for the family planning programme, under which will function the District Family Planning Board with the civil surgeon (who is the district health chief) as the chairman. The proposed arrangement is expected to provide maximum co-ordination between the health and family planning programmes, without merging the latter in the health programme.

In conformity with the government's population policy it has been suggested that efforts shall be made to reduce the present high growth rate of population (3·15 per cent) to as low as 1 per cent in three plan periods. Within the framework of this objective it is proposed to organise family planning efforts during the first five year plan in such a way that the present birth rate of 47 per thousand is reduced to 40·5 per thousand at the end of the plan period while the death rate falls from 17 to 14·50 giving a growth rate of 2·60 and involving prevention of 1·22 million births during the first plan period. As there has never been an instance of a country with a comparable level of development to Bangladesh achieving such a drastic fall in the growth rate, the target set appears rather optimistic. Nevertheless, according to experts this may be attainable if there is political commitment at the highest level and mobilisation of maximum effort at all levels to achieve the objective.

In the proposed reorganised family planning set-up, payment of money for motivational purposes will be dispensed with. The wide gap that exists between general awareness of the possibilities of family limitation and its actual practice will be bridged by an intensive couple-registration programme to be carried out by well-trained matriculate male and female field workers to motivate eligible couples for adoption of contraceptive methods. The field workers will be full-time employees of the programme with clearly defined responsibilities and schedule of work. They will act as motivators as well as agents for supply of non-clinical methods of family limitation and as guides for arranging clinical methods in the rural health complexes. It has been suggested that a two-member team consisting of one male and one female worker will be employed for every 5000 population (i.e. 1000 eligible couples). The work of the field workers will be supervised by the family planning authority through the thana health administrator. The thana health administrator and sub-divisional medical officer of health will remain over-all in charge of the programme in the rural and urban thanas respectively for implementation and supervision.

The thana health administrator will be responsible for providing the clinical methods of family limitation at the thana health complexes with the help of the doctors and other staff wherever clients ask for it or are referred to by the family planning workers of the areas. He will also ensure follow-up of all cases of I.U.D. insertions/ vasectomy with the help of the family planning programme workers and arrange to provide medical help wherever necessary.

Non-clinical methods of family limitation will be given due emphasis in the programme. Motivation for their use by those who do not want to adopt clinical methods will be geared up by educating eligible couples through mass media and personal contact as well as by ensuring ready availability of conventional contraceptives.

It is essential to provide a built-in mechanism in the programme for its periodic evaluation on the basis of actual number of births prevented and not on the number of contraceptives supplied, I.U.D. inserted and vasectomy done as in the case of the previous programme.

It is also most important to test the efficiency and performance of the family planning programme periodically so as to modify institutional arrangements and the working of the programme if these are called for to produce optimum results.

It has been tentatively worked out in the Planning Commission that a takas 1000 million expenditure during the first plan will provide the infrastructure and meet the recurring cost of the programme during the first plan. Considering that the benefit–cost ratio of the family planning programme is one of the highest on record, this investment or even a higher amount is entirely worth while.

V. SOCIAL WELFARE

Social welfare had been one of the most neglected sectors in former East Pakistan. The allocations to this sector increased nominally over successive plan periods, but in terms of actual utilisation there was in fact a decline. In the context of the present socio-economic conditions of Bangladesh a major emphasis needs to be placed on this sector. The major objectives of the social welfare sector for the first plan may be stated:

  (i) To arrange meaningful rehabilitation of victims of the war of liberation and natural disasters such as cyclones, floods, tornadoes, land erosion, to which this region is particularly prone.
 (ii) To help all physically, mentally and socio-economically handicapped members of the society, so that they can overcome their handicaps and become useful citizens.
(iii) To organise a child care programme.
 (iv) To harness all available youth power for constructive work for the betterment of society and to prevent it from being a disruptive force against the social order.
  (v) To provide, as a long-term policy, comprehensive social, security against hunger, disease, and unemployment through inter-sectoral collaboration for development and appropriate programmes.

In view of widespread destitution and limitation of resources it will be necessary to proceed cautiously in this sector. As in many other fields, social welfare has been neglected in rural areas except for providing relief to victims of natural disasters from time to time. A major aim of the programmes will be to extend the services to the rural areas to create dynamic rural communities by infusing the concept of self-help. This will require close collaboration between the social welfare sector and other socio-economic sectors such as health, education, family planning, manpower and employment, housing, transport and communications, and rural development.

At the urban level, existing urban programmes – in particular the community development programmes – must be revitalised so as to reorganise the urban communities on a self-help basis to meet the essential needs of these communities through expert assistance and collaboration with other programmes.

It is clear that entire financial support for the social welfare programmes cannot be met at this stage of our economy. Resources from the private sector have to be drawn up liberally to give coverage to the entire group of needy persons in every community. It will, therefore, be necessary to motivate, encourage and give guidance to the private social workers and organisations for maximum participation and co-ordinated efforts in the social welfare programmes.

Destitution due to natural disasters. In so far as natural disasters, such as cyclones and floods, will continue to recur before these can be effectively controlled, the existing machinery for meeting the impact of these disasters must be improved. In a paper prepared by a number of senior officials of the UNROD[1] a number of excellent recommendations have been made. These include building up of a stock of relief supplies at thana headquarters for use in emergency, clearly defined responsibility among officials for distribution of supplies, supervision of relief, deployment of military personnel in relief work and rehabilitation of victims of disasters so as to prevent permanent destitution.

Rehabilitation of war-affected destitute women and children. The devastating war of liberation has caused a number of urgent socio-economic problems, among which a very important one is that of dis-honoured and destitute women and children. The Government of Bangladesh gave highest priority to this problem and a number of social welfare agencies, including the Social Welfare Department of the Government of Bangladesh, initiated programmes to rehabilitate these unfortunate and helpless women and children. The ongoing government programme 'Care, Protection, Education, Training and Rehabilitation of Orphans and Destitute Women' which was started after liberation will continue during the plan period. The programme envisages setting up 60 units all over the country at a total cost of takas 285 million. Most of the units have been already established and a sum of takas 9·4 million has been spent so far. It is proposed to spend during the plan period a sum of takas 185 million. One important result of the programme will be building up of an infrastructure for social welfare work which was missing so long.

Destitution due to a social or physical handicap. Apart from destitute women and children whose plight is due to war there will be many women and children and others whose destitution will be due

[1] 'Destitution and dependency in Bangladesh', by Ahmadulla Mia, David French and K. M. Zaman.

to various misfortunes and physical handicap. All these persons will require care and assistance.

For the war-affected destitute women and children and other physically and socially handicapped persons the authors of the UNROD study make a number of recommendations which deserve close consideration. They do not in general advocate institutional care except for those who are completely without relatives or whose disability requires institutional care, and they would in most cases like to limit institutional care to a period necessary for training and rehabilitation. They advocate foster families in place of orphanages for small children and hostels for children without family support at the thana level. They advocate that destitute women and orphaned children should remain with their kinship group wherever practicable and be provided assistance through a public assistance programme aimed at providing a minimum income to the family by making available work opportunities, subsidy of food and clothing and provision for education, vocational training, health care and family counselling. In this way the destitutes will be assisted and rehabilitated without imposing an impossible burden on society.

A large part of destitution due to unemployment and underemployment; the answer to this problem is rapid development of the economy, particularly emphasis on labour-intensive programmes. In the short and medium run an expanded works programme may be one of the major instruments for countering destitution due to unemployment.

A number of projects covering the social welfare sector have been in operation – viz., those relating to youth, beggars, delinquents, old and infirm, etc. – which touch only a fringe of the problem. These will have to be strengthened, expanded and co-ordinated with other programmes. The planning machinery in the social welfare sector is weak, there being no Planning Cell in the Ministry of Social Welfare. There is an urgent necessity for assessment and evaluation of programmes. There is also a certain amount of duplication between government programmes and programmes run by some autonomous organisations and private bodies. There is obviously a need for co-ordination between the different agencies operating in the same field.

While a comprehensive social security scheme covering such risks as sickness, old age, unemployment, widowhood and orphanhood must remain a long-term goal, there is a great deal more than what has been done in the past that must be attempted even within the present resource constraints. The ridiculously low expenditure made in this sector in the past regime must be increased several fold in order to provide the minimum that will be considered acceptable in a country which is committed to socialism and welfare of the masses.

VI. SUMMARY

It is clear that in Bangladesh, as one of the poorest developing countries, there is a great need for social services. These social services partly take the form of human capital formation, as in the case of education. They partly take the form of the maintenance of human capital, as in the case of health. They partly take the form of diminishing the demands for physical capital and for investment in human capital, as in the case of family planning. They partly arise from the needs to mitigate the most severe effects of poverty, war and disaster.

The central question of policy in this field is just how far a very poor country can go in meeting these needs and of investing in human capital formation at the same time that it attempts to meet the similarly urgent needs for capital formation in the development of new industries, in improving transportation, energy supplies, and other infrastructure, and raising the living standards of the population generally.

Table 12.1 shows for the year 1968–9 what the area that is now Bangladesh was then spending on social services, and relates it to the G.N.P. of the region.

TABLE 12.1

EXPENDITURES ON SOCIAL SERVICES
(U.S. $ billions at 1968–9 prices)

	1968–9	%
Gross national product	6·27	100·0
Total investment	0·87	13·9
Domestic saving	0·66	10·6
Private consumption	5·19	82·8
Public consumption	0·21	3·3
of which: education	0·05	0·7
health	0·02	0·3
family planning	0·01	0·1

Discussion of the Paper by
A. F. A. Husain

COMMENTS ON THE PAPER BY AUSTIN ROBINSON

In this last session we come to social expenditure and investment in human resources. Professor Husain's paper makes clear the immense need for more expenditure in this field. He points out the appallingly low level of literacy; the high levels of mortality, due to preventible diseases, despite the modern improvements of the past fifty years; extensive absenteeism arising from sickness; the immense need which most of us here feel for a more active and effective population policy.

The only question to my mind is just how far, just how fast can one afford to go at once, in this first plan. That seems to me to depend on three things: what resources we have, what priority we attach to social expenditure, and what cost must be involved in the social expenditure. I would like to say a little about each of these three.

First, what resources have we for development? I have been worried throughout the conference as to whether we are really facing up to the full difficulties and problems of developing Bangladesh and to the limits of available resources. At this time of year (January) Bangladesh looks beautiful and gives the impression of fertility and abundance. But it is a country with immense difficulties. It has either too much or too little rainfall, and there is great uncertainty about when it will come. Population density is very great and income per head is exceptionally low. I accept Professor Pajestka's point that we must raise the target of the absolute level of income, but his point applies equally to other poor countries and would not alter the relative position of Bangladesh.

What resources can we hope to make available? Horvat and Pajestka have stressed the underutilisation of capacity. This does indeed exist in some sectors, e.g. cotton textiles, but this is a temporary phenomenon due to the lack of supply of cotton yarn. In a broader sense, of course, there is excess capacity in the form of underutilised manpower.

I absolutely agree that the first task is to achieve maximum utilisation of all capacity, and I agree that the plan should evoke maximum effort but I remain sceptical that a growth rate of 7 to 10 per cent is at all realistic. My own guess is that 5·5 per cent is a reasonably optimistic target.

Planning is not an amusing guessing game, it is a psycho-technical exercise in getting maximum results. It is in one sense better to aim at 8 per cent growth and get 6 per cent than to aim at 4·5 per cent and get 4·5 per cent. I would say forget all those tiresome financial journalists and United Nations commentators who will criticise you for failing to make your target. What does matter, however, is the general effect on the national morale and the political situation of failing to achieve a target. In the United Kingdom where critics – and especially economic critics – abound, if we announce 4 per cent growth and get 3 per cent growth there is an outcry and governments fall. In Bangladesh I do not pretend to understand what the psychological and political reaction will be if an ambitious target fails. Is it better politics to announce a bold and exciting plan and muster enthusiasm behind it, and be prepared for achievement to fall short? Or is that politically dangerous? Would it disunite the nation and discourage people?

Let us consider how much you can hope to devote to development expenditure. In 1968–9 about 14 per cent of the national resources were devoted to investment, of which about 10·5 per cent represented domestic savings and 3·5 per cent foreign capital. That is, capital inflow from abroad was a big addition to local savings. Consumption in that year accounted for 83 per cent of G.N.P. – and produced a very low standard of living. Public expenditure was only approximately 3 per cent of G.N.P. In other words, public consumption was a very small proportion of total expenditure. Less than 1 per cent of G.N.P. is spent on public education and at most only 1·5 per cent of G.N.P. is spent on total education, both public and private. Compare these figures with UNESCO's recommendation of 4 per cent.

Over the short period of the next three or four years real G.N.P. and real income per head are likely to be below the 1969–70 level. A. R. Khan kindly prepared for me a few guesses about the near future which will give us some idea of the orders of magnitude. His guesses are presented below in index form, in which 1969–70 = 100.

	G.N.P.	Population	G.N.P. per head
1969–70	100	100	100
1972–3	85	103	82
1973–4	103	106	97
1974–5	108	108	100
1978–9	135	120	112·5

These figures indicate that in 1973–4 real G.N.P. per head still will be 3 per cent less than it was four years earlier. If G.N.P. rises to 135 by 1978–1979, which would be a considerable achievement, most of the gain would be absorbed by the rising population, and in consequence income per head would be only 12–13 per cent higher than in the benchmark year. Thus we must not start thinking that Bangladesh will be able to spend generously on development.

What are, what should be, the priorities in claims on resources? Investment for agricultural development comes very high: tubewells, fertilisers, extension services. Infrastructure, particularly transport and energy, merits high priority. Then there is capital investment in the most needed industrial developments. This might include cotton spinning, pharmaceuticals, the building of country boats and possibly diesel engines for pumps. There is a case, however, for restraining over-ambitious industrial development in the first plan.

After these priority needs are met what is left for social investment? The most that can be done in the short term, I suspect, is to raise public consumption expenditure to about 5 per cent of G.N.P. A significant proportion of this can be devoted to social expenditure, provided the government is able to save on defence, on previously improper public expenditures and on transfers to the other wing.

Given the limited amount that can be spent on the social services, it is important, if possible, to provide education, health services and family planning facilities very much more cheaply than is usual. We should investigate whether it really is necessary to pay high stipends to attract teachers, doctors and others to work in the villages. Alternatively, it may be possible to establish a National Development Service of some kind with students doing two years of work in the villages after they graduate. Again, we should examine whether it is possible to throw onto the villages the costs of providing schools, dispensaries, and the housing and feeding of teachers and visiting medical staff.

The question I am raising is whether the government can draw on the leisure of the people of the villages, and on their enthusiasm, to create an imaginative scheme of local social services without having to devote national, central resources to finance it. I don't know whether these are nonsense suggestions, but something of this sort will be necessary if ambitious goals are to be achieved.

DISCUSSION

There was general discussion of how social policies should be integrated into the general development effort. Almost all the participants concentrated on education, neglecting other social services such as health, and many suggestions for improving the educational system were made.

Ilya Redko said there must be no objective contradiction between the government's economic and social policies. The way to assimilate new technology is to utilise the scientific achievements of the advanced countries by adapting them to local conditions. This requires a high priority on education. The most urgent task is to train managerial staff for the public enterprises and the administrative apparatus of the state. Unless there are trained management personnel nationalisation of industry cannot be successful. In fact, training should precede nationalisation. The eradication of illiteracy was less important than technical training. *Konstantin Kolev* also argued that progressive social development is not possible without development in the material sector. Social development is closely connected to material development and priority should be given to the latter. The way to improve the health of the population, for example, was to create conditions in which malaria, malnutrition, etc., could not exist. Within education, it is important to reorganise the curriculum so that it corresponds with the present stage of development of the country.

Paul Streeten remarked that we economists are tempted to emphasise financial aggregate targets and the volume of expenditure on inputs. What is important is not the inputs but the output, the results. The composition and direction of expenditure, the division between capital and recurrent expenditure, education of adults versus education of children, of men versus women – these are the crucial problems, not expenditure ratios. Especially in the field of social development the links between expenditure and results are tenuous. Much depends on the social structure. In family planning, for instance, more or less expenditure is less important than the social institutions and the general environment in which expenditure occurs.

The cultural and ethnic unity of Bangladesh is a great advantage. *Akira Takahashi* pointed out that apart from Japan, no other Asian country had such a large homogeneous population as Bangladesh. This creates a potentially large domestic market for cultural products. It was important here not to split the educational system into two levels, one using the local language and the other a foreign language. The language of education should be the language of the people, even at the higher levels of education. It is essential not to allow an elite to monopolise culture, science and education; one must avoid creating 'cultural compradors'.

Nurul Islam then asked if we should translate a massive amount of literature and books into Bengali. Would not this result in a short-run deterioration of quality in education? *Takahashi* replied that yes, perhaps the quality of elitist education would decline temporarily, but this price is worth paying. Translation is expensive and skill-intensive but it must be done. *Professor Husain* noted that already Bengali is required of all university lecturers; the development of the national language is moving ahead very fast.

Muzaffar Ahmad said that at Dacca University the classrooms were used on average less than two hours a day. There is tremendous under-utilisation of physical resources throughout the country. He, and others, suggested that schools be run in shifts. *Esra Bennathan*, however, was sceptical. The staff of the universities are grossly overworked in terms of hours of effort and teaching conditions are extremely difficult.

According to *Vladimir Kondratiev*, there is a tendency to exaggerate the need for high-level personnel in underdeveloped countries. It is the training of technicians and cadres that is vital. This is one of the weakest points in the educational system of many underdeveloped countries, and as a result the educational pyramid is distorted.

Austin Robinson asked whether the real problem isn't in the villages. *René Dumont* agreed and suggested that much could be learned from Cuba's programme of adult education. *Gustav Ranis* said we really must take advantage of the energy which resides in the villages. Some success in doing this has occurred in Indonesia and Taiwan. The problem is that unleashing the villagers goes against the procedures of the civil service; perhaps middle level civil servants should be required to spend a couple of years in a village. *Bennathan* said that Thailand has been particularly successful in obtaining local participation in primary education. The central government provides only takas 10 per pupil for a two-month course which occurs in the inter-harvest period; the rest of the finance comes from local funds. Simple botany, geography, literacy, etc., are taught and the cost to the central government was exceptionally low; local demand was immense. *Professor Brody* said that the time-lags and costs of building up human capital in the usual way are large. The pipelines are a half to two-thirds empty and a tremendous amount of resources is needed to fill up the pipe-line without producing much very quickly. Professor Robinson's suggestions should be supported as a possible way of overcoming this problem.

Professor Husain, replying to the discussion, stressed that education is complementary to other development expenditure, not an alternative to it. This was particularly evident in the case of middle level technicians, the products of technical high schools and of technical institutes. This type of education, in turn, requires a broad base of literacy. It is the aim of the government to attain universal primary education as soon as possible, say within ten years. The government also are considering a mass literacy programme for adults integrated with an agricultural development programme.

At present there is a severe problem of dropouts at the primary school level. The reason for this is essentially economic: the parents need their children to work. In addition, there are the problems of the isolation of the villages, the prejudice against mixing the two sexes in the same school and the lack of highly motivated and dedicated teachers. It is hoped to overcome some of the problems by synchronising school vacations with peak rural activities, introducing a school lunch programme and improving transport. Sooner or later, however, compulsory education will be needed.

The progress of vocational education has been extremely slow, largely because it has been too institutionalised. In future it is expected that much more emphasis will be placed on on-the-job training. This should be relatively easy to do within the nationalised industry sector.

Clearly it is important to mobilise resources for primary education at the local level. The villagers must be given responsibility for organising and managing *their* schools and Professor Robinson's suggestions are very welcome.

He agreed with the participants who said that the ratio of expenditures on education to G.N.P. was not the main factor, but education in this country has been a residual claimant for resources. This cannot continue. We must raise the ratio because Bangladesh is so low compared with other countries. The distinction between capital and current expenditure on education may not be very meaningful. It is easier to obtain finance for 'development' projects, i.e. buildings and equipment, than for teachers' salaries, but teachers are more important than buildings.

Index

Entries in **bold type** under the names of participants in the Conference indicate their papers or discussions of their papers. Entries in *italics* indicate contributions by participants to the discussions.